K.Praveen

QTP

For Professionals

ACKNOWLEDGEMENT

Authors of this book sincerely thank Mr. Sudhakar Kakunuri of Semantic space Technologies for his Contribution, including the review. Mr. Sudhakar blogs on www.qtpsudhakar.com

A big thank you goes to Mr. Sridhar Mallepally of Parishta Inc. U.S.A for reviewing the book.

We thank all the software professionals who helped us support the development of this book, their valuable questions, insights, feedback and suggestions have directly and indirectly added value to the content of this book.

A book gets into people's hands only through a lot of behind -the- scenes hard work by a publisher's team. A special thanks to the fine people at Shroff who helped bring this book to fruition.

Table of Contents

AUTOMATION FUNDAMENTALS

Test Automation is the use of software to execute the tests. Test Automation involves automating manual execution of test cases for enhancing speed and reliability.

Automation Testing is nothing but simulation of Manual Actions. Automation testing includes an additional activity of writing test scripts after Test case Development.

Benefits of Automated Testing

Benefits of Automated Testing:	
Fast	Automation Scripts run significantly faster than manual test execution.
Reliable	Tests perform precisely the same operations each time they are run, thereby eliminating human error.
Repeatable	One can test how the web site or application reacts after repeated execution of the same operations.
Programmable	One can program sophisticated tests that bring out hidden information.

Reusable	One can reuse tests on different versions of a web site or application.

Pros and Cons of Automation

- If you have to run a set of tests repeatedly, automation is a huge win for you.
- It gives you the ability to run automation against code that frequently changes to catch regressions in a timely manner.
- It gives you the ability to run automation in mainstream scenarios to catch regressions in a timely manner.
- Aids in testing a large test matrix (different languages on different OS platforms).
- Automated tests can be run at the same time on different machines, whereas manual tests would have to be run sequentially.
- Automation Testing takes more initial investment to design and develop automation framework and automation test scripts.
- Can't automate Visual References. For example the Look and Feel of the application is a manual test.
- What you automate depends on the tools you use. If the tools have any limitations, those tests are manual.
- It may not be worth automating if the repetition of test case execution is minimal.

Criteria for automating

There are two sets of questions to determine whether automation is right for your test case:

Is this test scenario automatable?

1. Yes, and it will cost a little
2. Yes, but it will cost a lot
3. No, it is not possible to automate

How important is this test scenario?

1. I must absolutely test this scenario whenever possible
2. I need to test this scenario regularly
3. I only need to test this scenario once in a while

If you answered #1 to both questions – definitely automate that test.
If you answered #1 or #2 to both questions – you should automate that test.
If you answered #2 to both questions – you need to consider if it is really worth the investment to automate.
If you answered #3 to both questions – you should not automate that test.

What happens if you can't automate?

Let's say that you have a test that you absolutely need to run whenever possible, but it isn't possible to automate. Your options are:

- Re-evaluate – do I really need to run this test this often?
- What's the cost of doing this test manually?
- Look for new testing tools.

Automation Life Cycle

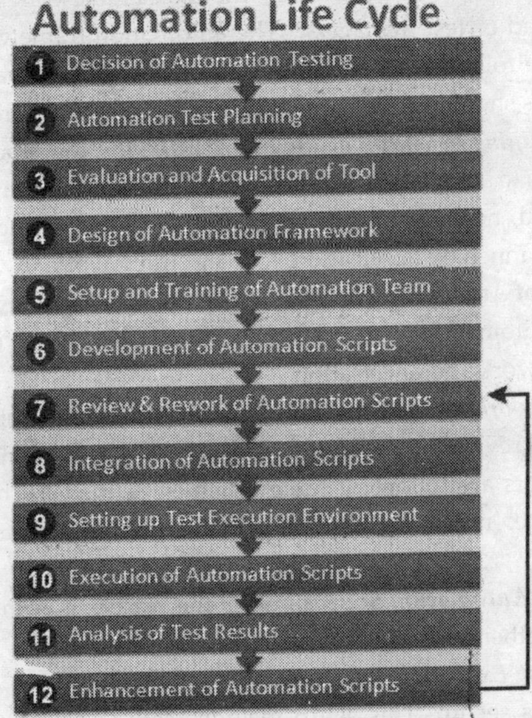

1. ***Decision of Automation Testing:*** The first phase of automation life cycle is to decide if the application under test can be given a nod for go ahead with automation. Usually this decision is taken by the client and test manager. Lot of factors like return on investment and future scope of the application are considered. After all calculations, if return on investment seems to be positive, automation of the application under test is approved.
2. ***Automation Test Planning:*** Once the decision to automate is confirmed the next step involves deciding on the automation plan. In this phase the planning team which is

generally comprised of Client, Test manager and Automation lead, decide on the automation test planning. This plan involves decisions like how to automate, what to automate and when to automate.

3. ***Evaluation and Acquisition of Tool:*** Once the automation plan is set up, the next phase is to decide on which tool to pick up from the market. In general the evaluation team which consists of the Client, Test Manger, and Automation Lead, together discuss and evaluate the various tools available in the market. Various factors such as cost of the tool, compatibility of the tool with the application and skilled resources required are considered to decide on the tool.
4. ***Design of Automation Framework:*** Once the tool is decided next step is to design appropriate framework supported by the tool. Framework is generally designed by automation lead or test managers. The automation framework consists of the rules that should be followed in automation. The automation framework design defines how the scripts should be developed, integrated, executed and maintained.
5. ***Setup and Training of Automation Team:*** Once the tool and framework is decided, the next step is to select team members of the automation team. In this phase after the team is formed, necessary setup (in terms of hardware and software) and training sessions are planned on application, tool and framework.
6. ***Development of Automation Scripts:*** Once the training phase is over, the next phase involves the automation team to start building scripts based on the training provided on tool, framework and application.
7. ***Review & Rework of Automation Scripts:*** After developing the scripts the next phase involves reviewing the scripts. The factors that are considered while reviewing are if the scripts are following the guidelines defined in the framework. Once the review is done, necessary rework is done on the scripts based on the review comments.
8. ***Integration of Automation Scripts:*** Once the rework is completed all the scripts are integrated together for the execution phase.
9. ***Setting up Test Execution Environment:*** After integration of scripts the execution environment is set up. This setup includes setting up of the number of systems, setting up of automation tool, setting up of application under test and setting up the data and environment required for execution of the scripts.
10. ***Execution of Automation Scripts:*** Final scripts (reviewed and reworked) are executed.
11. ***Analysis of Test Results:*** After execution phase the result reports generated are analyzed based on the pass/fail status of the scripts.
12. ***Enhancement of Automation Scripts:*** In this phase, scripts might be modified because there might be few changes in the existing functionality of the application.

Also for the new functionality added, scripts are developed. Since addition and modification of scripts takes place in this stage review and rework should be done again as shown in the figure with loop back.

Types of Test Tools

There are many testing tools available today. Some tools are designed only to fulfill a very specific role in the Testing environment, while other tools can adequately perform multiple tasks. Test tools are classified under the activity to which they most closely belong.

Following is the list of a few tools:

Functional Automation Test Tools

These tools are used to automate the functionality of an application by sending keyboard and mouse actions to the application. This functional automation is possible by creating and executing the test automation script using the language/s supported by Functional Automation Test Tool. Many commercial and open source Functional Automation Test Tools are available with an inbuilt record and play back feature that generates automation script automatically. Commonly repetitive test cases like Regression Testcases are automated using these tools.

Few Functional Automation Tools are

- Quick Test Professional
- WinRunner
- SilkTest
- Rational Functional Tester
- Test Partner
- Selenium

Performance Test Tools

Performance Testing Tools helps ensure your enterprise applications can meet heavy user loads during peak hours and have high uptime in production. Performance testing can help you identify bottlenecks in your application code and eliminate them proactively. This type of tool comprises of two components- Load Generation and Response Time Measurement. Response Time is the time taken by the application for various user actions like logging into the application, opening an email etc.. Load Generation is commonly performed by simulating load on the application. The number of transactions performed this way, are then logged. Performance test tools will commonly be able to display reports and graphs of load against response time.

Few Performance Test Tools are:

- Load Runner
- Silk Performer
- Rational Performance Tester
- WebLoad
- Web Application Stress Tool (WAS)
- OpenSTA

Test Management Tools

Test Management Tools commonly have multiple features. Test Management is mainly concerned with the management, creation and control of test documentation. More advanced tools have additional capabilities such as 'result logging' and 'test scheduling'.

Few Test Management Tools are:

- Quality Center
- QADirector
- SilkCentral Test Manager
- Rational Test Manager
- QaTraq
- Test Link

Configuration Management Tools

Although not strictly a Testing type of tool, they are useful in version control of software development. When we write automation scripts using various functional and performance automation tools these have to be managed for changes using Configuration Management Tools.

Few Configuration Management Tools are:

- VSS (Visual Source Safe)
- CVS (Concurrent Version)
- SVN (Sub Version)
- SCCS(Source Code Control System)
- Clear case

Coverage Measurement

This type of tool provides objective measures of structural test coverage when the actual tests are executed. Before the programs are compiled, they are first instrumented. Once this has been completed they can then be tested. The instrumentation process allows the coverage data to be logged whilst the program is running. Once testing is complete, the logs can provide statistics on the details of the tests covered.

Few Coverage Measurement Tools are:

- GCov
- JCov
- Rational Pure Coverage
- Optimizeit
- Clover

Review Questions

1. What are the Pros and Cons of Automation?
2. How will you decide whether a particular scenario can be automated or not?
3. Explain Different Testing Tools available?
4. Explain Automation Life Cycle?

Automation life cycle.

INTRODUCTION TO QTP

QuickTest Professional (QTP) often referred to as QuickTest is a functional automation tool created by the HP subsidiary Mercury Interactive that allows the automation of user actions on a web or desktop computer application. It is primarily used for functional regression test automation. QTP uses a scripting language built on top of VBScript to specify the test procedure, and to manipulate the objects and controls of the Application Under Test (AUT).

Features of QTP

QTP has got so many features that enable even an inexperienced tester to work with it. Some of the key features are:

- Record n Playback for quick and easy script identification
- Enhanced Script Life through excellent Object identification mechanism using Normal and Smart Identification
- Runtime Check of Application objects and Data using various check points
- Excellent data driven testing features like Data table, Action Parameterization

- Runtime Data Capturing using Output values
- Excellent Error Handling and Script recovery through Recovery scenario mechanism
- Keyword Driven Testing through keyword view
- Automation support to even non technical people like business analysts through Active Screen and Keyword View
- Easy and Effective programming using VB Script in Expert view
- Excellent Results management in the form of an XML tree
- Good support for Microsoft Object Models like Excel, MS Word, Outlook
- QTP is Unicode compliant according to the requirements of the Unicode standard, enabling you to test applications in many international languages.

System Requirements

The following table describes the system requirements for installing the latest version - QTP 10.0

CPU	A PC with a Pentium III or higher microprocessor(Pentium IV or higher recommended)
Operating System	• Windows 2000 Professional Service Pack 4 Update Rollup 1 for Windows 2000 Service Pack 4 • Windows XP Professional 32-Bit Edition Service Pack 2 or Service Pack 3 • Windows XP Professional 64-Bit Edition Service Pack 2 • Windows Server 2003 32-Bit Edition Service Pack 2 • Windows Server 2003 R2 (32-Bit x86) • Windows Vista 32-Bit Edition or Windows Vista 32-bit Edition Service Pack 1 • Windows Vista 64-Bit Edition or Windows Vista 64-bit Edition Service Pack 1 • Windows Server 2008 32-Bit Edition • Windows Server 2008 64-Bit Edition **Note:** The Quality Center client does not support 64-bit operating systems. Therefore, QuickTest-Quality Center integration functionality is not

	supported when working with 64-bit operating systems.
Memory (RAM)	Minimum of 512 MB. Minimum of 1 GB when using the Save movie to results option to capture movies during run sessions.
Color Settings	Minimum of High Color (16 bit).
Graphics Card	Graphics card with 4 MB video memory (8 MB and above recommended).
Free Hard Disk Space	650 MB of free disk space for application files and folders, when only the default add-ins are installed. 800 MB (recommended 1 GB) when all add-ins are installed. You must also have an additional 120MB of free disk space on the system disk (the disk on which the operating system is installed). If you are not installing all of the QuickTest add-ins, less free disk space is required. The free disk space requirements do not include disk space required for any prerequisites that may need to be installed before installing QuickTest. After QuickTest Professional is installed, it is recommended to have at least 150 MB free disk space on the system disk for the operating system and QuickTest Professional to run correctly.
Browser	To use QuickTestProfessional, you must have one of the following Microsoft Internet Explorer versions installed on your computer. Microsoft Internet Explorer6.0 Service Pack1 Microsoft Internet Explorer7.0 Microsoft Internet Explorer8.0 Beta 2

Source:
https://h10078.www1.hp.com/cda/hpms/display/main/hpms_content.jsp?zn=bto&cp=1-11-127-24%5E9674_4000_100__

Add-in Manager

To test applications developed in various environments, you must ensure that the relevant QuickTest add-in is installed and loaded on the computer on which you create and run your tests and components. When you start QuickTest, the Add-in Manager dialog box opens. To start QuickTest, select **Programs > QuickTest Professional** from the Start menu, or double-click the Quick Test Professional icon shortcut on your desktop. It displays a list of all installed add-ins and the license used for each add-in. Loading the relevant add-in enables QuickTest to work with the corresponding environment.

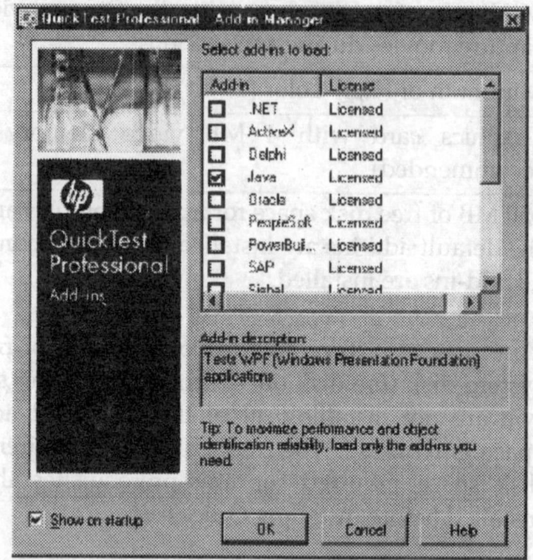

Supported Technologies:

The following are the technologies that are supported by QTP 10.0

- Web
- Java(Core and Advanced)
- .Net
- WPF
- SAP
- Oracle
- Siebel
- PeopleSoft
- Delphi
- Power Builder
- Stingray 1
- Terminal Emulator
- Flex
- Mainframe terminal emulators

QTP Versions

The following is the list of QTP versions released in the market starting from the latest version to the first release:

- 10.0 - Released in 2009
- 9.5 - Released in 2007
- 9.2 - Released in 2007
- 9.0 - Released in 2006
- 8.2 - Released in 2005
- 8.0 - Released in 2004
- 7.0 - Never released.
- 6.5 - Released in 2003
- 6.0 - Released in 2002
- 5.5 - First release. Released in 2001

Supported Browsers

The following are the list of browsers that are supported by QTP 10.0:

- Internet Explorer 5.5 SP2,6,7,8
- Netscape 6.1,6.22,6.33,7.01,7.02,7.1,8,8.1,8.1.3,9
- AOL 9
- Firefox 1.5,2.0,3.0.X,3.5,4

QTP License Types

Three types of licenses are available for QTP from HP:

1. **Demo License:** This is a 14-day demo license. You can register and download QTP 10.0 from HP site at the link below:
   https://h10078.www1.hp.com/cda/hpms/display/main/hpms_content.jsp?zn=bto&cp=1-11-127-24%5E1352_4000_100__
2. **Seat License:** Seat License refers to assigning QTP to one machine. If we take 5 seat licenses QTP will be installed only in 5 computers and can be used only from these 5 computers.
3. **Concurrent (Floating) License:** Concurrent License allows a license to be shared between machines at any given point in time. If we take 5 Concurrent licenses QTP can be installed in any number of computers. But only 5 users can login and use QTP at a time. License Server will be installed to monitor number of users logged in.

If your company wants to automate and run test scripts with a 4 members team - 2 in India and 2 in US better to go for 2 concurrent licenses and use time zone effectively than having 4 Seat Licenses, though Cost of one Seat license is lower than cost of one Concurrent license.

Automation Process in QTP

Testing process in QuickTest involves the following six main stages:

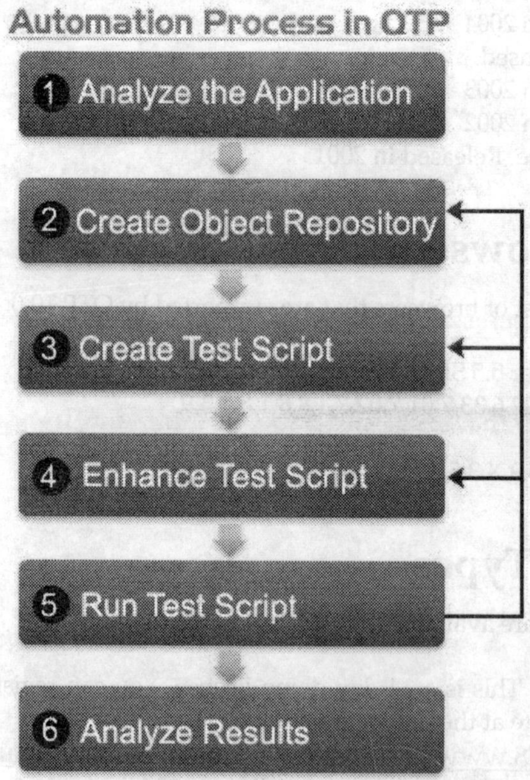

1) **Analyze the application:** Before developing scripts the first step is to analyze the application. Analyzing the application involves determining the required add-ins (like Web, .Net, Java) based on the environment the application is developed on, understand the functionality of the application and analyze how to create small, easier and modular scripts.

2) **Create object repository:** After analyzing the functionalities and behavior of the application the next step is to create object repository. The object repository consists

of objects on which the operations are performed. These objects are called as test objects.

3) **Create Test Script:** In this stage test scripts are generated. Scripts are constituted of steps where each step is one operation that is performed on the application. This step can be added in an action in two ways - either by entering the keywords in the table-like keyword view or by programming a line of VBScript in expert view.

4) **Enhance Test Script:** The basic scripts generated in stage 3 can further be modified using features of QuickTest such as checkpoints, output values, parameterization and synchronization.

5) **Run Test Script:** The next stage involves execution of the scripts. When the scripts are run starting from the first step the script is executed till the last step of the script. Each step performs one operation on the application. After running the scripts if any further modifications are required you can loop back to the relevant stage as shown in the figure above.

6) **Analyzing Results:** After the scripts are executed results are displayed on the test results window. In this stage the results window is analyzed by viewing either summary or detailed report.

Review Questions

1. Brief about the installation requirements of QTP
2. List out the Browsers supported by QTP
3. List out the add ins supported by QTP
4. Explain automation process in QTP
5. Discuss various licensing options of QTP

A GLANCE AT QTP

In this chapter we will discuss various tabs and menu items available in QTP window and their significance. The first time you start QuickTest, the Add-in Manager dialog box opens as shown in the figure below, displaying the currently installed add-ins. Select the add-ins that have to be loaded. The default license consists of 3 add-ins shown in the figure below. If any additional add-in is required we must purchase them from HP and install them. After installation, the add-in manager displays another check to select with add-in name.

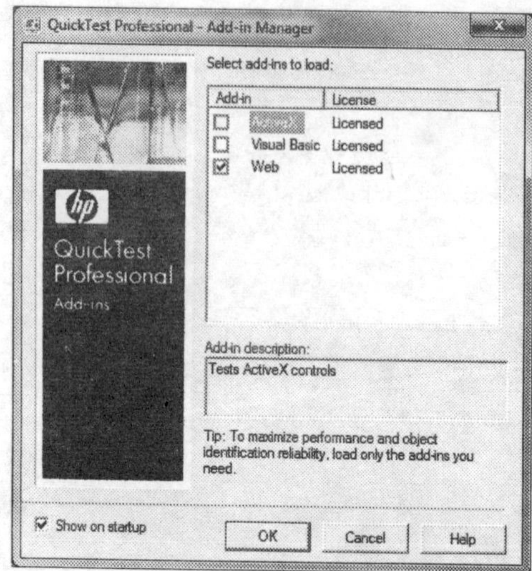

After selecting the required add-in, click **OK**. QuickTest is launched and the QTP window opens displaying the Start Page and a blank test. To access a blank test, click the Test tab.

Quick Test Window

The following figure displays the QuickTest window:

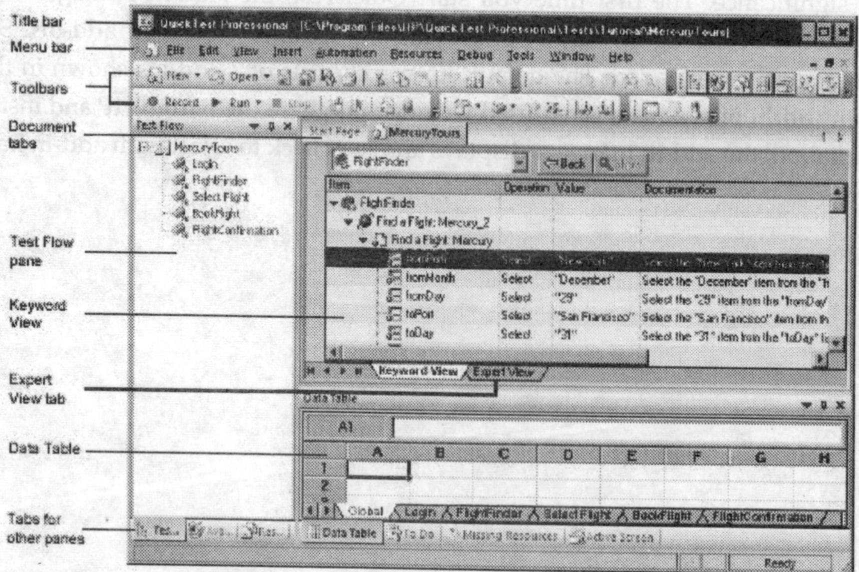

QuickTest window by default will have two tabs - Start Page and Test.

- **Start page** is just a welcome page it contains 4 sections
  1. *Welcome:* A Welcome message from HP to their customers
  2. *Process Guidance List:* In QTP we can define our own process and follow these steps while creating and running the scripts. This section shows the process available. By default we will find Keyword Driven testing process which is in-built. Anyhow users can define their own process.
  3. *Recently Used Files:* All Tests recently used for quick opening.
  4. *What's New:* Brief Explanation to all new features in the current release.
- **Test:** Enables you to create, view, and modify your test in Keyword View or Expert View (described below).

Key elements in the Quick Test window

The QuickTest window contains the following key elements:

- **QuickTest title bar**: Displays the name of the active document. If changes have been made since it was last saved, an asterisk (*) is displayed next to the document name in the title bar.
- **Menu bar:** Displays menus of QuickTest commands.
- **Tool Bars**
  - **Standard toolbar:** Contains buttons to assist you in managing your document.

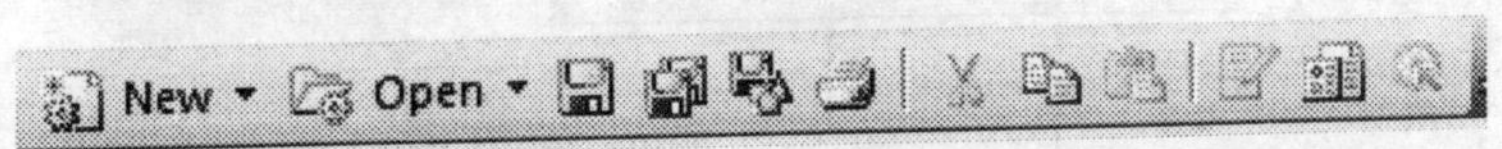

  - **Automation toolbar:** Contains buttons to assist you in the testing process.

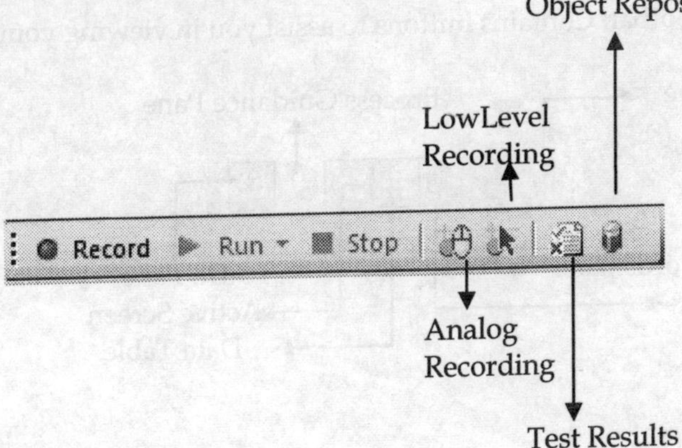

  - **Debug toolbar:** Contains buttons to assist you in debugging your document. (Not displayed by default).

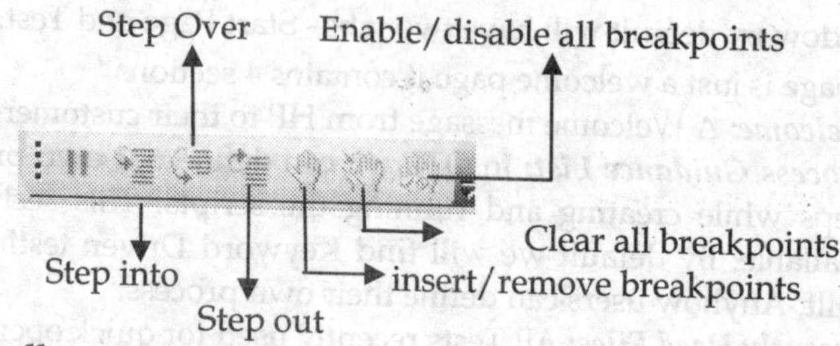

- **Edit toolbar:** Contains buttons to assist you in editing your test or function library.

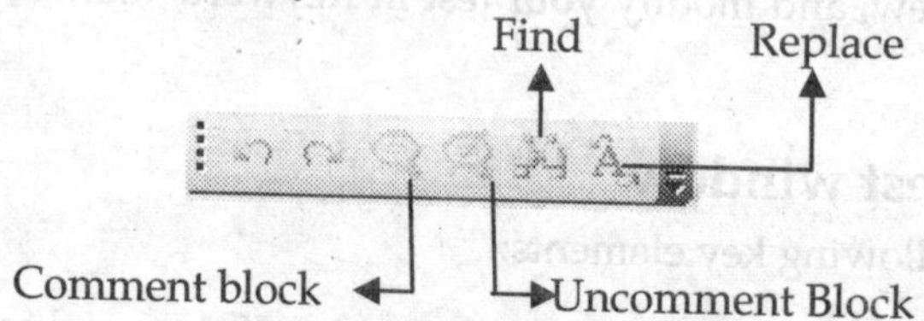

- **Insert toolbar:** Contains buttons to assist you when working with steps and statements in your test or function library.

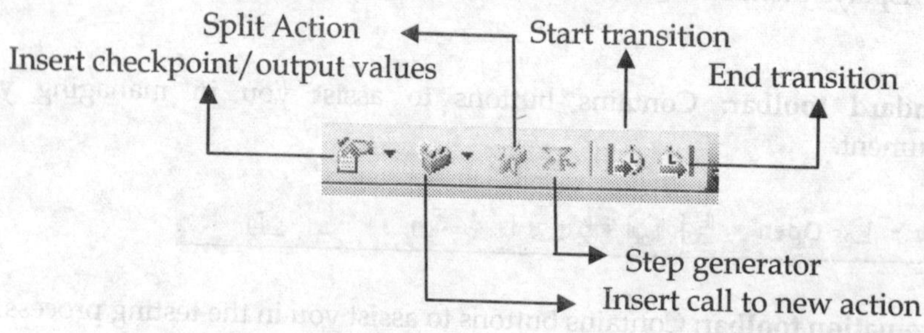

- **View toolbar:** Contains buttons to assist you in viewing your document.

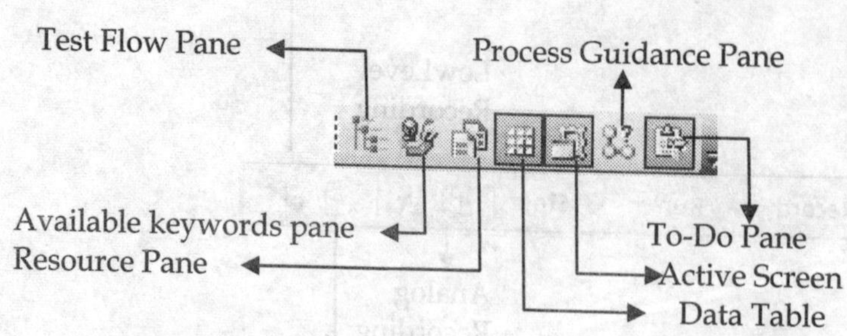

- **Tools toolbar:** Contains buttons with tools to assist you in the testing process.

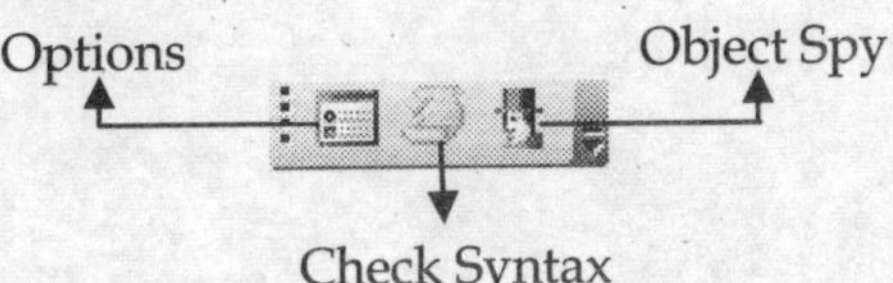

- **Action toolbar:** Contains buttons and a list of actions, enabling you to view the details of an individual action or the entire test flow. (not displayed by default).

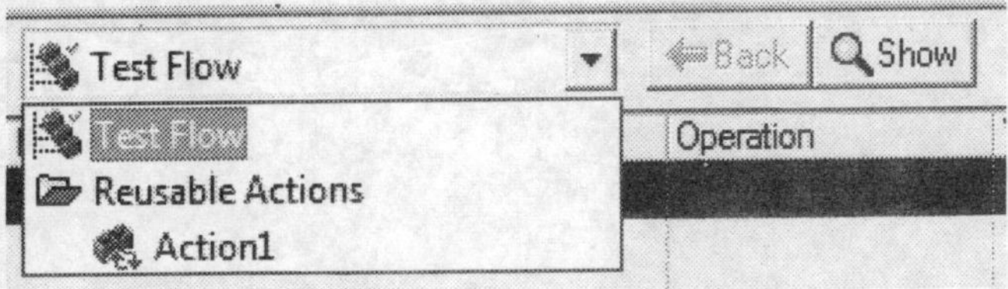

- **Keyword View:** Contains each step, and displays the object hierarchy, in a modular, icon-based table.
- **Expert View:** Contains each step as a VBScript line. In object-based steps, the VBScript line defines the object hierarchy.
- **Status bar:** Displays the status of the QuickTest application and other relevant information. You can show or hide the Panes like Active Screen, Data Table, Debug Viewer.

Review Questions

1. What are the different toolbars in the QuickTest window?
2. What does the start page of QuickTest contain?
3. What is the importance of add-in manager?
4. What does the keyword view of QuickTest contain?

RECORD AND PLAYBACK

Introduction

Using record option of QuickTest users can build automation scripts automatically without any knowledge of scripting. From the moment the record button is clicked till the stop button is clicked QuickTest records all the user actions as you navigate through your Web site or application and generates a script. User actions can be seen in the Keyword View and in the Expert View as steps in the script. A step is anything a user does that changes the content of a page or object in your application, for example, clicking a link or typing data in an edit box. During a run session, QuickTest uses the recorded steps to replicate the operations you performed while recording. While you record your test steps, QuickTest creates test objects representing the objects in your application on which you perform operations. This enables QuickTest to identify the objects in your application both while creating a test and during a run session.

Record and Playback is used to record the user actions in the form of script and Play them back at a later time by running the script.

Recording Modes

There are three recording modes in QuickTest:

- Normal
- Analog
- Low level

Normal recording mode

This is the default and most commonly used recording in QTP. This records the actions performed by the user on the application objects like Edit boxes, List boxes and Links. As the user performs actions on the objects QTP records each action as one step in the QTP script. Step is nothing but one line in the code.

To Record a Test using Normal Recording mode:

1) Launch QuickTest.
2) Create a new test: select **File>New>Test**
3) Click the Record button or select **Automation > Record** or press the Record command shortcut key **F3**.
4) The Record and Run Settings (**Automation > Record and Run Settings**) dialog box opens as shown below:

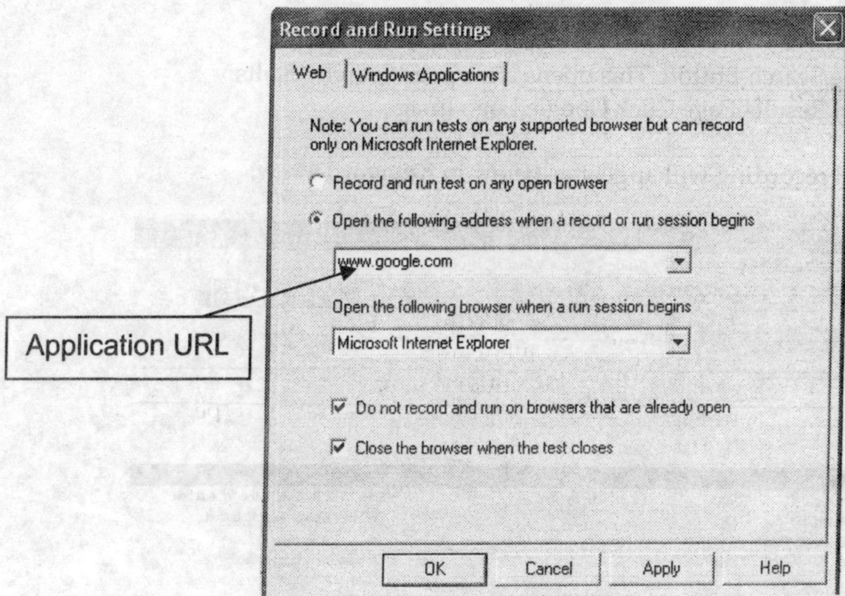

5) Enter Application URL in the Record and Run Settings Dialog as shown above.
6) Navigate through your application. QuickTest records each step you perform and displays it in the Keyword View and Expert View.
7) When you complete your recording session, click the Stop button or select **Automation>Stop**, or press the Stop command shortcut key **F4.**
8) To save your test, click the **Save** button or select **File > Save**. In the **Save QuickTest Test** dialog box, assign a name to the test.
9) Run the Test by clicking **Run**.

Example:
Perform the steps below on Google Application:

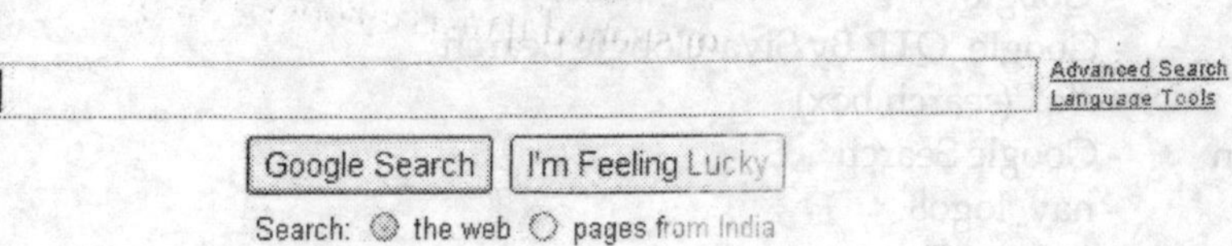

1. From Google Home Page enter text "QTP By Siva" in the Search Box

2. Click Google Search Button. This opens New page Search results
3. From Search Results Page Click Google Logo Image

Script created in Normal recording will appear as below in **Keyword View:**

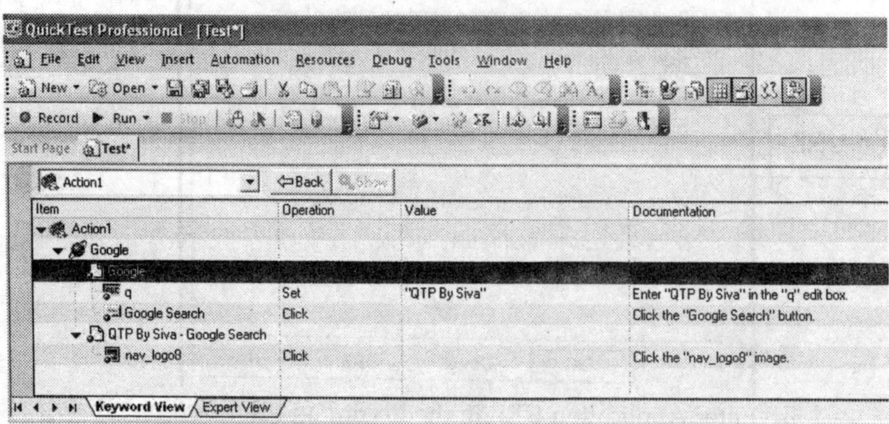

Script created in Normal recording will appear as below in **Expert View:**

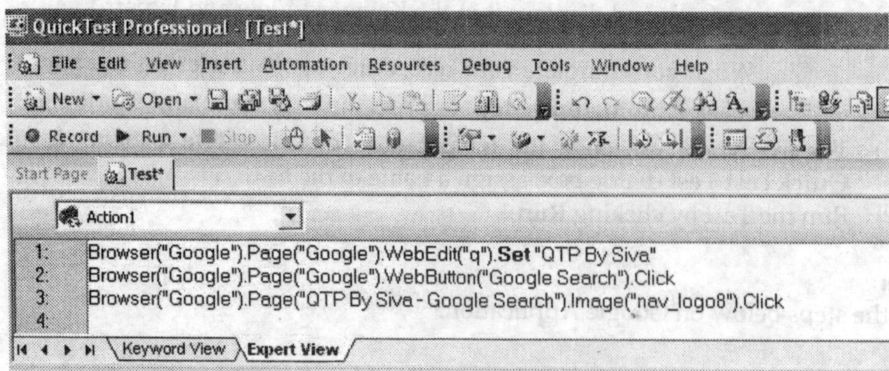

In the above script we can observe following object classes with names of objects as below:

Browser	– Google
Page	- Google, QTP By Siva-Google Search
WebEdit	- "q" (search box)
WebButton	- Google Search
Image	- nav_logo8

We can easily map Actions performed by the user with Steps Created by QTP as below:

S.No	Step	Code	Remarks
1	From Google Home Page enter text "QTP By Siva" in Search Box	*Browser("Google").Page("Google").WebEdit("q"). Set "QTP By Siva"*	Set method is used to write into WebEdit search box "q"
2	Click Google Search Button	*Browser("Google").Page("Google").WebButton("Google Search").Click*	Click method is used to click on the WebButton *"Google Search"*
3	From Search Results Page Click Google Logo Image	*Browser("Google").Page("QTP By Siva - Google Search").Image("nav_logo8").Click*	Click on the Image named *"nav_logo8"*

Analog Recording mode

This mode enables you to record the exact mouse and keyboard operations you perform in relation to either the screen or the application window. In this recording mode, QuickTest records and tracks every movement of the mouse as you drag the mouse around a screen or window. This mode is useful when you want to record mouse movements, for example, recording a signature or drawing performed by dragging the mouse.

To Record a Test using Analog Recording mode:

1) You can switch to Analog Recording mode only while recording i.e from Normal Recording.
2) To record in Analog Recording mode start normal recording by clicking the Record button and then click the Analog Recording button or select Automation > Analog Recording.
3) The Analog Recording Settings dialog box opens.

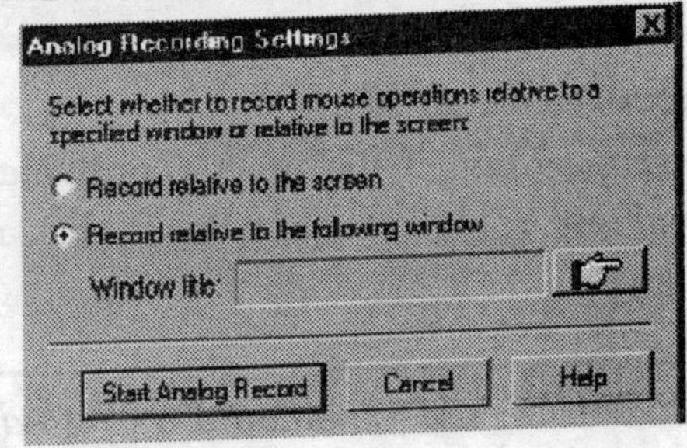

Select from the following options:

Record relative to the screen: QuickTest records any mouse movement or keyboard input relative to the top left coordinates of your screen (i.e desktop).

Record relative to the following window: QuickTest records any mouse movement or keyboard input relative to the coordinates of the specified window.

NOTE: Record relative to window is a better option because your script works properly even though window position or screen resolution is changed.

4) If you choose to Record relative to the following window, click the pointing hand and click anywhere in the window on which you want to record in Analog Recording mode. The title of the window you clicked is displayed in the window title box. Click Start Analog Record.
5) Perform the operations you want to record in Analog Recording mode. All of your keyboard input, mouse movements, and clicks are recorded and save.
6) When you are finished and want to return to normal recording mode, click the Analog Recording button or select **Automation > Analog Recording** to turn off the option.

If you chose to Record relative to the screen, QuickTest inserts the RunAnalog step as:

Desktop.RunAnalog "Track1"

If you chose Record relative to window, QuickTest inserts the RunAnalog step as:

Window("Microsoft Internet Explorer").RunAnalog "Track1"

> 1. *Analog Recording Mode should be used only when Mouse Movement is essential like signatures and drawings.*
> 2. *Track represents the track of the coordinates traversed by mouse during Analog Recording.*

Low level Recording mode

Use low-level recording if the exact coordinates of the operation on the object are important for your test. You may require this to click at some exact coordinate in the window or application object.

> *Low Level Recording Mode should be used only when exact coordinate of operation is essential.*

To Record a Test using Low Level recording mode:

1) If you are not already recording, click the Record button to begin a recording session.

2) Click the Low Level Recording button or select **Automation > Low Level Recording**. The record mode changes to Low Level Recording.
3) Click on any object/s.
4) When you are finished and want to return to normal recording mode, click the Low Level Recording button or select **Automation > Low Level Recording** to turn off the option.

Example:

Perform Low Level recording as above to click on Cancel button of font dialog in Notepad.

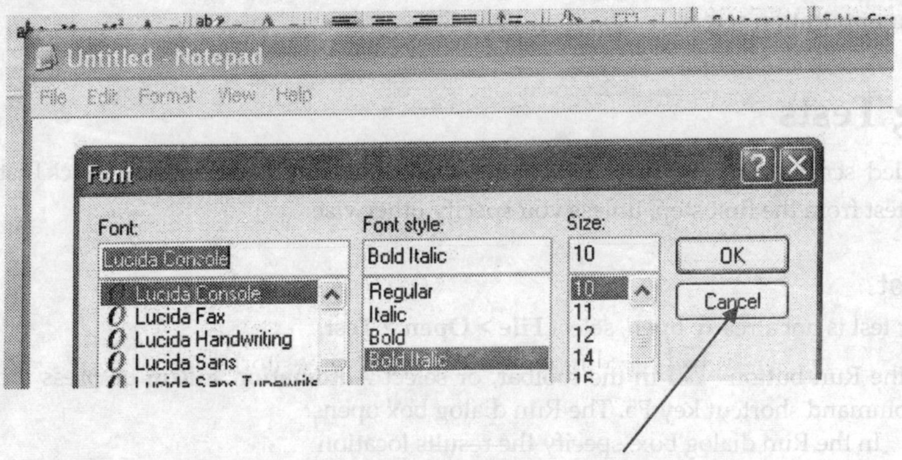

Code Created will be as below in **LowLevel Recording.**
Window("Notepad").Window("Font").WinObject("Cancel").Click 40,11

For the same operation code will be as below in **Normal Recording**
Window("Notepad").Dialog("Font").WinButton("Cancel").Click

Observe that in Low Level recording code clearly shows we clicked cancel button at coordinate 40, 11. This coordinate is measured taking Top Left Corner of the object (In this case Cancel Button) as Reference (0,0). It is important to note that coordinate of operation is not shown Normal Recording.

The user can switch between any recordings any number of times by clicking appropriate recording buttons. For Example if the user is in Low-level Recording he/she can switch to Analog Recording by clicking Analog Recording Button or to Normal Recording by clicking Low-level Recording button again.

Choosing the Recording mode

Consider the following guidelines when choosing Analog Recording \ Low Level Recording:

- Use analog recording or low-level recording **only when** normal recording mode does not accurately record your operation.
- Use analog recording for applications in which the actual movement of the mouse is what you want to record. These can include drawing signatures or working with drawing applications by dragging the mouse.
- Use low-level recording when you need to record the exact location of the operation on your application screen.

Running Tests

The recorded scripts can be run several times using the play back option. QuickTest always runs a test from the first step, unless you specify otherwise.

To run a test

1) If your test is not already open, select **File > Open > Test.**
2) Click the Run button in the toolbar, or select **Automation > Run** or press the Run command shortcut key F5. The Run dialog box opens.
   - ✓ In the Run dialog box, specify the results location

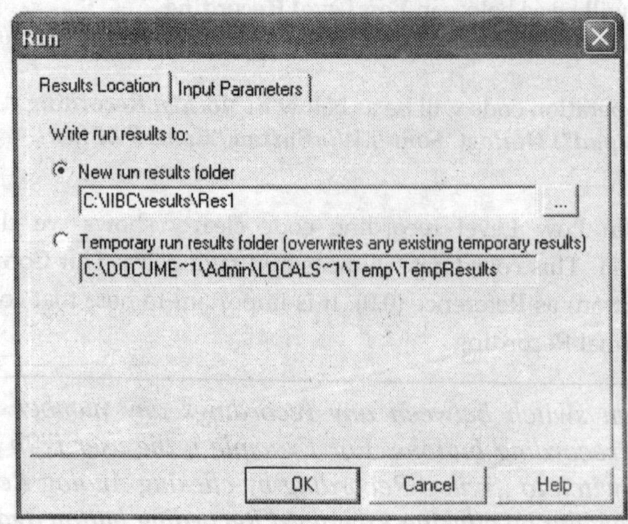

Temporary run results folder: Saves the run results in a temporary folder. This option overwrites any results previously saved in this folder.

3) Click OK. The Run dialog box closes and the run session starts. By default, when the run session ends, the Test Results window opens.

Test Results Window

When a run session ends, you can view the run session results in the Test Results window. By default, the Test Results window opens automatically at the end of a run.

You can also open the Test Results window as a standalone application from the Start menu. To open the Test Results window, select **Start > Programs > QuickTest Professional > Test Results Viewer.**

The following figure shows the results of a test with three iterations:

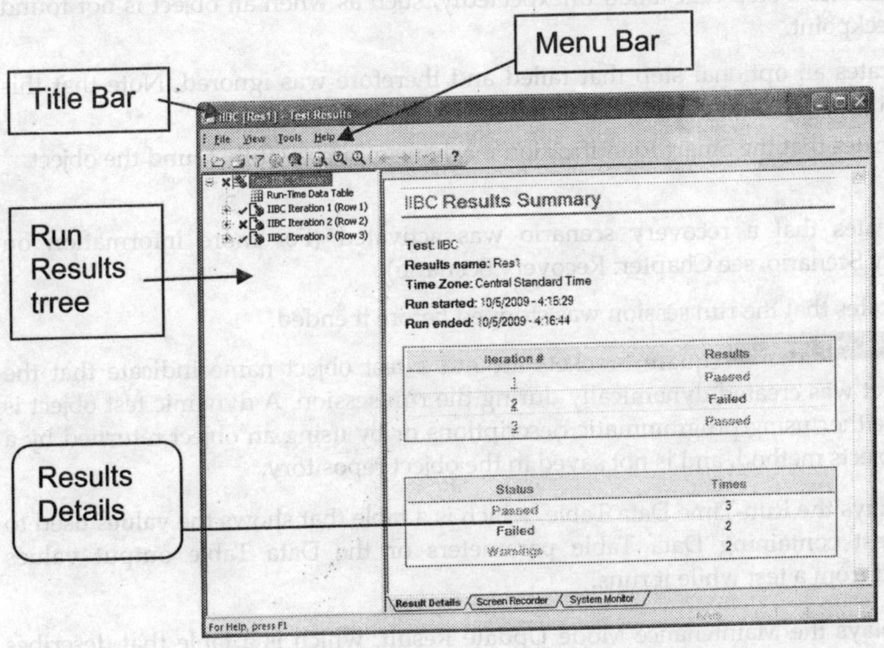

The Test Results window contains the following key elements:

- ✓ **Title bar.** Displays the name of the test.
- ✓ **Menu bar.** Displays menus of available commands
- ✓ **Run results tree.** Contains a graphic representation of the test results in the run results tree. The run results tree is located in the left pane in the Test Results window.

✓ **Result Details tab.** Contains details of the selected node in the run results tree. The Result Details tab is located in the right pane in the Test Results window.

Some Icons of Run Results Tree and Their Importance

The left pane in the Test Results window displays the run results tree; a graphical representation of the test results:

✓ ✔ indicates a step that succeeded. Note that if a test does not contain checkpoints, no icon is displayed.

✓ ✖ indicates a step that failed. Note that this causes all parent steps (up to the root action or test) to fail as well.

✓ ! indicates a warning, meaning that the step did not succeed, but it did not cause the action or test to fail.

✓ ! indicates a step that failed unexpectedly, such as when an object is not found for a checkpoint.

✓ i indicates an optional step that failed and therefore was ignored. Note that this does not cause the test to fail.

✓ indicates that the Smart Identification mechanism successfully found the object.

✓ indicates that a recovery scenario was activated (For more information on Recovery Scenario, see Chapter: Recovery Scenario) .

✓ indicates that the run session was stopped before it ended.

✓ [password].SetSecure square brackets around a test object name indicate that the test object was created dynamically during the run session. A dynamic test object is created either using programmatic descriptions or by using an object returned by a ChildObjects method, and is not saved in the object repository.

✓ displays the Run-Time Data Table, which is a table that shows the values used to run a test containing Data Table parameters or the Data Table output values retrieved from a test while it runs.

✓ displays the Maintenance Mode Update Result, which is a table that describes the Action taken by Maintenance Run Wizard on a failed step and its Details. This is displayed only for tests run in Maintenance Run Mode (For more information on Maintenance Run Mode, see Chapter: Maintaining Tests).

Advantages of Recording

Recording can be useful in the following situations:

- Recording is useful for novice Quick Test users. It helps you to learn how Quick Test interprets the operations you perform on your application and how it converts them to Quick Test objects and built-in operations.
- Recording can be useful when you need to quickly create a test that tests the basic functionality of an application or feature and does not require long-term maintenance.

Limitations of Recording

- Although recording makes it easier to create tests quickly, such tests are harder to maintain when the application changes and often require re-recording large parts of the test.
- Using recording we cannot program sophisticated tests that bring out hidden information.
- When you record tests, you may not notice that new objects are being added to the local object repository. This may result in many testers maintaining local object repositories with copies of the same objects.

Guidelines to be followed when recording a test

- Before you start to record, close all applications not required for the recording session.
- Decide how you want to open the application or Web browser when you record and run your test. You can choose to have Quick Test open one or more specified applications, or record and run on any application or browser that is already open. This can be done using Record and Run Settings Dailog.

Record and Run Settings Dialog

Before you record or run a test on an application, you can use the Record and Run Settings dialog box to instruct QuickTest, which applications to open when you begin to record or run your test. The Record and Run Settings dialog box always contains the Windows Applications tab. It may contain other tabs corresponding to add-ins that are loaded.

Windows Applications Tab

As shown below in Windows Applications Tab we can find 2 radio buttons. If we select First One QTP records and runs test on any application and if we select a second one we can specify the applications on which QTP should record or run test.

- Checkbox **Applications opened by QuickTest** indicates that QTP records only on those applications opened from QTP.
- Checkbox **Applications opened via the Desktop** indicates that QTP records only on those applications opened by double clicking on the aplication icon placed on the Desktop.
- Checkbox **Application specified below** indicates that QTP records only on those applications selected using + icon.

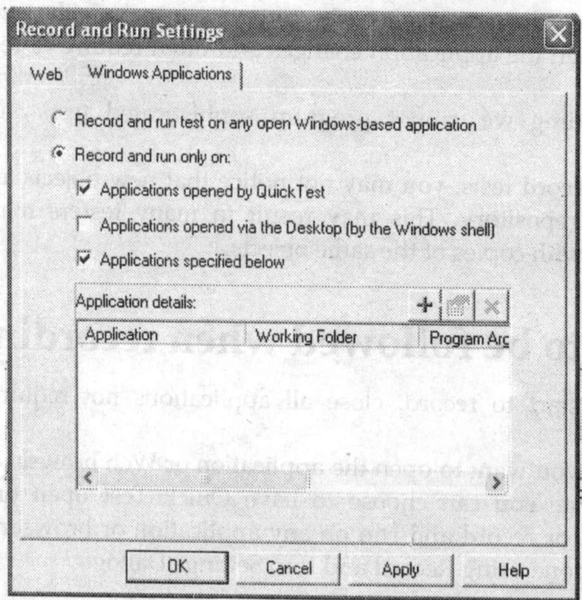

Web Tab

As shown below, in Web Tab also we can find 2 radio buttons. If we select the first One, QTP records and runs test on application opened on any browser and if we select second one, QTP records and runs test by opening application in a new browser of the specified type. Please note that QTP run tests on any supported browser (See Chapter: **Introduction to QTP** for supported browsers) but **records only on Microsoft Internet Explorer**.

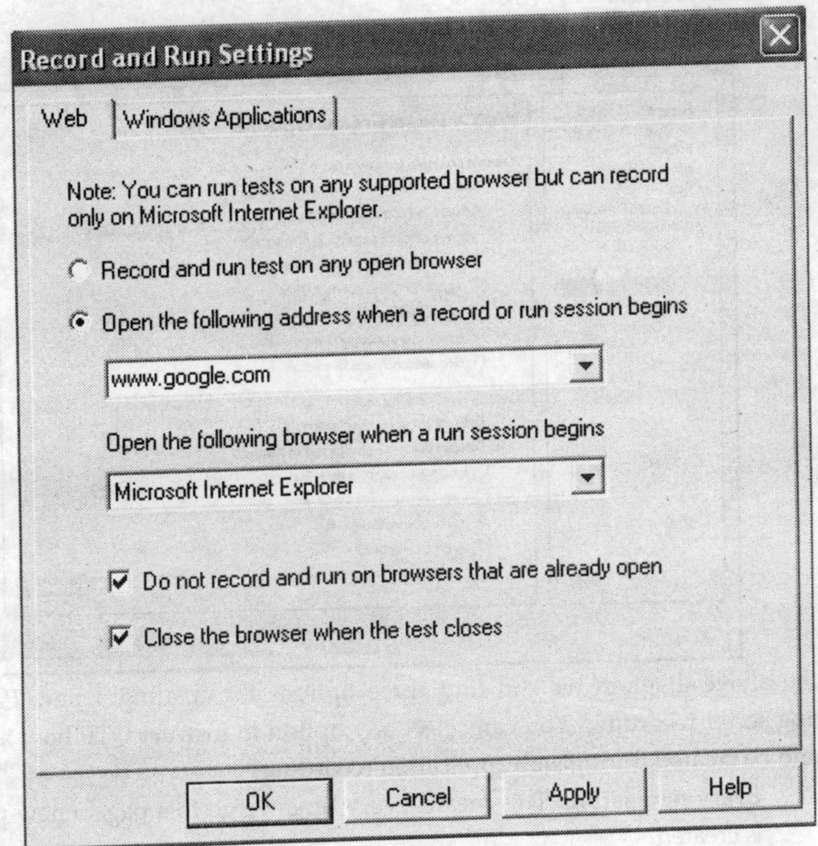

Web Record Settings

- You can instruct Quick Test to ignore recording or running on a specific browser using **Tools->Options->Web->Ignore the following Browsers.**
- You can also instruct Quick Test how to create new pages during recording through **Tools->Options->Web->Page/Frame Options**

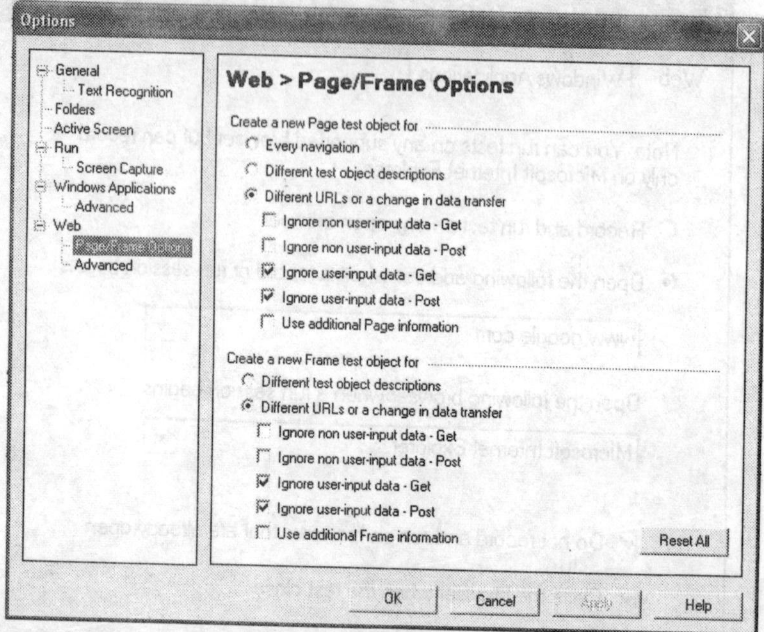

In the above diagram we can find three options for creating a new Page/Frame during script recording. You can select any option to instruct QTP how a new page should be created during web application recording.

1. **Every navigation**: This means every time we go to a page a new page object is created.
2. **Different Test Object Descriptions**: This means a new page will be created only if the new page has an object which is not there in the previous pages. For Example if logo is there in all pages of application, clicking logo in any page will not be treated as a new page since it is already available in previous pages.
3. **Different URLs or a Change in Data Transfer**: Every new URL is treated as a new page. Also every refresh creates new page in recording the URL is same.

Review Questions

1. Discuss Advantages and Disadvantages of Recording?
2. What are different types recording?
3. Which is the preferred recording and Why?
4. When to use Analog Recording?
5. How Coordinates in Low Level Recording are measured?

OBJECT REPOSITORY

Introduction

An object is an element that is present in the application. All the elements of the application are considered as objects. Each object belongs to particular class like list box, edit box, button, image, links etc.

Have a look at the Google Home Page below:

Some of the important objects present in the Google Home Page and their classes are

Object Name	Class Type
Images	Link
Maps	
News	
Orkut	
Books	
Gmail	
More	
iGoogle	
Advanced Search	
Language Tools	
Search Box	Web Edit
Google India Logo	Image
Google Search	WebButton
I'm Feeling Lucky	
the Web	Web Radio Group
pages from India	

Working with Object Repository

When QuickTest works on any of the objects in the application it adds the description of the object into the object repository.

Object repository acts as a container to store test objects. Test object is the object created by QuickTest in the test script to represent the object present in the application.

To open an Object Repository choose **Resources->Object Repository.** Object Repository looks like this (see below):

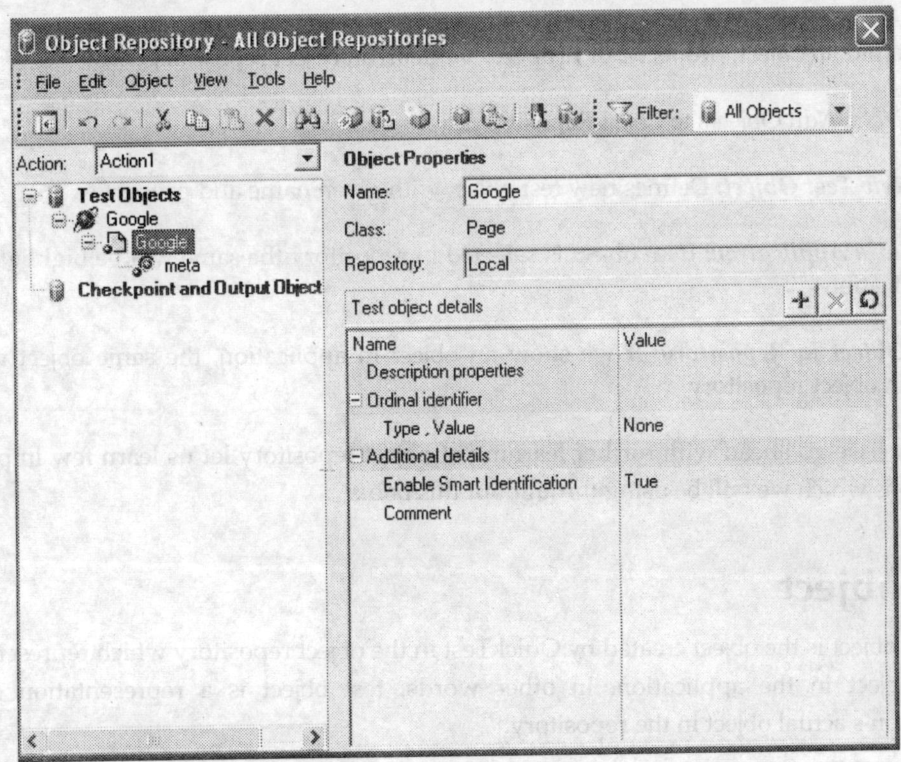

Object Repository along with storing objects, can also be used to add, delete and find the objects. Below is the tool bar of object repository with important icons:

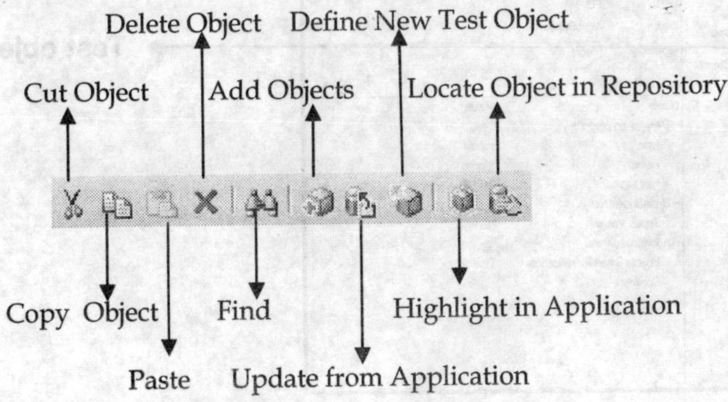

Cut&Paste: Will Cut and Paste object from one place to another place in an object repository.

Copy&Paste: Will Copy and Paste object from one place to another place in an object repository.

Delete: Deletes the object from repository.

Find: To find an object, property, or property value in an object repository.

Add Objects: Add Objects to Local Repository.

Define New Test Object: Defines new test object with given name and properties

Highlight in Application: If an object is selected in repository the same will be highlighted in the application

Locate Object in Repository: If we show an object in application, the same object will be located in object repository

Before we go ahead with further learning of object repository let us learn few important definitions which we will be using throughout this book.

Test object

Test object is the object created by QuickTest in the object repository which represents the actual object in the application. In other words, test object is a representation of the application's actual object in the repository.

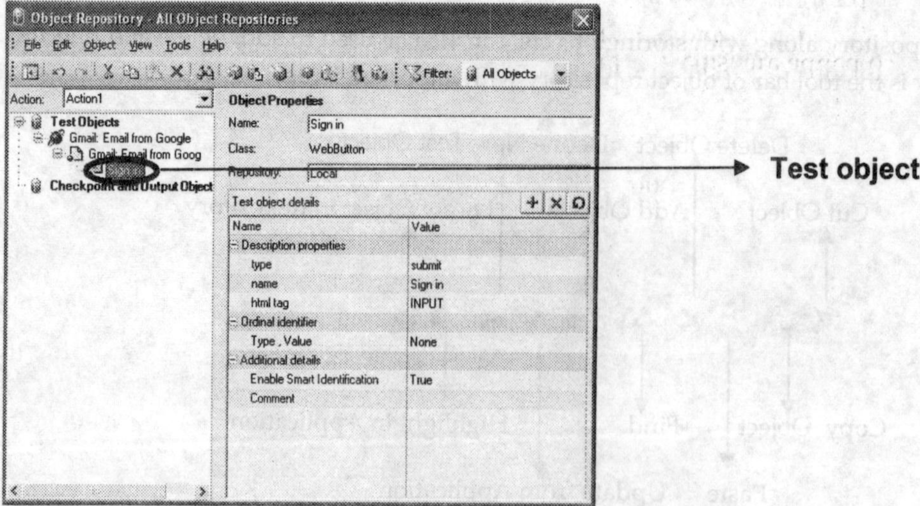

For example consider that the sign in button is clicked in Gmail. The representation of this sign in button is stored in object repository as shown in figure above and is called as test object.

Run-time object

The actual object that is present in the application on which the QuickTest performs an operation. For example signin button of Gmail application on which quick test clicks when the test runs is referred as **Run Time** object as shown in figure below.

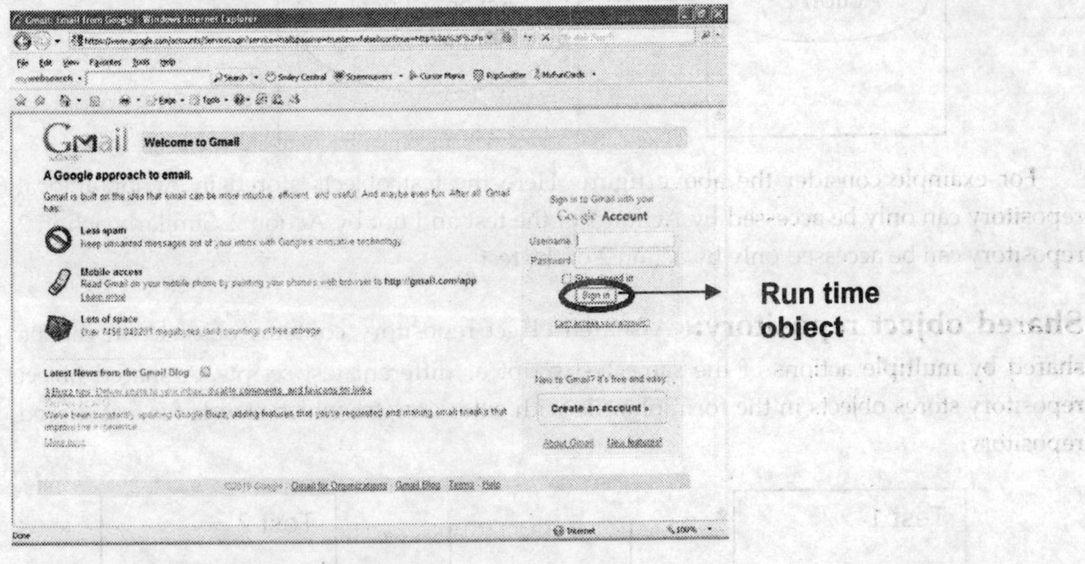

Object Repository types

Depending on the way objects are stored and used by QTP Test Script, Object repositories are divided in to two types.

1. Local Object Repository
2. Shared Object Repository

Local object repository: In this type of repository, the objects are stored for a particular action and only that particular action can access the stored objects. An action is nothing but few lines of code in the QTP Script. One script can contain multiple actions. If you are recording some operations on the application first you must choose in which action of the QTP script the steps must be recorded. By default, during recording all objects corresponding to user actions are automatically stored in the corresponding action's local object repository.

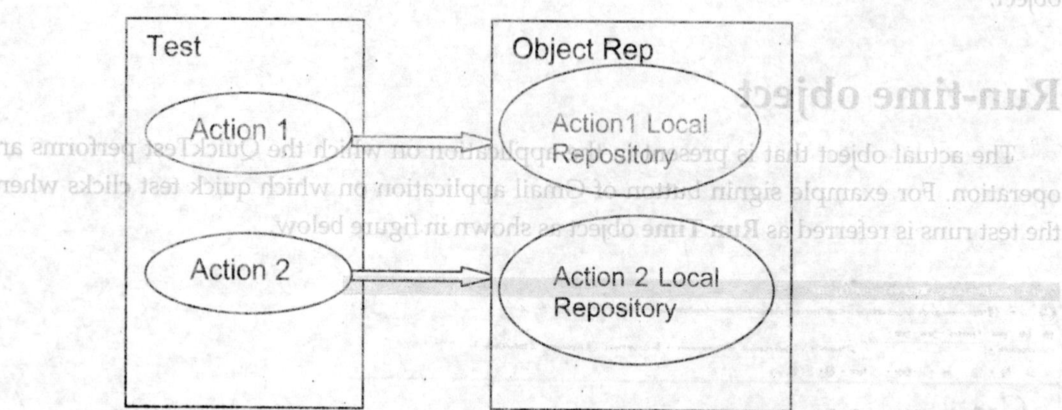

For example consider the above figure. Here the test objects stored in Action 1 local repository can only be accessed by Action 1 of the test and not by Action 2. Similarly action 2 repository can be accessed only by action 2 of the test.

Shared object repository: A shared object repository contains objects that can be shared by multiple actions of the same test script or different test scripts. A shared object repository stores objects in the form of a file with extension **.tsr** which stands for test shared repository.

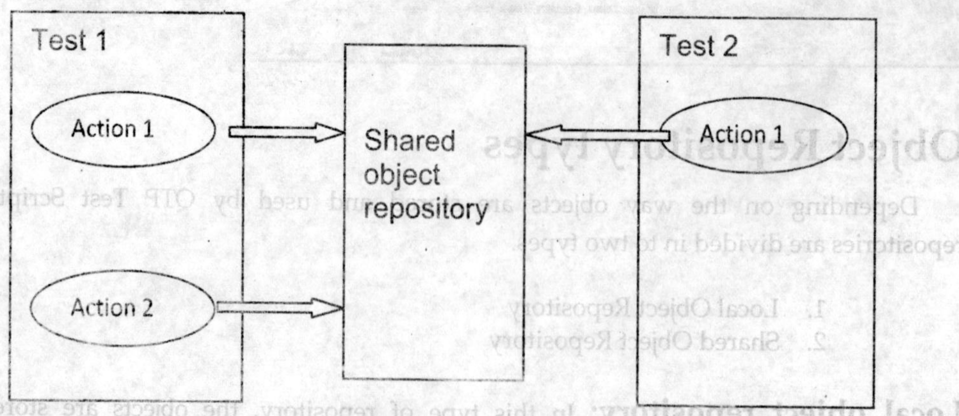

For example consider the above figure; as shown there are two tests which require the same objects so instead of creating three local repositories(one each for action 1,action 2 of test 1 and one for action1 of test2) with the same objects a shared repository is created and accessed by all the three actions. As shown in the figure not only multiple actions of a test can access a shared repository, also multiple tests can access the shared repository.

Points to remember:

- *When a test is recorded objects are by default stored in local object repository.*
- *A test can use a combination of repository types. That is a test can use both local and shared repository together.*
- *If an object with the same name is located in both the local object repository and in a shared object repository, the action will use the local object definition.*
- *A test can be associated with many shared repositories.*
- *If an object with the same name is located in more than one shared object repository, the object is used from the first occurrence of the object, according to the order in which the shared object repositories are associated with the action.*

Local Vs Shared Object Repository

It is always preferred to use Shared repository over local repository since every object is present only once and it can be shared by all required actions. Since we are avoiding multiple copies of object it is very easy to maintain the changes present in the object properties.

Creating a Local Repository

Test objects can be added to local repositories in two ways:

- Test objects are automatically stored into local repository in recording mode.
- Objects can be added to the local repository manually by following the steps below:

1. Click on the object repository button from the automation toolbar or alternatively select **Resources > Object Repository** The Object Repository window opens.
2. Click the Add Objects to Local toolbar button and select the object to be added to the repository.
3. If the selected object does not consist of any child object in the test object hierarchy, it is added directly to the repository. For example let us add the Google search button. Follow steps 1-2 from above. Object selection dialog box appears as shown in the figure below.

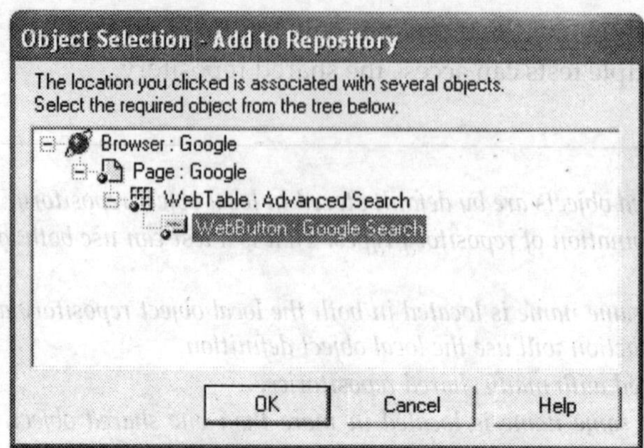

As seen in the figure above, the Google search button does not contain any child object hence it is added directly to the repository by clicking OK.

4. Alternate to step 3, if the selected object is a parent of an object then QuickTest will prompt an **Define Object Filter** dialog box with the following four options:

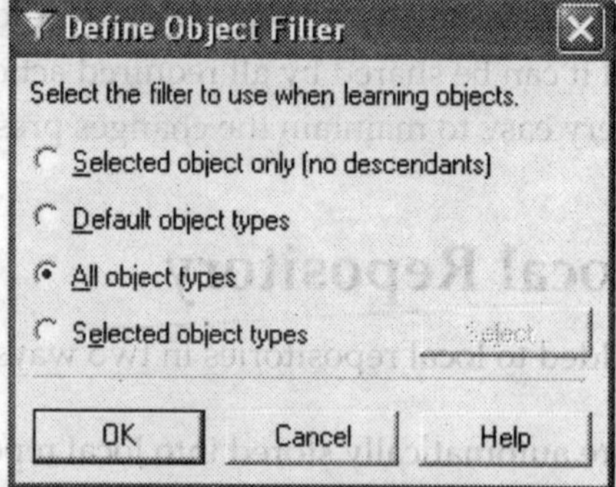

- ✓ **Selected object only (no descendants):** Adds only parent object
- ✓ **Default object types**: Adds all default objects in the parent.
- ✓ **All object types**: Adds all the objects including custom objects.
- ✓ **Selected object types**: Adds objects of only selected type.

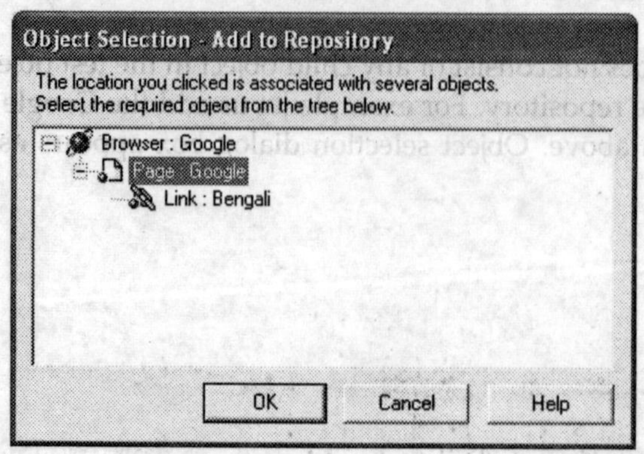

For example if Google search page is to be added then clicking on the page you find that the page object has a child object. When you select the page object and click OK the Define Object Filter dialog box will be opened.

5. Select the required option and click **OK**, The object will be added to the repository.

Exporting Local Objects to a Shared Object Repository

The first step involved in creating a shared repository is to export the objects from the local repository to a shared repository. This can be done in two ways.

1. The **Export Local Objects** option will export all the local objects to shared file which will be stored in a physical location.
2. The **Export and Replace Local Objects** option exports the local objects to a shared object repository and associates the new shared object repository with the action, and automatically deletes the objects in the local object repository of that action.

Steps to export local objects to a new shared object repository:

1) Select **File > Export Local Objects**, or **File > Export and Replace Local Objects** in the object repository window. The **Save Shared Object Repository** dialog box opens as shown in the figure below.

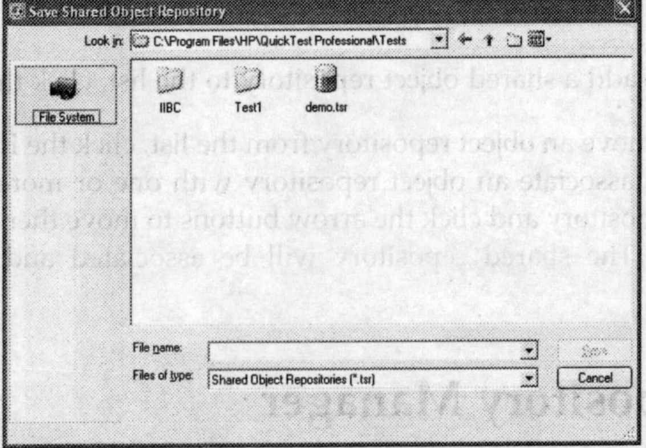

2) Select the location where the file should be saved.
3) Enter the filename and Click Save. QuickTest saves the object repository with a **.tsr** extension.

Associating Shared Object Repository to Action

Once the shared object repository is created by exporting the local objects the next step is to add the created shared repository to the action.

To add shared repository to an action:

- Click on Associate Repositories button or alternatively select **Resources > Associate Repositories**. The Associate Repositories dialog box opens.

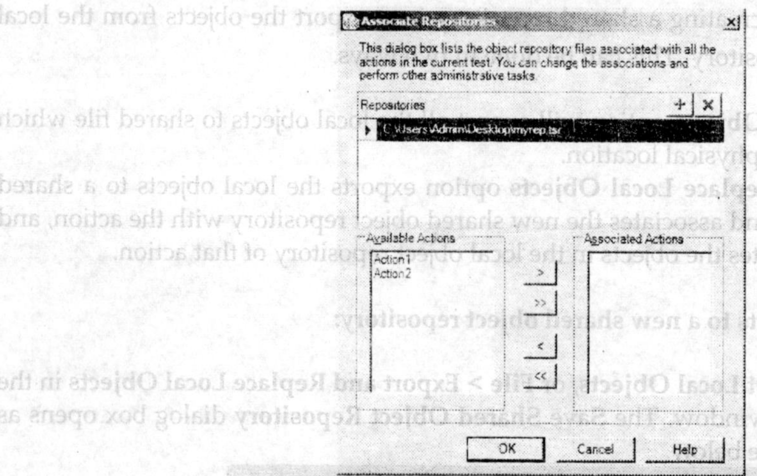

  - To add a shared object repository to the list, click the Add button and to remove an object repository from the list, click the Remove button.
  - To associate an object repository with one or more actions select the object repository and click the arrow buttons to move them between the Actions.
- Click OK. The shared repository will be associated and displayed in the object repository.

Object Repository Manager

Object repository manager is used to manage the shared object repositories. Using this object repository manager, shared repositories can be created and edited. The edit operations that can be done are add, delete, rename and move objects of the shared repositories from one repository to another.

Editing shared object repository

Follow the steps below to edit shared object repository:

1) In the Object Repository Manager, select ***File*** > ***Open.*** Select Shared Repository from file selection dialog.
2) If repository opened is non-editable, Select ***File*** > ***Enable Editing***. The object repository becomes editable.
3) Modify any objects information similar to the way you did in local repository.
4) Click **Save** to save changes.

Remember the following with local object repository

- By default QuickTest creates a new empty local object repository for every action in a test.
- If a child object is added to a local object repository, and its parent objects are in a shared object repository, its parent objects are automatically added to the local object repository.
- If QuickTest learns the same object in your application in two different actions, the test object is stored as a separate test object in each of the local object repositories.
- When you save your test, all of the local object repositories are automatically saved with the test as part of each action within the test.
- The local object repository cannot be stored as a separate file.

Remember the following with shared object repository

- If QuickTest comes across an object that already existing in local/shared repository, QuickTest uses the existing information instead of adding again to the repository.
- When QuickTest learns a new object, it automatically adds to local repository and not the shared repository.

Object repository-Comparison tool

The object repository comparison tool is used to compare two repositories for similarities and variations among the objects. This tool compares for different object names, descriptions (properties and values of each object) in the two repositories.

After the compare process the tool generates a report which displays graphical representation of the objects of the repositories. In this report objects that have differences and the objects that are present in one repository are highlighted.

Object repository-Merge tool

The Object Repository Merge Tool is used to merge two object repositories into a single repository.

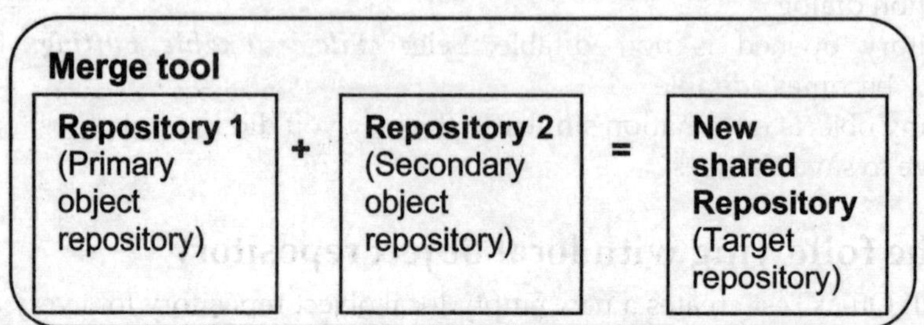

Objects in the primary and secondary object repositories are automatically compared and then added to the target object repository.

The Object Repository Merge Tool:

✓ *Merges two selected object repositories.*

✓ *Enables you to merge objects from the local object repository of one or more actions into a shared object repository.*

Steps to merge two object repositories:

1) In the Object Repository Manager, select Tools > Object Repository Merge Tool. The following New Merge window will be opened

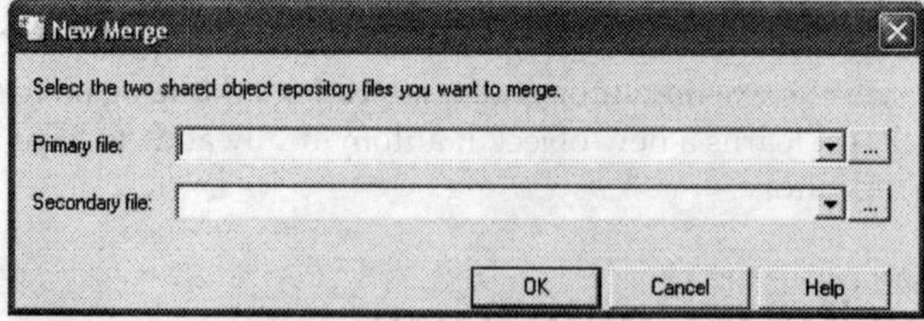

2) Select the files that have to be merged.
3) Click **OK**. The Object Repository Merge Tool automatically merges the selected object repositories into a new target object repository.
4) Click on close.

Review Questions

1. Why is an object repository required?
2. How many types of repositories are available and what are the differences between them?
3. What are the activities that can be performed with Object repository?
4. What are the activities that can be performed with Object repository Manager?
5. What is the difference between Local and Shared Repositories?

- Action
- Test object
- Object Repository
- Local object Repository
- shared object Repository (.tsr)
-
- ✓ object Repository manager
- ✓ object repository – Comparison tool.
- object repository merge tool.

OBJECT IDENTFICATION

Introduction

QuickTest performs actions on the objects of an application by learning and identifying the objects in the application. The process of uniquely identifying an object from the application window is called as object identification. QuickTest uses two modes of object identification to recognize the objects uniquely.

- Normal Identification mode.
- Smart Identification mode.
- Ordinal Identifiers

Normal Identification

In this mode of identification QuickTest has two lists of properties based on which it will identify the object uniquely. The first list is the list of mandatory properties. QuickTest learns these default property values and checks if any object matches the description. If no object in the application is identified uniquely it adds properties from the second list called as assistive properties. All the properties in the assistive list are added one by one till an unique object is identified.

If both Mandatory and Assistive properties fail to uniquely recognize the object, QTP uses **ordinal identifiers (location** and **index**) to recognize the object uniquely. During a run session, QuickTest searches for a *run-time object* that exactly matches the description of the test object it learned while recording. It expects to find a perfect match for both the mandatory and any assistive properties it used to create an unique description while recording. As long as the object in the application does not change significantly, the description generated during recording is almost always sufficient for QuickTest to uniquely identify the object.

Mandatory properties are properties that QuickTest always learns for a particular test object class.
Assistive properties are properties that QuickTest learns only if the mandatory properties are not sufficient to create an unique description.

Ordinal Identifiers

Even after using mandatory and assistive properties if the object is not uniquely identified then QuickTest uses the ordinal identifiers to identify the object uniquely.

There are three types of ordinal identifiers:

1. ***Index***: this identifier indicates the order in which the object appears in the application code. This order is unique even though identical objects are present.
2. ***Location:*** this identifier indicates the order in which the object appears within the window, frame or dialog box irrespective of objects with identical description.
3. ***Creation time:*** this identifier is applicable only to web applications. This identifier indicates an unique id in the order in which the browsers were opened. This identifier is handy in identifying the browser to be worked on when a group of identical browsers are open.

Smart Identification

When normal identification fails (that is, no unique object is identified or more than one object is matched) to identify an unique object, QuickTest switches to the next mode of identification called smart identification. For QuickTest to switch to this mode, the smart identification mode must be enabled for the test.

The Smart Identification mechanism uses two lists of properties:

- **Base filter properties**: This list of properties contain the most fundamental properties of a particular test object class whose values cannot be changed without changing the original object. For example, if a Web link's tag was changed from <A> to any other value, you could no longer call it a web link.
- **Optional filter properties:** Other properties that can help identify objects of a particular class as they are unlikely to change on a regular basis, but which can be ignored if they are no longer applicable.

Smart Identification Process

The Smart Identification mechanism during a run session follows the following process to identify the object:

1. QuickTest "forgets" the recorded test object description and creates a new ***object candidate*** list containing the objects (within the object's parent object) that match all of the properties defined in the base filter property list.
2. From that list of objects, QuickTest filters out any object that does not match the first property listed in the Optional Filter Properties list. The remaining objects become the new object candidate list.
3. QuickTest evaluates the new object candidate list based on following conditions:

   - ✓ If the **new object candidate list still has more than one object**, QuickTest uses the new (smaller) object candidate list to repeat step 2 for the next optional filter property in the list.
   - ✓ If the **new object candidate list is empty**, QuickTest ignores this optional filter property, returns to the previous object candidate list, and repeats step 2 for the next optional filter property in the list.
   - ✓ If the object **candidate list contains exactly one object**, then QuickTest concludes that it has identified the object and performs the statement containing the object.

4. QuickTest continues the process described in steps 2 and 3 until it either identifies one object, or runs out of optional filter properties to use.

If, after completing the Smart Identification elimination process, QuickTest still cannot identify the object, then QuickTest uses the recorded description plus the ordinal identifier to identify the object.

Configuring object identification

When QuickTest learns an object, it learns a set of properties and values that uniquely describe the object within the object hierarchy. In most cases, this description is sufficient to enable QuickTest to identify the object during the run session. If you find that the description QuickTest uses for a certain object class is not the most logical one for the objects in your application, or if you expect that the values of the properties in the object description may change frequently, you can configure the way that QuickTest learns and identifies objects.

Steps to configure mandatory and assistive properties

1) Select **Tools > Object Identification**. The Object Identification dialog box opens as shown below

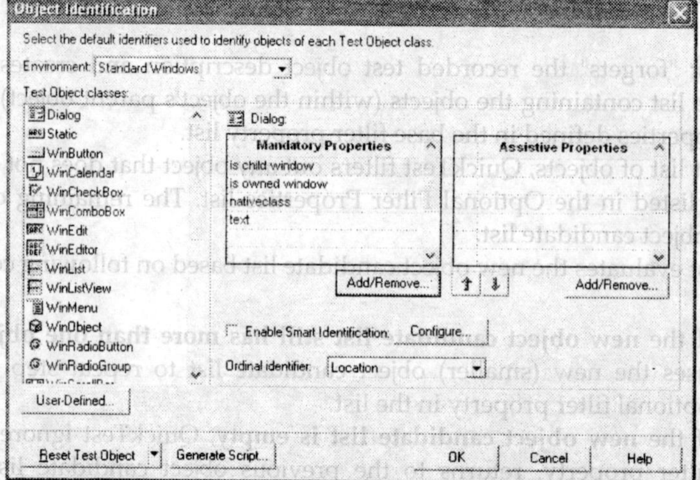

2) Select the appropriate environment in the Environment list.
3) In the Test Object classes list, select the test object class you want to configure.
4) In the Mandatory Properties list, click **Add/Remove**. From the Add/Remove Properties dialog opened select the properties you want to include. Click **OK** to close the Add/Remove Properties dialog box. Note that you can also add new properties by clicking New button.

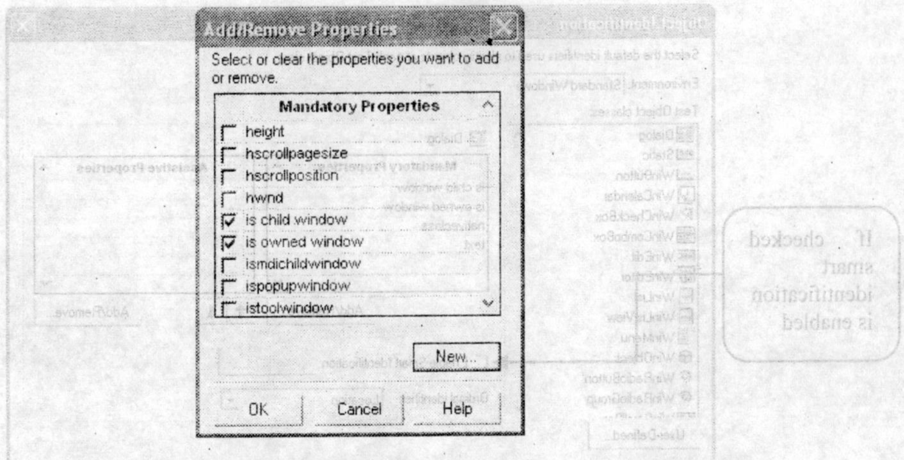

5) In the Assistive Properties list, click **Add/Remove**. Select the properties you want to include in the assistive properties.

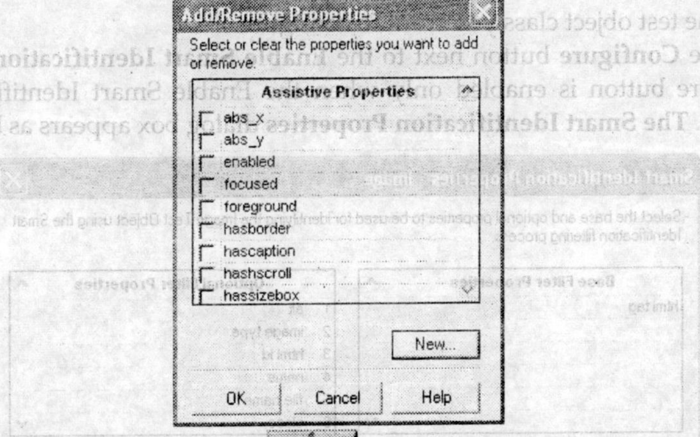

6) Use the up and down arrows to set your preferred order for the assistive properties. Click **OK** to close the Add/Remove Properties dialog box. The properties are displayed in the Assistive Properties list.

Steps to configure smart identification properties

Select **Tools > Object Identification**. The Object Identification dialog box opens as shown below. Select the appropriate environment in the Environment list.

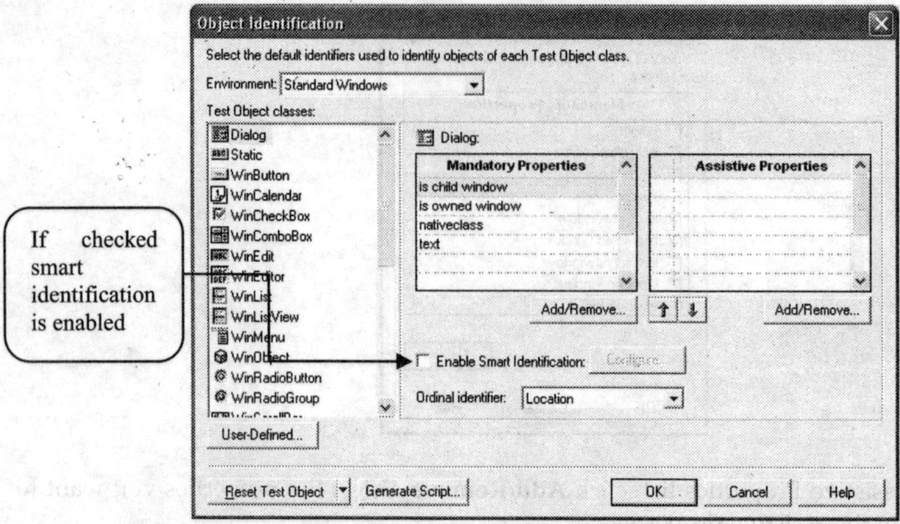

2) Select the test object class you want to configure.
3) Click the **Configure** button next to the **Enable Smart Identification** check box. The Configure button is enabled only when the Enable Smart Identification option is selected. **The Smart Identification Properties** dialog box appears as below:

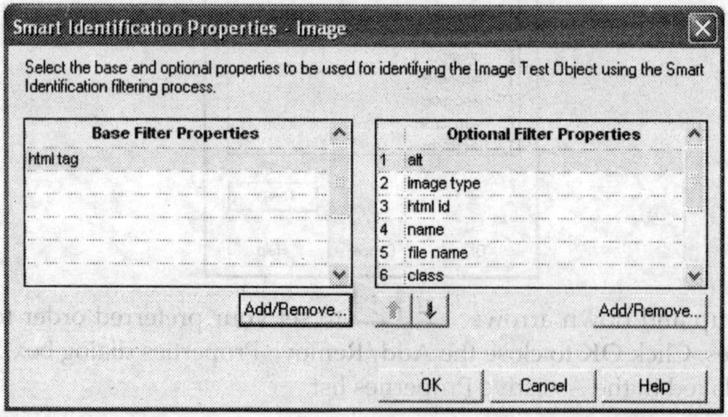

4) In the **Base Filter Properties** list, click **Add/Remove**. The Add/Remove Properties dialog box for base filter properties opens. Select the properties you want to include in the Base Filter Properties. Click **OK** to close the Add/Remove Properties dialog box.

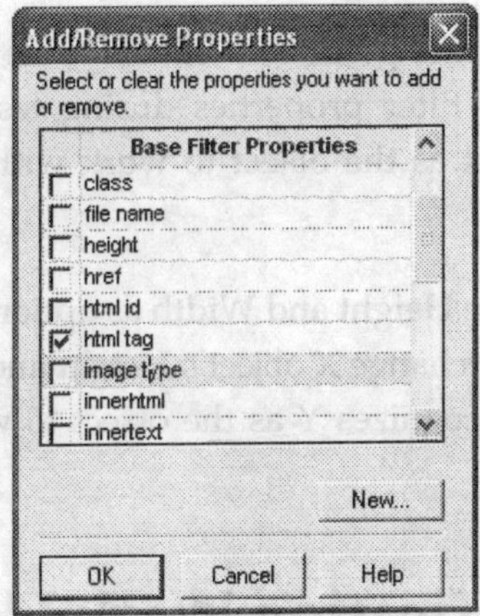

5) In the **Optional Filter Properties** list, click **Add/Remove**. The Add/Remove Properties dialog box for optional filter properties opens. Select the properties you want to include in the Optional Filter Properties list.

6) Use the up and down arrows to set your preferred order for the optional filter properties. Click **OK** to close the **Add/Remove** Properties dialog box.

Normal Vs Smart Identification

Even though both normal and smart identification are used for identifying the object, normal identification is used by QTP before switching to smart identification. Moreover normal identification must fail to identify the Object before QTP uses Smart Identification. The good thing about normal identification is, if it identifies an object in the application it always identifies the correct object. This is because during test run, normal identification uses all properties recorded at recording time to identify the object. In other words, Smart Identification uses one by one filter properties during test run and if any one property matches, it considers that object as the object to work with. Sometimes this might lead to wrong object Identification.

For example let's say, we use Height and Width as optional filter properties to identify an object X. Let's say the developer change X object's Height and creates a new object Y with the same Height of X. Now tool recognizes Y as the object to work instead of X and performs operation on that.

QTP Object Identification Work Flow

Let us consider a step from QTP Script which clicks Google Search Button from Google Home Page. The step looks as below:

```
Browser("Google").Page("Google").WebButton("Google Search").Click
```

In the above step QTP must Identify Google Search button from the application before it performs click operation. Anyways QTP must also identify Google Search Button's parent objects Page and Browser before Identifying Google Search Button. To Identify Google Search Button object, QTP follows the 3 steps approach as shown below.

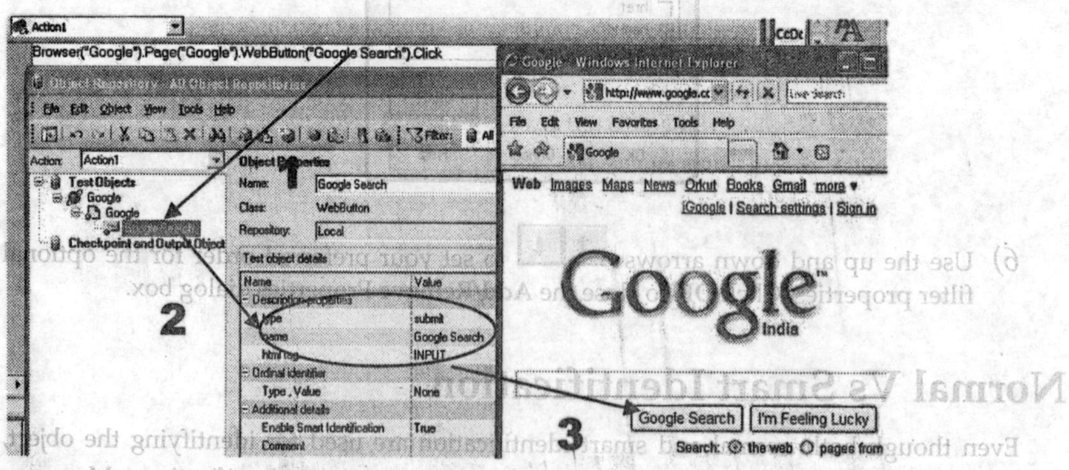

Step1:

Map Logical Name of the object in the script with Logical name of the object in Repository. In the above example "Google Search" is the logical name of the "Google Search" web button. Even though in the above example Logical Name is the same as the Actual name of the object, it need not always be so. If Logical Name is not found in the object repository, the following error dialog will appear indicating the object was not found in the repository. Otherwise QTP proceeds to the next step.

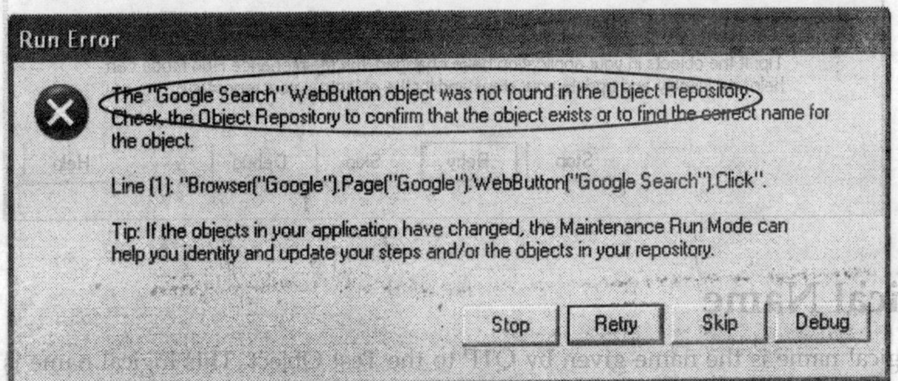

Step2:

Here QTP reads Test Object Description which is nothing but all the properties required to identify the Test Object. For Example for the Google Search button, below is the Test Object description in the Object Repository:

Name	Value
⊟ Description properties	
type	submit
name	Google Search
html tag	INPUT

Step 3:

Using the above properties, QTP goes to application and tries to recognize an unique object which is matching the test object description. If the object was not found, the following error will be displayed indicating the object was not found in the application with specified properties of the object in the repository. Note that the dialog below will be displayed only if smart identification was disabled or set to false for this object. In case smart identification is enabled, QTP will go to smart identification and try to recognize the object using smart identification mechanism.

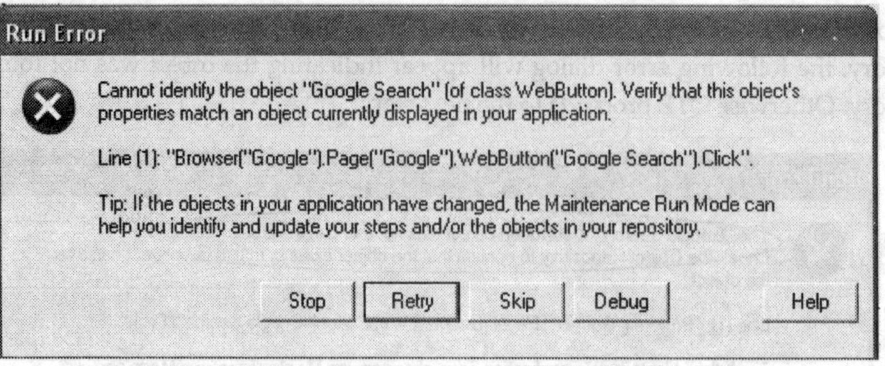

Logical Name

Logical name is the name given by QTP to the Test Object. This logical name is used in QTP script and Object Repository to map test object from script to Object Repository. It is important to note that Logical name of all objects of a particular class under a particular parent must be unique. This means if we have a Google home page with logical name "Google Home", all links under this page name in object repository must be unique. Anyhow we can have objects of two different classes under a particular parent with same logical name. For example we can have an edit box with logical name "**Login**" and also a button with the logical name "**Login**" under the same parent and it is perfectly acceptable. The only requirement to keep in mind always is if X is the logical name of the object in object repository, name X must be used in the QTP script.

The advantage of Logical name is it can be changed for better readability of the script and also it helps in better maintenance of the script for application changes. For example to identify a button Google Search we are using its **name** property value "**Google Search**". Let us say later the name property value has been changed by the developer to "**My Google Search**". This will not affect the existing script because we will only change the name property value in the object repository to "**My Google Search**" and the script will get the updated Test Object Description through logical name mapping as shown in Step1 of the previous section.

Name	Value
− Description properties	
type	submit
name	Google Search
html tag	INPUT

Custom to Standard Class Mapping

If the application under test contains objects that do not belong to a particular class type, such objects are recorded as WinObjects and are called as custom objects.

Such custom objects can be mapped to an existing standard windows class. While mapping remember that the custom object behavior should be comparable to the standard class being mapped to.

Steps to map an unidentified or custom class to a standard Windows class:

1. Choose **Tools > Object Identification**. The Object Identification dialog box opens.
2. Select **Standard Windows** in the **Environment** box. The **User-Defined** button becomes enabled.
3. Click **User-Defined**. The Object Mapping dialog box opens as shown below.

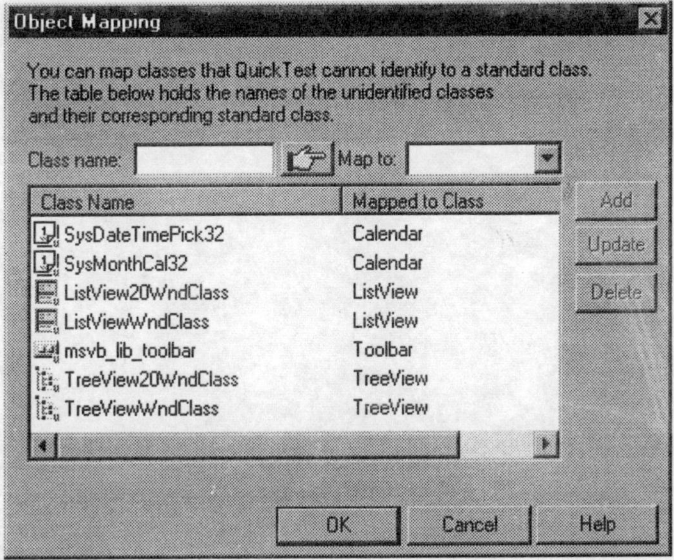

4. Click the pointing hand and then click the object whose class you want to add as a user-defined class. The name of the user-defined object is displayed in the **Class Name** box.
5. In the **Map to** box, select the standard object class to which you want to map your user-defined object class and click **Add**. The class name and mapping is added to the object mapping list.
6. If you want to map additional objects to standard classes, repeat steps 4 & 5 for each object.

7. Click **OK**. The Object Mapping dialog box closes and your object is added to the list of Standard Windows test object classes as a user-defined test object. Note that your object has an icon with a red U in the corner, identifying it as a user-defined class.

Review Questions

1. Name the different Identification Modes supported by Tool and their working differences.
2. How will you configure Normal Identification properties?
3. What are Normal and Smart Identification merits and demerits?
4. What is the difference between Standard and Custom Class?
5. What are the advantages of Logical Name

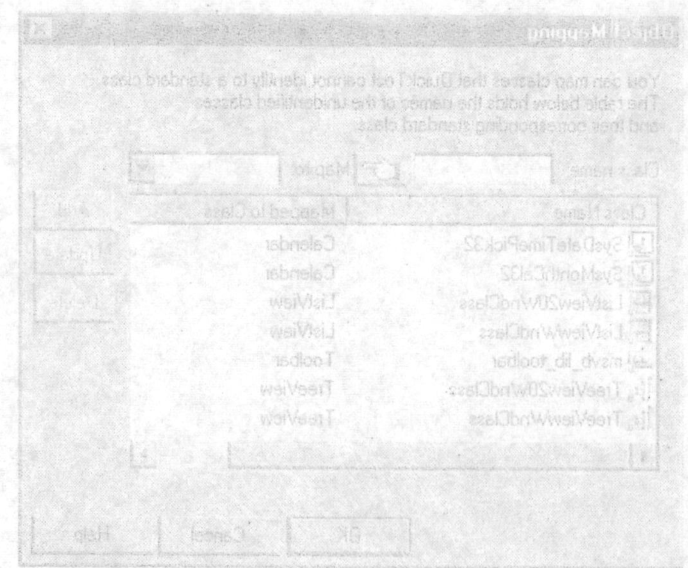

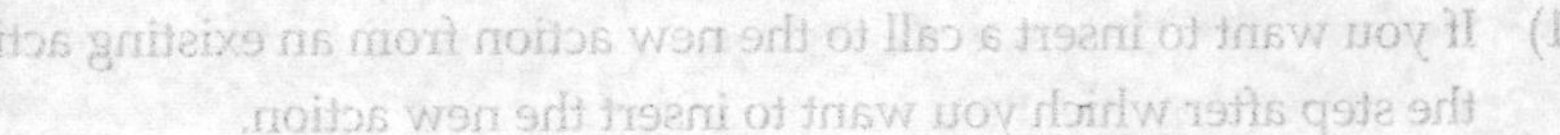

ACTIONS

You can divide your test into actions to streamline the process of testing your application. Actions help divide your test into logical units. When you create a test, it includes one action. All the steps you add and all the modifications you make while editing your test are part of a single action.

You can divide your test into multiple actions by:

- ✓ creating new actions and inserting calls to them
- ✓ inserting calls to existing actions
- ✓ splitting existing actions.

The actions used in the test, and the order in which they are run, are displayed in the Test Flow pane.

Types of Actions

There are three kinds of actions:

1) **Reusable action:** An action that can be called multiple times by the test with which it is stored (the local test), as well as by other tests.

2) **Non-reusable action:** An action that can be called only once in the test with which it is stored, and cannot be used by other tests.

3) **External action:** A reusable action stored with another test. External actions are read-only in the calling test, but you can choose to use a local, editable copy of the Data Table information for the external action.

Creating New Action

1) If you want to insert a call to the new action from an existing action in your test, click the step after which you want to insert the new action.

2) Select **Insert > Call to New Action** or click the Insert Call to New Action button on the Insert toolbar. The Insert Call to New Action dialog box opens.

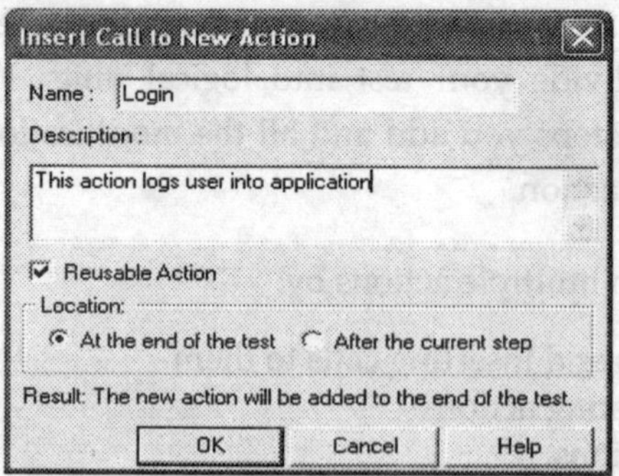

3) In the Name box, type a new action name or accept the default name.
4) In the Description box, add a description of the action. You can also add an action description at a later time using the Action Properties dialog box.
5) Ensure **Reusable Action** is selected if you want to be able to call the action from other tests or multiple times from within this test. By default, this option is selected.
6) Decide where to insert the call to the action by selecting **At the end of the test** or **After the current step**.
7) Click **OK**. A new action is stored with your test.

Setting Action Properties

The Action Properties dialog box enables you to define options for the stored action. These settings apply each time the action is called. You can modify an action name, add or modify an action description, and set an action as reusable or non-reusable.

You can open the Action Properties dialog box while recording or editing your test by:

- Choosing **Step > Action Properties** from the Keyword View when an action node is highlighted or by Right-clicking an action node in the Keyword View and selecting **Action Properties**.

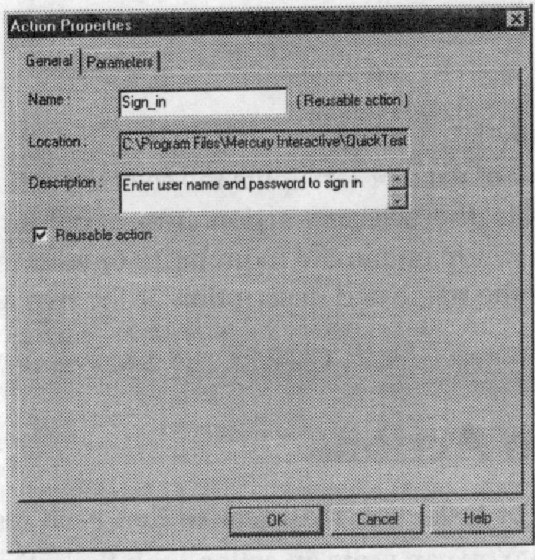

You can use the General tab of the Action Properties dialog box to modify the name of an action, add or edit an action's description, or change the reusability status of the action.

Splitting Actions

You can split an action that is stored with your test into two sibling actions or into parent-child nested actions.

When you split an action in your test that uses a local object repository:

- The two actions have identical local object repositories containing all of the objects that were in the original local object repository.

Steps to Split an action

1) Select the step before which you want the new (second) action to begin.
2) Select **Edit > Action > Split Action**. The Split Action dialog box opens as shown in the figure below: 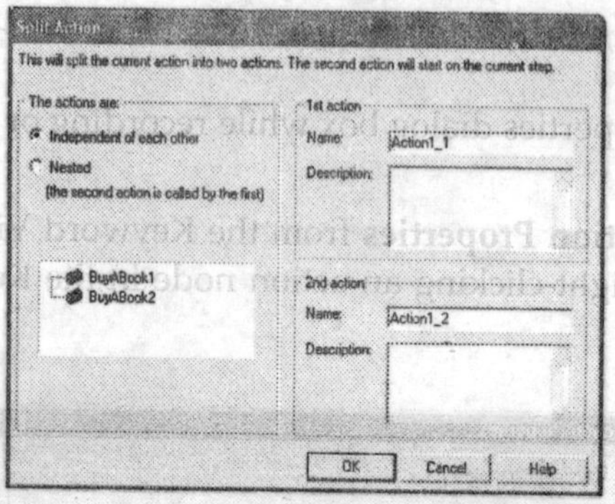
3) Select one of the following options:
   - ✓ **Independent of each other**: Splits the selected action into two sibling actions.
   - ✓ **Nested**. Splits the selected action into a parent child action. By nesting actions, you can maintain the modularity of your test.
4) If you want, modify the name and description of the two actions - use the **Name** and **Description** boxes.

Inserting Calls to Actions

When you plan a suite of tests, you may realize that each test requires some identical activities, such as logging in. You can write an action with the activities required and you can insert calls to this action into other tests.

You can insert calls to an existing action by inserting a **call to a copy of the action**, or by inserting a **call to the existing action**.

Inserting Call to Copy of Action

When you insert a call to a copy of an action into a test, the original action is copied in its entirety, including local repository, checkpoints, parameterization, the corresponding action tab in the Data Table, plus any defined action parameters.

If the test into which you are copying uses a shared object repository, the copied action will use the same shared object repository as the calling test. Before running the test, confirm that the shared object repository contains all the objects that are in the copied action. Otherwise, the test may fail.

Steps to call the Copy of Action in your test:

1. While recording or editing your test, choose **Insert > Call to Copy of Action.** The Select Action dialog box opens.

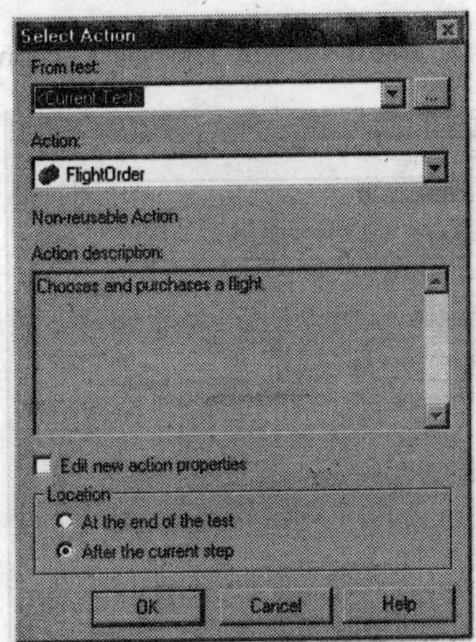

2. Use the **From test** browse button to select the test.
3. Use the **Action** drop down to select a reusable action.
4. Decide where to insert the call to the copy of the action and select **At the end of the test** or **After the current step.**
5. Click **OK**. The action is inserted into the test as a copy of the action.

Inserting Call to an Existing Action

You can insert a call to a reusable action that is stored in your current test (local action), or in any other test (external action). Inserting a call to an existing action is like linking to it. You can view the steps of the action in the action view, but you cannot modify them. If you call an external action, you can choose, however, whether you want the data from the action's data sheet to be imported as a local, editable copy, or whether you want to use the (read-only) data from the original action.

If the test calling an action uses local repository mode, the called action's object repository is read-only (as are the steps of the called action) in the test calling the action. If the test calling an action uses a shared object repository, the called action uses the same shared object repository as the calling test. In this case, before running the test, confirm that the shared object repository of the calling test contains all the objects that are in the called action. Otherwise, the test may fail.

Steps to insert a call to an existing action:

1. Choose **Insert > Call to Existing Action.** The Select Action dialog box opens.

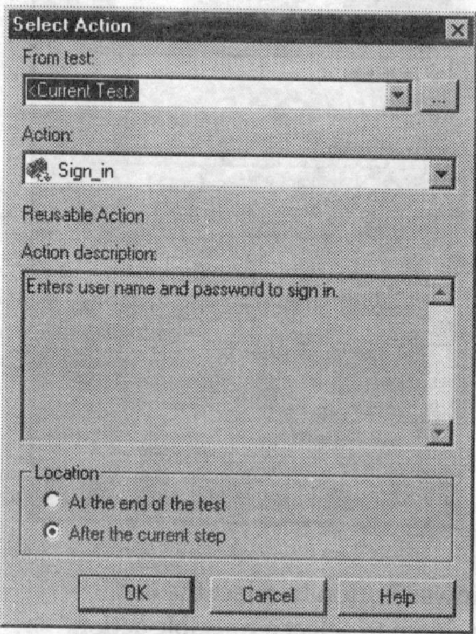

2. Use the **From test** browse button to find the test that contains the action you want to call. The **Action** box displays all reusable actions in the test you selected.
3. In the Action list, select the action you want to call.
4. Decide where to insert the call to the action and select **At the end of the test** or **After the current step**.
5. Click **OK**. A call to the action is inserted into the test flow.

Action Syntax in the Expert View

Calling Actions without Parameters:

In the Expert View, a call to an action with no parameters is displayed with the following basic syntax:

RunAction ActionName, IterationQuantity

For example, to call the **Select Flight** action and

- ✓ run it one iteration:

  RunAction "Select Flight", oneIteration

- ✓ run on all rows:

  RunAction "Select Flight", allIteration

- ✓ Run on a specified range of rows 1-4

  RunAction "Select Flight", "1 - 4"

Calling Actions with Parameters

If the action you are calling has input and/or output parameters defined, you can also supply the values for the input parameters and the storage location of the output parameters as arguments of the RunAction statement. Input parameters are listed before output parameters. An action call with parameters has the following syntax:

RunAction ActionName, IterationQuantity, Parameters

For example: Suppose you call Action2 from Action1, and Action2 has one input and one output parameter defined. The following statement supplies a string value of MyValue for the input parameter and stores the resulting value of the output parameter in a variable called MyVariable.

RunAction "Action2", oneIteration, "MyValue", MyVariable

Storing Action Return Values

If the action called by the RunAction statement includes an **ExitAction** statement, the RunAction statement can return the value of the **ExitAction** statement as below.
MyRetVal=RunAction(ActionName,IterationQuantity, Parameters)

Exiting an Action

You can add a line in your script in the Expert View to exit an action before it runs in its entirety. There are four types of exit action statements you can use:

- ✓ **ExitAction**: Exits the current action, regardless of its iteration attributes.
- ✓ **ExitActionIteration**: Exits the current iteration of the action.
- ✓ **ExitRun**: Exits the test, regardless of its iteration attributes.
- ✓ **ExitGlobalIteration**: Exits the current global iteration. You can view the exit action node in the Test Results tree.

Review Questions

1. What are the different types of Actions?
2. What is the difference between calling an existing action and copy of action?
3. Difference between **ExitActionIteration** and **ExitGlobalIteration?**

CHECK POINTS

Introduction

A checkpoint is one of the options provided by Quicktest to enhance the scripts. Check points in Automation Test Script are analogous to view and check activity of Manual Testing.

For example let's say from the country list box of registration page you want to check whether it has India by default through manual testing. You will open the Registration Page and view the country list box and then decide whether check is pass or fail. If the country list box has India as the selection then the check is passed else the check is failed.

You should notice few important points from the above manual action.

1. **You are viewing the Default Selected item in the country list box.**
2. **You have an expected value in your brain as "India".**
3. **Your eyes will see the actual value in the application's country list box which informs your brain the actual value present in the object.**
4. **Your brain compares the expected and actual value and decides whether the check is passed or failed.**

In Automation Testing your Brain is nothing but QTP Script. Hence Expected value is the value present in QTP script and Actual value anyways is the value present in the application. Hence in QTP (a checkpoint is a step of the test which compares the values of a specific property of an object during run time with the values that are stored in the test.) If the comparison turns positive the checkpoint passes and if the comparison is negative the checkpoint fails.

Checkpoints are verification points used to compare actual value with the expected value.
Actual value: Value that is present in the application.
Expected value: Value that is supposed to be in the application.

Adding a New Checkpoint to a test

Types of Checkpoints

Depending on the type of information we check, QuickTest provides the following types of checkpoints:

Checkpoint	Description	Example
Standard Check Point	Checks object's Property	Checks that a button is enabled
Bitmap Check Point	Checks the content of a bitmap	Check whether Logo is correct
Image Check Point	Checks the property values of an image	Check whether the image has ToolTip
Text Check Point	Checks whether Text present in the page is correct	Check whether the Welcome message after login is proper
Text Area Check Point	Checks whether Text present in the specified area is correct	Checks whether the total amount on bottom right side of the page is correct
Database Check Point	Check whether the contents of a record set is correct	Checks whether the username in the database is correct
Table Check Point	Checks the data present in the Table	Check whether the book name in the table cell is correct
Page Check Point	Check the contents of a Webpage	Checks whether all the links in the page are pointing to the correct destination

Accessibility Check Point	Checks whether the Web Page is adhering to Accessibility Rules	Checks that there are no Applets in the Webpage
XML Check Point From Application	Checks the XML Content displayed in the Webpage	Checks whether the attributes of a root element is correct
XML Check Point From Source	Checks whether the XML Content in an XML file is correct	Checks whether an XML element has correct child elements

Let us look at the above listed checkpoints in detail:

Standard Checkpoint

Standard checkpoint compares property values of an object in the application with the expected values. Objects such as list boxes, combo boxes, buttons can be checked using standard checkpoints.

Steps to insert standard checkpoint:

1) Click **Record** and select **Insert> Checkpoint > Standard Check Point**
2) Click the object to be checked in the application.
3) Checkpoint Properties Dialog will appear as shown in the figure below.

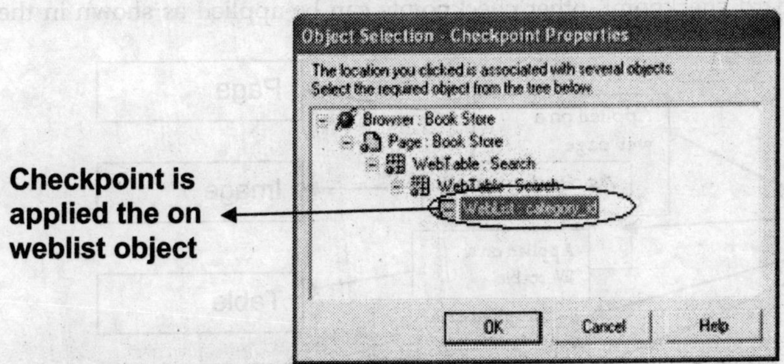

4) Select the object and Click **OK**
5) Checkpoint Properties dialog will appear as shown in figure below.

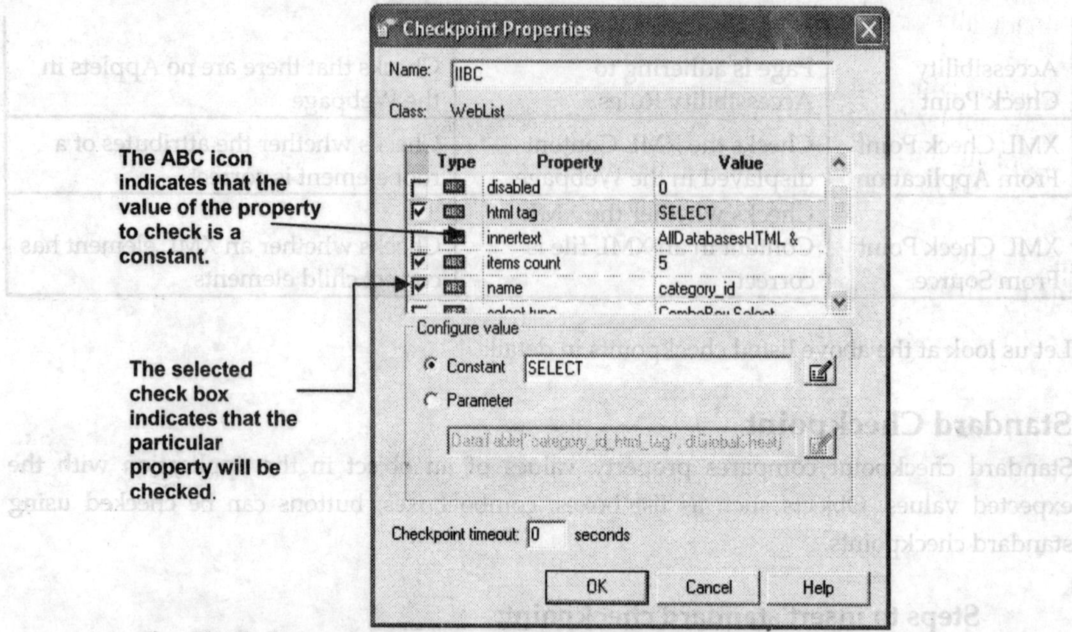

6) Check the properties to be checked as shown in figure above
7) Set the expected value for the property in the constant field.
8) Click **OK**.

Note: Using standard checkpoint, other checkpoints can be applied as shown in the figure below.

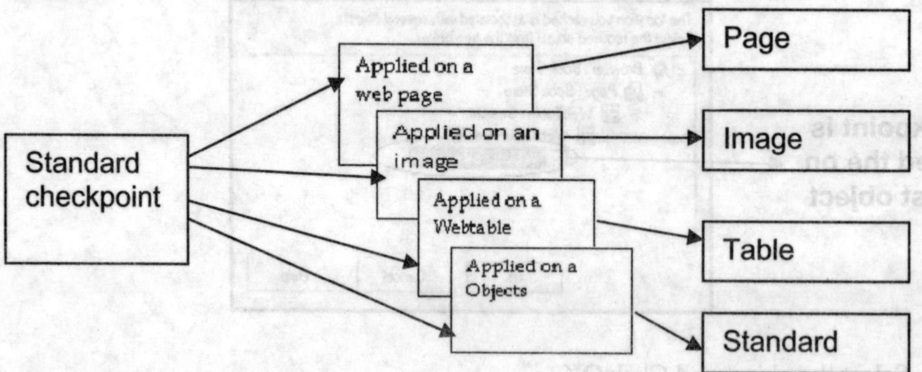

Image Checkpoint

Image Checkpoint is used to check for the values of an image. An image checkpoint can be created by inserting a standard checkpoint on an image object.

Steps to insert an Image checkpoint:

1) Click **Record** and select **Insert> Checkpoint > Standard Check Point**
2) Click the image object you want to check in the application.
3) Checkpoint Properties Dialog will appear as shown in the figure below.

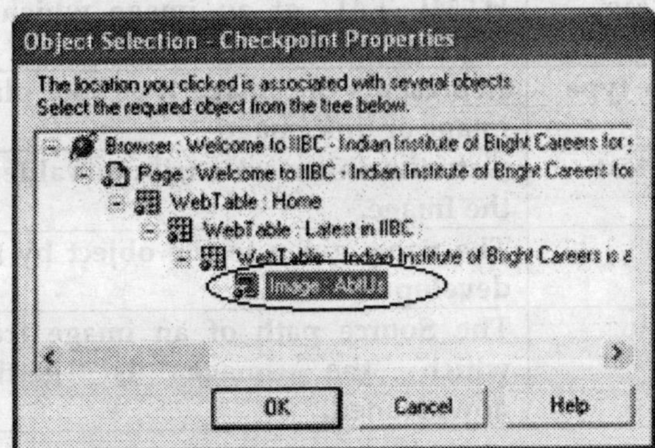

4) Select the image object as highlighted in figure above and click **OK**
5) Image Checkpoint Properties dialog will appear as shown in figure below.

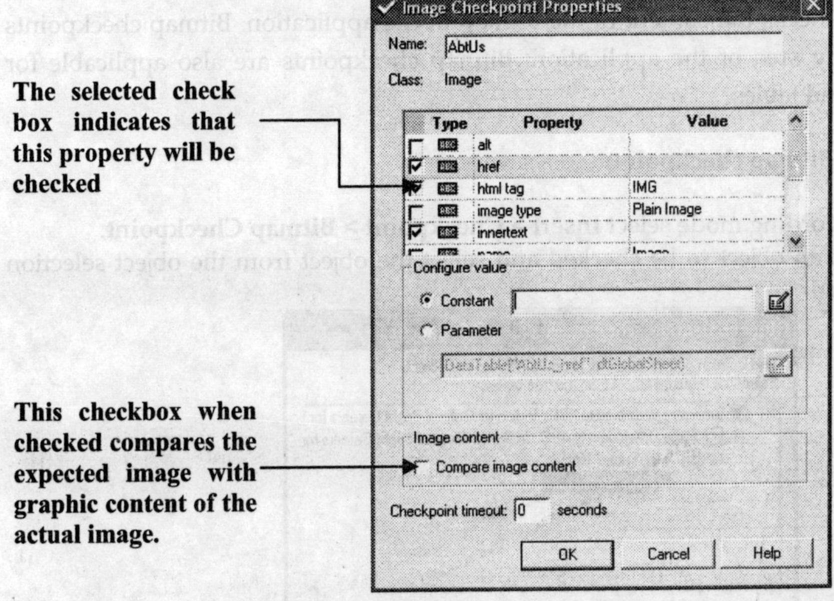

6) Check the properties to be checked and enter the expected value in the constant field. The table below shows some of the important properties of an object and their description.

Property	Description
alt	ToolTip of an image
href	Hyper Text Reference; i.e the URL of the page that opens when we click on this image
html tag	HTML TAG of an image which is nothing but IMG
image type	Represents the image type like plain image or link image
innertext	Gets the innertext attribute value of the Image.
name	The name given to the object by the developer.
src	The Source path of an image from which the image is getting downloaded.

7) Click **OK**. Image checkpoint will be placed into the test.

Bitmap Checkpoint

This checkpoint checks the content of the bitmap in the application. Bitmap checkpoints can be placed for any area of the application. Bitmap checkpoints are also applicable for buttons, text boxes, and tables.

Steps to insert a Bitmap checkpoint:

1) In recording mode select **Insert > Checkpoint > Bitmap Checkpoint.**
2) Click an object to be checked and select the object from the object selection dialog.

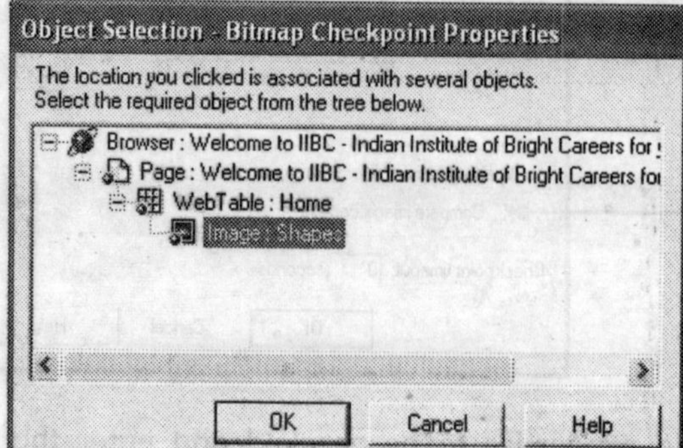

3) Select the image and click OK.
4) Bitmap Checkpoint Properties Dialog will appear as shown below.

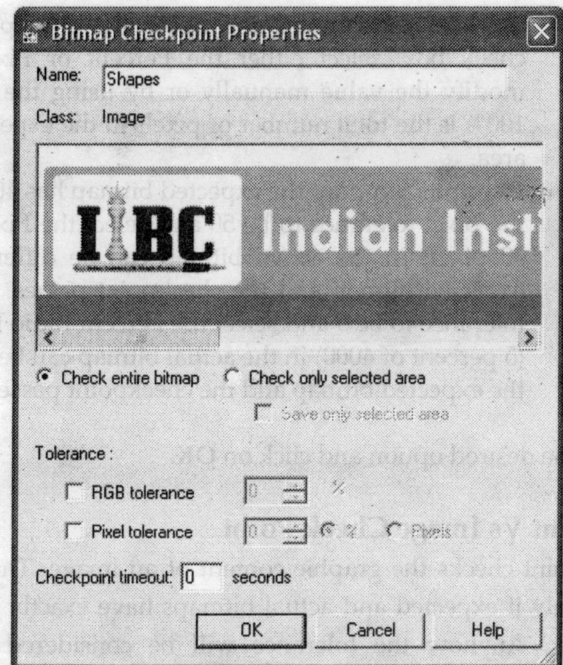

✓ **Check entire bitmap / Check only selected area**:
This option allows the user to select if a specific area or entire area of the bitmap is compared.

✓ **Save only selected area**:
This option will save the selected area of the bitmap within the test to save disk space.

Bitmap Checkpoint Tolerance Options:

✓ **RGB tolerance**: This option is limited to bitmaps with a color depth of 24bits.The RGB (Red, Green, Blue) tolerance determines the percent by which the RGB values of the pixels in the actual bitmap can differ from those of the expected bitmap and allow the checkpoint to pass.
Example: A bitmap checkpoint on identical bitmaps could fail if different display drivers are used when you create your checkpoint and when you run your test. Suppose one display driver displays the color white as RGB (255, 255, 255) and another driver displays the color white as RGB (231, 231, 231). The difference between these two values is about 9.4%. By setting the RGB tolerance to 10%, your checkpoint will pass when running your test with either of these drivers.

✓ **Pixel tolerance:** The pixel tolerance determines the number or percentage of pixels in the actual bitmap that can differ from those in the expected bitmap and allow the checkpoint to pass.Select the check box, select either the Percent or Pixels radio button, and modify the value manually or by using the up and down arrows. 100% is the total number of pixels in the expected bitmap or selected area.

Example: Suppose the expected bitmap has 4000 pixels. If you define the pixel tolerance to be 50 and select the Pixels radio button, up to 50 pixels in the actual bitmap can be different from those in the expected bitmap and the checkpoint passes. If you define the pixel tolerance to be 5 and select the Percent radio button, up to 200 pixels (5 percent of 4000) in the actual bitmap can be different from those in the expected bitmap and the checkpoint passes.

5) Set the desired option and click on **OK.**

Bitmap Check Point Vs Image Check Point

Bitmap Check Point checks the graphic content of an image. This means Bitmap check point is successful only if expected and actual bitmaps have exactly same number of pixels with the same color. Anyhow the tolerance will be considered appropriately if it is configured.

Image check point checks the properties of an Image like alt, src, image Type, href, etc. Even though image check point can be used to check the graphic content of an image more advanced options like pixel tolerance, checking part of an image are not available.

Table Checkpoint

Table checkpoints are applied on webtables and are used to check the content within the tables. This checkpoint is applied through standard checkpoint. Table checkpoints are also supported for some list view objects, such as WinListView and VbListView.

Steps to insert a Table checkpoint:

1) In recording mode select **Insert > Checkpoint > Standard Checkpoint**
2) Click the table to be checked

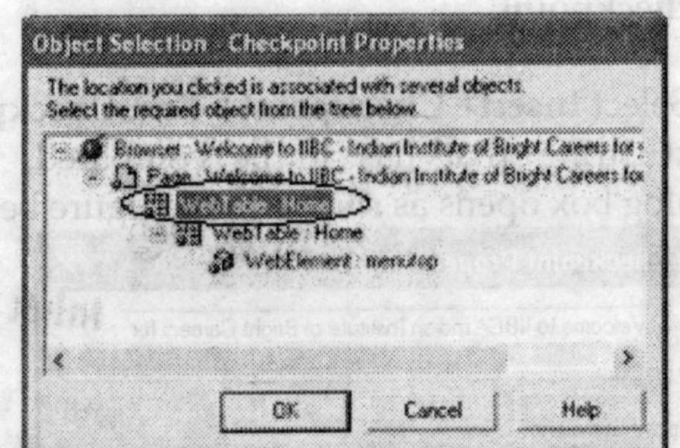

3) Select a table item from the displayed object tree as highlighted in the figure above and click **OK**. The Table Checkpoint Properties dialog box opens as shown below.

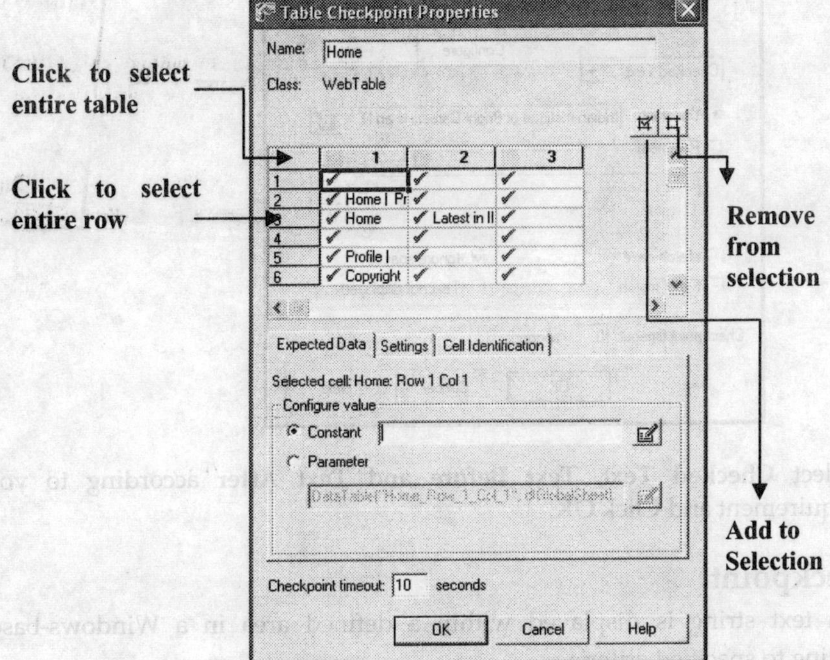

4) In the Table Checkpoint Properties dialog box, specify the settings for the checkpoint.
5) Click **OK** to close the dialog box. A checkpoint statement is added for the selected object.

Text Checkpoint

It is used to check if a text string is displayed in the appropriate place on a Web page or application.

Steps to insert a text checkpoint:

1) Click Record.Select **Insert> Checkpoint >Text Checkpoint**
2) Click the text string that has to be compared. The **Text Checkpoint Properties** dialog box opens as shown in the figure below.

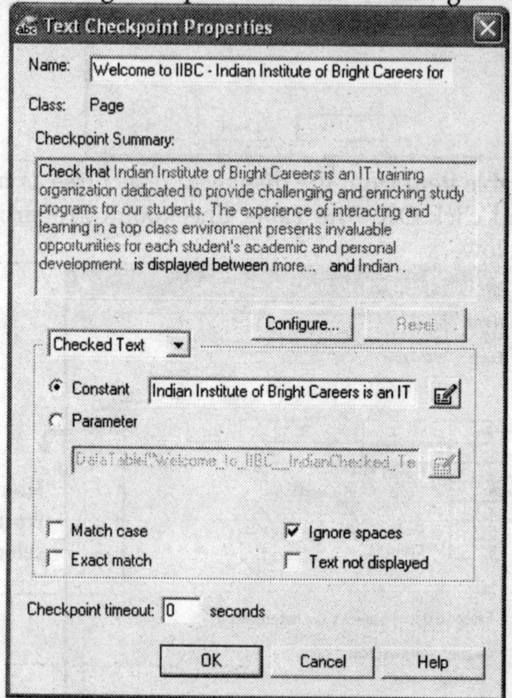

3) Select **Checked Text, Text Before** and **Text After** according to your requirement and Click **OK.**

Text Area Checkpoint

Checks that a text string is displayed within a defined area in a Windows-based application, according to specified criteria.

Steps to add a text area checkpoint:

1) Select **Insert > Checkpoint > Text Area Checkpoint.**
2) Define the area containing the text you want QuickTest to check by clicking and dragging the crosshairs pointer.
3) Select the object for which you are creating the checkpoint. The Text Area Checkpoint Properties dialog box opens.
4) Specify the checkpoint settings.
5) Click **OK** to close the dialog box. A checkpoint statement is added for the selected object.

Accessibility Checkpoint

Identifies areas of your Web site that may not conform to the World Wide Web Consortium (W3C) and Web Content Accessibility Guidelines (WCAG). Web Content Accessibility Guidelines are part of a series of Web accessibility guidelines published by the W3C's Web Accessibility Initiative. They consist of a set of guidelines on making content accessible, primarily for disabled users, but also for all user agents, including highly limited devices, such as mobile phones. The current version is 2.0

Steps to add an Accessibility checkpoint:

1) Configure the guidelines to be checked by the accessibility checkpoint in **Tools->Options->Web**. Select **Advanced** option and select the guidelines to be checked.

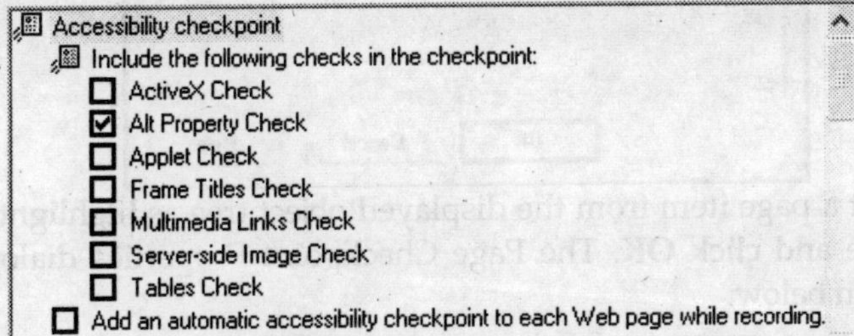

2) Click Record. Select **Insert-> Checkpoint ->Accessibility Checkpoint**
3) Click the page to be checked.
4) Accessibility Checkpoint Properties dialog will be opened with the options checked while configuring as mentioned in step 1.

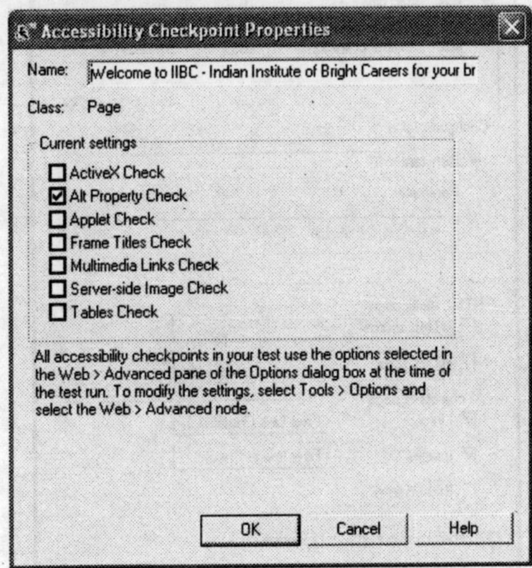

5) Click **OK**. Accessibility Checkpoint will be created.

Page Checkpoint

It is used to check the characteristics of a Web page. For instance, you can check load time the Web page takes to load or whether a Web page contains broken links.

Steps to insert a Page checkpoint:

1) In recording mode select **Insert > Checkpoint > Standard Checkpoint**
2) Click the web page you want to check.

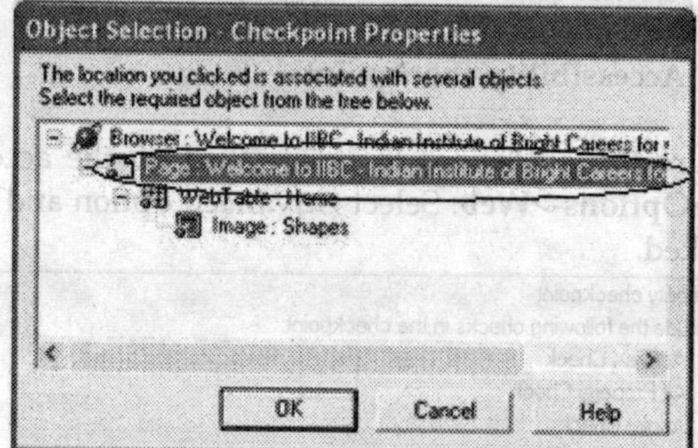

3) Select a page item from the displayed object tree as highlighted in the figure above and click **OK**. The Page Checkpoint Properties dialog box opens as shown below.

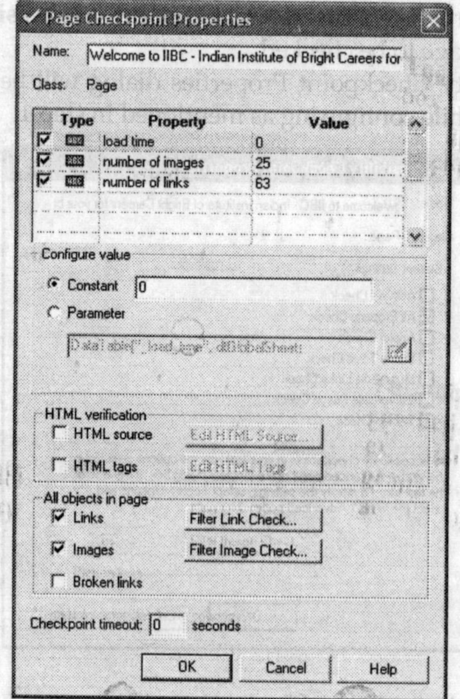

4) In the page Checkpoint Properties dialog box, specify the settings for the checkpoint.
HTML Source: Checks the entire HTML Source including HTML Tags and the text of the page. Even a single word change in the web page will change the HTML Source.
HTML tags: Only checks the tags of an HTML file.
Links: Checks whether each link is pointing to the correct URL
Images: Checks whether all images are downloading from the correct source.
Broken Links: Checks whether all links in the page are active or any of the links are broken. Broken link is the one clicking on which throws **page not found** error.

5) Click **OK** to close the dialog box. A checkpoint statement is added for the selected object.

Database Checkpoint:

It is used to check the contents of a database accessed by your application.

Steps to add a database checkpoint:

1) Select **Insert > Checkpoint > Database Checkpoint**. The Database Query Wizard opens.

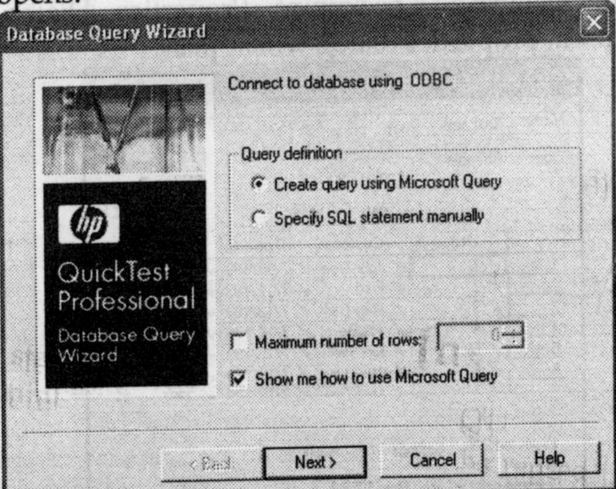

2) Select your database selection preferences. You can choose from the following options:

- **Create query using Microsoft Query:** This option is available if Microsoft Query is installed in the system. This feature will open a Microsoft query to create a new query.
- **Specify SQL statement manually:** This option will allow the user to manually define a query after connecting to a database using the connection string option.

> **Maximum number of rows**: Select this check box if you would like to limit the number of rows to be selected.

3) After clicking **Next,** the screen that opens depends on the option you selected in the previous step. Select option **Specify SQL Statement** and click **Next**. The Screen below appears:

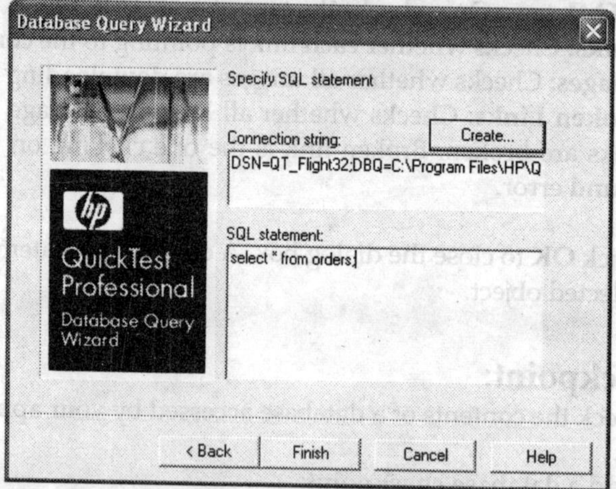

4) Create **Connection string** and **SQL statement** as shown above and Click **Finish**. Database Checkpoint Properties Dialog similar to the table checkpoint properties dialog will appear.

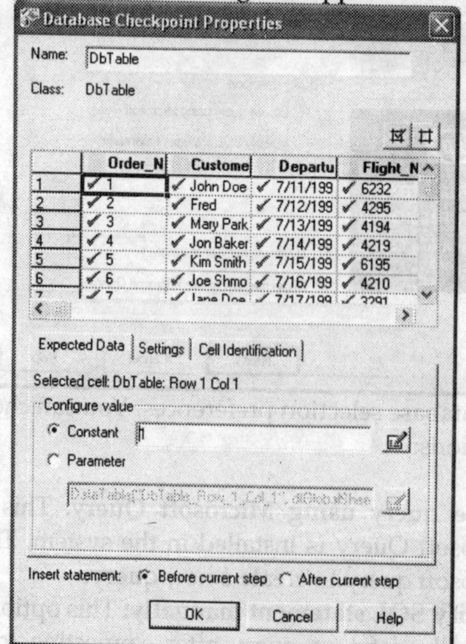

5) Select the checks and click **OK**. Database Checkpoint properties dialog will close and checkpoint will be inserted in the test.

XML Checkpoint (from Resource)

Checks the data content of XML documents in XML files.

Steps to add an XML checkpoint:

1) Click record. Select **Insert-> Checkpoint ->XML Checkpoint (from Resource)**. XML Checkpoint from file dialog will open.
2) Select the file to check and click OK. XML Check point properties dialog will open.

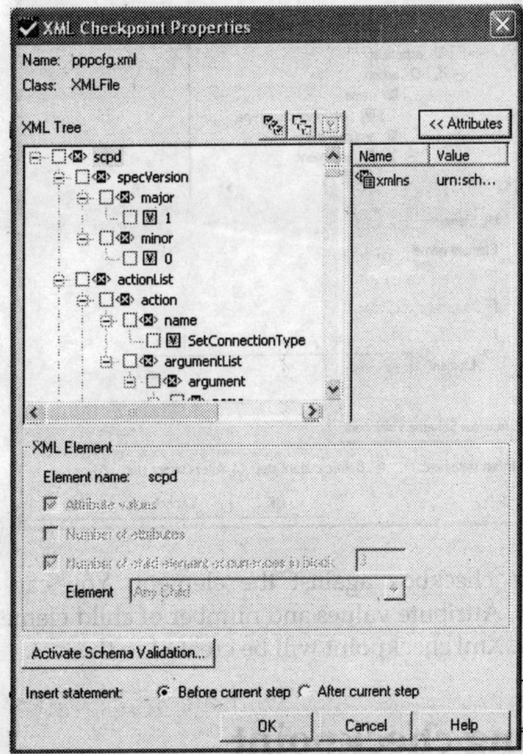

3) Select the checkbox against the element. You can check the number of attributes, Attribute values and the number of child elements.
4) Click **OK.** Xml checkpoint will be created in the test.

XML Checkpoint (from Application)

Checks the data content of XML documents in Web pages and frames.

Steps to add an XML checkpoint:

1) Click record. Select **Insert-> Checkpoint ->XML Checkpoint (from Application)**. XML Checkpoint from Application will open.
2) Click on the XML document opened in the web browser. XML Check point properties dialog will open.

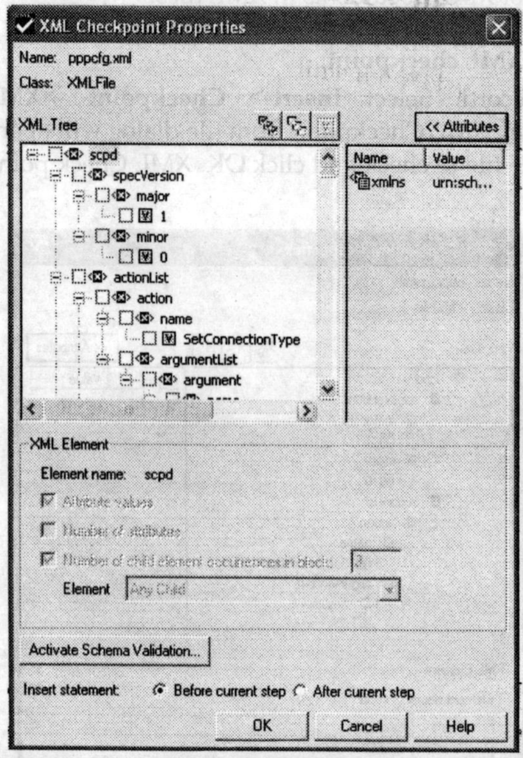

3) Select the checkbox against the element. You can check the number of attributes, Attribute values and number of child elements.
4) Click **OK.** Xml checkpoint will be created in the test.

Insert an existing checkpoint

QTP 10.0 allows users to reuse the existing checkpoints defined in the test. Checkpoints can be reused in instances where the application contains the organization logo on every page, application contains multiple edit boxes, etc.

Steps to insert an existing checkpoint:

1) Select the action which requires the checkpoint to be inserted.

2) Select **Insert > Checkpoint > Existing Checkpoint**. The add existing checkpoint dialog box appears as shown in the figure below:

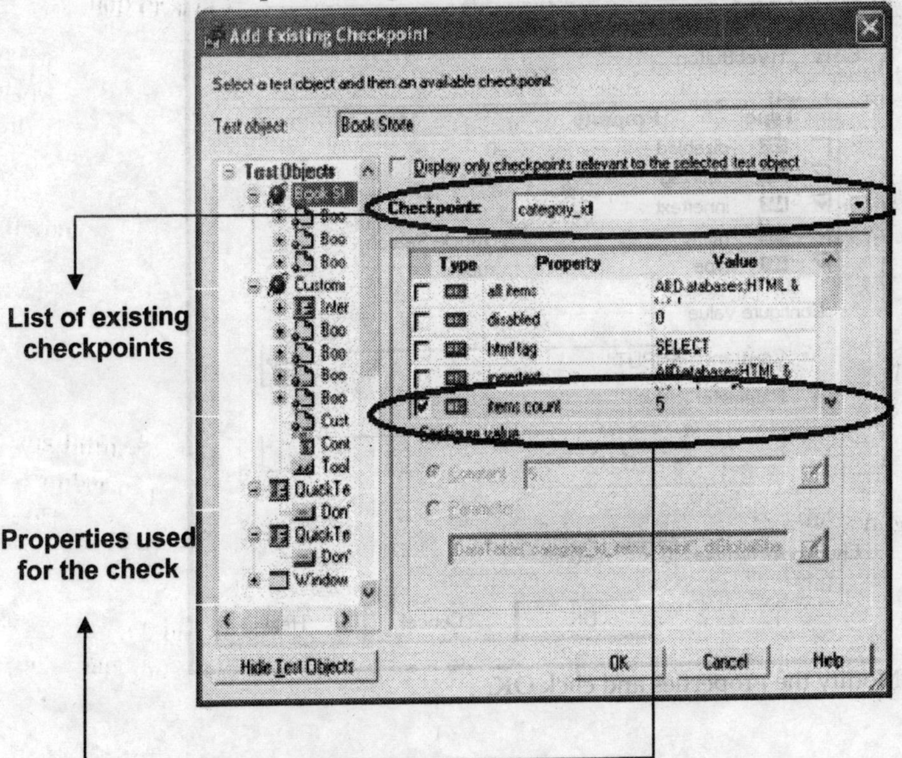

3) Select the object from the test object tree and from the list of checkpoints select the checkpoint.
4) Click **OK**. The checkpoint is inserted after the current step.

Modify the inserted checkpoint

QuickTest allows the user to modify the checkpoints that are already inserted in the test.

Steps To modify the checkpoints:

1) Right click on the inserted checkpoint to be modified or select the step containing the checkpoint and select **Edit > Step Properties> Checkpoint Properties**. The checkpoint dialog opens.

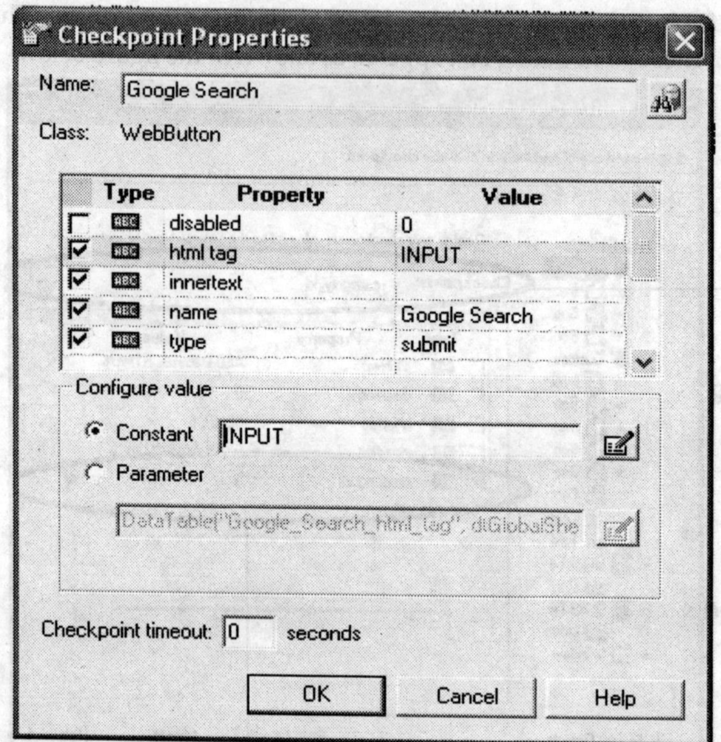

2) Modify the properties and click **OK**.

Review Questions

1. How are check points helpful in QTP script?
2. Discuss various check points and their purpose?
3. What is the difference between image and bitmap check point?

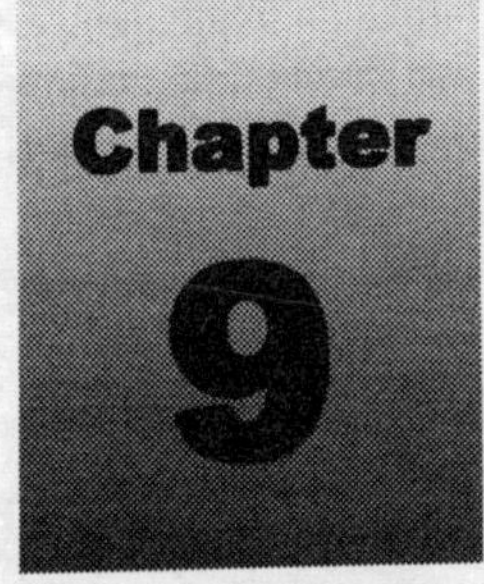

PARAMETERIZATION

The process of replacing fixed value with parameter is called as parameterization where a parameter is a value that is assigned by external data source or generator.

QuickTest enables you to expand the scope of a basic test by replacing fixed values with parameters. This process is known as parameterization, which greatly increases the power and flexibility of your test.

Types of parameters

Depending on the source of data, parameterization is divided into 4 categories.

- Data Table parameterization
- Test/Action parameterization
- Environment variable parameterization
- Random number parameterization

Data Table Parameterization

This enables you to create a *data-driven* test that runs several times using the data you supply. In each repetition, or *iteration*, QuickTest uses different values from the Data Sheets of the Data Table.

The Data Table has two types of data sheets—**Global** and **Action**.

Data Table

A1

	A	B	C	D	E
1					
2					
3					
4					
5					
6					
7					

Global | Action1

- Global sheet contains the data that is available to all actions.
- Action sheet contains the data that is available to specific action.

Below is the script to search a specified keyword from Google Search:

```
1 Browser("Google").Page("Google").WebEdit("q").Set "QTP"
2 Browser("Google").Page("Google").WebButton("Google Search").Click
3 Browser("Google").Page("Google").Image("nav_logo13").Click
4 Browser("Google").Page("Google").Sync
```

Observe that in Line1 we are searching for the keyword QTP. Let us say we also want to search for other key words IIBC, Testing, Siva. The best approach for this is to parameterize the search keyword "QTP" in such a way that for different executions it has different keywords to search.

The example below explains how to do data table parameterization of the above requirement using the Global Sheet.

1. To do this From Keyword view, select the cell which contains QTP and Click on symbol.

q Set "QTP"

2. Value Configurations Option Dialog as shown below will be displayed. Select the parameter as **Data Table**; Sheet as **Global Sheet** and Name of the column to store data as **SearchKeyword** as shown below and click the OK button.

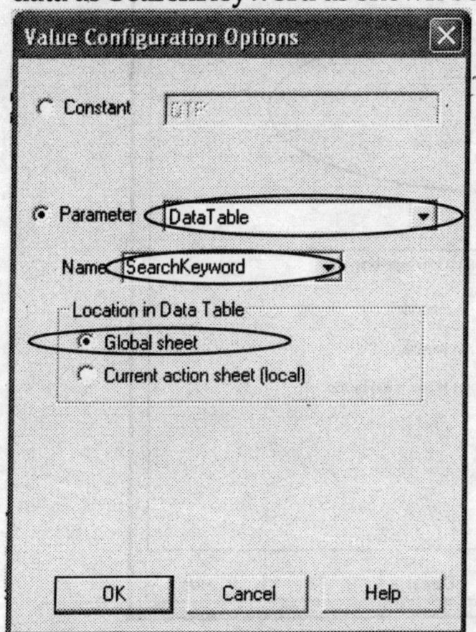

3. A new column **SearchKeyword** will be created in the Global sheet. Add keywords to search in this column. After entering the data, the Global sheet looks as below:

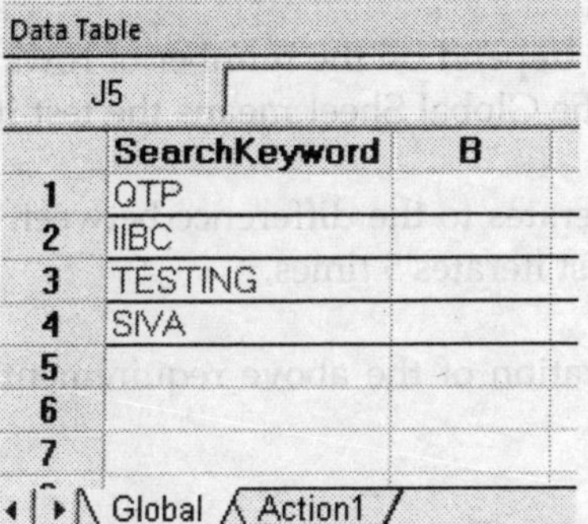

	SearchKeyword	B
1	QTP	
2	IIBC	
3	TESTING	
4	SIVA	
5		
6		
7		

4. Click Run button. You can see that the test runs 4 iterations and each iteration uses one search keyword from the list above.
5. The number of iterations the test runs can be controlled from **File>Settings>Run** dialog.

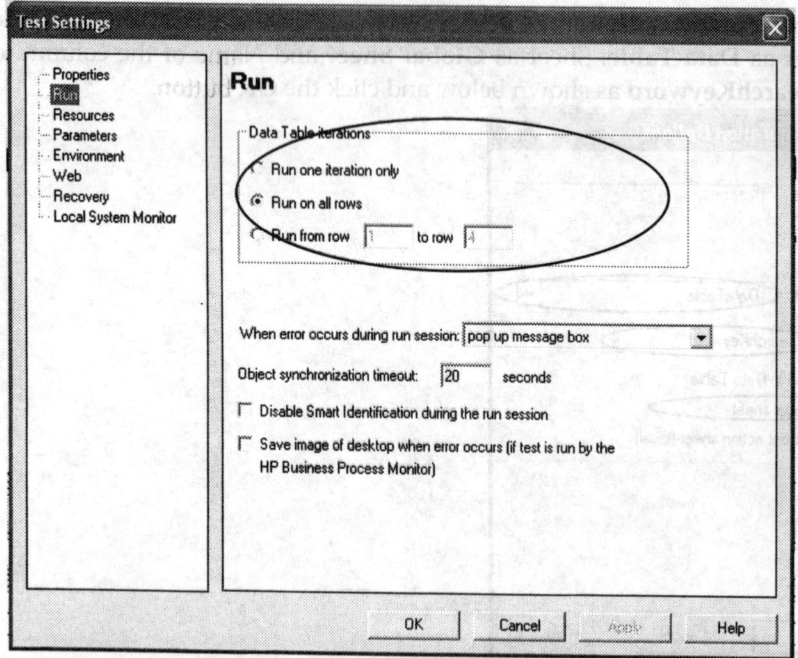

Run one Iteration only: Runs Test Script one iteration only irrespective of the number of rows in the Global sheet

Run on all rows: Test Script iterations depend on the number of rows in the Global Sheet. For example 4 rows in the Global Sheet means the test iterates for 4 times.

Run from row X to row Y: The test iterates to the difference between X and Y. if Y is 10 rows and X is 5 rows the test iterates 5 times.

Explained below is how to do data table parameterization of the above requirement using Action Sheet:

1. Repeat step1 and 2 above and select Sheet as **Local Sheet.**
2. A new column **SearchKeyword** will be created in the Local Sheet-Action1. Add keywords to search in this column. After entering the data, Action1 sheet looks like below:

Data Table

G6

	SearchKeyword	B
1	QTP	
2	IIBC	
3	TESTING	
4	SIVA	
5		
6		
7		

Global | Action1

3. Click Run button and observe that the script searches for only the first keyword in the column. This is because iteration settings of action points to **Run One Iteration Only** by default.
4. To change the action iteration settings:
   a. Select **View>Test Flow**. This opens the Test Flow Pane. Right click on Action node in the Test Flow Pane and select Action Call Properties from the menu.

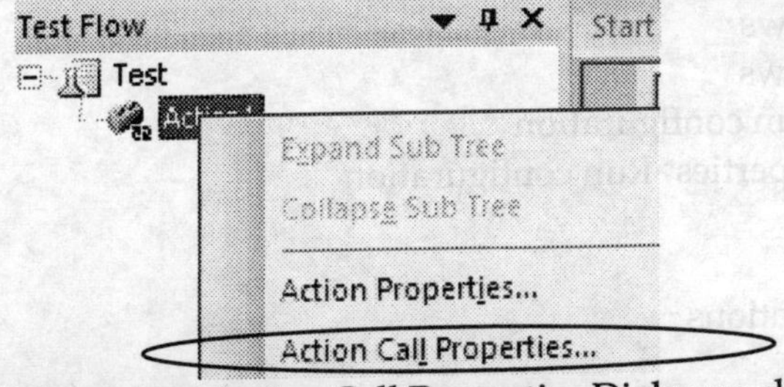

   b. This opens Action Call Properties Dialog as shown below.

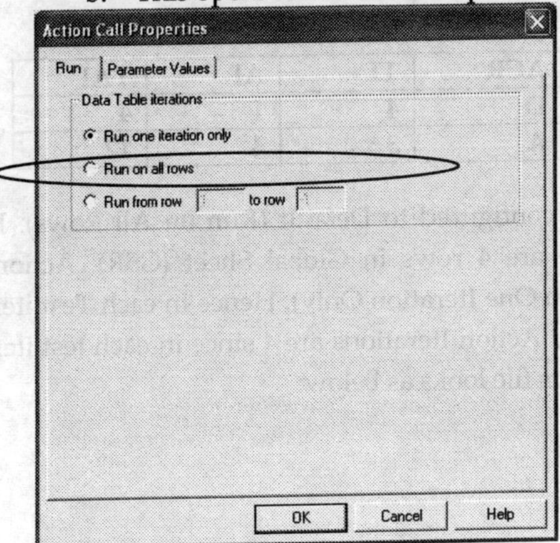

c. Observe that by default setting allows the action to run only one iteration. So the action took test data from only one row. Now Select **Run on All rows** and click OK.

5. Now run the script and observe that the script searches for all keywords.

Action Iteration Vs Test Iteration

Action Iteration means running once from the first step to the last step of an action.Test Iteration means running at least once from the first action to the last action.

For Example if a test has 3 actions A1, A2 and A3, then One Test iteration could be equal to 2A1+10A2+A3. This means A1 iterated 2 times, A2 iterated 10 times and A3 iterated only once. Similarly One Test iteration could also be equal to A1+A2+A3. This means A1 iterated only once, A2 iterated only once and A3 also iterated only once.

The following table displays how many times the Test Iterates and how many times the Action iterates depending on data table values and Run settings.

GSR – Global Sheet Rows
ASR – Action Sheet Rows
FSR – File>Settings>Run configuration
ACR – Action Call properties>Run configuration
TI – Test Iterations
AI – Action Iteration
TAI – Total Action Iterations
D – Default
A – All Rows

GSR	ASR	FSR	ACR	TI	AI	TAI
4	3	D	D	4	1	4
3	4	D	A	3	4	12

In the first row File>Settings>Run is configured to Default (Run on All Rows). Hence Test iterates (TI) for 4 times since there are 4 rows in Global Sheet (GSR). Action Call properties>Run configured to Default (Run One Iteration Only). Hence in each Test iteration Action iterates (AI) only once. Hence Total Action Iterations are 4 since in each test iteration only one action iteration is there. The results file looks as below:

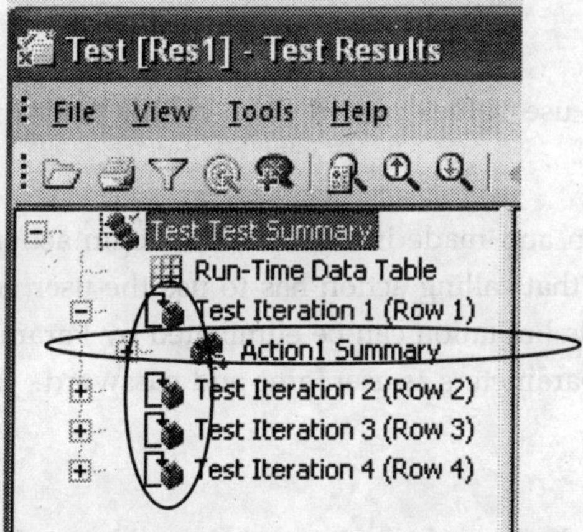

In the first row File>Settings>Run is configured to Default (Run on All Rows). Hence the Test iterates (TI) for 3 times since there are 3 rows in Global Sheet (GSR). Action Call properties>Run configured to All Rows. Hence in each Test iteration Action iterates (AI) for 3 times since there are 3 rows in the Action Sheet (ASR). Hence Total Action Iterations are 12 since in each test iteration, 4 action iterations are there.

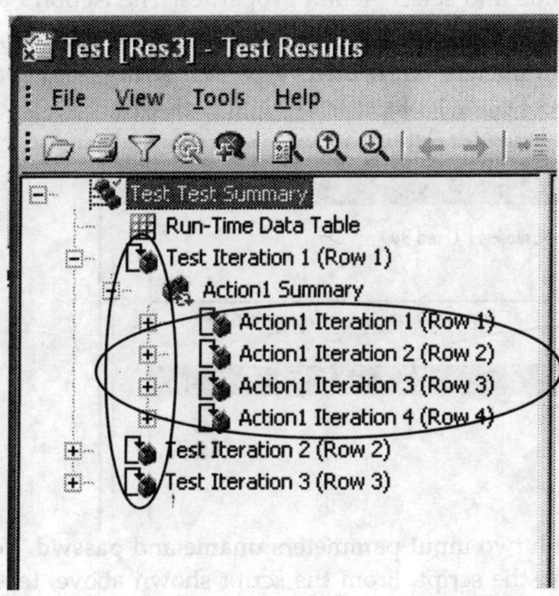

Test/Action Parameters

Test/Action Parameters enable you to use values passed from calling action to called action.

For example if we create a **login** action and made it reusable, this login action can be called from any other action. Limitation is that calling action has to use the user name and password which is part of **login** action. This limitation can be eliminated by Parameterising the action in such a way that it takes input parameters as username and password.

Steps to achieve the above are…

1. Create a **login** action. For Gmail login code looks as below where **siva** is the username and **4be86e6dbb98c6d2edd63b3ef935** is the encrypted password

```
1 Browser("Google").Page("Gmail").WebEdit("Email").Set "siva"
2 Browser("Google").Page("Gmail").WebEdit("Passwd").SetSecure
  "4be86e6dbb98c6d2edd63b3ef935"
3 Browser("Google").Page("Gmail").WebButton("Sign in").Click
```

2. Right Click on the Action Node and select Action Properties. The Action Properties Dialog box will appear. Select Parameters>Input Parameters and Click + and add **uname** and **passwd** as parameters and their type as **string** and **password** respectively. Action Properties Dialog looks as below and click OK.
NOTE: if you want, you can also enter default values.

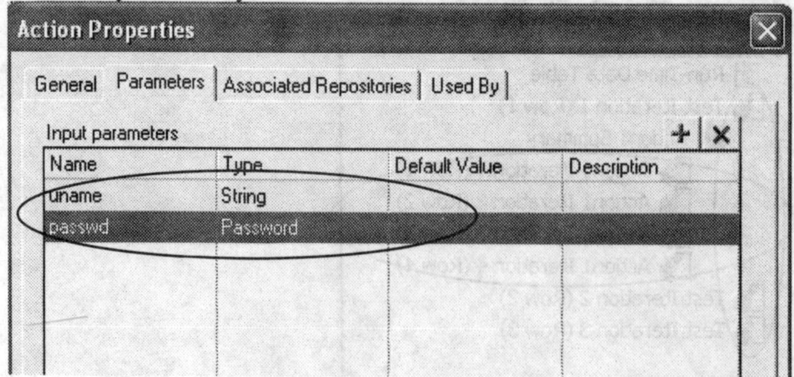

3. Now your action is ready with two input parameters **uname** and **passwd.** You must use these input parameters in the script. From the script shown above, text **siva** in Line 1 must be parameterized with **uname** and text **4be86e6dbb98c6d2edd63b3ef935** in Line 2 must be parameterized with **passwd**.
4. To do this From Keyword view, select the cell which contains **siva** and Click on symbol.

5. Value Configurations Option Dialog as shown below will be displayed. Select parameter as **Test/action parameter** and parameter name as **uname.**

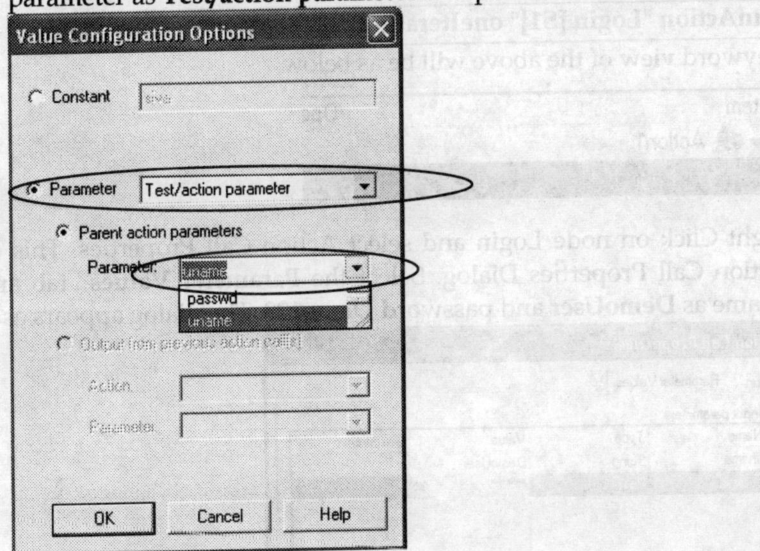

6. Similarly repeat steps 4,5 for password also.
7. Now the action with parameters is ready to use by any calling action. Save this in a script S1.
8. Now Let us call the Login Action of script S1 from script S2 and pass the parameter values. Steps for this are as below.
   a. Create new script S2 and select **Insert>Call To Existing Action.**
   b. From **Select Action** dialog select the **From test** as S1 and **Action** as Login. The dialog looks as below.

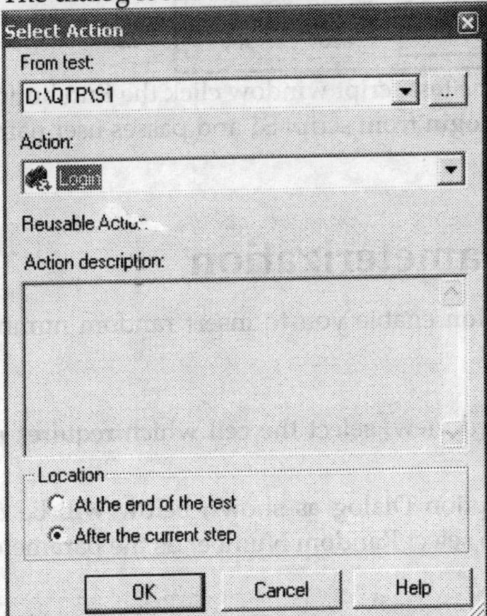

c. Click OK. This adds a statement to call login action of script S1 from S2. The statement will be as below:

```
RunAction "Login [S1]" oneIteration
```

d. Keyword view of the above will be as below

e. Right Click on node Login and select Action Call Properties. This displays Action Call Properties Dialog. Select the **Parameter Values** tab and enter uname as **DemoUser** and password **Demo123.** The dialog appears as below:

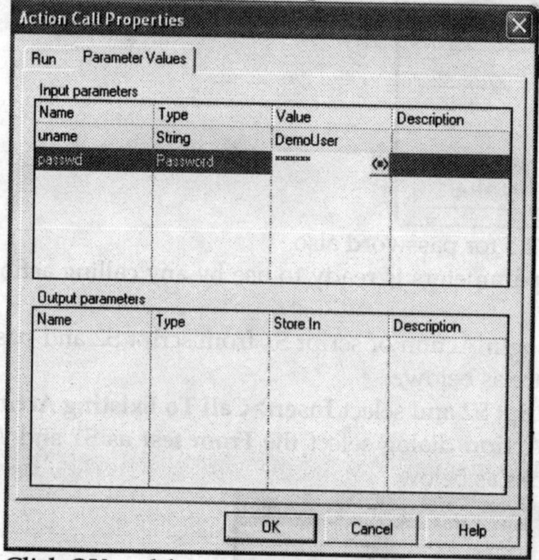

f. Click OK and from the test script window click the Run button.

9. Now Script S2 calls Action **Login** from script S1 and passes user name and password as Demo User and Demo123.

Random Number Parameterization

Random number parameterization enable you to insert random numbers as values in your test.

1. To do this From Keyword view, select the cell which requires random number and Click on symbol.
2. Value Configurations Option Dialog as shown below will be displayed. This dialog box enables you to select Random Number as the parameter type.

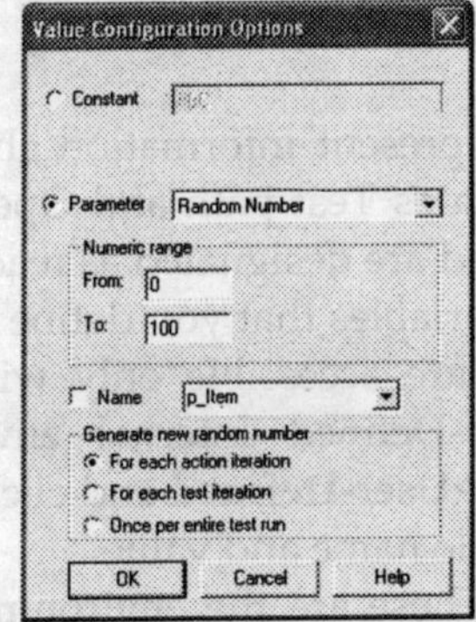

3. The following options are available for configuring random number parameters:
   - ✓ **Numeric range:** Specifies the range from which the random number is generated.
   - ✓ **Name:** Assigns a name to your parameter. Assigning a name to a random parameter enables you to use the same parameter several times in your test.
   - ✓ **Generate new random number:**
     i) **For each action iteration:** Generates a new number at the end of each action iteration.
     ii) **For each test iteration:** Generates a new number at the end of each global iteration.
     iii) **Once per entire test run:** Generates a new number the first time the parameter is used. The same number is used for the parameter throughout the test run.

4. Select appropriate setting and Click OK.
5. When you run the script you can see that the script is getting random values during execution.

Environment variable parameterization

Environment variable parameters enable you to use variable values from environment variables.

QuickTest can insert a value from the Environment variable list, which is a list of variables and corresponding values. Throughout the test run, the value of an environment variable remains the same, regardless of the number of iterations, unless you change the value of the variable programmatically in your script.

There are several types of environment variables:

- **Built-in:** Variables that represent information about the test and the computer on which the test is run, such as Test path and Operating system. These variables are accessible from all tests, and are designated as read-only.
- **User-Defined Internal**: Variables that you define within the test. These variables are saved with the test and are accessible only within the test in which they were defined. To Create User-Defined Internal environment variables choose **File->Settings->Environment->User-Defined** and click Add symbol. This opens a dialog to add environment variable name and value.
- **User-Defined External:** These are the environment values present in the external XML File.

Using Environment Variable Parameters

1. To do this From Keyword view, select the cell which requires parameterization using Environment variables and Click on symbol.
2. Value Configurations Option Dialog as shown below will be displayed. Select the parameter as **Environment.**

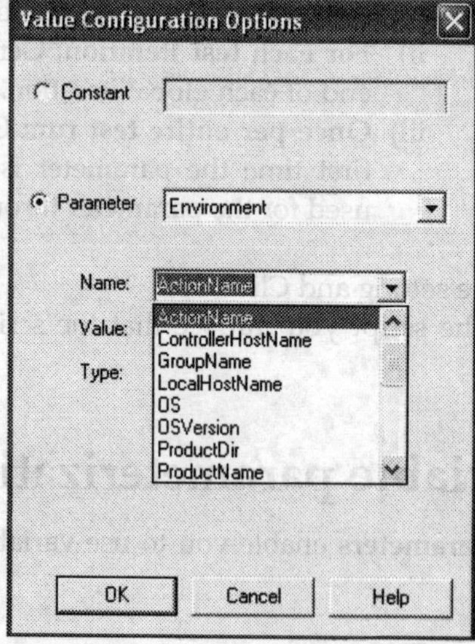

3. Select the name of the environment variable and click OK.
4. Run the test and observe that the value in the test has been replaced with environment variable value.

Steps to create an external environment variable file:

1) Create an **xml file** using the editor of your choice.
2) Type **<Environment>** on the first line.
3) Type each variable **name-value** pair within **<Variable>** elements in the following format:

<Variable>

<Name>This is the first variable's name </Name>

<Value> This is the first variable's value </Value> <Description>

This text is optional and can be used to add comments. It is shown only in the XML not in QuickTest

</Description>

</Variable>

4) Type </Environment> on the last line.
5) Save the file in a location that is accessible from the QuickTest computer. The file must be in .xml format with an .xml file extension.

Example: Your environment variables file may look like this:

```
<Environment>
    <Variable>
        <Name>Address1</Name>
        <Value>Near reliance  fresh</Value>
    </Variable>
    <Variable>
        <Name>Address2</Name>
        <Value>Banglore</Value>
    </Variable>
    <Variable>
        <Name>Name</Name>
        <Value>IIBC</Value>
    </Variable>
    <Variable>
        <Name>Telephone</Name>
        <Value> 080-23608385</Value>
    </Variable>
</Environment>
```

Steps to select the external environment variables file:

1) Select **File > Settings** to open the Test Settings dialog box.
2) Click the **Environment** node.
3) Select **User-defined** from the **Variables type** list.
4) Select the **Load variables and values from the external file** check box.

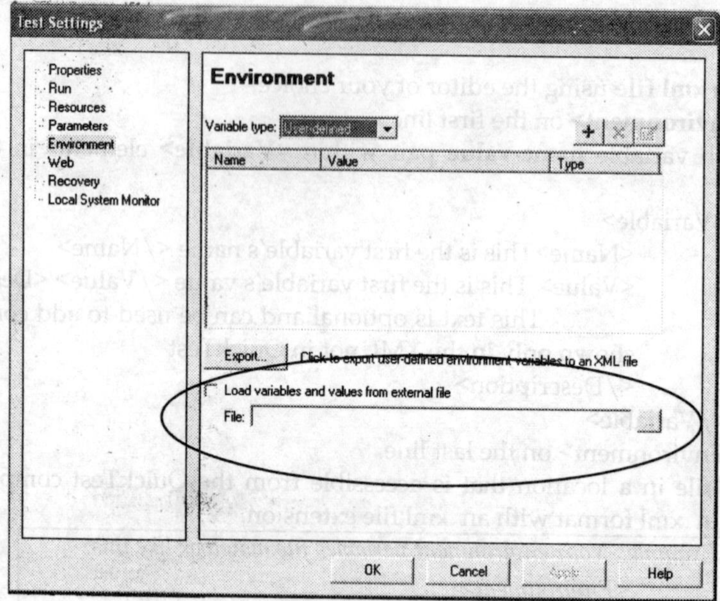

5) Use the browse button or enter the full path of the external environment variables file you want to use with your test. The variables defined in the selected file are displayed in blue in the list of user-defined environment variables.

Where do we use Parameterization?

Using parameterization you can:

- ✓ Parameterize values in steps
- ✓ Parameterize values of action parameters
- ✓ Parameterize values in steps and checkpoints while working with your test.
- ✓ Also parameterize identification property values of test objects in the object repository using repository parameters.

Review Questions

1. What is the advantage of parameterization?
2. What are the different parameterizations available and their purpose?
3. What are the types of Environment variables?
4. Discuss about Action Iteration and Test Iteration.

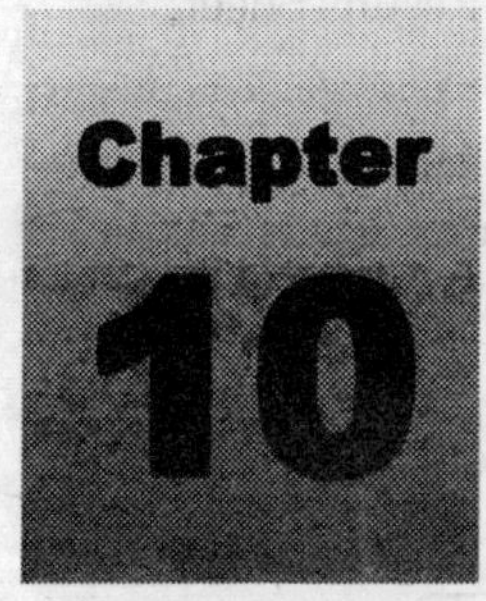

OUTPUT VALUES

Introduction

Sometimes there might exist a scenario where the few steps of the test depend on the run time value of the current step. For such instances QuickTest allows users to retrieve run time values in the test and store them to use as input to steps at a different stage in the run session. Output values are stored only for the duration of the run session. When you define an output value, you can specify where and how each value is stored during the run session.

An output value step is a step in which one or more values are captured at a specific point in your test and stored for the duration of the run session. The values can later be used as input at a different point in the test run.

You can output a value to:

- a test or action parameter
- the run-time Data Table
- an environment variable

Design Time Data Table

The Data table which is present in QTP before running the script is called Design Time Data Table. This contains various data to be used in the script while the script is under execution.

Run Time Data Table

This is the data table you see while QTP script is under execution. At the starting of the script execution QTP copies the data from Design Time Data Table to Run Time Data Table and add, delete or change the data in the Run Time Data Table during script execution. At the end of script execution QTP exports the Runtime Data table to the Test Results Sheet.

Why Run Time Data Table?

If QTP directly modifies data in the Design Time Data Table we cannot use same data table for the next execution of the script since the data has been modified from initial execution. Hence to ensure that the same script can be executed without modifying data in the data table QTP does changes to the data only in Run Time Data Table without affecting the Design Time Data Table.

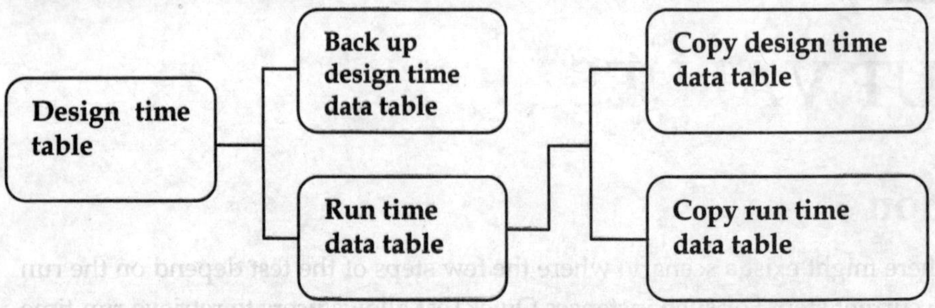

Using QTP you can create the following categories of output values:

- Standard Output Values
- Text and Text Area Output Values
- Database Output Values
- XML Output Values

Standard Output values

Using standard output values the property values of the objects can be output. You can use standard output values to output the property values of most objects. For example, after reserving a ticket, it must be confirmed. In this case confirming the ticket number is required which is generated during run time. You could create an output value in your test to store the ticket number after it is generated during run time.

Steps to create standard output values:

1) Select **Insert > Output Value > Standard Output Value.**
2) Click the object for which output value must be generated.

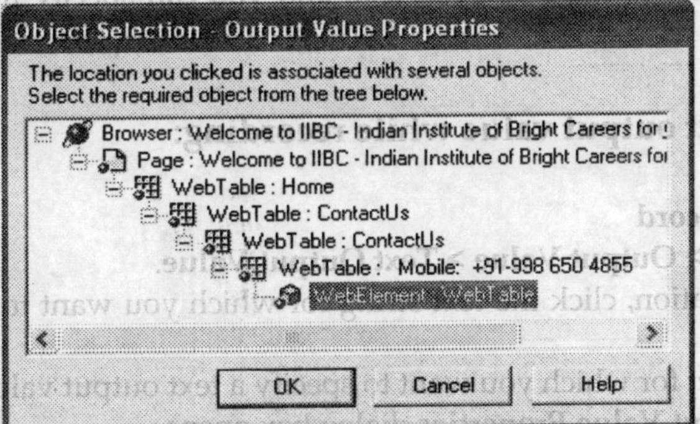

3) In the Object Selection dialog box, select the object for which you want to specify an output value, and click **OK**. The Output Value Properties dialog box opens for the selected object.

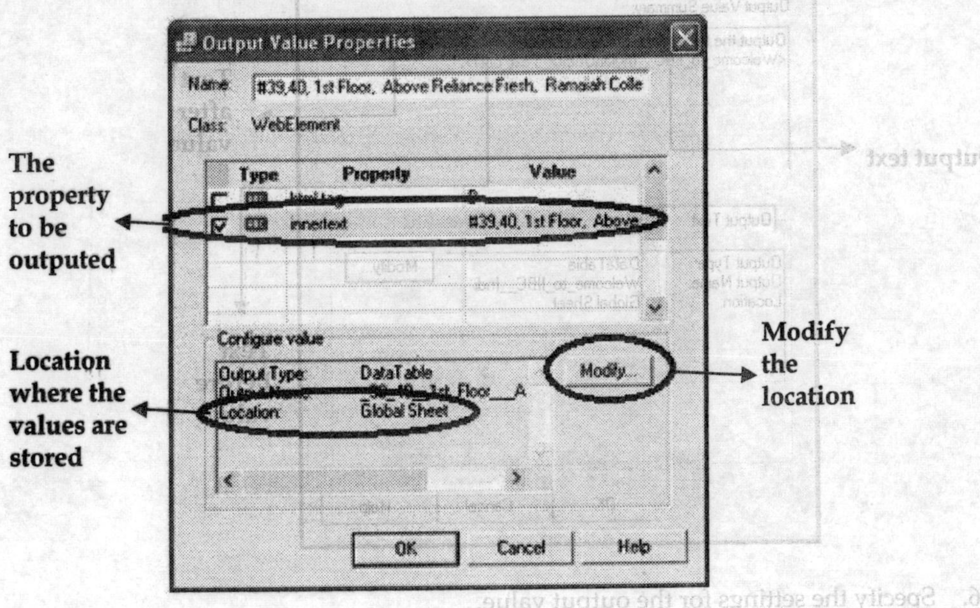

4) Specify the property values to output and their settings.

5) When you finish defining the output value details, click **OK**. QuickTest inserts an output value step in your test.

Outputting Text Values

You can create a text output value from a text string displayed in a screen. You can define the output value as part of the displayed text, and you can specify the text before and/or after the output text.

Steps to create a text output value while recording:

1. Select **Test>Record**
2. Choose **Insert > Output Value > Text Output Value**.
3. In your application, click the text string for which you want to specify a text output value.
4. Select the object for which you want to specify a text output value, and click **OK**.
5. The **Text Output Value Properties** dialog box opens.

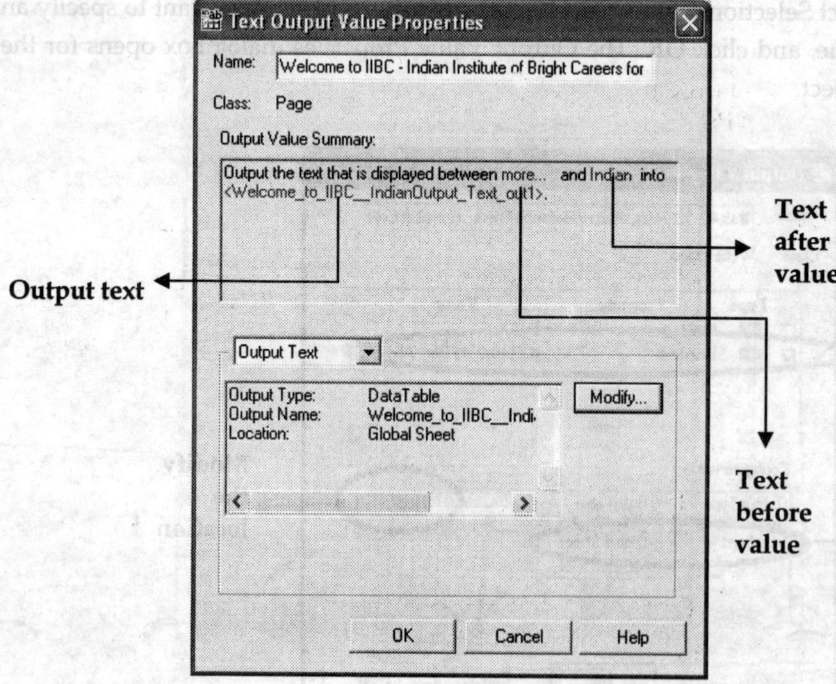

6. Specify the settings for the output value.
7. When you have finished defining the text output value details, click **OK**. QuickTest inserts an output value step in test.

NOTE: Use the same steps to create text area output value. The only difference is using cross hire to select a rectangle area of text.

Database Output Values

You can use database output values to output the value of the contents of database cell.

Steps to create database output values:

1. Choose **Insert>Output Value >Database Output Value**. The Database Query Wizard opens.
2. Use the wizard to define a query to retrieve the data that you want to output. Follow the instructions specified for creating a database checkpoint.
3. When you have finished defining your query, the Database Output Value Properties dialog box opens.
4. Specify the values to output and their settings.
5. When you have finished defining the output value details, click **OK**. QuickTest inserts an output value step in your script.

Outputting XML Values

You can create XML output values from any XML document contained in an XML Web page or frame, or directly from an XML file. You can output element and/or attribute values in an XML output value step.

Steps to create XML output values from an XML file:

To create XML output values from an XML file:

1) Choose **Insert > Output Value> XML Output Value (File)**. The XML Output Value from File dialog box opens.
2) In the XML File box, enter file path of the XML file.
3) Click **OK**. The **XML Output Value Properties** dialog box opens.
4) Specify the values to output and their settings.
5) When you have finished defining the output value details, click **OK**. QuickTest inserts an output value step in your test.

Adding Existing Output Values to a Test

QTP 10.0 allows users to reuse the existing output value. Every time the output value step is run the older values are replaced with the new one.

Steps to insert an existing output value in your test:

1) Select the step after which you want to insert the existing output value. Select **Insert > Output Value > Existing Output Value**. The Add Existing Output Value dialog box opens as shown below.

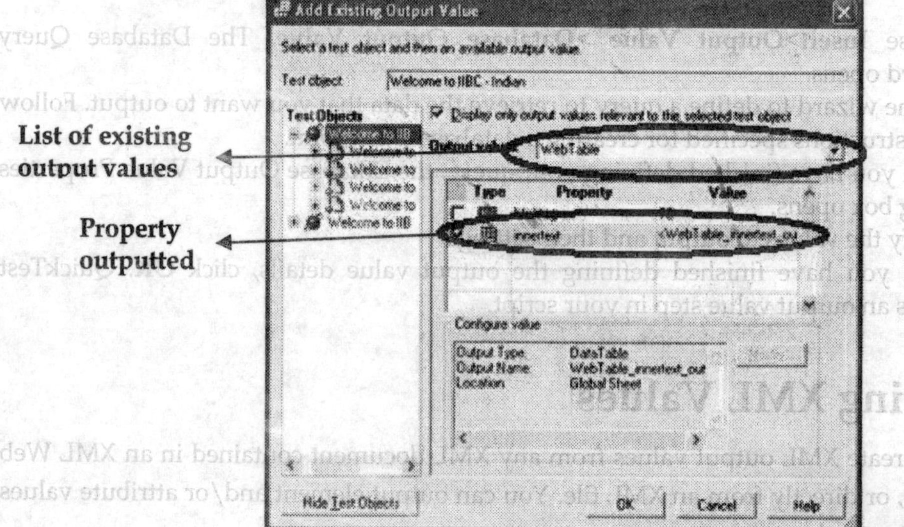

2) From the Output values list, select the output value that should be inserted.
3) Click **OK**. The output value step is inserted after the selected step.

Review Questions

1. How do output values and Check points differ?
2. How many types of output values are available and what is their purpose?
3. What is a Runtime value?
4. What is the difference between Design time and Runtime Data Table?

SYNCHRONISATION

Sometimes scripts fail when they are run because of the speed mismatch between QuickTest and the application. QuickTest is always faster than the application; as a result the application responds to Quicktest slower than expected and the test fails. Instances where the application responds slower than expected include for a progress bar to reach 100%,for a status message to appear, for a button to become enabled and for a window or pop-up message to open.

These speed mismatch problems can be handled by synchronizing the test. Synchronizing the test involves making the QuickTest wait until the application is ready for performing the next step.

> *Synchronization is used to match the speed of test script execution with the speed of the application.*

A test can be synchronized in the following ways:

By modifying the default time settings for a test in QuickTest

QuickTest provides some time setting for the test which makes QuickTest wait for the mentioned time in the setting.

1) ***Browser navigation timeout:*** This setting makes QuickTest wait for the web page to load completely for the specified amount of time. By default the maximum wait time specified by QuickTest is 60 seconds. This setting can further be modified by the user based on the requirement. This setting is found in **File>settings>Web>Browser navigation** timeout. This setting is applicable only for web applications.
2) ***Object synchronization timeout:*** this setting makes QuickTest wait for the specified amount of time for the objects to appear. By default the time setting is 20 seconds which can be modified by the user according to their requirement. This setting can be found in File**>Settings>Run>Object synchronization timeout**.

By inserting wait / exist statements

These statements can be inserted to make QuickTest wait until an object exists.

Wait statement: When a wait statement is encountered, QuickTest pauses its script execution for the specified amount of time. Once the specified amount is lapsed, QuickTest proceeds with execution of the next step.

Syntax: wait(n): This statement pauses QuickTest for n seconds (where n can be any integer value) before proceeding to the next step.

Example: wait(5): This statement when encountered, QuickTest halts the script execution for 5 seconds.

Exist statement: When an exist statement is inserted it checks if the object exists or not in the application under test and returns a Boolean value for the same. Based on the return value, appropriated steps can be taken to handle the timing mismatch.

For example: You can combine wait and exist statements within a loop to instruct QuickTest to wait until the object exists before continuing with the test as shown below:

```
If Browser("Yahoo").Page("Home").Link ("weather").Exist Then
        Browser("Yahoo").Page("Home").Link("weather").Click
Else
        wait(10)
End if
```

By inserting a synchronization point

A synchronization point can be inserted which makes QuickTest pause the test until an object property achieves a specified value. Synchronization point is often referred to as intelligent wait statement.

Inserting a Synchronization point:

1) Start a recording session. Select **Insert > Synchronization Point**.
2) Click the object in your application for which you want to insert a synchronization point.
3) Select the object for which you want to insert a synchronization point, and click **OK**.

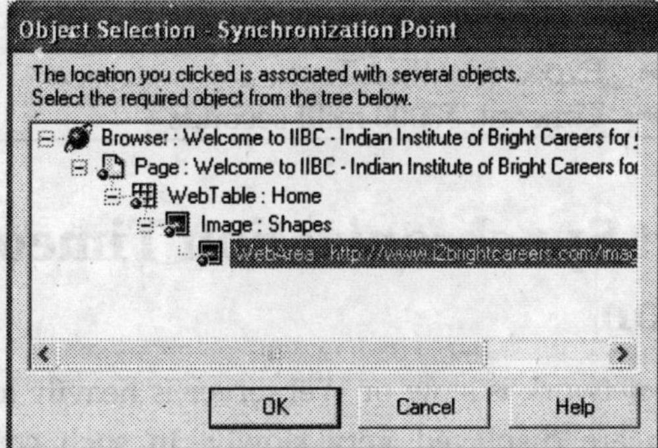

4) The **Add Synchronization Point** dialog box opens as shown in figure below:

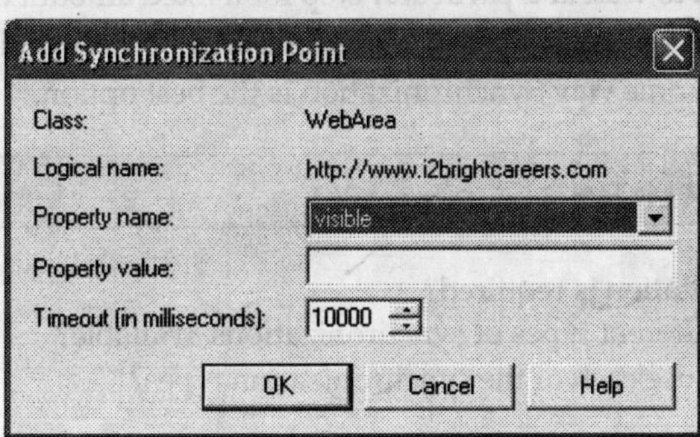

- ✓ The **Property name** contains the list of properties of the object. Select the property name you want to use for the synchronization point.
- ✓ **Property value** is the value for which QuickTest should wait before continuing to the next step in the test.
- ✓ **Timeout (in milliseconds)** specifies the maximum amount of time to wait for the specified property to be achived. Quicktest proceeds to the next step once this time is lapsed irrespective whether the value is achieved or not.

5) Enter all the required values in **Add Synchronization Point** dialog and Click **OK**. A **WaitProperty** step is added to the test.

Example: A synchronization point is applied on the web button **sign in** of Yahoo home page.

Browser("Yahoo").Page("Home").WebButton("SignIn").WaitProperty "Enabled",True,50000

In the above statement;

- Waitproperty is the method which represents the synchronization point.
- Property name: Enabled
- Expected value: True
- Timeout: 50000 milli seconds

Wait Vs Object Synchronization Timeout Vs Synchronization

In the situations like network is slow or Webserver is heavily loaded; pages and objects in the entire application are displayed very slowly. In such contexts modifying Object Synchronization Timeout value is a best option since you want the test to wait for more time at each step. If we want to wait at a particular step for a fixed amount of time like Application Initialization using wait statement is the best option. In all other conditions where the object property is changed in some way Synchronization is the best option.

Review Questions

1. Why synchronization is required?
2. What are the different types of synchronizations available?
3. When will you use each of the synchronization types?

STANDARD, CUSTOM AND VIRTUAL OBJECTS

According to QTP, objects in the application are divided into the following three types.

Standard Object: Object in the application which is identified by QTP and also whose class is standard (recognized) to QTP like Listbox, Editbox, Button, Link and Image.

Custom Object: Object in the application which is identified by QTP and whose class is not standard to QTP. Usually these are the objects which are specially designed by developers like Date Field with Day/Month/Year that takes day between 1-31 and Month between 1-12.

Virtual Object: Object in the application which is not identified (not seen) by QTP. Since object itself is not visible to QTP there is no need to talk about its class.

As an automation programmer your automation complexity will not be dependent on either the number of pages in the application or on the number of objects in the page. It just depends on the identification of the objects in the application by your automation tool. If more objects are not standard objects to the tool, the more complex it is to automate your application.

So when you look at application objects it is better to determine how many objects are not standard to your tool and take some steps to make the tool to identify your objects. In QTP we have two approaches to achieve this.

1. Mapping Custom Objects To Standard objects
2. Creating Virtual Objects.

Mapping Custom Objects To Standard objects

The Object Mapping dialog box enables you to map an object of an unidentified or custom class to a Standard Windows class. For example in the diagram below there is a Date editbox in the Flight Reservation application which is behaves like a normal Edit Box.

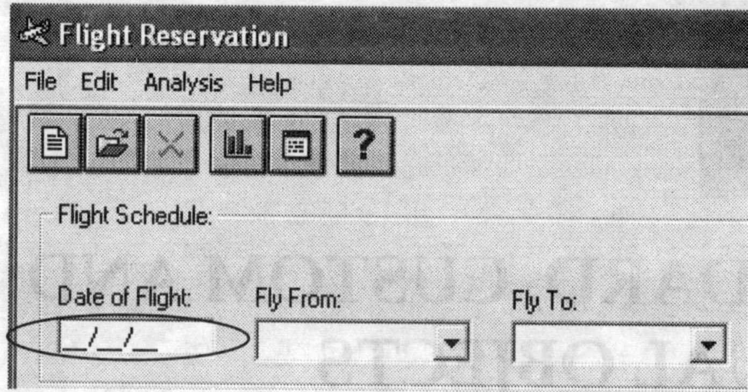

The steps below will map the Date object as an Editbox:

1. In QTP Select **Tools>Object Identification>User-Defined;** Object Mapping dialog box will appear.
2. Click the Hand symbol and show the Date field from the application.
3. From Map to dialog, select **Single Line Edit**. The dialog looks as below:

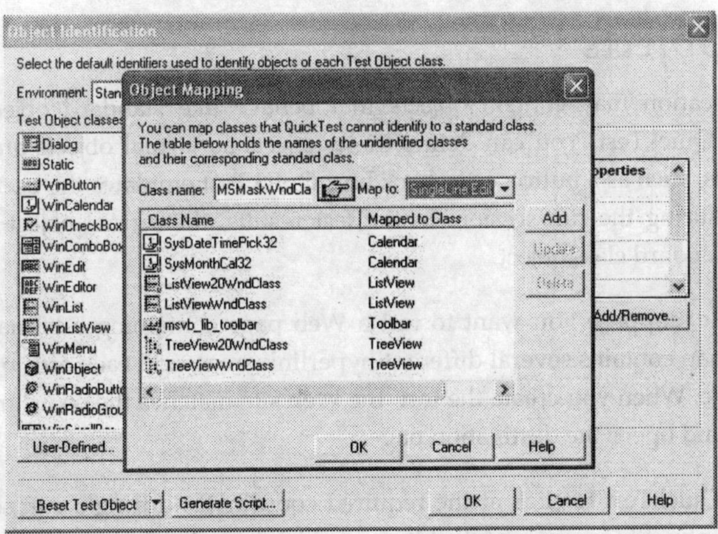

4. Click Add button
5. Click OK and close Object Mapping Dialog and Object Identification Dialog.
6. Now Custom object Date is mapped to Standard object WinEdit.

Code before Mapping:

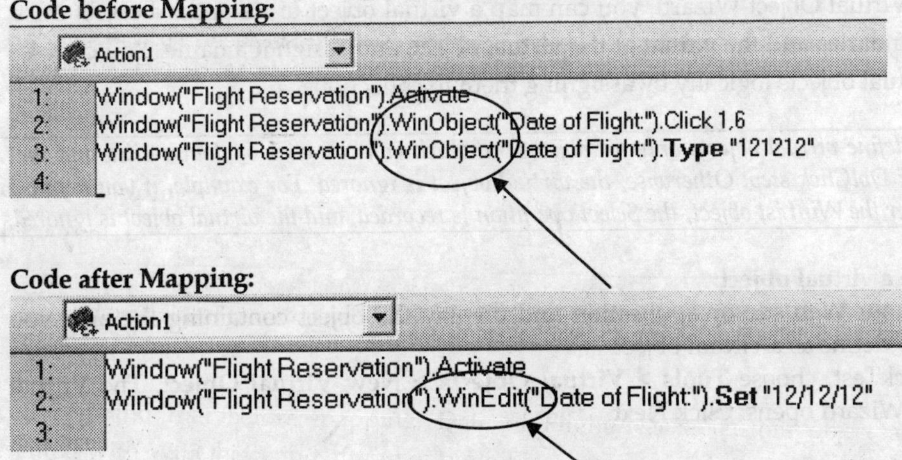

You can find that before mapping, Date of Flight was a custom object and hence represented with WinObject and after mapping it is a standard object and hence represented with WinEdit.

In web technology custom objects are identified as **WebElement**.

Virtual Objects

Your application may contain objects that behave like standard objects but are not recognized by QuickTest. You can define these objects as virtual objects and map them to standard classes, such as a button or a check box. QuickTest emulates the user's action on the virtual object during the run session. In the test results, the virtual object is displayed as though it is a standard class object.

For example, suppose you want to test a Web page containing a bitmap that the user clicks. The bitmap contains several different hyperlink areas, and each area opens a different destination page. When you create the test, the Web site matches the coordinates of the click on the bitmap and opens the destination page.

To enable QuickTest to click at the required coordinates during a run session, you can define a virtual object for an area of the bitmap, which includes those coordinates, and map it to the button class. When you run the test, QuickTest clicks the bitmap in the area defined as a virtual object so that the Web site opens the correct destination page.

Defining a Virtual Object

Using the Virtual Object Wizard, you can map a virtual object to a standard object class, specify the boundaries and the parent of the virtual object, and assign it a name. You can also group your virtual objects logically by assigning them to collections.

> ***Note:*** *You can define virtual objects only for objects on which you can click or double-click and that record a Click or DblClick step. Otherwise, the virtual object is ignored. For example, if you define a virtual object over the WinList object, the Select operation is recorded, and the virtual object is ignored.*

Steps to define a virtual object:

1) Open your Web site or application and display the object containing the area you want to define as a virtual object.
2) In QuickTest, choose **Tools > Virtual Objects > New Virtual Object**. The Virtual Object Wizard opens. Click **Next**.

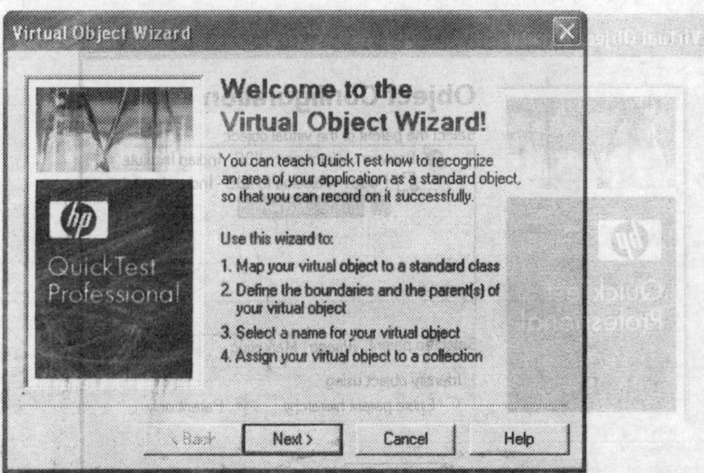

3) Select a standard class to which you want to map your virtual object.

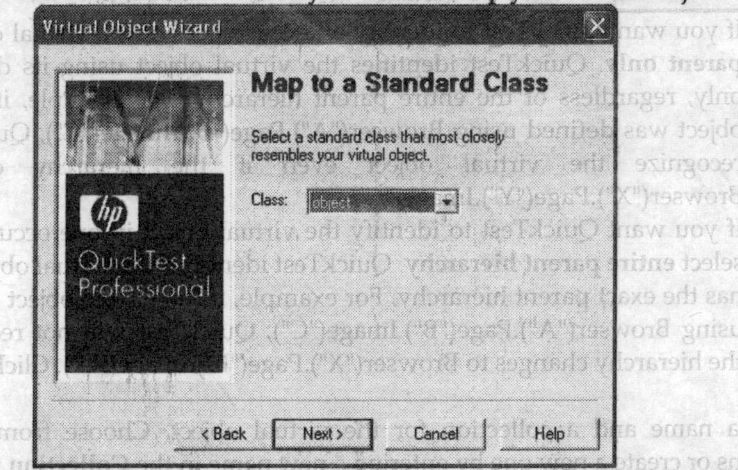

If you select the list class, specify the number of rows in the virtual object. For the table class, select the number of rows and columns. Click **Next**.

4) Click **Mark Object**. QTP displays cross hire symbol. Use the crosshairs pointer and mark the area of the virtual object. Click **Next**.
5) Select parent from below dialog displayed. The coordinates of the virtual object outline are relative to the parent object you select.

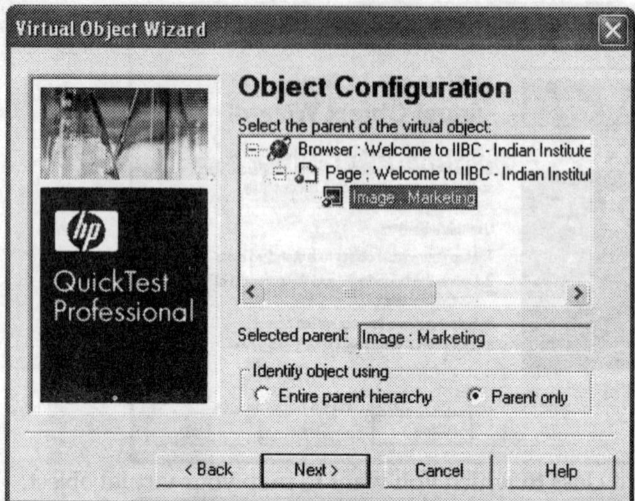

a. If you want QuickTest to identify all occurrences of the virtual object, select **parent only**. QuickTest identifies the virtual object using its direct parent only, regardless of the entire parent hierarchy. For example, if the virtual object was defined using Browser("A").Page("B").Image("C"), QuickTest will recognize the virtual object even if the hierarchy changes to Browser("X").Page("Y").Image("C").

b. If you want QuickTest to identify the virtual object in one occurrence only, select **entire parent hierarchy**. QuickTest identifies the virtual object only if it has the exact parent hierarchy. For example, if the virtual object was defined using Browser("A").Page("B").Image("C"), QuickTest will not recognize it if the hierarchy changes to Browser("X").Page("B").Image("C"). Click **Next**.

6) Specify a name and a collection for the virtual object. Choose from the list of collections or create a new one by entering a new name in the **Collection name** box.
7) To add the virtual object to the Virtual Object Manager and close the wizard, select **No** and then click **Finish**.
8) To add the virtual object to the Virtual Object Manager and define another virtual object, select **Yes** and then click **Next**. The wizard returns to the Map to a Standard Class screen, where you can define the next virtual object.

Virtual Object Manager

The Virtual Object Manager contains all the virtual object collections defined on your computer. From the Virtual Object Manager, you can define and delete virtual objects and collections. Invoke virtual object Manager through

Tools >Virtual Objects > Virtual Object Manager

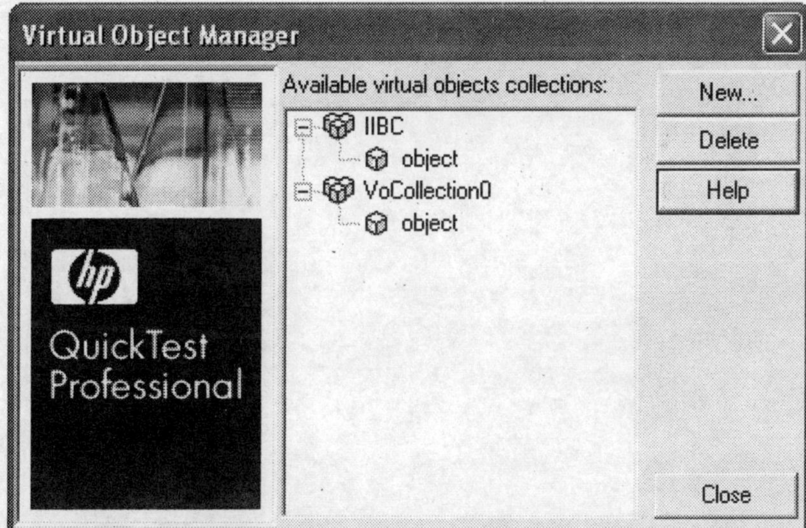

The virtual object collections displayed in the Virtual Object Manager are stored in your computer and not with the tests that contain virtual object steps. This means that if you use a virtual object in a test step, the object will be recognized during the run session only if it is run on a computer containing the appropriate virtual object definition. To copy your virtual object collection definitions to another computer, copy the contents of your **<QuickTest installation folder>\dat\VoTemplate** folder to the same folder on the destination computer.

Review Questions

1. What is the difference between Standard, Custom and Virtual Objects?
2. Why do you need Virtual Object Configuration? Discuss with example?

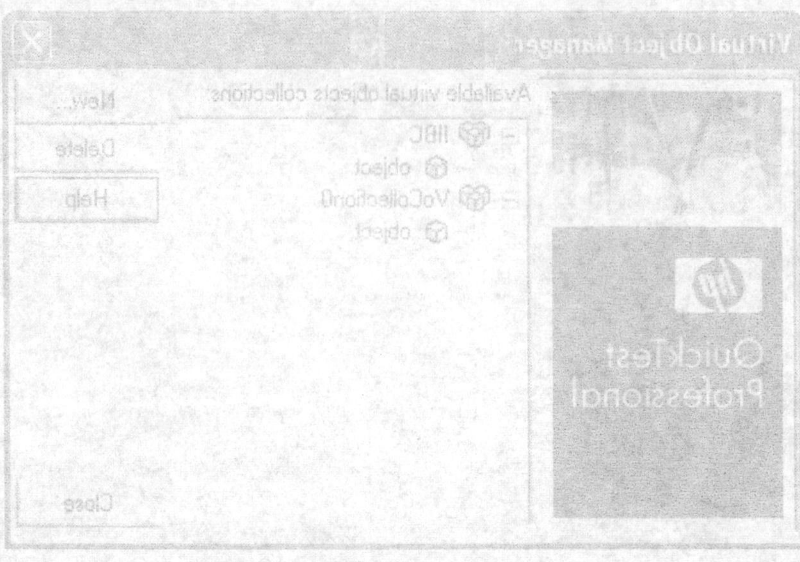

PROGRAMMING WITH VBSCRIPT

Introduction to VBScripting

VbScript stands for Visual basic Scripting. This scripting language was launched in 1996 by Microsoft. Initially this scripting language was developed targeting web developers. Over these years VBScript has advanced itself into many versions each time evolving itself into a strong language for automation tools. VBScript is an interpreted language.

VBScript has been installed by default in every desktop release of Microsoft Windows since Windows 98; as part of Windows Server since Windows NT 4.0 Option Pack. A VBScript program must be executed within a host environment, of which there are several provided with Microsoft Windows, including: Windows Script Host (WSH), Internet Explorer (IE), Internet Information Services (IIS). Additionally, The VBScript hosting environment is embeddable in other programs, through technologies such as the Microsoft Script control (msscript.ocx).

Data types

VBScript has only one data type called a **Variant**. A **Variant** is a special kind of data type that can contain different kinds of information, depending on how it's used. Because **Variant** is the only data type in VBScript, it's also the data type returned by all functions in VBScript.

At its simplest, a **Variant** can contain either numeric or string information. A **Variant** behaves as a number when you use it in a numeric context, that is, when you do not include the value within double quotes, and as a string when you use it in a string context, that is, when you include the value within double quotes.

Beyond the simple numeric or string classifications, a **Variant** can make further distinctions about the specific nature of numeric information. Most of the time, you can just put the kind of data you want in a **Variant**, and the **Variant** behaves in a way that is most appropriate for the data it contains. These different categories of information that can be contained in a **Variant** are called subtypes.

The following table shows the subtypes of data that a **Variant** can contain.

Subtype	Description
Empty	**Variant** is uninitialized. Value is 0 for numeric variables or a zero-length string ("") for string variables.
Null	**Variant** intentionally contains no valid data.
Boolean	Contains either **True** or **False**.
Byte	Contains integer in the range 0 to 255.
Integer	Contains integer in the range -32,768 to 32,767.
Currency	-922,337,203,685,477.5808 to 922,337,203,685,477.5807.
Long	Contains integer in the range -2,147,483,648 to 2,147,483,647.
Single	Contains a single-precision, floating-point number in the range -3.402823E38 to -1.401298E-45 for negative values; 1.401298E-45 to 3.402823E38 for positive values.
Double	Contains a double-precision, floating-point number in the range -1.79769313486232E308 to -4.94065645841247E-324 for negative values; 4.94065645841247E-324 to 1.79769313486232E308 for positive values.
Date (Time)	Contains a number that represents a date between January 1, 100 to December 31, 9999.

String	Contains a variable-length string that can be up to approximately 2 billion characters in length.
Object	Contains an object.
Error	Contains an error number.

Note:
- ➢ You can use conversion functions to convert data from one subtype to another.
  Example: CBool, CByte, CCur, CInt, etc.
- ➢ The VarType and TypeName functions can be used to identify the datatype of a variable.
  Syntax: VarType(*variable name)*
  TypeName(*variable name)*

The VarType and TypeName functions can return one of the following values:

Value	Meaning	Description
0	vbEmpty	Indicates Empty (uninitialized)
1	vbNull	Indicates Null (no valid data)
2	vbInteger	Indicates an integer
3	vbLong	Indicates a long integer
4	vbSingle	Indicates a single-precision floating-point number
5	vbDouble	Indicates a double-precision floating-point number
6	vbCurrency	Indicates a currency
7	vbDate	Indicates a date
8	vbString	Indicates a string
9	vbObject	Indicates an automation object
10	vbError	Indicates an error
11	vbBoolean	Indicates a Boolean
12	vbVariant	Indicates a variant (used only with arrays of Variants)
13	vbDataObject	Indicates a data-access object
17	vbByte	Indicates a byte
8192	vbArray	Indicates an array

Note: If the variable is an array, VarType() returns 8192 + VarType(array_element). **Example:** for an array of integer VarType() will return 8192 + 2 = 8194.

Comments

Comments are the non executable line of a script. Comments are used in scripts for better readability and maintenance. In VBScripting comments can be provided in two ways. Use '(Single Quote) or **REM**

Example 1: Program to print Variable type using VarType function

Script:

```
1.  'Program to Print Variable Type
2.  x="I am string"
3.  y=2.54
4.  print(VarType(x))
5.  print(VarType(y))
```

Description:

Line 2: x is assigned with String

Line 3: y is assigned with Floating Number

Line 4,5: Print Sub Data types of variables stored in Variant using VarType Function. Line 4 output is 8 (vbString) and Line 5 output is 5 (vbDouble)

Output:

QuickTest Pri...

File

8

5

Variables

A variable is a convenient placeholder that refers to a computer memory location where you can store program information that may change during the time your script is running.

There are two ways you can declare your variables:

1) **Explicit declaration**: You declare variables explicitly in your script using:
   - ✓ **Dim** statement: Variables declared with Dim at the script level are available to all procedures within the script. At the procedure level, variables are available only within the procedure.
   - ✓ **Public** statement: Variables declared using the Public statement are available to all procedures in all scripts of all projects.
   - ✓ **Private** statement: Private variables are available only to the script in which they are declared.

2) **Implicit declaration:** You can also declare a variable implicitly by simply using its name in your script. In this method directly the name of the variable is used and a value is assigned to a variable whenever required. Formal declaration of variables is not done here.

Note:

- ✓ You declare multiple variables by separating each variable name with a comma. For example: Dim iibc, istq, infics
- ✓ Declaration of variables is Optional i.e. you can directly assign value to a variable without declaration. This kind of implicit declaration is not generally a good practice because misspelling of the variable name in one or more places, can cause unexpected results when your script is run. To avoid such instance we have an option to force explicit declaration of all the variables used in the script by using the Option Explicit statement. This Option Explicit statement should be the first statement in your script.

Constants

The values that do not alter during the entire execution of the program are called as constants. These fixed values are defined in the script using the **Const** statement.

Example: **Const** myname="iibc"

Following are the constants that are built into VBScript, You don't have to define them before using them. Use them anywhere in your code to represent the values shown for each.

Constant	Value	Description
1) Color constants		
vbBlack	&h00	Black
vbRed	&hFF	Red
vbGreen	&hFF00	Green
vbYellow	&hFFFF	Yellow
vbBlue	&hFF0000	Blue
vbMagenta	&hFF00FF	Magenta
vbCyan	&hFFFF00	Cyan
vbWhite	&hFFFFFF	White
2) Date and Time Constants		
vbSunday	1	Sunday
vbMonday	2	Monday
vbTuesday	3	Tuesday
vbWednesday	4	Wednesday
vbThursday	5	Thursday
vbFriday	6	Friday
vbSaturday	7	Saturday
3) String Constants		

vbCr	Chr(13)	Carriage return.
VbCrLf	Chr(13) & Chr(10)	Carriage return–linefeed combination.
vbFormFeed	Chr(12)	Form feed; not useful in Microsoft Windows.
vbLf	Chr(10)	Line feed.
vbNewLine	Chr(13) & Chr(10) or Chr(10)	Platform-specific newline character; whatever is appropriate for the platform.
vbNullChar	Chr(0)	Character having the value 0.
vbNullString	String having value 0	Not the same as a zero-length string (""); used for calling external procedures.
vbTab	Chr(9)	Horizontal tab.
vbVerticalTab	Chr(11)	Vertical tab; not useful in Microsoft Windows.
4) Date format constants		
vbGeneralDate	0	Display a date and/or time. For real numbers, display a date and time. If there is no fractional part, display only a date. If there is no integer part, display time only. Date and time display is determined by your system settings.
vbLongDate	1	Display a date using the long date format specified in your computer's regional settings.
vbShortDate	2	Display a date using the short date format specified in your computer's regional settings.
vbLongTime	3	Display a time using the long time format specified in your computer's regional settings.
vbShortTime	4	Display a time using the short time format specified in your computer's regional settings.

Naming Restrictions

Variable names follow the standard rules for naming anything in VBScript. A variable name:

- Must begin with an alphabetic character.
- Cannot contain a period.
- Must not exceed 255 characters.
- Must be unique in the scope in which it is declared.

Operators

VBScript has a full range of operators, including arithmetic operators, comparison operators, concatenation operators, and logical operators.

Operator Precedence

When several operations occur in an expression, each part is evaluated and resolved in a predetermined order called operator precedence. You can use parentheses to override the order of precedence and force some parts of an expression to be evaluated before others. Operations within parentheses are always performed before those outside. Within parentheses, however, standard operator precedence is maintained.

When expressions contain operators from more than one category, arithmetic operators are evaluated first, comparison operators are evaluated next, and logical operators are evaluated last. Comparison operators all have equal precedence; that is, they are evaluated in the left-to-right order in which they appear. Arithmetic and logical operators are evaluated in the following order of precedence.

Arithmetic		Comparison		Logical	
Exponentiation	^	Equality	=	Logical Negation	Not
Unary Negation	-	Inequality	< >	Conjunction	And
Multiplication	*	Less than	<	Disjunction	Or
Division	/	Greater than	>	Exclusion	Xor
Integer Division	\	Less than or equal to	<=	Equivalence	Eqv
Modulus arithmetic	**Mod**	Greater than or equal to	>=	Implication	Imp
Addition	+	Object Equivalence	**Is**		
Subtraction	-				
String Concatenation	&				

Conditional Statements

Conditional statements are used to control the flow of the program. These statements in the program are executed when certain condition is true.

In VBScript we have four conditional statements:

➤ **If statement** – Using this statement we can execute a single or block of statements when a condition is true.

Example:

✓ In the following example you need not end the **if** block with **End if** statement since a single statement is executed if the given condition is true.

```
If i=10 Then msgbox "Hello"
```

✓ If you want to execute more than one statement when a condition is true, you must put each statement on separate lines and end the statement with the keyword **End If**

```
If i=10 Then
    msgbox "Hello"
    i = i+1
End If
```

➢ **if...then...else statement** :Using the conditional statement block of statements are executed if the condition is true else alternate block of statements are executed if the condition is false.

Example: If you want to execute a statement if a condition is true and execute another statement if the condition is not true, you must add the "Else" keyword:

```
If i=10 then
    Print "Condition is true"
    msgbox "Hello"
Else
    Print "Condition is false"
    msgbox "Goodbye"
End If
```

The first block of code will be executed if the condition is true, and the other block will be executed otherwise (if i is not equal to 10).

➢ **If...Then...Elseif statement**: Using this statement multiple conditions are evaluated and appropriate block of if/else statements are executed.

Example: You can use the if...then...elseif statement if you want to select one of many blocks of code to execute:

```
if payment="Cash" then
    msgbox "You are going to pay cash!"
elseif payment="Visa" then
    msgbox "You are going to pay with visa."
elseif payment="AmEx" then
    msgbox "You are going to pay with American Express."
else
    msgbox "Unknown method of payment."
end If
```

➢ **Select Case statement:** Using this statement one of several groups of statements are executed based on the expression value.

Example: You can use the SELECT statement if you want to select one of many blocks of code to execute.

```
Select case payment
    Case "Cash"
        msgbox "You are going to pay cash"
    Case "Visa"
        msgbox "You are going to pay with Visa"
    Case "AmEx"
        msgbox "You are going to pay with American Express"
    Case Else
        msgbox "Unknown method of Payment"
End Select
```

This is how it works: First we have a single expression (more often a variable), that is evaluated once. The value of the expression is then compared with the values for each Case in the structure. If there is a match, the block of code associated with that Case is executed.

Looping statements

Using looping statements a group of statements can be executed repeatedly. Loops are used when a statement or set of statements are to be executed repeatedly.

- **For Loop:**

  A For Loop is used for special situations when you need to do something over and over again until some condition statement fails.

Example: The following example will print out the counter variable to the browser after each successful loop.

```
For count = 0 to 3
    Print (count)
Next
```

You can exit a For...Next statement with the Exit For keyword.

- **For Each Loop:**

  VBScript For Each Loop is useful when you want to go through every element in an array, but you do not know how many elements there are inside the array.

Example: The following example creates an array and then prints out every element.

```
Dim myCloset(2)
    myCloset(0) = "Coat"
    myCloset(1) = "Suit"
    myCloset(2) = "Boxes"
For Each item In myCloset
    Print(item)
Next
```

- **While Loop:**
  A While Loop is a simple loop that keeps looping while something is true.

Example: The following code creates the while loop to create a simple VBScript countdown.

```
Dim counter
    counter = 10
While counter > 0
    print(counter)
    counter = counter - 1
Wend
```

- **Do...Loop**
  You can use Do...Loop statements to run a block of code when you do not know how many repetitions you want. The block of code is repeated while a condition is true or until a condition becomes true.

Example:

✓ **Repeating Code While a Condition is True:**

You use the While keyword to check a condition in a Do...Loop statement.

```
Do While i>10
    Print(i)
Loop
```

If **i** is less than 9, the code inside the loop above will never be executed.

```
Do
    Print(i)
Loop While i>10
```

The code inside this loop will be executed at least one time, even if **i** <10.

✓ **Repeating Code Until a Condition Becomes True:**

You use the Until keyword to check a condition in a Do...Loop statement.

```
Do Until i=10
    Print(i)
Loop
```

If **i** equals 10, the code inside the loop will never be executed.

```
Do
    Print(i)
Loop Until i=10
```

The code inside this loop will be executed at least one time, even if **i** =10.

You can exit a Do...Loop statement with the Exit Do keyword.

Arrays

Introduction to Arrays

So far you've learned what a variable is, how to create a variable, and what you can store inside. A variable containing a single value is a scalar variable. But if you want to store a set of variables you might be wondering if there is some easy way to group variables together in a single variable. This is certainly feasible through the use of arrays. Using Arrays you can create a variable that can contain a series of values. Array variables and scalar variables are declared in the same way, except that the declaration of an array variable uses parentheses ( ) following the variable name. Arrays are useful when you're storing sets of similar data because they often make it easier to manipulate the data together. For example, say you have a shopping list that you want to store and write out to the screen. You could store these in a simple variable like this:

```
item1 = "Bananas"
item2 = "Bread"
item3 = "Pasta"
```

This will work fine. But one problem with this approach is that you have to write out each variable name whenever you need to work with it. Also, you can't do things like, loop through all your variables. If these values were stored in an array, you could save yourself a lot of time by manipulating an array. Also in instances where you really don't know ahead of time how many pieces of information you have, array comes to the rescue.

A VBScript array is a special type of variable that allows you to store multiple values against a single variable.

How Does an Array Look Like?

Arrays can be visualized as a stack of elements. Each element has an index number (left column) and a value (right column).

Note: In VBScript arrays are zero-based i.e. they always start their numbering at zero.

Array	
0	Bananas
1	Bread
2	Pasta

Features of Arrays

- **Arrays in VBScripting are Zero-Based:**
  Example: *Dim Myarray(5)*
  Here even though the parenthesis is enclosed with 5 the number of elements the array can store is 5+1 since arrays in VBScript is zero based and in a zero-based array, the number of array elements is always the number shown in parentheses plus one.

- **Arrays in VBScript can have a maximum of 60 dimensions:**

Arrays aren't limited to a single dimension. You can have as many as 60 dimensions. Multiple dimensions can be declared by separating an array's size numbers in the parentheses with commas as depicted in the following example.

Example: *Dim Myarray(5,10)*

Here Myarray is an array variable which is a two-dimensional array consisting of 6 rows and 11 columns

- **If no value is assigned for an array element it consists of NULL value by default**

Example:
```
dim Myarray(3)
    Myarray(0)="hi"
    Myarray(2)= "welcome"
```
Here Myarray(1) is considered as NULL by default since no value is entered for it.

- **Arrays can not only hold similar kind of data but can have combinations of types of data:**

Example:
```
dim Myarray(3)
    Myarray(0)="hi"
    Myarray(1)= 16
    Myarray(2)= "welcome"
    Myarray(3)=72872
  For each e in Myarray
      print e
  Next
```
In this example Myarray is constituted with both numeric and string values.

Creating Arrays in VBScript

VBScript arrays are created by

- ✓ first assigning an array object to a variable name.
  Synatx:*Dim arrayName(No.Of Elements)*
- ✓ by assigning values to the array.
```
arrayName(0) = "Array element 1"
arrayName(1) = "Array element 2"
arrayName(2) = "Array element 3"
```

So, using our prior example, we could write:
```
Dim shoppingList(3)
shoppingList(0) = "Bananas"
shoppingList(1) = "Bread"
shoppingList(2) = "Pasta"
```

Accessing Array Data

You can access data in an array by referring to the name of the array and the element's index number.

Display a Single Array Element

This example displays the second element of the array named *shoppingList* (remember that VBScript array index numbers begin at zero). In this case, the value would be *Bread*

```
Print(shoppingList(1))
```

Example: With respect to our previous example, you could use the following code to declare an array, assign values, then output the contents to the screen.

```
Dim shoppingList(3)
    shoppingList(0) = "Bananas"
    shoppingList(1) = "Bread"
    shoppingList(2) = "Pasta"
For each item in shoppingList
        Print(item)
Next
```

Modify the Contents of an Array

You can modify the contents of an array by specifying a value for a given index number:

```
shoppingList(1) = "Whole meal Bread"
```

Now, the value of the second element will be:

Whole meal Bread

In built functions applicable to Arrays

- **UBound function**

  This will return an integer of the highest subscript or item position in the array.

Example:

```
Dim myArray(3), arraySize
arraySize = UBound(myArray)+1
Print arraySize
```

- **LBound function**

  This will return an integer of the lowest subscript or item position in the array.

  Example:

```
Dim myArray(3), arraySize
arraylbound = LBound(myArray)  'Returns zero
Print arraylbound
```

- **Array()**

  The array function takes comma as delimiter and list as its arguments and returns an array to an ordinary variable.

  Example:

  ```
  Dim arrTest
  arrTest = Array("elem0","elem1","elem2")
  ```

- **Isarray**

  This function will return boolean value True if the variable is an array.

  Example:

  ```
  Dim a
  a=array("jha",1,1)
  check=isarray(a)
  If check="True" Then
          Print "a is an array variable"
  Else
          Print " a is not an array variable"
  End If
  ```

- **Erase**

  The erase function either reinitializes a fixed array or de-allocates the memory used by a dynamic array. If using a dynamic array then you must use the ReDim statement to re-initialize the array.

  ```
  Dim fixedArray(2)
  Erase fixedArray
  ```

Types of Arrays

There are two types of arrays in VBScript:

Static or fixed size arrays

An array that has a fixed number of elements within it is called as Fixed or Static array. The size of a static array does not change; it remains the same throughout. Static array sizes cannot be varied.

Example: Dim myarray (10)

Here an array variable called *myarray* is created with fixed elements of 11, since arrays in VBScript are zero based.

Dynamic arrays

You can also declare an array whose size changes during the time your script is running. This is called a dynamic array. Dynamic arrays are used when you are not sure about the size of an array when you are coding. Dynamic arrays are created in the same way as static arrays but the only difference is that no upper bound will be defined in the declaration.

Example: Dim MyArray()

The array is initially declared using either the *Dim* statement or using the *ReDim* statement. However, for a dynamic array, no size or number of dimensions is placed inside the parentheses.

ReDim: To use a dynamic array, you must subsequently use ReDim to determine the number of dimensions and the size of each dimension. ReDim statement is used to "re-dimension" the array to as many elements you specify. ReDim takes dimensions the same way Dim can. There is no limit to the number of times you can resize a dynamic array, although if you make an array smaller, you lose the data in the eliminated elements.

Example: In the following example, Dim statement is used to define a dynamic array followed by **ReDim** which sets the initial size of the dynamic array to 25. A subsequent **ReDim** statement resizes the array to 30

```
Dim MyArray()
ReDim MyArray(25)
.
.
ReDim MyArray(30)
```

Preserve Statement

In the above example when Myarray is redefined to 30 all the previous contents of the array are lost since the array is redefined. In instances where you have to retrieve the previous contents of the array even after redefining you can make use of preserve statements. The **Preserve** keyword is used to preserve the contents of the array as the resizing takes place. If the preserve keyword is not used then all the previous array elements will be lost.

Example:

```
Dim MyArray()
ReDim MyArray(25)
.
.
ReDim preserve MyArray(30)
```

Example: The following code will create a dynamic array and read and print array elements

```
Dim myarray()
n= inputbox("Enter Size of array")
Redim myarray(n)

For i=0 to n
```

```
        Myarray(i)=inputbox("Enter array element: ")
    Next
    For i=0 to n
        Print myarray(i)
    Next
```

Multi Dimensional Arrays

You can have as many as 60 dimensions, although most people can't comprehend more than three or four dimensions. Multiple dimensions are declared by separating an array's size numbers in the parentheses with commas. In the following example, the *MyTable* variable is a two-dimensional array consisting of 6 rows and 11 columns:

Example: To define a two dimensional static array.

```
Dim MyTable(5, 10)
```

Example: To define multidimensional array dynamically.

```
Dim myarray()
ReDim myarray(1,1)
```

Review Questions

1. Explain Data Types in VbScript?
2. What is difference between for loop and for each loop?
3. Difference between static and dynamic arrays and how you create them?
4. What is the use of preserve statement?

WORKING WITH LIBRARIES

Introduction

Library is a place holder of reusable procedures. Procedures are a set of statements that are enclosed within a group. This group of statements performs a specific task. Once a procedure is defined it can be called from different locations in the program as many times as required by the program. The main purpose of using procedure is to maintain modularity and reusability. In VBScript there are two kinds of procedures; the **Sub** procedure and the **Function** procedure.

Advantages of procedures

- **Modularity**: By dividing our scripts into procedures we can maintain and write programs by segregating the code into smaller and manageable blocks
- **Reusable**: Procedures help us to reduce the number of lines of the code by allowing re usage of the code.
- **Generalization**: Once a procedure is defined it can be used by different tests.
- **Recursive**: Procedures can call themselves any number of times.

Sub procedures

Sub procedure is a series of VBScript statements, enclosed by **Sub** and **End Sub** statements that perform actions. The Sub procedures don't return any value.

The following **Sub** procedure uses two intrinsic, or built-in, VBScript functions, **MsgBox** and **InputBox**, to prompt a user for some information. It then displays the results of a calculation based on that information. The calculation is performed in a **Function** procedure created using VBScript. The **Function** procedure is shown after the following discussion.

```
Sub ConvertTemp()
    temp = InputBox("Please enter the temperature in degrees F.", 1)
    MsgBox "The temperature is " & Celsius(temp) & " degrees C."
End Sub
```

Function Procedures

A **Function** procedure is a series of VBScript statements enclosed by the **Function** and **End Function** statements. A **Function** procedure is similar to a **Sub** procedure, but the only difference is that it can also return a value. A **Function** returns a value by assigning a value to its name. The return type of a **Function** is always a **Variant**.

Example: In the following example, the Celsius function calculates degrees Celsius from degrees Fahrenheit. The result of the calculation is returned to the caller.

```
Function Celsius(fDegrees)
        Celsius = (fDegrees - 32) * 5 / 9
End Function
```

Scope of Procedures

A procedure can be scoped as private, public or default. If not explicitly specified using either Public or Private, procedures are Public by default.

- **Public:** Indicates that the procedure is accessible to all other procedures in all scripts.
- **Private:** Indicates that the procedure is accessible only to other procedures within the script where it is declared.
- **Default:** Used only with the Public keyword in a Class block to indicate that the Function procedure is the default method for the class. An error occurs if more than one Default procedure is specified in a class.

Syntax:
[Public [Default] | Private] [Function |Sub] [(arglist)]
  [statements]
  End [Function | Sub]

Arguments of Procedures

- A procedure can have 0 to n number of arguments where n is a positive integer.
- Commas are used to separate multiple variables. This list of variables representing arguments are passed to the procedure when it is called.
- Arguments can be passed in two modes to a procedure
  - ✓ **By Value:** Indicates that the argument is passed by value. ByVal is used only to pass value to the procedure
    Syntax: ([ByVal] varname)
    Example: [Function | Sub] PassVal(Byval x)
  - ✓ **By Reference:** Indicates that the argument is passed by reference. ByRef is used even to get return value from the procedure. This is the default mode of passing arguments.
    Syntax: ([ByRef] varname)
    Example: [Function/Sub] Passbyref(x)
    Since by default procedure pass arguments by reference mode, you need not to mention the keyword ByRef

Call Statement

Call statement is used to pass program execution control to a procedure. Procedure can be called without using a call statement. In such scenarios whenever the program encounters a procedure name it will automatically pass control to the Procedure. However, if you use the Call keyword to call a procedure that requires arguments, argument list must be enclosed in parentheses. If you omit the Call keyword from the procedure call, you must also omit the parentheses around argument list.

Syntax: Call [Procedure name] [Argument list]

Example: The following example shows two calls to the MyProc procedure. One uses the Call statement in the code; the other doesn't. Both do exactly the same thing.

Call MyProc(firstarg, secondarg)
MyProc firstarg, secondarg

Notice that the parentheses are omitted in the call when the Call statement isn't used.

Note:

- **If you remove the Call statement but fail to remove the parentheses from a call to a procedure with a single argument, then that argument is passed by value mode rather than by reference mode. This might result into unwanted consequences.**
- **The optional Call statement can be used when function procedures do not have any return values.**
- **A procedure name cannot be assigned to a variable and set this variable as an argument to the Call statement.**

Example: The following is invalid usage of call statement

```
Dim myVar
pmyVar="myProc"
call myProc(myarg)
```

Exit Statement

The code within a procedure is executed until the last line of the procedure i.e. End statement is encountered. In instances where the user wants to exit the procedure when certain conditions are met; exit statements come into use. Exit statements when encountered within a procedure body exits the procedure unconditionally.

Syntax: Exit [Procedure]

Creating Library Files

Library is nothing but a file which contains function procedures and sub procedures. These library files can be associated to any script in QTP, so that the script in QTP can call or reuse the procedures present in the library file.

Library files can have 3 extensions as below

- .txt
- .vbs
- .qfl

Creating Library file with extension .txt

1. Open Notepad.
2. Paste existing procedures or create new procedures
3. Click Save. From the file dialog opened give any name like mylib and click OK.
4. Library file is ready with extension .txt

Creating Library file with extension .vbs

1. Open Notepad.

2. Paste existing procedures or create new procedures
3. Click Save. From the file dialog opened give any name like mylib.vbs and click OK.

   Note: You must give double quotes around file name Ex:"mylib.vbs" to save the file with vbs extension
4. Library file is ready with extension .vbs

Creating Library file with extension .qfl

1. From QTP Select File>New>Function Library. Opens a new function library to write functions.
2. Place procedures in the function library script editor. After placing procedures script editor looks like below.

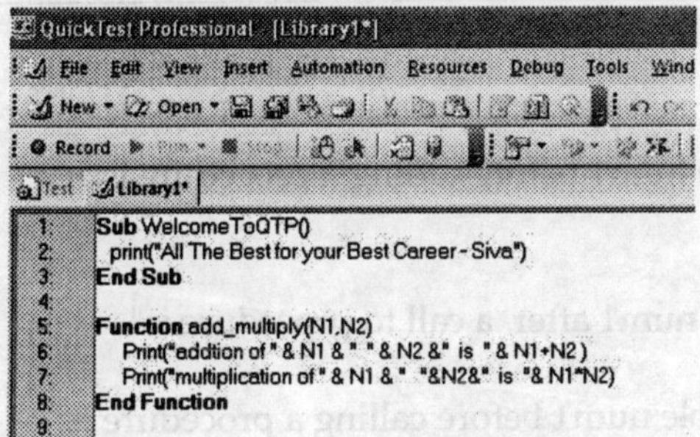

3. Click Save icon. From Dialog opened enter your file name like mylib.qfl and click OK.
4. Library file is ready with extension .qfl

Associating/Adding Libraries to QTP

To add library files created above to QTP follow below steps.

1. Select File>Settings. Test Settings Dialog will open.

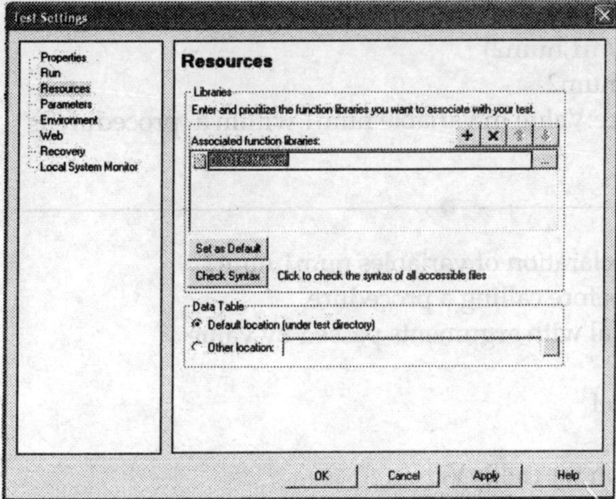

2. Click + to add a library file. A file browse button will be displayed.
3. Click on browse button and select the file.
4. Automatic Relative Path conversion dialog appears. Select Yes to close the Automatic Relative Path dialog and click OK to close the Test Settings Dialog.
5. Click Check Syntax button to validate the syntax of functions in the library file.

Scripting Examples

1. Program to demonstrate ByVal and ByRef

```
1  Dim num1,num2
2   num1=10
3   num2=20
4    print("pass by Value: Value in variable num1 before calling a procedure is:"
   &space(1)&num1)
5  call  passByVal(num1,num2)
6   print("Pass by Value: Value in variable num1 after  a call to procedure is"
   &space(1)&num1)
7   print("pass by reference:Value in variable num1 before calling a procedure is:"
   &space(1)&num1)
8   call passByRef(num1,num2)
9   print("Pass by reference:Value in variable num1 after  a call to procedure is"
   &space(1)&num1)
10 Function passByVal(ByVal num1,ByVal num2)
11           num1=num1+num2
12           Print("Pass by Value:Value in variable num1 within a  procedure is"
   &space(1)&num1)
13  End Function
14 Function passByRef(num1,num2)
15           num1=num1+num2
16  Print("Pass by reference:Value in variable num1 within a  procedure is"
   &space(1)&num1)
17  End Function
```

Line1-3:Initialization and declaration of variables num1,num2
Line4: Print value of num1 before calling a procedure.
Line5:Call function passByVal with arguments passed by value
Line6-7:Print value of num1
Line8:Call function passByRef
Line9: Print value of num1
Line10-13: Function definition for callByVal
Line14-17: Function definition for callByRef

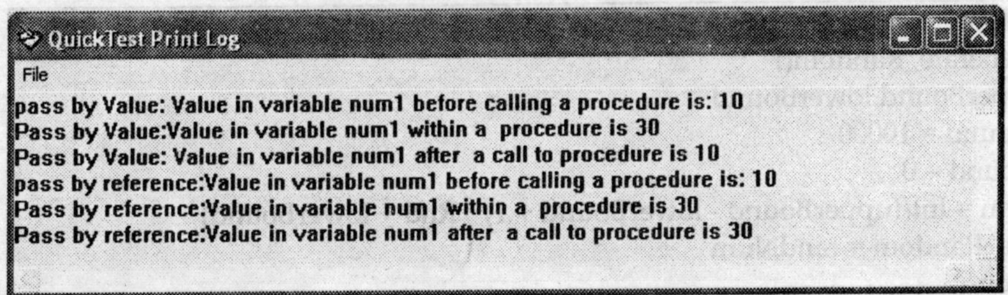

Program 2: Program to Exit a procedure if user input is 10 or less than 10

```
1  Call exitDemo
2  Sub exitDemo()
3    Dim counter, myNum
4    counter = 0
5    myNum = inputbox("Enter a number greater than 10(not less that or equall to 10:")
6    If myNum<10 or myNum=10 Then
7            Print("Procedure exiting....Entered number is less than or equall to 10")
8            Exit Sub
9    End If
10   Do While myNum > 10
11     myNum = myNum - 1
12     counter = counter + 1
13   Loop
14   MsgBox "The loop made" & counter & " repetitions."
15 End Sub
```

Line1: Call the procedure exitDemo

Line3-15: definition of a sub procedure.

Line 8: Exit the sub procedure without executing remaining lines if the user input is 10 or less than 10

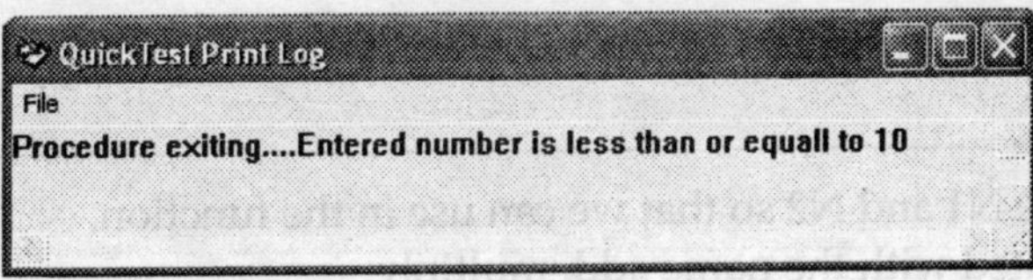

Program 3: Program to write a function to return a random number

```
1  Dim randNum
2  Function generate_Random()
3      Dim upperBound,lowerBound
4      upperBound = 10000
5      lowerBound = 0
6      randNum = Int((upperBound - lowerBound + 1) * Rnd + lowerBound)
7      generate_Random = randNum
8  End Function
9  randNum = generate_Random()
10 print(" The random number generated is:    " & Cstr(randNum))
```

Line2: Function is created with the name generate_Random.
Line3: Declaring local variables within the function.
Line4-5: Assigning value 10000 to upperBound and 0 to lowerBound.
Line6: Some calculation using random number and storing it in randNum.
Line7: Storing the randNum to the name of the function i.e., generate_Random.
Line9: Assigning the name of the function generate_Random to randNum in the Main program

QuickTest Print Log

File

The random number generated is: 7056

Program 4: Program to write a function to add and multiply two numbers.

```
1  Dim N1, N2
2  Function add_multiply(N1,N2)
3      Print("addtion of " & N1 & "  " & N2 &"  is  " & N1+N2 )
4      Print("multiplication of " & N1 & "   "&N2&"  is  "& N1*N2)
5  End Function
6  add_multiply 4,3
```

Line1: Declare variable N1 and N2 so that we can use in the function.
Line2: Function is created with the name add_multiply.
Line3: Printing after addition.
Line4: Printing after multiplication.
Line5: Ending the function.
Line6: Call the function with arguments 4, 3

QuickTest Print Log

File

addtion of 4 3 is 7
multiplication of 4 3 is 12

Program 5: Program to write a sub procedure to add and multiply two numbers.

```
1 Option Explicit
2 Dim N1, N2
3 Sub add_multiply(N1,N2)
4    Print("addition of " & N1 & " " & N2 &" is " & N1+N2 )
5    Print("multiplication of " & N1 & " "&N2&" is "& N1*N2)
6 End Sub
7 add_multiply 4,3
```

Line1-2 : Declaring the variables using Option Explicitly.
Line3 : add_multiply is the Sub Procedure.
Line4 : Prints after addition.
Line5 : Prints after multiplication.
Line6 : Ending the Sub Procedure.
Line7 : Calling Sub Procedure with value 4 & 3 from the main program.

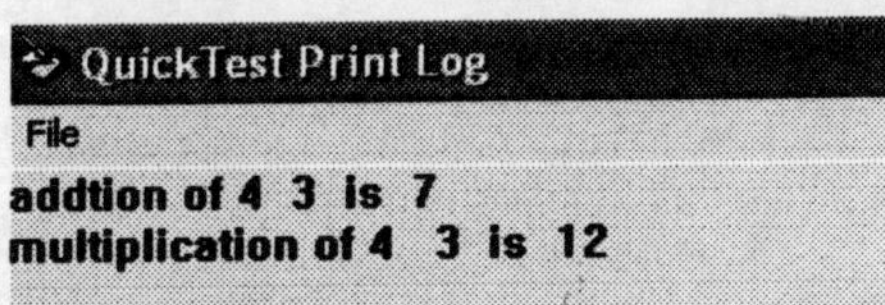
QuickTest Print Log
File
addtion of 4 3 is 7
multiplication of 4 3 is 12

VBSCRIPT BUILT-IN FUNCTION LIBRARY

Every Programming language comes with in built functions to enhance the speed of development. Even VB Script has many inbuilt functions that can be categorized as follows.

- Conversion Functions
- String Functions
- Array Functions
- Date and Time Functions
- Math Functions
- Other Functions

Below is the brief explanation of commonly used functions from each category

Conversion Functions

Function	Description
Asc	Returns ASCII value of a character
Chr	Returns Character corresponding to ASCII value
CBool	Converts an expression to a variant of subtype Boolean
CByte	Converts an expression to a variant of subtype Byte
CCur	Converts an expression to a variant of subtype Currency
CDate	Converts a valid date and time expression to the variant of subtype Date
CDbl	Converts an expression to a variant of subtype Double
CInt	Converts an expression to a variant of subtype Integer
CLng	Converts an expression to a variant of subtype Long
CSng	Converts an expression to a variant of subtype Single
CStr	Converts an expression to a variant of subtype String
Hex	Returns the hexadecimal value of a specified number
Oct	Returns the octal value of a specified number

String Functions

Function	Description
Len	Returns the number of characters in a string
Mid	Returns a specified number of characters from a string
InStr	Returns the position of the first occurrence of one string within another. The search begins at the first character of the string
InStrRev	Returns the position of the first occurrence of one string within another. The search begins at the last character of the string
LCase	Converts a specified string to lowercase
UCase	Converts a specified string to uppercase
Left	Returns a specified number of characters from the left side of a string
Right	Returns a specified number of characters from the right side of a string
LTrim	Removes spaces on the left side of a string
RTrim	Removes spaces on the right side of a string
Trim	Removes spaces on both the left and the right side of a string

Replace	Replaces a specified part of a string with another string a specified number of times
Space	Returns a string that consists of a specified number of spaces
StrComp	Compares two strings and returns a value that represents the result of the comparison
String	Returns a string that contains a repeating character of a specified length
StrReverse	Reverses a string

Array Functions

Function	Description
Array	Returns a variant containing an array
Filter	Returns a zero-based array that contains a subset of a string array based on a filter criteria
IsArray	Returns a Boolean value that indicates whether a specified variable is an array
Join	Returns a string that consists of a number of substrings in an array
LBound	Returns the smallest subscript for the indicated dimension of an array
Split	Returns a zero-based, one-dimensional array that contains a specified number of substrings
UBound	Returns the largest subscript for the indicated dimension of an array

Date and Time Functions

Function	Description
Date	Returns the current system date
Month	Returns a number that represents the month of the year (between 1 and 12, inclusive)
MonthName	Returns the name of a specified month
Year	Returns a number that represents the year
Day	Returns a number that represents the day of the month (between 1 and 31, inclusive)
Weekday	Returns a number that represents the day of the week (between 1 and 7, inclusive)
WeekdayName	Returns the weekday name of a specified day of the week such as Sunday, Monday

Time	Returns the current system time
Hour	Returns a number that represents the hour of the day (between 0 and 23, inclusive)
Minute	Returns a number that represents the minute of the hour (between 0 and 59, inclusive)
Second	Returns a number that represents the second of the minute (between 0 and 59, inclusive)
Now	Returns the current system date and time
DateAdd	Add specified time interval to a date and returns new date
DateDiff	Returns the time interval between two dates
IsDate	Returns a Boolean value that indicates if the evaluated expression is a date

Math Functions

Function	Description
Abs	Returns the absolute value of a specified number
Atn	Returns the arctangent of a specified number
Cos	Returns the cosine of a specified number (angle)
Exp	Returns *e* raised to a power
Hex	Returns the hexadecimal value of a specified number
Log	Returns the natural logarithm of a specified number
Oct	Returns the octal value of a specified number
Rnd	Returns a random number less than 1 but greater or equal to 0
Sgn	Returns an integer that indicates the sign of a specified number
Sin	Returns the sine of a specified number (angle)
Sqr	Returns the square root of a specified number
Tan	Returns the tangent of a specified number (angle)

Other Functions

Function	Description
CreateObject	Creates an object of a specified type
Eval	Evaluates an expression and returns the result

GetLocale	Returns the current locale ID
GetObject	Returns a reference to an automation object from a file
GetRef	Allows you to connect a VBScript procedure to a DHTML event on your pages
InputBox	Displays a dialog box, where the user can write some input and/or click on a button, and returns the contents
IsEmpty	Returns a Boolean value that indicates whether a specified variable has been initialized or not
IsNull	Returns a Boolean value that indicates whether a specified expression contains no valid data (Null)
IsNumeric	Returns a Boolean value that indicates whether a specified expression can be evaluated as a number
IsObject	Returns a Boolean value that indicates whether the specified expression is an automation object
LoadPicture	Returns a picture object. Available only on 32-bit platforms
MsgBox	Displays a message box, waits for the user to click a button, and returns a value that indicates which button the user clicked
RGB	Returns a number that represents an RGB color value
Round	Rounds a number
ScriptEngine	Returns the scripting language in use
ScriptEngineBuildVersion	Returns the build version number of the scripting engine in use
ScriptEngineMajorVersion	Returns the major version number of the scripting engine in use
ScriptEngineMinorVersion	Returns the minor version number of the scripting engine in use
SetLocale	Sets the locale ID and returns the previous locale ID
TypeName	Returns the subtype of a specified variable
VarType	Returns a value that indicates the subtype of a specified variable

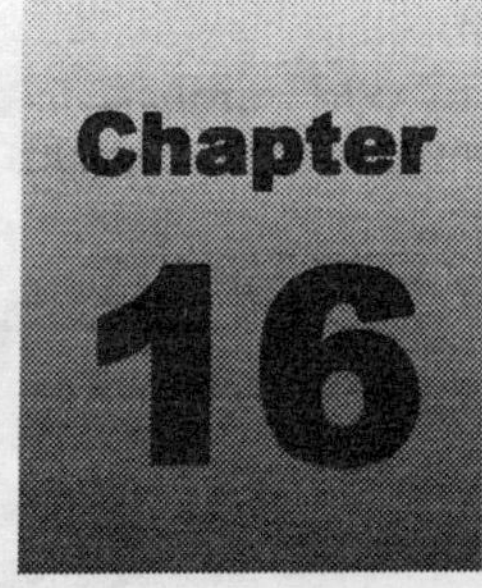

VBSCRIPTING SOLVED EXAMPLES

This chapter contains lots of examples developed using VBScript and their detailed explanation.

1. Print Hello World

```
print("Hello World
```

Print is a utility statement that displays information in Quicktest Print Log Window during run session

Output:

QuickTest Print Log

File

Hello World

2. Find whether the given number is an odd or even number

```
1  Dim n
2  n=inputbox("enter the number")
3  n=cint(n)
4  If (n mod 2) = 0 Then
5      print( n & " is even number" )
6   Else
7      print ( n & " is odd number" )
8  End If
```

Line 1: Declare variable n

Line 2: Displays dialog box for the user to input text, returns a string value

Line 3: Converts input expression into an Integer and assigns that value to n.

Line 4: If the number is divisible by 2 number is an 'even number' else it is an 'odd number'.

Line 5: Prints if number is an even number

Line 7: Prints if number is an Odd number

Line 8: End of If statement

Input:

n = 4 (First Time of execution)

n = 9 (Second Time of execution)

Output:

QuickTest Print Log

File

4 is even number
9 is odd number

3. Print odd numbers between a given range of numbers

```
1  Dim N1,N2,N,odd_Numbers
2  N1=inputbox("Enter the starting number")
3  N2=inputbox("Enter the ending number")
4  N1=Cint(N1)
5  N2=Cint(N2)
6  Print("The odd numbers between " & N1 &" and "& N2& " are ")
7  oddNumbers=""
8  For N=N1 to N2
9  If (N mod 2) <> 0 Then
10     oddNumbers = oddNumbers &cstr(N) & vbtab
11 End If
12 Next
13 print(oddNumbers)
```

Line 1: Declare variables N1, N2, N, odd_Numbers

Line 2: Displays a dialog box for user to input the starting Number, returns a string value

Line 3: Displays a dialog box for user to input the Ending Number, returns a string value
Line 4: Converts input expression N1 into an Integer and assigns that value to N1.
Line 5: Converts input expression N2 into an Integer and assigns that value to N2.
Line 6: Prints the number of Odd numbers present between N1 & N2
Line 7: Equate variable oddNumbers to NULL value
Line 8: For loop that runs for all the inputs between N1 & N2
Line 9: Check whether each value of N is Divisible by 2, if (N Mod 2) <>0 then the number is an odd number.
Line 10: Values of odd numbers will be evaluated as follows in different iterations

Iteration	oddNumbers	Expression Details
1	1	“”&1&VbTab
2	1	Evaluates false since 2 Mod2 is 0
3	1 3	1 &3&VbTab
4	1 3	Evaluates false since 4 Mod2 is 0
5	1 3 5	1 3&5&VbTab

After 15 iterations oddNumbers variable contains data as follows:

1 3 5 7 9 11 13 15

VbTab: Prints Tab space in the output Window
Line 13: Prints all Odd Numbers between N1 & N2

Input:

N1 = 1
N2 = 15

Output:

QuickTest Print Log

File

The odd numbers between 1 and 15 are
1 3 5 7 9 11 13 15

4. Find the factorial of a given number

```
Dim N,factorial
N=inputbox("Enter the number")
N=Cint(N)
duplicateNumber=N
factorial=1
If N < 0 Then
print("No factorial for Negative Numbers")
elseif (N=0) or (N=1) then
print(" Factorial of " & cstr(N) + " is 1")
```

```
10 else
11 While N > 1
12     factorial=factorial * N
13     N=N-1
14 Wend
15 print(" Factorial of " & cstr(duplicateNumber) & " is "& cstr(factorial))
16 end if
```

Line 1-5: Variable declarations, assignment and Input Reading
Line 6-7: if the Number entered is a negative number then no factorial
Line 8-9: if the Number entered is 0 or 1 then factorial value is 1
Line 10-13: If N>1 then factorial =factorial times N(factorial=factorial * N).
Multiply all values until the given input number.
Line 15: Prints the factorial value
For input value 8

Iteration	NVal	factorial
1	8	1*8
2	7	1*8*7
3	6	1*8*7*6
4	5	1*8*7*6*5
5	4	1*8*7*6*5*4
6	3	1*8*7*6*5*4*3
7	2	1*8*7*6*5*4*3*2

Input:

N = 8

Output:

QuickTest Print Log

File

Factorial of 8 is 40320

5. Find the factors of a given number

```
Dim N,factors
N=inputbox("Enter the number")
N=Cint(N)
If N <= 0 Then
   print("No factors for Negative Numbers or zero")
End If
   factors=""
   print(" The factors of " & Cstr(N) & "are ")
   For i=1 to N
```

```
10        If (N mod i) = 0 Then
11       factors = factors & cstr(i)& vbtab
12    End If
13    Next
14    print(factors)
```

Line 1: Declare variables
Line 2-3: Takes input and convert them to integers
Line 4-5: If number N <=0 then print No factors .End of If statement
Line 6: A variable is declared to store data for formatting.
Line 9 -13: Divide N with all the numbers from 1 to N. If N is divisible by any number i.e. Modulus is equal to zero then that number is a factor of N.
Line 14: Print all the factors

Input:

N = 28

Output:

```
QuickTest Print Log
File
The factors of 28are
1        2        4        7        14        28
```

6. Print prime numbers between a given range of numbers

```
Dim N1,N2, N,primeNumbers,flag
N1=inputbox("Enter the starting number")
N2=inputbox("Enter the ending number")
N1=Cint(N1)
N2=Cint(N2)
Print("The prime numbers between " & N1&" and "& N2& " are ")
primeNumbers=""
For N=N1 to N2
   flag=0
   For i=2 to N -1
      If (N mod i) = 0 Then
         flag=1
         Exit for
      End If
   Next
   If flag=0 Then
      primeNumbers = primeNumbers&cstr(N) & vbtab
   End If
Next
print(primeNumbers)
```

Line 1-7: Initialize variables
Line 8: Loop through all the values between two given numbers
Line 9: flag=0 means we are assuming that the number is a prime number
Line 10-19: Divide a given number with all the numbers from 2 to a number one less than that. If it is divisible then it's not a prime number. For example if 7 is divisible by 2,3,4,5,6 then it is not a prime number. Since 7 is NOT divisible by any of these numbers 2,3,4,5,6 we consider 7 as a prime number. Incase if a given number is divisible by any number then **Exit for** statement in line 13 will exit inner for loop and goes to external for loop to loop through the next number.
Line 20: Prints prime numbers

Input:

N1 = 2
N2 = 20

Output:

```
QuickTest Print Log
File
The prime numbers between 2 and 20 are
2    3    5    7    11    13    17    19
```

7. Swap 2 numbers without a temporary variable

```
1  Dim N1,N2
2  N1=inputbox("Enter the number")
3  N2=inputbox("Enter the number")
4  N1=Cint(N1)
5  N2=Cint(N2)
6  print(" Numbers before swapping  N1= "& N1 & vbtab &"N2= "& N2)
7  N1=N1+N2
8  N2=N1-N2
9  N1=N1-N2
10 print(" Numbers after swapping     N1= "& N1 & vbtab &"N2= "& N2)
```

Line 1-5 : Initialization
Line 7: N1=5+9 i.e N1= N1+N2 = 5+9 = 14
Line 8: N2= 14-9 i.e N2=5
Line 9: N1=14-5 i.e N1=9

Input:

N1 = 5
N2 = 9

Output:

QuickTest Print Log

File

Numbers before swapping N1= 5 N2= 9
Numbers after swapping N1= 9 N2= 5

8. Write a program to Perform specified Arithmetic Operation on two given numbers

```
1  Dim N1, N2, ch
2  N1=inputbox("Enter the number")
3  N2=inputbox("Enter the number")
4  N1=Cint(N1)
5  N2=Cint(N2)
6  ch=inputbox("1.  Addition"  &  vbnewline  &"2.Subtraction"  &  vbnewline
   &"3.Multiplication" & vbnewline &" 4.Division "& vbnewline &"Enter your choice")
7  Select Case ch
8  Case 1
9      print(" Addition of " & N1&" and "& N2&" is "& N1+N2)
10 Case 2
11     print(" Subtraction of "& N1&" and "& N2&" is "& N1-N2)
12 Case 3
13     print(" Multiplication of " & N1 &" and "&N2&" is "&N1*N2)
14 Case 4
15     print(" Division of " & N1&" and "& N2&" is "& N1/N2)
16 Case default
17    print("Wrong Choice")
18 End Select
```

Line 1- 5: Initialise Variables
Line 6: Displays input box for user choice. VbNewLine breaks the text to next line. '_' is inline character. This will be used if VbScript statement is long and we want to write the statement in multiple lines.
Line 7: Select case statement evaluates the expression and finds case value. In given input ch value is 3. So control switches to case 3 i.e. 13th line in the program.
Line 13: Prints the value of the expression
Line 16: Incase the input value doesn't match with any case value, control shift to default case.

Input:

N1 = 6
N2 = 3
ch = 3

Output:

QuickTest Print Log

File

Multiplication of 6 and 3 is 18

9. Find the length of a given string

```
1 Dim str,lengthStr
2 str= inputbox("Enter the String")
3 lengthStr=len(str)
4 print("Length of String "& str &" is " & Cstr(lengthStr))
```

Line 1-2: Initialises string
Line 3: Calculates the Length of the String using **'len'** function.
Input:

Str = Hello

Output:

QuickTest Print Log

File

Length of String Hello is 5

10. Reverse given string

```
1 Dim str,lengthStr
2 str= inputbox("Enter the String")
3 reverseStr=strreverse(str)
4 print("Reverse of String "& str &" is "& reverseStr)
```

Line 1-2: Initialises string
Line 3: Reverse the String using **strreverse** function.
Line 4: Prints reversed string
Input:

Str = "hai how are you"

Output:

QuickTest Print Log

File

Reverse of String hai how are you is uoy era woh iah

11. Find how many alpha characters are present in a string

```
1  Dim str, noOfAlphaChars, lengthStr,ch
2  str= inputbox("Enter the String")
3  lengthStr=len(str)
4  noOfAlpahChars=0
5  For i=1 to lengthStr
6     ch=mid(str,i,1)
7     If StrComp(ch,"[A-Za-z]") = 1 Then
8       noOfAlphaChars=noOfAlphaChars+1
9     End If
10 Next
11 print("Number of Alpha Characters in " & str & " is "& noOfAlphaChars)
```

Line 1-4: Initialization of Variables
Line 5: **For loop** iterates from first character to last character of the input string
Line 6: Read one by One character as follows

Iteration	Character	Mid Parameters
1	R	str,1,1
2	A	str,2,1
3	2	str,3,1

Mid function takes three arguments: string, character to start, how many characters to Read
Line 7: Check whether the character is an alphabet. **StrComp** function compares each character of string with alphabet.
Line 8: increment number of alphabets if alphabet is found
Line 11: prints number of alpha characters
Input:

Str = "ra23tr5b"

Output:

QuickTest Print Log

File

Number of Alpha Characters in ra23tr5b is 5

12. Find occurrences of a specific character in a string

```
Dim str,noOfOccurences,lengthStr,ch,inCh
str= inputbox("Enter the String")
inCh=inputbox("Enter the Character")
lengthStr=len(str)
noOfOccurences=0
For i=1 to lengthStr
```

```
7           ch=mid(str,i,1)
8           If ch=inCh Then
9                noOfOccurences=noOfOccurences+1
10          End If
11     Next
12     print("Number of Occurrences of  given Character  " & inCh & " in " & str & " are " &
       noOfOccurences)
```

Line 1: Declaration Of variables.
Line 2-3: Read the String and character to check from user
Line 4: Calculates the Length of the String using 'len' function
Line 5: Initialising the variable "noOfOccurences =0 ". This variable keeps the count of number of times the given characters occurs in the given string.
Line 6 : **For** loop runs from first character to last character
Line 7: mid function reads 1character each time from the string, since in this line length of characters to return is given as 1.
Line 8 : Checks if read character (ch) matches the given Character (inCh).
Line 9: If the Character matches with the given Character, then noOfOccurences is incremented by 1.
Line 12 : Displays the number of times the given character is present in the given string.
Below is the iteration flow for character 'm' in string 'madam'

Iter	Character	Mid(madam,i,1)	noOfOccurences
1	m	madam,1,1	1
2	a	madam,2,1	1(not incremented)
3	d	madam,3,1	1(not incremented)
4	a	madam,4,1	1(not incremented)
5	m	madam,5,1	2

Input:

Str = "madam"
inCh = m

Output

QuickTest Print Log
File
Number of Occurences of given Character m in madam are 2

13. Replace space with tab in between the words of a string

```
Dim str,outStr
str= inputbox("Enter the String")
print("String before replacing space with tab is:     " + str)
```

```
4 outStr=Replace(str," ",vbtab)
5 print("String after replacing space with tab is:     " + outStr)
```

Line 1: Declaration Of variables.
Line 2: Initializes the String .
Line 3: Displays the actual String given by the user without inserting the space.
Line 4: Replace function Returns a string in which a specified substring has been replaced with another substring a specified number of times.
Line 5: Displays the String with the Space inserted between the given string .

Input:

Str = "All The Best by Siva"

Output:

QuickTest Print Log

File

String before replacing space with tab is: All The Best by Siva
String after replacing space with tab is: All   The   Best   by   Siva

14. Write a program to return ASCII value of a given character

```
1 Dim inCh,inChAscii
2 inCh= inputbox("Enter the Character")
3 inChAscii=Asc(inCh)
4 print("Ascii value of " & inCh & " is " & Cstr(inChAscii))
```

Line 1: Declaration Of variables.
Line 2: Initializes the String.
Line 3: **Asc** function Returns the ANSI character code corresponding to the character entered by user

Input:
inCh = b

Output:

QuickTest Print Log

File

Ascii value of b is 98

15. Write a program to return a character corresponding to the given ASCII value

```
Dim inCh,inChAscii
inChAscii= inputbox("Enter the Character")
```

```
3 inCh=Chr(inChAscii)
4 print("Corresponding Character For a given ASCII value "& Cstr(inChAscii) & "  is  " &inCh)
```

Line 1: Declaration Of variables.

Line 2: Initialises the String.

Line 3: **Chr** function Returns the character associated with the specified ANSI character code.

Input:

inChAscii = 105

Output:

QuickTest Print Log

File

Corresponding Character For a given ASCII value 105 is i

16. Convert a string to Upper Case

```
1 Dim Str,ucaseStr
2 Str= inputbox("Enter the String")
3 print(" Given String is:    " + Str )
4 ucaseStr=ucase(Str)
5 print(" String After Converting into uppercase is:    " + ucaseStr )
```

Line 1: Declaration of variables.

Line 2: Initialises the String .

Line 3: Displays the Given String entered by the user.

Line 4: **Ucase** function Returns a string that has been converted to uppercase

Input:

Str = "hello"

Output:

QuickTest Print Log

File

Given String is: hello
String After Converting into uppercase is: HELLO

17. Convert a string to lower case

```
Dim Str,lcaseStr
Str= inputbox("Enter the String")
print(" Given String is:    " + Str )
lcaseStr=lcase(Str)
print(" String After Converting into lowercase is:    " + lcaseStr )
```

Line 1: Declaration Of variables.
Line 2: Initializes the String .
Line 3: Displays the Given String entered by the user.
Line 4: **Lcase** function Returns a string that has been converted to lowercase

Input:
Str = "HELLO"

Output:

QuickTest Print Log

File

Given String is: HELLO
String After Converting into lowercase is: hello

18. Write a program to Replace a word in a string with another word

```
1 Dim str,outStr
2 str= inputbox("Enter the String")
3 inWord=inputbox(" Enter the word to search for")
4 replaceWord=inputbox("Enter the word to replace with")
5 print("String before replacing is:    " + str)
6 outStr=Replace(str,inWord, replaceWord)
7 print("String after replacing is:     " + outStr)
```

Line 1: Declaration Of variables.
Line 2: Initialises the String .
Line 3-4: Enter the word to be searched and enter the word to be replaced with.
Line 5: Displays the given string before replacing .
Line 6: Replace function Returns a string after replacing specified substring with another substring.

Input:

Str = "how are you how do you do"
inWord = "do"
rlaceWord = "done"

Output

QuickTest Print Log

File

String before replacing is: how are you how do you do
String after replacing is: how are you how done you done

19. Check whether the string is a PALINDROME

```
1 Dim str,revStr
2 str= inputbox("Enter the String")
3 print(" The Given String is :  " +str)
4 revStr = StrReverse(str)
5 If StrComp(str,revStr) = 0 Then
6      print(" The Given String is a Palindrome")
7 else
8      print(" The Given String is not a Palindrome ")
9 End If
```

Line 1: Declaration Of variables.
Line 2: Initialises the String.
Line 3: Displays the given String.
Line 4: **StrReverse** function Returns reverse of the string
Line 5: **StrComp** function compares the given two strings i.e., string given by the user and the String that is reversed.If two Strings are same the StrComp function returns 0.

Input:

Str = "madam"

Output:

```
QuickTest Print Log
File
The Given String is :  madam
The Given String is a Palindrome
```

20. Verify whether the given two strings are equal

```
1  Dim instring1,instring2
2  instring1= inputbox("Enter the String")
3  instring2=inputbox("Enter the String")
4  print(" The String1 is :   " +instring1)
5  print(" The String2 is :   " +instring2)
6  If StrComp(instring1,instring2) = 0 Then
7     print(" The Strings are equal ")
8  else
9     print(" The Strings are not equal ")
10 End If
```

Line 1: Declaration Of variables.
Line 2-3: Initialises the String.
Line 4-5: Displays the given two Strings.

Line 5: StrComp function compares the given two strings. If the two Strings are the same the StrComp function returns 0.

Input:

instring1 = "hai"
instring2 = "hello"

Output:

QuickTest Print Log
File
The String1 is : hai
The String2 is : hello
The Strings are not equal

21. Print all values from an Array

```
1 Dim inputArray, index
2 inputArray=array(10,"20.5","IIIBC","QTP","Siva")
3    print("Elements of inputArray are")
4 For index=lbound(inputArray) to ubound(inputArray)
5    print(inputArray(index ))
6 Next
```

Line 1: Declaration Of variables.
Line 2: array Function Returns a variant containing an array. If no arguments are specified, an array of zero length is created.
Line 4: For loop ranges from lbound to ubound of the array.Lbound function returns the lower bound of the array i.e 0 and Ubound function returns the higher bound of the array i.e 4.

Output:

QuickTest Print Log
File
Elements of inputArray are
10
20.5
IIIBC
QTP
Siva

22. Sort Array elements

```
Dim inputArray,index, index1,index2,elements
inputArray=array(10,9,2,8,5,1)
Print("Array elements before sorting are:   ")
elements = ""
For index=lbound(inputArray) to ubound(inputArray)
```

```
6     elements = elements & Cstr(inputArray(index)) & vbtab
7  Next
8  print(elements)
9  For index1=lbound(inputArray) to ubound(inputArray)
10     For index2=index1+1 to ubound(inputArray)
11         If inputArray(index1) > inputArray(index2) Then
12             temp = inputArray(index1)
13             inputArray(index1) = inputArray(index2)
14             inputArray(index2) = temp
15         End If
16     Next
17 Next
18 Print("Array elements after sorting are:  " )
19 elements = ""
20 For index=lbound(inputArray) to ubound(inputArray
21     elements = elements & Cstr(inputArray(index)) & vbtab
22 Next
23 print(elements)
```

Line 1: Declaration Of variables.
Line 2: array Function Returns a variant containing an array. If no arguments are specified, an array of zero length is created.
Line 4: Initializing the elements variable to null i.e empty.
Line 5: **For Loop** ranges from Lbound to Ubound of the array .
Line 6: Each element is added to the list of existing elements. **Cstr** Converts element represented by array in to string. vbtab inserts the space after each element.
Line 8: Displays the Array elements before sorting.
Line 9: For a Loop to iterate through the array , for loop ranges from lbound to ubound of the array.
Line 10:For a loop to iterate through the array from the next element of the array to the last element of the array. This is used to compare the previous element with the next element of the array.
Line 11-14: The comparison is made with array elements i.e, if the first element of the array is greater than the next element then the two elements are swapped using the temporary variable "temp".
Line 20-22:To print the elements of the array that is sorted

Output

QuickTest Print Log
File
Array elements before sorting are:
10 9 2 8 5 1
Array elements after sorting are:
1 2 5 8 9 10

23. Write a program for Dynamic declaration of an array

```
1  Dim inputArray(),index,element,elements
2  N=Inputbox("Enter the size of the array")
3  ReDim inputArray(N)
4  For index=0 to N-1
5      element = inputbox("Enter the " & Cstr(index+1) & "  element of array")
       inputArray(index) = element
6  Next
7  Print("The array elements are ")
8  elements = ""
9  For index=lbound(inputArray) to ubound(inputArray)
10        elements = elements & Cstr(inputArray(index)) & vbtab
11 Next
12 print( elements )
13
```

Line 1: Declaration Of variables.
Line 2: Initializing the variables.
Line 3: Dynamic declaration of array. For dynamic declaration we have to create an array without specifying its size as shown in line 1. Then we have to create an array of required size during program execution using **ReDim** function as shown in this line.
Note: use **Preserve** keyword if you are expanding size of array further using Redim. This Preserve keyword helps in retaining the values of array elements in new array.
Line 4-6: For Loop ranges from zero to N-1, this for loop is used to enter the array elements. Array elements entered by the user are stored in inputArray.
Line 10: For Loop is used to display the array elements. For loop ranges from lbound to ubound of the array.

Input:

N = 3
First Element = 9
Second Element = 3
Third Element = 7

Output:

QuickTest Print Log

File

the array elements are
9 3 7

24. Add two 2X2 matrices

```
Dim Matrix1(1,1),Matrix2(1,1),resultMatrix(1,1),rowElements
Matrix1(0,0) = 2 : Matrix1(0,1) = 5 : Matrix1(1,0) = 3 : Matrix1(1,1) = 8
```

```
3  Matrix2(0,0) = 7 : Matrix2(0,1) = 4 : Matrix2(1,0) = 6 : Matrix2(1,1) = 1
4  Print(" The Matrix1 Elements are ")
5  For i=0 to 1
6      rowElements = ""
7      For j=0 to 1
8          rowElements = rowElements & Cstr(Matrix1(i,j)) & vbtab
9      Next
10     Print(rowElements)
11 Next
12 Print("The Matrix2 Elements are")
13 For i=0 to 1
14     rowElements = ""
15     For j=0 to 1
16         rowElements = rowElements & Cstr(Matrix2(i,j)) & vbtab
17 Next
18 Print(rowElements)
19 Next
20 For i=0 to 1
21     For j=0 to 1
22         resultMatrix(i,j) = Cint(Matrix1(i,j)) + Cint(Matrix2(i,j))
23     Next
24 Next
25 print("Matrix after adding matrices is:")
26 For i=0 to 1
27     rowElements = ""
28     For j=0 to 1
29         rowElements = rowElements & Cstr(resultMatrix(i,j)) & vbtab
30     Next
31 Print(rowElements)
32 Next
```

Line 1: Declaration Of variables.

Line 2: Initializing the Matrix1 elements.

Line 3: Initializing the Matrix2 elements.

Line 5:For Loop to walk through the row of the Matrix1.

Line 7: For loop to walk through the column of the matrix1.

Line 10: prints the matrix1 elements.

Line 13:For Loop to walk through the row of the Matrix2.

Line 15: For loop to walk through the column of the matrix2.

Line 17: prints the matrix2 elements.

Line 20-22: For loop to perform the addition of matrix1 and matrix2 and store in resultMatrix.

Line 26-28: For Loops to walk through the row and column of the resultMatrix and print result. Line26: For loop to walk through the row of the resultMatrix. Line28: For loop to walk through the column of the resultMatrix.

Output:

```
QuickTest Print Log
File
The Matrix1 Elements are
2	5
3	8
The Matrix2 Elements are
7	4
6	1
Matrix after adding matrices is:
9	9
9	9
```

25. Multiply Two Matrices of size 2X2

```
Dim Matrix1(1,1),Matrix2(1,1),resultMatrix(1,1),rowElements,i,j,k, element
Matrix1(0,0) = 2 : Matrix1(0,1) = 5 : Matrix1(1,0) = 3 : Matrix1(1,1) = 8
Matrix2(0,0) = 7 : Matrix2(0,1) = 4 : Matrix2(1,0) = 6 : Matrix2(1,1) = 1
Print(" The Matrix1 Elements are ")
For i=0 to 1
    rowElements = ""
    For j=0 to 1
        rowElements = rowElements & Cstr(Matrix1(i,j)) & vbtab
    Next
    Print(rowElements)
Next
Print("The Matrix2 Elements are")
For i=0 to 1
    rowElements = ""
    For j=0 to 1
        rowElements = rowElements & Matrix2(i,j) & vbtab
    Next
    Print(rowElements)
Next
For i=0 to 1
    For j=0 to 1
        element = 0
        For k=0 to 1
        element = element + ( Cint(Matrix1(i,k)) *Cint(Matrix2(k,j)) )
    Next
        resultMatrix(i,j) = element
      Next
Next
print("Matrix after multiplying matrices is:")
For i=0 to 1
    rowElements = ""
    For j=0 to 1
rowElements = rowElements&resultMatrix(i,j) & vbtab
```

```
33         Next
34         Print(rowElements)
35     Next
36
```

Line 1: Declaration Of variables.
Line 2: Initializing the Matrix1 elements.
Line 3: Initializing the Matrix2 elements.
Line 5:For Loop to walk through the row of the Matrix1.
Line 7: For loop to walk through the column of the matrix1.
Line 10: prints the matrix1 elements.
Line 13:For Loop to walk through the row of the Matrix2.
Line 15: For loop to walk through the column of the matrix2.
Line 18: prints the matrix2 elements.
Line 20-22: For loop to perform the Multiplication of matrix1 and matrix2 and store in resultMatrix.
Line 29: For Loops to print the resultMatrix.
Line 30: For Loop to walk through the row of the resultMatrix.
Line 32: For loop to walk through the column of the resultMatrix.
Output:

```
QuickTest Print Log
File
The Matrix1 Elements are
2       5
3       8
The Matrix2 Elements are
7       4
6       1
Matrix after multiplying matrices is:
44      13
69      20
```

26. Convert a String into an array

```
1  Dim inputStr, outArray, index
2  inputStr = " QTP Complete Reference By Siva is Best Book for QTP "
3  outArray = Split(inputStr," ")
4  Print("The array elements are ")
5  For index = lbound(outArray) to ubound(outArray)
6      print(outArray(index))
7  Next
```

Line 1: Declaration Of variables.
Line 2: Initializing the variables.
Line 3: Split function Returns a zero-based, one-dimensional array containing a specified number of substrings with delimiter as space.
Line 5: For Loop ranges from lbound to ubound of the array and print the array elements

Output:

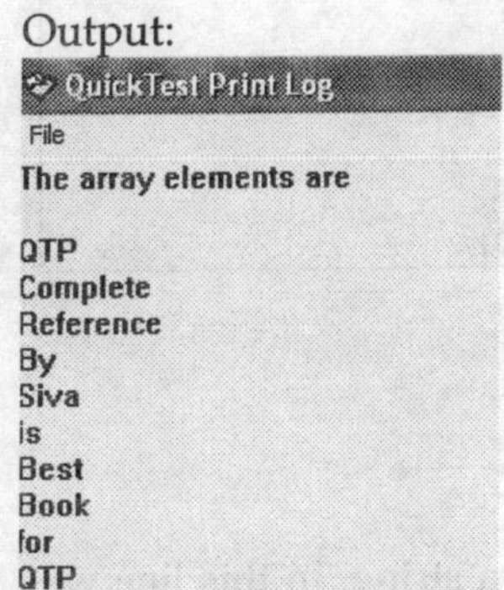
QuickTest Print Log
File
The array elements are
QTP
Complete
Reference
By
Siva
is
Best
Book
for
QTP

27. Convert a String in to an array using 'e' as delimiter

```
1 Dim inputStr, outArray, index
2 inputStr = " QTP Complete Reference By Siva is Best Book for QTP "
3 outArray = Split(inputStr,"e")
4 Print("The array elements are ")
5 For index = lbound(outArray) to ubound(outArray)
6     print(outArray(index))
7 Next
```

Line 1: Declares the variables.

Line 2: Initializing the variables.

Line 3: Split function Returns a zero-based, one-dimensional array containing elements created with delimiter 'e'.

Line 5: For Loop ranges from lbound to ubound of the array and print the array elements

Output:

```
QuickTest Print Log
File
The array elements are
 QTP Compl
t
 R
f
r
nc
 By Siva is B
st Book for QTP
```

28. Find number of words in a given string

```
Dim inputStr, character, noOfWords, lenInputStr, i
inputStr =Inputbox("Enter the String")
lenInputStr = len(inputStr)
noOfWords = 1
Print (" The Given String is:  " & inputStr)
For i = 1 to lenInputStr
    character = mid(inputStr,i,1)
```

```
8      If strcomp(character," ") = 0 Then
9          noOfWords = noOfWords + 1
10     End If
11 Next
12 Print (" The number of Words in given string  are" & noOfWords)
```

Line 1: Declaration Of variables.
Line 2: Initializing the variables.
Line 3: **Len** function returns the length of the string.
Line 5: Displays the given String that is entered by the user.
Line 6: For Loop ranges from 1 to length of the string .
Line 7: mid function Returns a specified number of characters from a string. In this line we are receiving 1 character at a time from string
Line 8-9: **strcomp** function Returns a value indicating the result of a string comparison. In this line **strcomp** is comparing the received character with space. If the character received from the mid function is space then **strcomp** returns true and noOfWords will be incremented by one.

Input:

inputStr = "QTP Complete Reference by Siva"

Output:

QuickTest Print Log
File
The Given String is: QTP Complete Reference by Siva
The number of Words in given string are 5

29. Write a program to reverse the words of a given string

```
1 Dim inputStr, index, outArray, wordsReverse
2 inputStr =Inputbox("Enter the String")
3 outArray=Split(inputStr," ")
4 wordsReverse = ""
5 Print (" The Given String is:  " & inputStr)
6 For index=Ubound(outArray) to Lbound(outArray) step -1
7     wordsReverse = wordsReverse + outArray(index) & " "
8 Next
9 Print (" The String after reversing the words is:  " & wordsReverse)
```

Line 1: Declaration of variables.
Line 2: Initializing the variables.
Line 3: Split function Returns a zero-based, one-dimensional array containing elements created with delimiter pace.
Line 5: Display the given string.

Line 6: For loop to print the array elements in the reverse order . For loop ranges from Ubound to lbound of the array.

Iterates	Word Reverse
4	Indian
3	an
2	be
1	to
0	proud

Input:

inputStr = "Proud to be an Indian"

Output:

QuickTest Print Log

File

The Given String is: Proud to be an indian
The String after reversing the words is: indian an be to Proud

30. Join elements of an array as a string

```
1 Dim inputArray, outString
2 inputArray = Array("QTP","Complete","Reference","by","Siva")
3 outString = Join(inputArray," ")
4 print("String formatted after joining array elements:  " & outString)
```

Line 1: Declaration of variables

Line 2: Initializing the array elements.

Line 3: **Join** function Returns a string created by joining substrings contained in an array

Output:

QuickTest Print Log

File

String formatted after joining array elements: QTP Complete Reference by Siva

31. Trim a given string from both sides

```
1 Dim inputStr
2 inputStr = inputbox("Enter the String")
3 inputStr = trim(inputStr)
4 print("String After trimming is:  " &inputStr)
```

Line 1: Declaration of variables.

Line 2: Initializing the variables.

Line 3: Trim function Returns a copy of a string without both leading and trailing spaces

Input:

inputStr = "   hai how are you   "

Output:

QuickTest Print Log

File

String After trimming is: hai how are you

32. Write a program to force the declaration of variables

```
1 Option Explicit
2 Dim inputStr
3 inputStr=Inputbox("Enter the string")
4 Print (" The String is:" & vbtab & inputStr)
```

Option Explicit is a keyword used to force the declaration of variables from the user. Observe that in Line 2 we are declaring variable **inputStr** before we use it in line 3. Else system will through an error **"Variable is Undefined"**

33. Program to check if variable is an array variable.

```
1 Dim a(3)
2 If isArray(a) Then
3     Print("The variable 'a'  is an array")
4 Else
5     Print("The variable 'a'  is not an array")
6 End If
```

is **Array** function in line2 checks whether variable 'a' is an array or not. If variable is Array then returns True, else returns False.

Output:

QuickTest Print Log

File

The variable 'a' is an array

34. Write a program to convert value into a currency

```
1 Dim number_Currency
2 number_Currency = FormatCurrency(1000)
3 print(number_Currency)
```

Line 1: Declaring variable for currency.

Line 2: **FormatCurrency** function Returns an expression formatted as a currency value using the currency symbol defined in the system control panel.
Line 3: Prints the currency after formatting

Output:

QuickTest Print Log
File
$1,000.00

35. Write a program to convert an expression to a date

```
Dim number_Date
number_Date = FormatDateTime(Date)
print(number_Date)
```

FormatDateTime function Returns an expression formatted as a date or time.

Output:

QuickTest Print Log
File
12/6/2007

36. Display current date and Time

```
1  currentDateTime = Now()
2  print(currentDateTime)
```

Line 1: **Now** function Returns the current date and time of your computer.
Line 2: Prints the Computer's system date and time

Output:

QuickTest Print Log
File
12/6/2007 12:58:38 PM

37. Find difference between the days of two dates

```
1  Dim Date1,Date2,Diff
2  Date1 = "10/07/2006"
3  Date2 = "11/07/2007"
4  Diff = DateDiff("d",Date1,Date2)
5  Print("Difference between given dates is  " & Cstr(Diff))
```

Line 1 : Declaring the variables.

Line 2-3 : Storing the two dates in different variables.
Line 4 : **DateDiff** function Returns the difference between the two dates.
Line 5 : Prints the number of dates difference between 2 dates.

Output:

QuickTest Print Log
File
Difference between given dates is 396

38. Add time interval to a date

```
1 Dim ResultDate,Date1
2 Date1 = Now
3 ResultDate = DateAdd("h",2,Date1)
4 Print("Current Date and Time is:   " & Now)
5 Print("Date and Time after adding 2hrs is:    " & ResultDate)
```

Line 1: Declaring the variables.
Line 2: **Now** function Returns the current date and time according to the setting of your computer's system date and time.
Line 3: **DateAdd** function Returns a date to which a specified time interval has been added. Since 'h' is the setting for hour, **DateAdd** function adds 2hrs to the current hour.
Line 4: Printing current date and time.
Line 5: Prints the Resultdate after adding 2hrs to current time.

Output:

QuickTest Print Log
File
Current Date and Time is: 6/16/2010 1:28:51 PM
Date and Time after adding 2hrs is: 6/16/2010 3:28:51 PM

39. Print current day of the week

```
1 Dim dayWeek,dayWeekName
2 dayWeek = Weekday(date)
3 dayWeekName =  WeekdayName(dayWeek)
4 Print("Date is :     " & date)
5 Print("Week day is:    " & dayWeek)
6 Print("Week day Name is:    " & dayWeekName)
```

Line 1 : Declaring the variables.
Line 2 : **Weekday** function Returns a whole number representing the day of the week.
Line 3 : **WeekdayName** function Returns a string indicating the specified day of the week.
Line 4-6: **date** function prints current date
Line 5: **dayWeek** function prints the number corresponding to current day in week. For Ex; 1-Sunday, 2-Monday

Line 6: **dayWeekName** function prints the name corresponding to current day in week.

Output:

QuickTest Print Log
File

Date is : 6/16/2010
Week day is: 4
Week day Name is: Wednesday

40. Find whether current month is a long month

```
1  Dim long_Months, monthNum, index, flag
2  long_Months = array(1,3,5,7,10,12)
3  monthNum = month(date)
4  Print("Date is:   " & Cstr(date))
5  flag = 0
6  For index=lbound(long_Months) to ubound(long_Months)
7      If Cint(monthNum) = Cint(long_Months(index)) Then
8          flag = 1
9          Exit For
10     End If
11 Next
12 If flag = 1 Then
13     Print(MonthName(monthNum) & "  is a long month")
14 Else
15     Print(MonthName(monthNum) & "  is NOT a long month")
16 End If
```

Line 1: Declaring the variables.
Line 2: Array containing the Long Month Numbers as elements (i.e., months having 31 days).
Line 3: Month function Returns a whole number between 1 and 12.
Eg. If date = 12/6/2007
monthNum = 12
Line 4: Printing the current date.
Line 5: Initializing flag to zero.
Line 6-11: For loop goes through every element of long month array and checks whether current month num equals to one of the long month numbers. If CInt(monthNum) returns 12, then 12 will be checked with one of the elements of an array through each iteration

Iterations	Cint(long_Months(index))	Cint(monthNum) = Cint(long_Months(index))
0	Cint(long_Months(0)) = 1	12 <> 1
1	Cint(long_Months(1)) = 3	12 <> 3
2	Cint(long_Months(2)) = 5	12 <> 5
3	Cint(long_Months(3)) = 7	12 <> 7

4	Cint(long_Months(4)) = 10	12 <> 10
5	Cint(long_Months(5)) = 12	12 = 12

Line 8-9: From the above, iteration 5 matches the given month as long month. So flag will be assigned to 1 and for loop will be exited.

Line 12 -16: Checking for the flag,
If flag is '1' then printing month as a long month.
If flag is '0' then printing it month as not a long month

Output:

QuickTest Print Log

File

Date is: 12/6/2007
December is a long month

41. Find whether given year is a leap year

```
1 Dim yy
2 yy = inputbox("Enter the Year. Format of year should be 'yyyy'")
3 yy = CInt(yy)
4 If (yy mod 4) = 0 Then
5       Print ( " The Year '" & Cstr(yy) &"' is a leap year")
6 Else
7       Print ( " The Year '" & Cstr(yy) &"' is not a leap year")
8 End If
```

Line 1: Declaring the variables.
Line 2: Enter the year to check for leap year. For Ex:2007.
Line 4: Condition which verifies the given year is a leap year or not by dividing with "4".
Line 5-7: Prints whether year is a leap year or not based on the evaluation of the if condition.
Input:
yy = 2007
Output:

QuickTest Print Log

File

The Year '2007' is not a leap year

42. Format Number to specified decimal places

```
Dim InputNum
InputNum = Inputbox("Enter the number with decimal places  Eg: 12.45678")
Print(" The Given Number is:    " & inputNum)
InputNum = Round(inputNum,2)
Print(" Number after rounding:    " & inputNum)
```

Line 1: Declare the variables.
Line 2: Enter the number in an inputbox with decimals Eg. 12.45678
Line 3: Cstr is a function that converts Integer to String, and prints the entered number.
Line 4: Round function Returns a number rounded to a specified number (i.e. 2) of decimal places.
Line 5: Prints the rounded to 2 decimal places in QuickTest Print Log Window during run session.

Input:

inputNum = 24.67890

Output:

QuickTest Print Log

File

The Given Number is: 24.67890
Number after rounding: 24.68

43. Write a program to generate a Random Number

```
1 Dim randNum,upperBound,lowerBound
2 upperBound = 100000
3 lowerBound = 0
4 randNum = Int((upperBound - lowerBound + 1) * Rnd + lowerBound)
5 Print(" The random number generated is:   " & randNum)
```

Line 1: Declaring variables.
Line 2: Initialize the UpperBound to 10000.
Line 3: Initialize the LowerBound to 0.
Line 4: **Rnd** function Returns a random number which always below 1. Equation in Line 4 returns any random number between **upperBound** and **lowerBound**. **Int** function Returns the integer portion of a Random number.
Line 5: Prints Random Number

Output:

QuickTest Print Log

File

The random number generated is: 70555

44. Write a program to find subtype of a variable

```
1 Dim InputValue,sType
2 InputValue = 5
3 sType = typename(inputValue)
4 Print("The Sub Type of value " & Cstr(inputValue) & " is:   " & sType)
```

Line 1: Declaring the variables.

Line 2: Assigning Value 5 to the variable InputValue.
Line 3: **Typename** is the function that returns a string that provides Variant subtype information of a variable.
Line 4: Print the type of variable used for InputValue

Output:

QuickTest Print Log
File
The Sub Type of value 5 is: Integer

45. Write a program to print the decimal part of a given number

```
1 Dim inputValue,decimalValue,resultArray
2 inputValue = inputbox("Enter the number with decimal value   Eg: 12.5123")
3 resultArray = split(inputValue,".")
4 decimalValue = resultArray(1)
5 print(" Decimal Part  in  the number " & inputValue& " is: " & decimalValue)
```

Line 1: Declaring the variables.
Line 2: Enter 15.2349 in dialog box waits for user to input text , returns a string value
Line 3: Since " . " is used as delimeter **split** function splits the number in to integer and decimal parts and stores in resultArray
Line 4: Assigning the second element of resultArray to variable decimalValue
Line 5: Print the number which is after decimal point
Input:

InputValue = 15.2349

Output:

QuickTest Print Log
File
Decimal Part in the number 15.2349 is: 2349

DEBUGGING

Debugging is the process of locating and fixing errors in the computer program code. After you create a test, you should check that it runs smoothly, without errors in syntax or logic. Set the breakpoints in the program to stop program execution and to isolate defects. When the test stops at a breakpoint, you can use the Debug Viewer to check and modify the values of VBScript objects and variables.

1. *By controlling and debugging your run sessions, you can identify and handle problems in your tests, function libraries, and registered user functions.*
2. *Breakpoints are used to break the script execution.*

How to Debug?

Step 1: Add/Delete Breakpoints

- ✓ Click a step or a line in the test where you want the run to stop.
- ✓ Choose **Debug > Insert/Remove Breakpoint**
- ✓ To remove a single breakpoint, click a line in your test or component with the breakpoint symbol and choose **Debug > Insert/Remove Breakpoint**
- ✓ To remove all breakpoints, choose **Debug > Clear All Breakpoints**

Step 2: Begin Running the Test, Control will stop at first break point encountered

Step 3: Select **View->Debug Viewer** to display debug viewer as shown below. This is used to view the values of variables, and to watch the results of expression and also to execute commands.

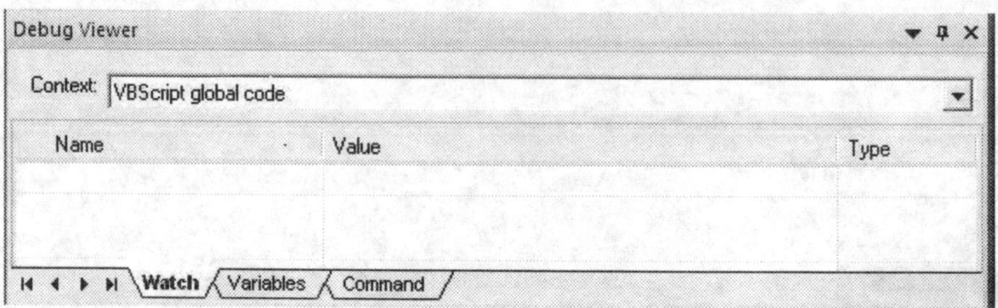

- **Watch** tab: Displays the current values and types of variables and VBScript expressions that you add to the Watch tab, and enables you to modify the values of displayed variables and properties.
- **Variables** tab: Displays the current values and types of all variables in the main script of the current action, or in a selected subroutine, and enables you to modify their values.
- **Command** tab: Enables you to run VBScript commands in your paused run session.

Step 4: Run line by Line

Choose Step Over (Debug > Step Over): To run the step. If step is the function, the entire function is completed and control goes to the next line of the test.

Choose Step Into (Debug > Step Into): To run the step. If step is the function and control goes to the function and stops at first line of the test.

Choose Step Out (Debug > Step Out): If you are inside the function and want to come out of the function.

Step 5: Check the Value of the Variables in the Debug Viewer Pane

Step 6: Modify the Value of a Variable Using the Command Tab.

Important points to remember before debugging

1) You must have the **Microsoft Script Debugger** installed to run tests in debug mode. If it is not installed, you can use the QuickTest Additional Installation Requirements Utility to install it:
   Select **Start > Programs > QuickTestProfessional > Tools > Additional Installation Requirements.**
2) While the test and function libraries are running in debug mode, they are read-only. You can modify the content after you stop the debug session, not when you pause it.
3) If you perform a file operation the debug session stops.
   For example: you open a different test or create a new test.
4) If a file is called using an **ExecuteFile** statement, you cannot debug the file or any of the functions contained in the file. In addition, when debugging a test that contains an **ExecuteFile** statement, the execution marker may not be displayed correctly.
5) In QuickTest, when you open a test, Quick Test creates a local copy of the external resources that are saved to your Quality Center project. Therefore, any changes you apply to any external resource that is saved in your Quality Center project, such as a function library, will not be recognized in the test until the test is closed and reopened.
   An external resource is any resource that can be saved separately from the test, such as a function library, a shared object repository, or a recovery scenario. In contrast with this, any changes you apply to external resources saved in the file system, such as function libraries, are implemented immediately, as these files are accessed directly and are not saved as local copies when you open your test.

Review Questions

1. Why do you need debugging?
2. What is the difference between **Step into** and **Step Over**?
3. At break point does control stop before running the step or after running the step?
4. What are the tabs in Debug Viewer and their purpose?

RECOVERY SCENARIO

Introduction

While a test is running unexpected events, errors and application crashes will interrupt the run session. For example, an advertisement may appear while writing an email in a web based email application. This is a problem particularly when tests run unattended – the test pauses until you perform the operation needed to recover. To handle such situations QuickTest has provided an option for you to create recovery scenarios and associate them with specific tests.

The Recovery Scenario Manager provides a wizard that guides you through the process of defining a recovery scenario, which includes a definition of an unexpected event and the operations necessary to recover the run session.

Recovery Scenario is used to instruct QuickTest to recover from unexpected events and errors that occur in your testing environment during a run session.

Recovery scenarios are saved in recovery scenario files. A recovery scenario file is a logical collection of recovery scenarios, grouped according to your own specific requirements.

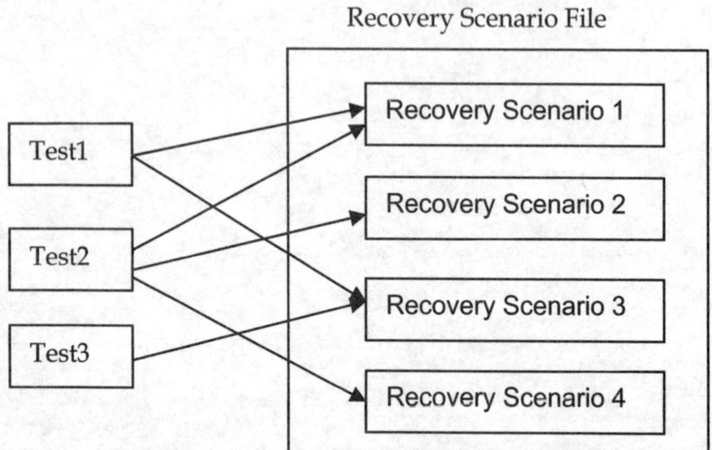

In the above diagram Test 2 is using Recovery Scenarios 1, 2 and 4. Test 1 is using Recovery scenario 1 and 3 and Test 3 is using Recovery Scenario 3.

When to use Recovery Scenario?

Recovery scenarios are intended for use only with events that you cannot predict in advance, or for events that you cannot otherwise synchronize with a specific step in your test. For example, you could define a recovery scenario to handle printer errors. Then if a printer error occurs during a run session, the recovery scenario could instruct QuickTest to click the default button in the Printer Error message box.

You would use a recovery scenario in the above example because you cannot handle this type of error directly in your test. This is because you cannot know at what point the network will return the printer error. Even if you try to handle this event by adding an If statement in your test immediately after a step that sends a file to the printer, your test may progress several steps before the network returns the actual printer error.

If you can predict that a certain event may happen at a specific point in your test, it is highly recommended to handle that event directly within your test by adding steps such as If statements or optional steps, rather than depending on a recovery scenario. For example, if you know that an Overwrite File message box may open when a Save button is clicked during a run session, you can handle this event with an If statement that clicks OK if the message box opens or by adding an optional step that clicks OK in the message box.

Key Elements of Recovery Scenario

Below are the key elements that are part of a Recovery scenario:

- **Trigger Event:** The event that interrupts your run session. For example, a pop window or a QuickTest run error.
- **Recovery Operations:** The operations to perform to enable QuickTest to continue running the test after the trigger event interrupts the run session. For example, clicking an OK button in a pop-up window, or restarting Microsoft Windows.
- **Post-Recovery Test Run Option:** The instructions on how QuickTest should proceed after the recovery operations have been performed, and from which point in the test QuickTest should continue, if at all. For example, you may want to restart a test from the beginning, or skip a step entirely and continue with the next step in the test.

Creating Recovery Scenario

Open Recovery Scenario Manager **Resources > Recovery Scenario Manager**. In the Recovery Scenario Manager dialog box open the Recovery Scenario Wizard by clicking the **New Scenario** button. The Recovery Scenario Wizard leads you, step-by-step, through the process of creating a recovery scenario. The Recovery Scenario Wizard contains the following five steps:

- Defining the trigger event that interrupts the run session.
- Specifying the recovery operations required to continue.
- Choosing a post-recovery test run operation.
- Specifying a name and description for the recovery scenario.
- Specifying whether to associate the recovery scenario to the current test and/or to all new tests

There are four types of trigger events that disturb the script flow. They are:

Sl no	Event type	Raised due to:	Example
1	Pop up window	Unexpected pop up window	Work remainder window, Printer paper out pop up window
2	Test run error	Return value of test script statement	Item not available in list box
3	Object state	Change in property value of an object	A button enabled from disabled state.
4	Application crash	Crash of the application	Application is terminated by an operation during run time

Pop up window recovery scenario

QuickTest detects a pop-up window and identifies it according to the window title and textual content. For example, a message box may open during a run session, indicating that the username entered in the username field is invalid. QuickTest can detect this window and activate a defined recovery scenario to continue the run session.

Steps to create a pop-up window recovery scenario:

1) Choose **Tools > Recovery Scenario Manager**. The Recovery Scenario Manager Dialog box opens.

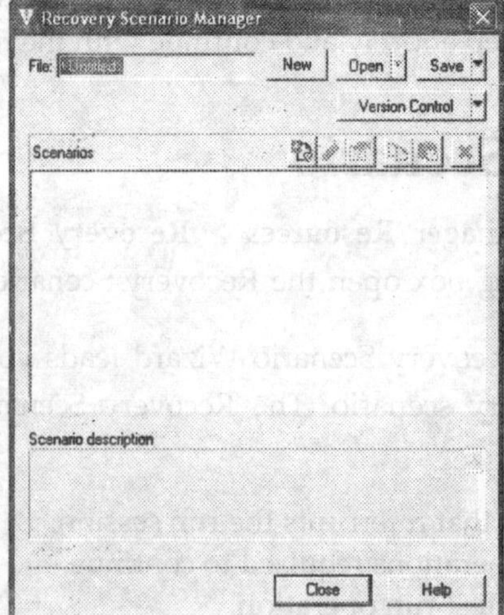

2) Open the Recovery Scenario Wizard by clicking the New Scenario button.
3) Click **Next** in Recovery Scenario Wizard. The Trigger Event Screen appears as shown in the figure below.

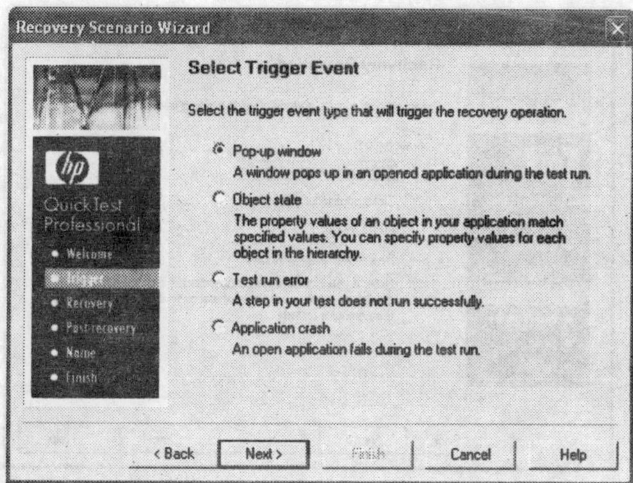

4) Select **Pop-up window** and click **Next**. **Specify pop-up window conditions** screen appears as shown below.

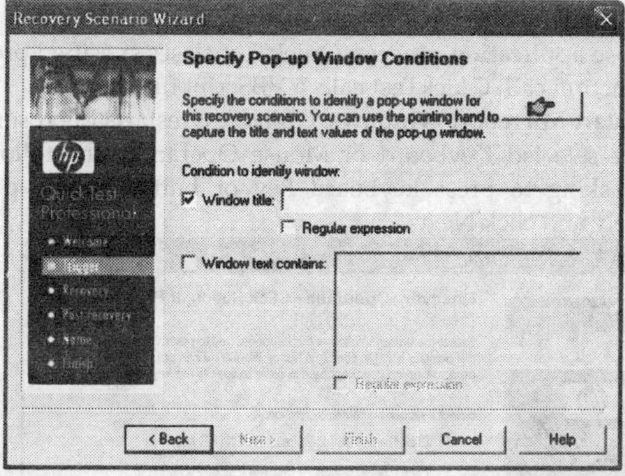

5) Specify the pop-up window that is interrupting the run session using the pointing hand and click on **Next**.
6) Select any operation type from the Recovery Operation screen as shown in the figure below. Select the default operation type **Keyboard or mouse operation** and click **Next.**

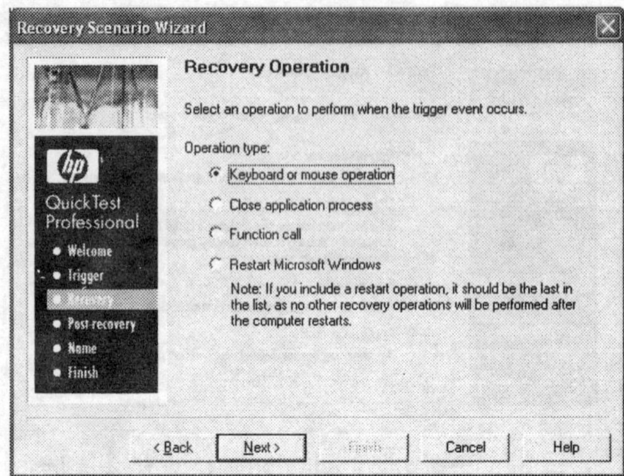

You can define the following types of recovery operations:

- ✓ **Keyboard or mouse operation**: QuickTest performs keyboard or mouse operation on the pop window like clicking OK button. This is a Commonly Selected Option.
- ✓ **Close application process**: QuickTest closes specified processes.
- ✓ **Function call**: QuickTest calls a VBScript function.
- ✓ **Restart Microsoft Windows**: QuickTest restarts Microsoft Windows.

7) If you have selected Keyboard or Mouse Operation, the following dialog will be displayed asking to press keyboard key or button in the pop window. Select appropriately and click Next.

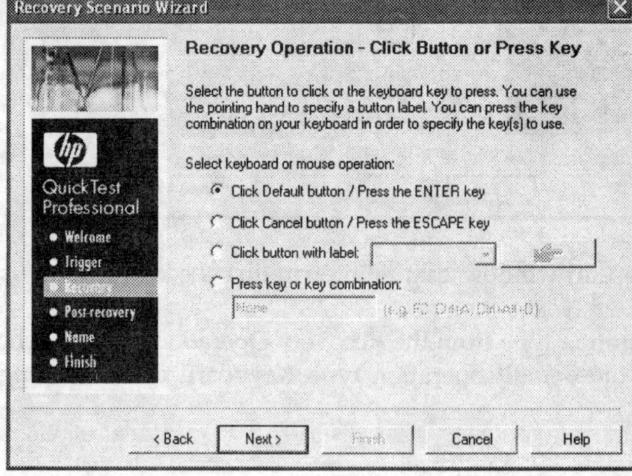

8) Post-Recovery Test Run Options Screen opens as shown in the figure below. Post-recovery test run options specify how to continue the run session after QuickTest has identified the event and performed all of the specified recovery operations.

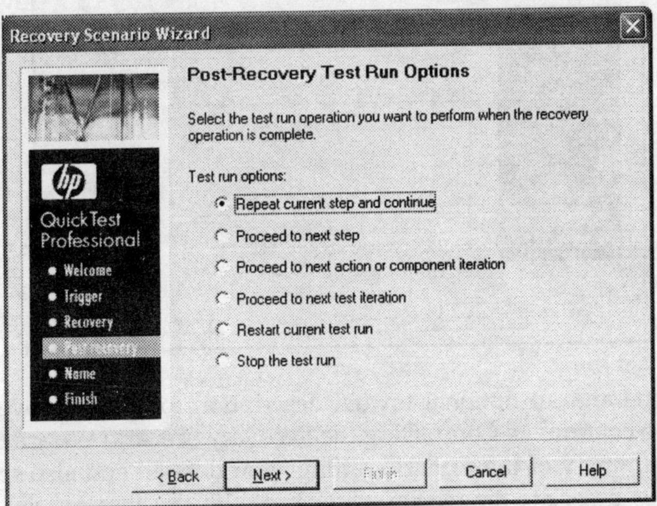

QuickTest can perform one of the following run session options after it performs the defined recovery operations:

- ✓ **Repeat current step and continue:** Run the same step where recovery scenario triggered.
- ✓ **Proceed to the next step:** Skips the step where recovery scenario is triggered and go to the next step.
- ✓ **Proceed to the next action or component iteration:** Stops performing steps in the current action and begins the next iteration from the beginning.
- ✓ **Proceed to the next test iteration:** Stops performing steps in the current action and begins the next QuickTest test iteration from the beginning.
- ✓ **Restart current test run:** Stops performing steps and re-runs the test from the beginning.
- ✓ **Stop the test run:** Stops the test execution.

9) Select one of the **Test run options** from the above screen and click **Next**. Name and Description Screen appears as shown below:

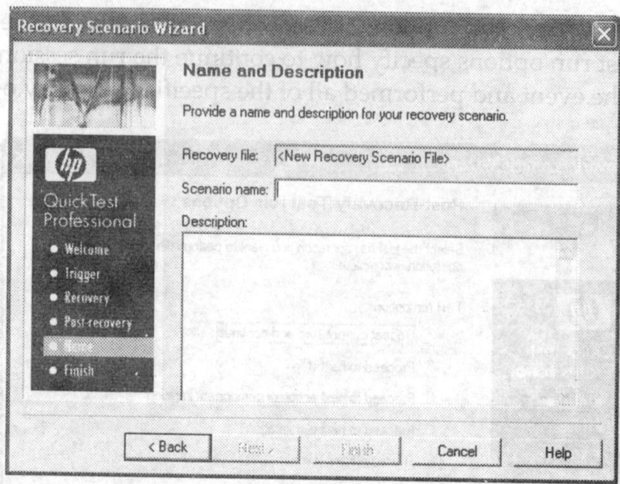

10) Enter a name and an optional textual description for your recovery scenario, and click **Next** to continue to Completing the Recovery Scenario Wizard Screen.
11) Review a summary of the scenario settings you defined and also specify whether to automatically associate the recovery scenario with the current test, and/or to add it to the default settings for all new tests. Click **Finish**.

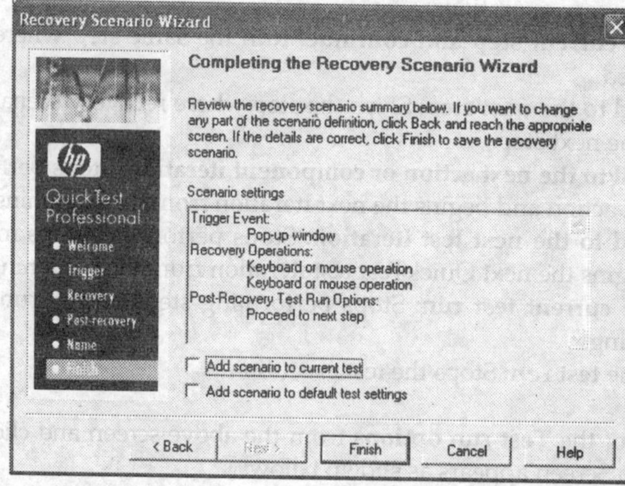

12) Quick Test Adds Pop-Up Recovery scenario to the pop up dialog and handles it every time the dialog appears.

Object State Recovery Scenario

1) Follow steps 1, 2 and 3 of **Steps to create a pop-up window recovery scenario.**
2) Select object state as your trigger event and click **Next.**

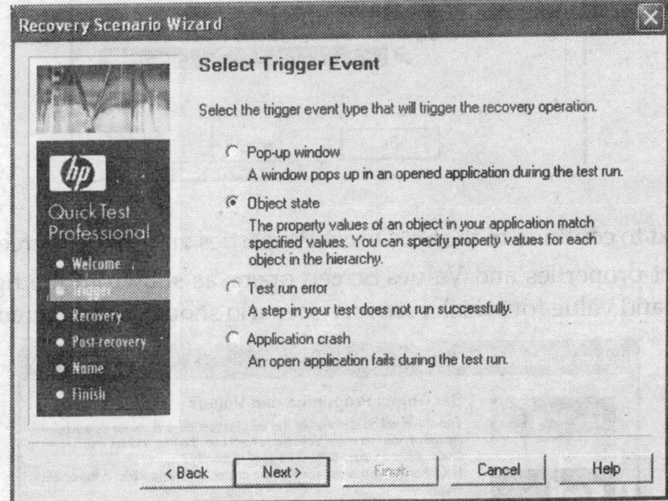

3) The select object screen is displayed as shown below

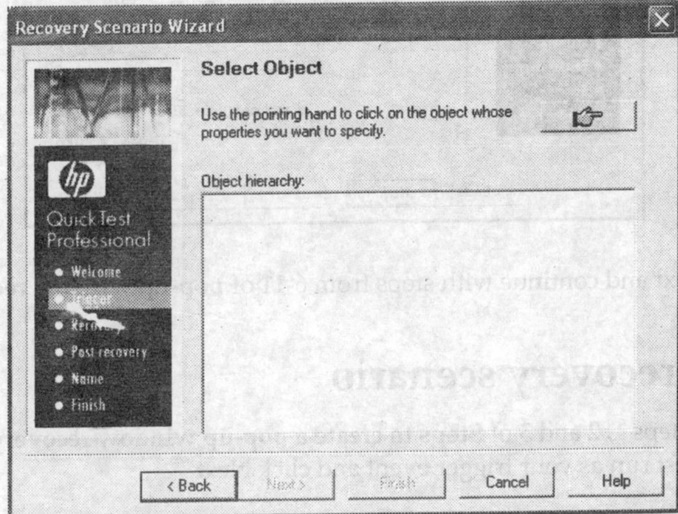

4) Click the pointing hand and then click the object whose properties you want to specify. Select the object whose properties you want to specify and click OK.

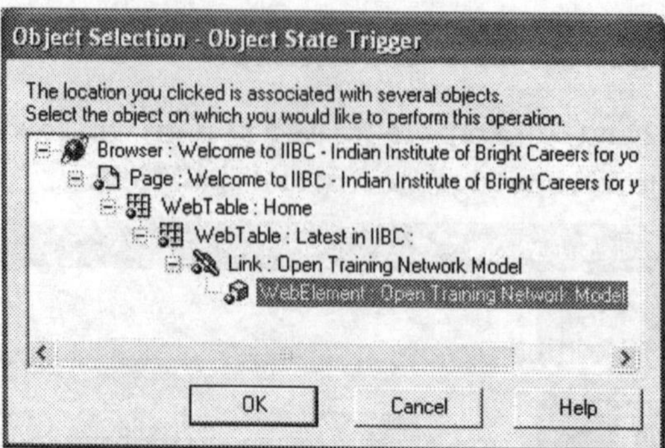

5) Click Next to continue to the Set Object Properties and Values Screen.
6) The object properties and Values Screen opens as shown in the figure below. Select property and value for which recovery scenario should be triggered.

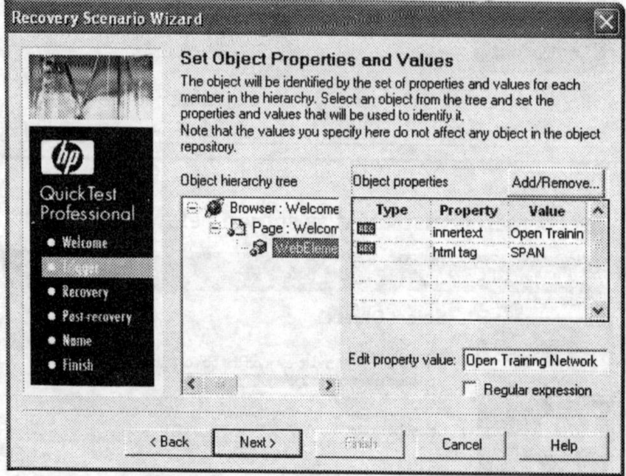

7) Click **Next** and continue with steps from 6-11 of **pop-up window recovery scenario**.

Test Run recovery scenario

1) Follow steps 1, 2 and 3 of **Steps to create a pop-up window recovery scenario**.
2) Select Test run as your trigger event and click **Next**.

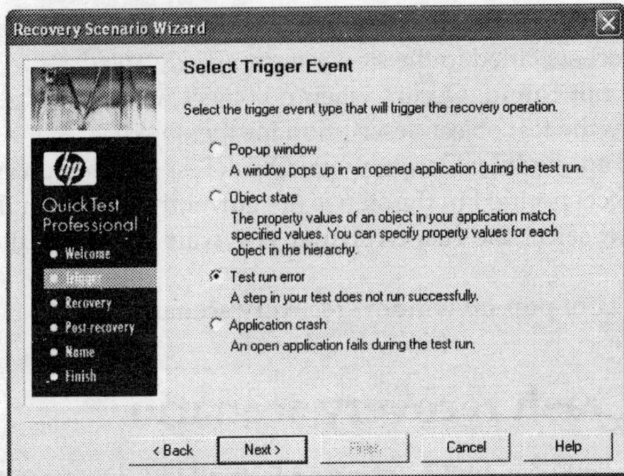

3) The Select Test Run Error screen appears as shown below.

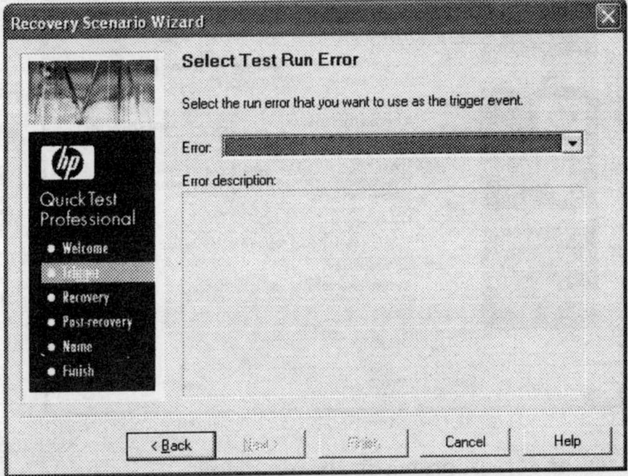

The Error list consists of the following options. You can select the run error that you want to use as the trigger event from this list:

- ✓ **Any error**: Any error code that is returned by a test object method.
- ✓ **Item in list or menu is not unique**: Occurs when more than one item in the list, menu, or tree has the name specified in the method argument.
- ✓ **Item in list or menu not found**: Occurs when QuickTest cannot identify the list, menu, or tree item specified in the method argument. This may be due to the fact that the item is not currently available or that its name has changed.
- ✓ **More than one object responds to the physical description**: Occurs when more than one object in your application has the same property values as those specified in the test object description for the object specified in the step

- ✓ **Object is disabled**: Occurs when QuickTest cannot perform the step because the object specified in the step is currently disabled.
- ✓ **Object not found**: Occurs when no object within the specified parent object matches the test object description for the object.
- ✓ **Object not visible**: Occurs when QuickTest cannot perform the step because the object specified in the step is not currently visible on the screen.

4) In the Error list, select the run error that you want to use as the trigger event and click **Next**.
5) Follow steps 6-11 of **pop-up window recovery scenario.**

Application Crash recovery scenario

1) Follow steps 1, 2 and 3 of **Steps to create a pop-up window recovery scenario**.
2) Select Application crash as your trigger event and click **Next**.

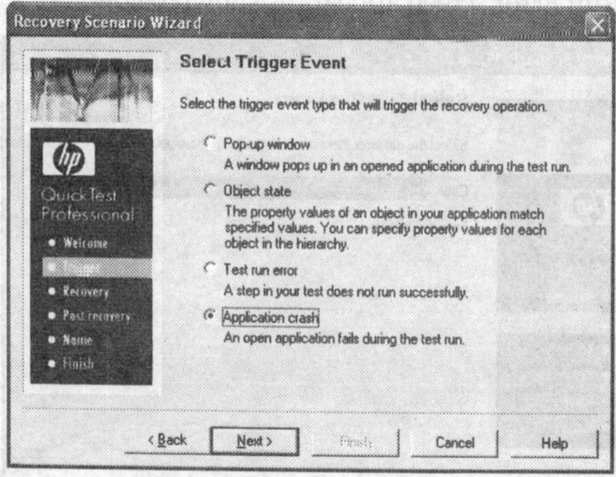

3) The **Select Processes** screen opens as shown below.

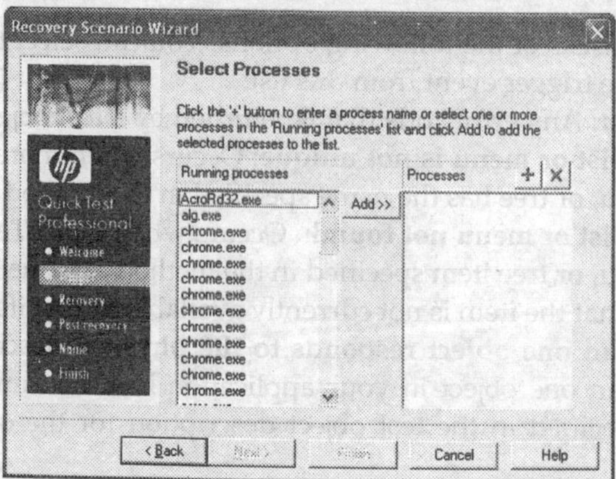

- The Running processes list displays all application processes that are currently running.
- The Processes list displays the application processes that will trigger the recovery scenario if they crash.
- You can add application processes to the Processes list by typing them in the Processes list or by selecting them from the Running processes list.

4) Click Next to continue to the Recovery Operations Screen.
5) Follow steps 6-11 of **pop-up window recovery scenario.**

Saving the Recovery Scenario in a Recovery File

After you create or modify a recovery scenario in a recovery file using the Recovery Scenario Wizard, you need to save the recovery file. If you have not yet saved the recovery file, and you click the Close button in the Recovery Scenario Manager dialog box, QuickTest prompts you to save the recovery file.

Steps to save a new or modified recovery file:

1) In the Recovery Scenario Manager dialog box (Resources > Recovery Scenario Manager) click the Save button. If you are using a new recovery file, the Save Recovery Scenario dialog box opens.

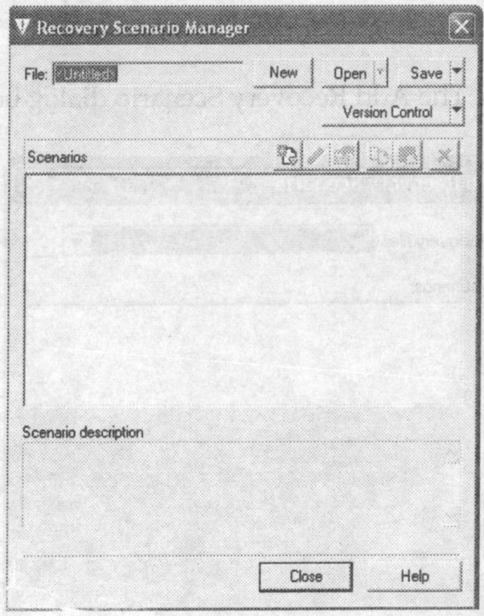

2) In the File name box, enter a name for the file and click **Save**.

Attaching Recovery Scenarios for Tests

After you have created recovery scenarios, you associate them with selected tests so that QuickTest will perform the appropriate scenario(s) during the run sessions if a trigger event occurs.

Steps To add a recovery scenario to a test:

1) Choose **File > Settings**. The Test Settings dialog box or Business Component Settings dialog box opens. Select the Recovery node.

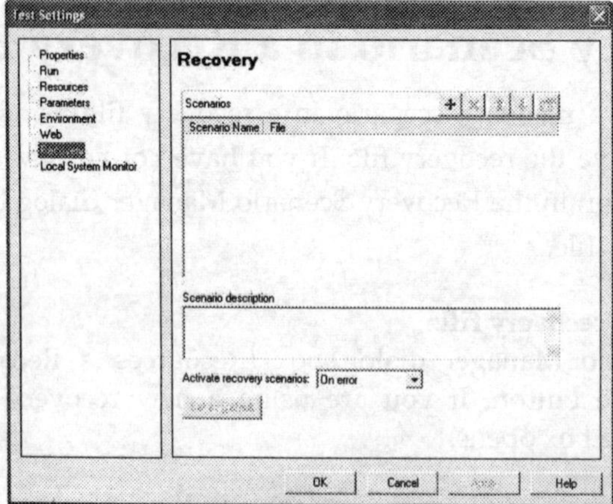

2) Click the **Add** button. The Add Recovery Scenario dialog box opens.

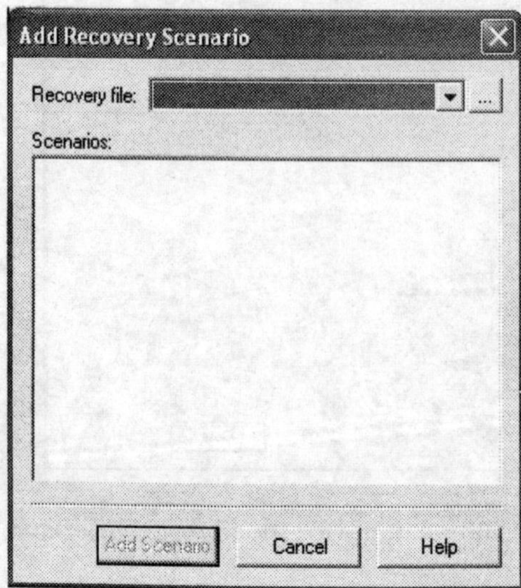

3) In the **Recovery file** box, select the recovery file containing the recovery scenario(s) you want to associate with the test or component. The **Scenarios** box displays the names of the scenarios saved in the selected file.
4) In the **Scenarios** box, select the scenario(s) that you want to associate with the test or component and click **Add Scenario**. The Add Recovery Scenario dialog box closes and the selected scenarios are added to the **Scenarios** list in the Recovery tab.

Review Questions

1. What is the Advantage of Recovery scenario?
2. What are the Different Types of recovery Scenarios?
3. Give 3 examples when you require Pop Recovery scenario?
4. What are the Key elements of Recovery Scenario?
5. When to use and When not to use recovery scenario? Explain with example?

QTP TOOLS AND PANES

QTP provides various tools for different purposes of automation. Indicated below is the most commonly used tools and their purpose:

Step Generator

The Step Generator enables you to add steps to your test by selecting step category and entering the required parameter values. Categories of Steps are:

- test object operations (tests only).
- Utility object operations.
- calls to library functions .

Steps to insert a step:

1) Invoke Step Generator as **Insert > Step > Step Generator**. The following dialog box appears.

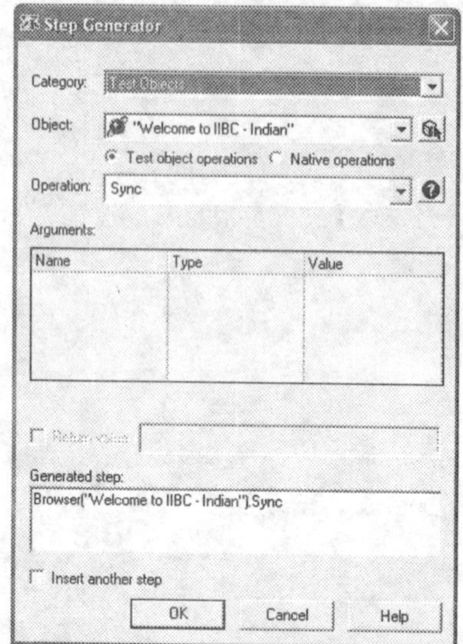

2) First select the type of step that you want to add to your test. In the Category list box, you can select one of the following options:
   - **Test Objects**: To write steps on objects such as Edit Boxes and buttons.
   - **Utility Objects**: Enables you to select a Utility object such as Data table and Random Number.
   - **Functions**: Enables you to select library functions.
3) Define all mandatory argument values for the current operation and click OK to write the step.

Silent Test Runner

Enables you to simulate the way a QuickTest test runs from LoadRunner and Business availability Center, and to verify that your QuickTest test is compatible with LoadRunner and Business Availability Center. To open Select the **Start > Programs > QuickTest Professional > Tools > Silent Test Runner** menu command.

You must close QuickTest and wait for its process to end before running your test using Silent Test Runner. You can invoke only one instance of Silent Test Runner and you can specify only one test to run. You cannot use the **ResultDir** QuickTest environment variable when running a test from Silent Test Runner.

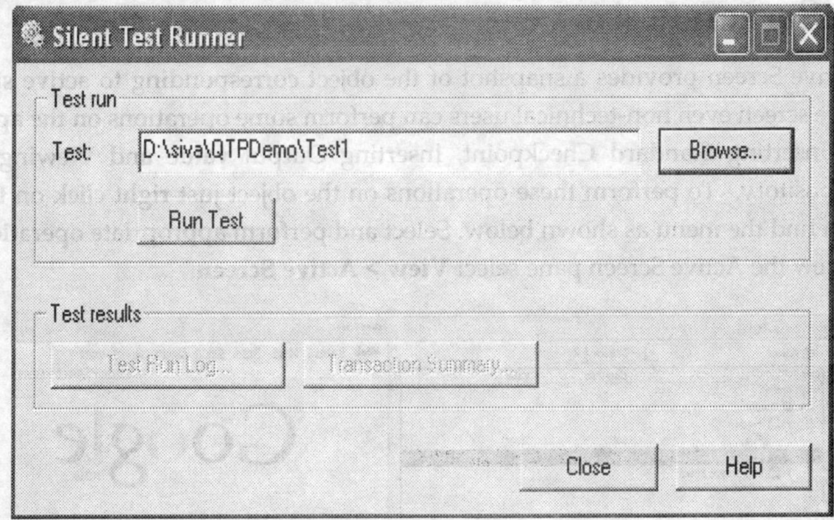

Silent Test Runner Dialog Box Options

Option	Description
Test	The full file system path of the test you want to run.
Run Test	When you click this button, the test runs without opening the QuickTest user interface. The text **Running test...** is displayed next to the **Run Test** button while the test is running. When the test run finishes, the text **Running test...** is replaced with the text **Test run completed**. If Silent Test Runner was unable to run your test, the text **Test could not be run** is displayed. **Note:** After you start a test run, you cannot stop the test run from Silent Test Runner. Even if you close Silent Test Runner, the test continues to run. To end the run, end the **mdrv.exe** process manually.
Test Run Log	Enables you to view the most recent run log for the selected test. Each time you run a test with Silent Test Runner, the previous log file is overwritten with the current run results.
Transaction Summary	Enables you to view the summary of the transactions in the test.

Active Screen

The Active Screen provides a snapshot of the object corresponding to active statement. Using Active screen even non-technical users can perform some operations on the application object like Inserting Standard Checkpoint, Inserting Output value and Viewing/Adding object in repository. To perform these operations on the object just right click on the object and you can find the menu as shown below. Select and perform appropriate operation on the object. To view the Active Screen pane select **View > Active Screen.**

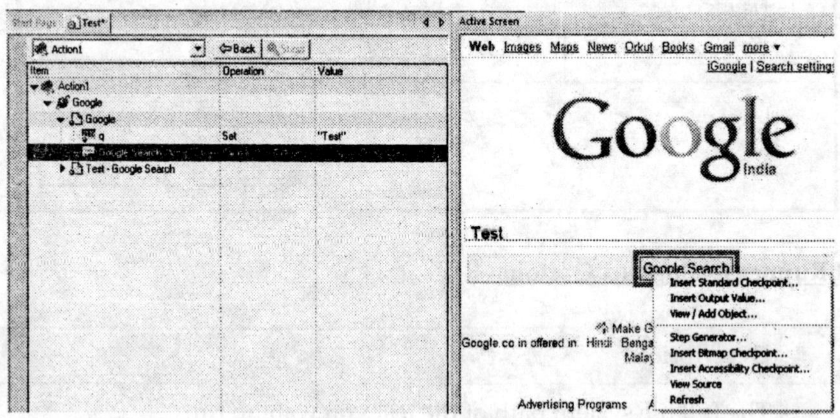

When you save the script images that are displayed corresponding to each object in the test, they are saved in the same folder of the QTP script. In case we are saving QTP script in quality center it requires lot of system and network resources to save and load the script because of huge memory occupied by images corresponding to test objects. Hence for better script performance, in general, the technical team doesn't want to enable this feature. To disable or configure some settings related to Active Screen, select Active Screen settings dialog through Tools>Options>Active Screen.

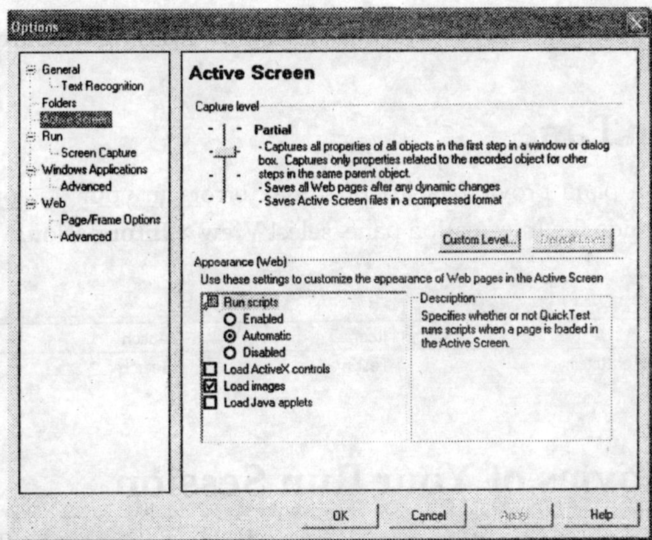

Moving the slider to completely down completely disables capturing of any active screen images.

Missing Resources Pane

If a test has resources that cannot be found during Test Run, QuickTest indicates this in the Missing Resources pane. QuickTest opens the Missing Resources pane, if the pane is not already open. The Missing Resources pane provides a list of all resources that are currently unavailable, along with the location where QuickTest is expected to find the resource, when available. Resources that can be indicated by Missing Resources Pane are:

- ✓ Missing action
- ✓ Missing environment variable file
- ✓ Missing function library
- ✓ Missing object repository
- ✓ Missing recovery scenario
- ✓ Repository parameters

Missing Resources Pane Looks as below:

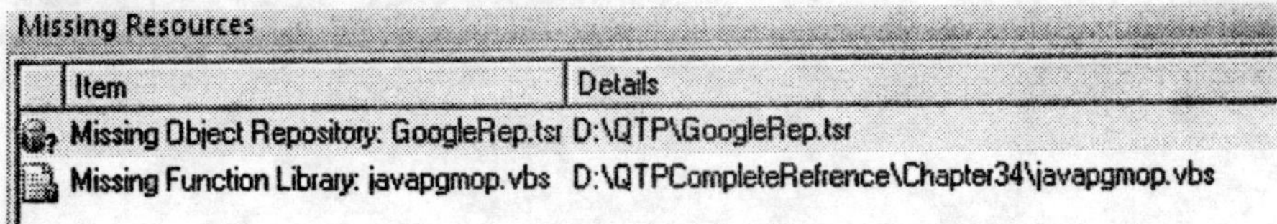

You can open the Missing Resources Pane through **View> Missing Resources.**

Information Pane

The Information pane provides a list of syntax errors in your or function library scripts. To show or hide the Information pane, select **View > Information.**

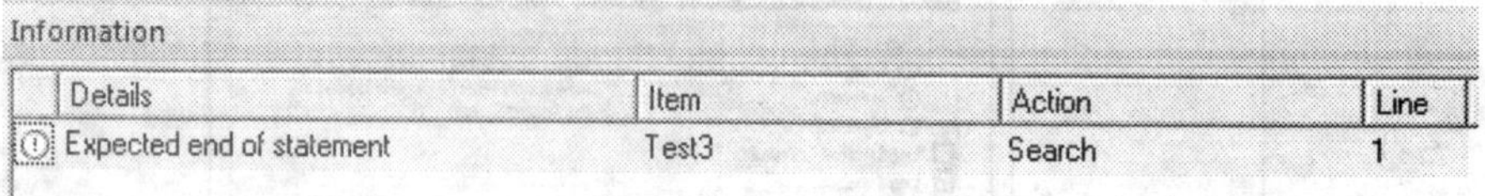

Viewing Movies of Your Run Session

QuickTest can save a movie of your application during a run session. This can be useful to help you see how your application behaved under test conditions or to debug your test.

You can customize the criteria QuickTest uses to save movies using the Save movies to results option in the Run > Screen Capture pane of the Options dialog box.

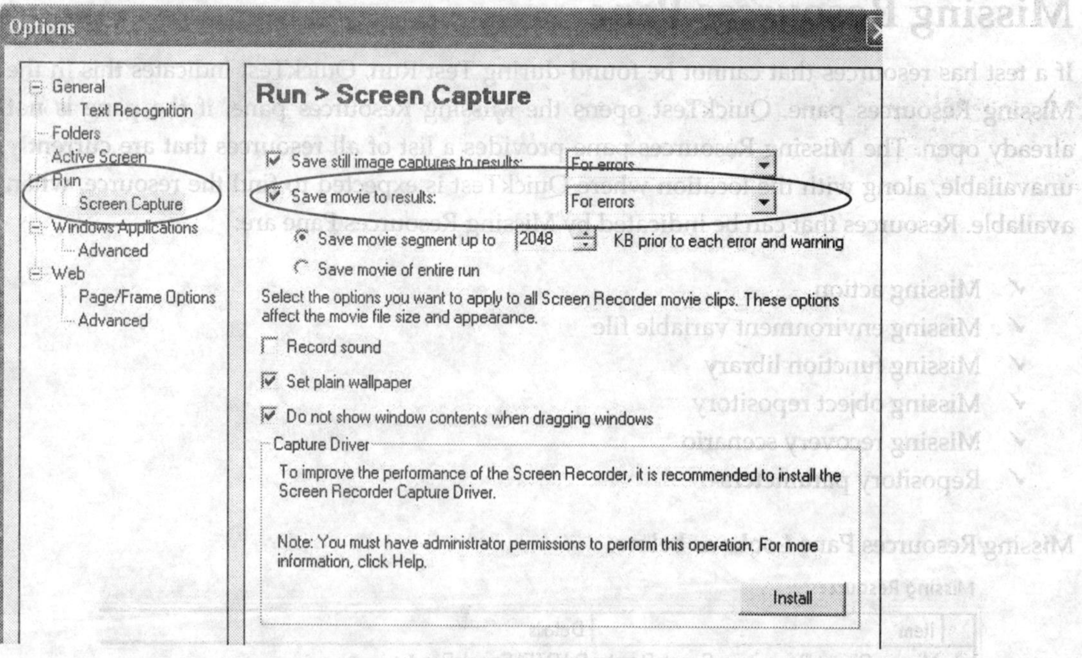

If we select the check box "Save movie to result" results will be saved in the Test results file like Movie. This movie can be opened from Test results by selecting **View>Screen Recorder**. Click Run button to run the movie.

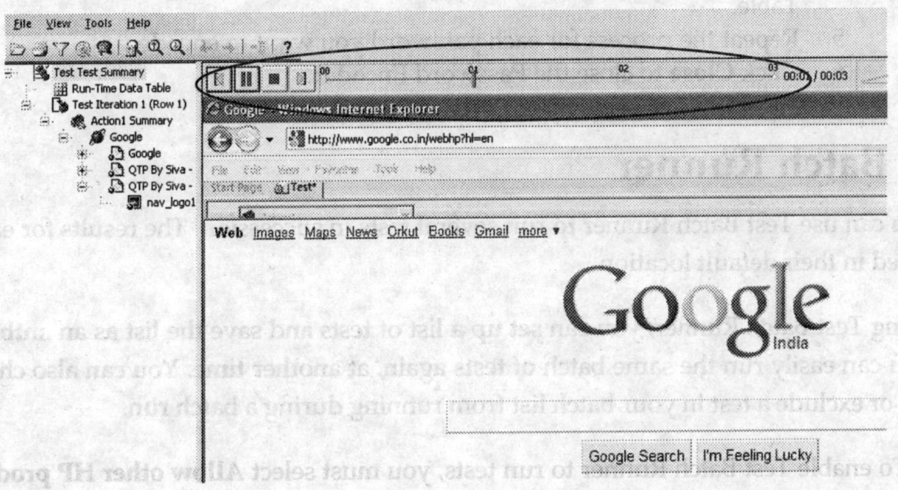

Password Encoder

This dialog is used to encode the password. For example, your Web site may include a form in which the user must supply a password. You may want to test how your site responds to different passwords, but you also want to ensure the integrity of the passwords. The Password Encoder enables you to encode your passwords and place secure values into the application.

1. To Open from the **Windows** menu, select **Start > Programs > QuickTest Professional > Tools > Password Encoder**. The Password Encoder dialog box opens.

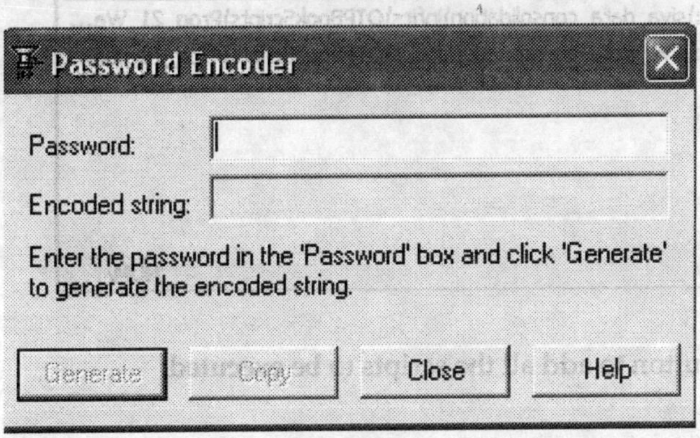

2. Enter the password in the **Password** box.
3. Click **Generate**. The Password Encoder encrypts the password and displays it in the **Encoded String** box.
4. Use the **Copy** button to copy and paste the encoded value into the Data Table.
5. Repeat the process for each password you want to encode.
6. Click **Close** to close the Password Encoder.

Test Batch Runner

You can use Test Batch Runner to run several tests in succession. The results for each test are stored in their default location.

Using Test Batch Runner, you can set up a list of tests and save the list as an **.mtb** file, so that you can easily run the same batch of tests again, at another time. You can also choose to include or exclude a test in your batch list from running during a batch run.

Note: To enable Test Batch Runner to run tests, you must select **Allow other HP products to run tests and components** in the Run pane of the Options dialog box.

To set up and run a test batch:

1. To Open from the **Windows** menu, select **Start > Programs > QuickTest Professional > Tools > Test batch Runner.** The Batch Runner dialog box opens.

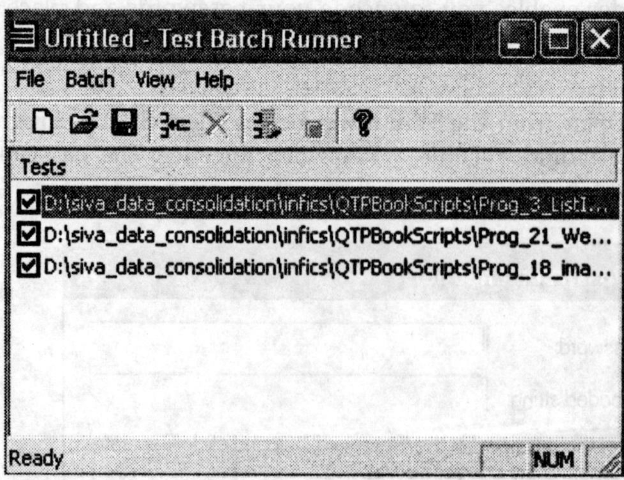

2. Click Add button to add all the scripts to be executed.

3. Click Save button to save the scripts added in a file with extension **mtb** for future reuse.
4. When you are ready to run your test batch, click the **Run** button or select **Batch > Run**. If QuickTest is not already open, it opens and the tests run sequence begins. After the batch run is complete, you can view the results for each test in its default test results folder (**<test folder>\res#\report**).

QuickTest Script Editor

The QuickTest Script Editor enables you to open and modify the scripts of multiple tests and function libraries, simultaneously. You can also create new function libraries. You can modify the script of a test, but you cannot create new tests, associate or remove associated function libraries, or change information such as existing test names, test settings, parameterization, or Data Table values.

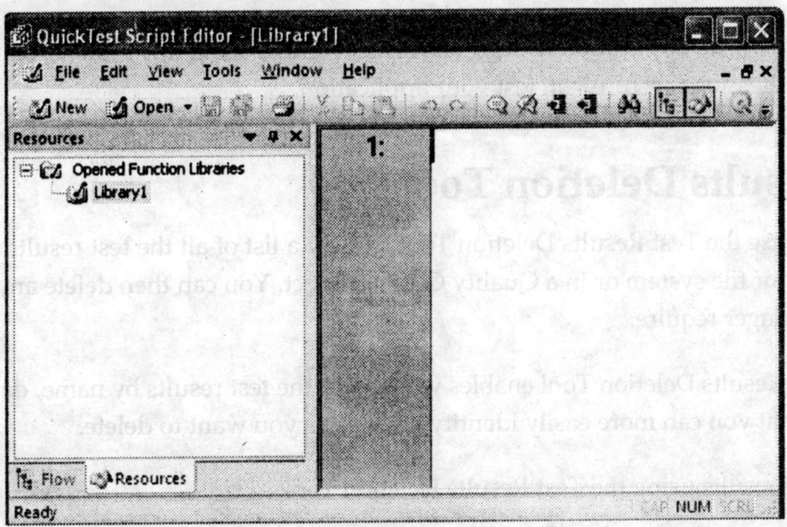

You open the QuickTest Script Editor by choosing **Start > Programs > QuickTest Professional > Tools > QuickTest Script Editor.**

Register New Browser Control

A browser control adds navigation, document viewing, data download, and other browser functionality to a non-Web application. This enables the user to browse the Internet as well as local and network folders from within the application.

QuickTest Professional cannot automatically recognize the objects that provide browser functionality in your non-Web application as Web objects. For QuickTest to record or run on these objects, the application hosting the browser control must be registered.

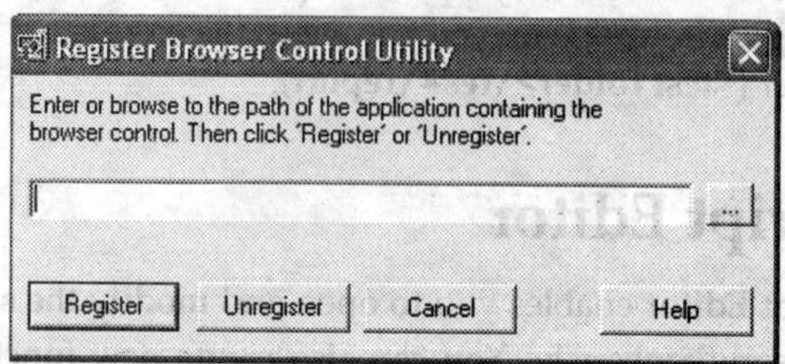

Enter the absolute path to the **.exe** file of the application hosting the browser control, and click **Register**. To remove a registered application, enter the absolute path and click **Unregister**.

After you register an application hosting a browser control using this utility, you must restart QuickTest Professional before you test your application.

Test Results Deletion Tool

You can use the Test Results Deletion Tool to view a list of all the test results in a specific location in your file system or in a Quality Center project. You can then delete any test results that you no longer require.

The Test Results Deletion Tool enables you to sort the test results by name, date, size, and so forth, so that you can more easily identify the results you want to delete.

To delete test results using the Test Results Deletion Tool:

1. Select **Start > Programs > QuickTest Professional > Tools > Test Results Deletion Tool** from the **Start** menu. The Test Results Deletion Tool window opens.

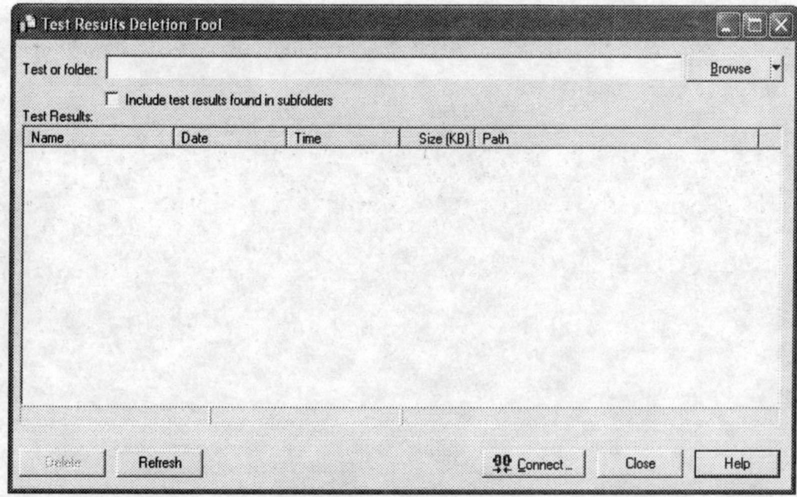

2. In the **Test or folder** box, specify the path from which you want to delete test results.
3. Select Include test results found in subfolders if you want to view all test results contained in subfolders of the specified folder.
4. Select the test results you want to delete. You can select multiple test results for deletion using standard Windows selection techniques.
5. Click **Delete**. The selected test results are deleted from the system and the Quality Center database.

Other tools

- **Remote Agent**: Activates the QuickTest Remote Agent, which enables you to configure how QuickTest behaves when a test is run by a remote application such as Quality Center.
  Programs > QuickTest Professional > Tools > Remote Agent

- **Additional Installation Requirements:** Opens the Additional Installation Requirements dialog box, which displays any prerequisite software that you must install or configure to work with QuickTest.
  Programs > QuickTest Professional > Tools > Additional Installation Requirements

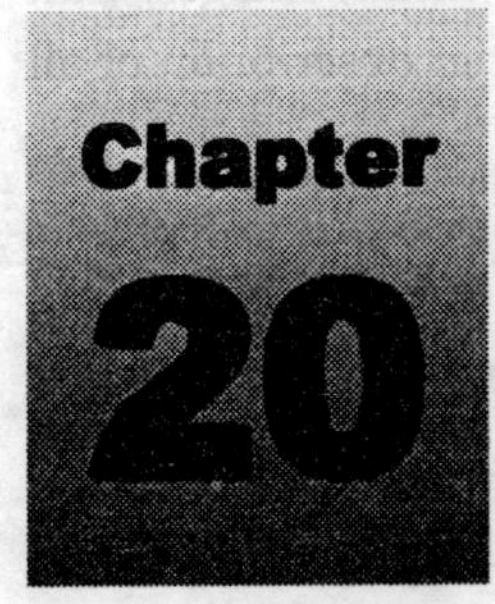

WINDOWS AND WEB OBJECTS

Objects supported by QTP can be divided in to 3 categories. Technology Objects, Utility Objects and Supplemental Objects.

Technology Objects

These objects represent the test objects of various technologies like Web, Windows and VB. For Example test objects WebEdit, WebList, WebButton belong to Web technology. Test objects WinEdit, WinButton, WinList belong to windows technology and Objects VBEdit, VBButton, VBList belong to VB technology. This also means WebButton is different from WinButton and VBButton.

Utility Objects

These objects are used commonly in all technologies. For Example Data Table is an object which is used to store the data required by test script. This object is used in all the technologies since Test Scripts are developed for windows, web and any other technology requires data for data driven of the test script.

Supplemental Objects

These are the additional objects which are part of QTP but do not belong to any specific environment.

In the rest of the chapter we will discuss windows and web objects that belong to technology specific objects.

Web Objects

A web object represents the object displayed on the Webpage like Links, Images, Edit boxes and Buttons as shown below. The following table gives you the brief description of all the web objects.

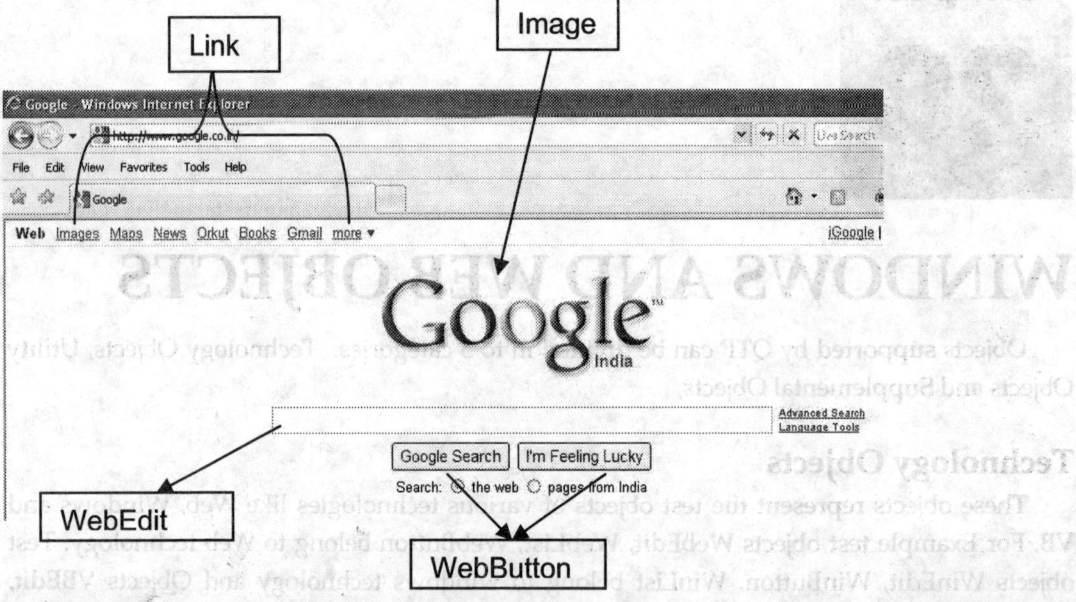

Object	Description
Browser	A Web browser (or browser tab).
Frame	An HTML frame.
Image	An image with or without a target URL link.
Link	A hypertext link.
Page	An HTML page.
ViewLink	A Viewlink object.
WebArea	A section of an image (usually a section of a client-side image map).

WebButton	An HTML button.
WebCheckBox	A check box with an ON and OFF state.
WebEdit	An edit box, usually contained inside a form.
WebElement	A general Web object that can represent any Web object.
WebFile	An edit box with a browse button attached, used to select a file from the File dialog box.
WebList	A drop-down box or multiple selection list.
WebRadioGroup	A set of radio buttons belonging to the same group.
WebTable	A table containing a variable number of rows and columns.
WebXML	An XML document contained in a Web page.

Windows Objects

Windows objects are the objects displayed on the desktop based applications developed using standard windows technology. Following table gives you the brief description of all the windows objects.

Object	Description
Desktop	An object that enables you to access top-level items on your desktop.
Dialog	A Windows dialog box.
Static	A static text object.
SystemUtil	An object used to control applications and processes during a run session.
WinButton	A Windows button.
WinCalendar	A Windows calendar.
WinCheckBox	A Windows check box.
WinComboBox	A Windows combo box.
Window	A standard window.
WinEdit	A Windows edit box.
WinEditor	A Windows multi-line editor.
WinList	A Windows list.
WinListView	A Windows list-view control.
WinMenu	A Windows menu.
WinObject	A standard (Windows) object.
WinRadioButton	A Windows radio button.

WinScrollBar	A Windows scroll bar.
WinSpin	A Windows spin box.
WinStatusBar	A Windows status bar.
WinTab	A Windows tab strip in a dialog box.
WinToolbar	A Windows toolbar.
WinTreeView	A Windows tree-view control.

Common Methods used in Web and Windows Objects

Method	Description
CaptureBitmap	Saves a screen capture of the object as a .png or .bmp image using the specified file name.
Check	Checks whether the actual value of an item matches the expected value.
CheckProperty	Checks whether the actual value of the specified object property matches the specified expected value within the specified timeout.
ChildObjects	Returns the collection of child objects contained within the object.
GetROProperty	Returns the current value of the test object property from the object in the application.
GetTOProperties	Returns the collection of properties and values used to identify the object.
GetTOProperty	Returns the value of the specified property from the test object description.
Output	Retrieves the current value of an item and stores it in a specified location.
RefreshObject	Instructs QuickTest to re-identify the object in the application the next time a step refers to this object.
SetTOProperty	Sets the value of the specified property in the test object description.
ToString	Returns a string that represents the test object.
WaitProperty	Waits until the specified object property achieves the specified value or exceeds the specified timeout before continuing to the next step.

How to program with Common Methods

CaptureBitmap Method

Saves a screen capture of the object as a .png or .bmp image, depending on the specified file extension.

Syntax: *object*.**CaptureBitmap** *FullFileName*, [*OverrideExisting*]

Argument	Description
object	A test object of type Window.
FullFileName	Required. A String value. The full path of the .png or .bmp image to save. If you specify a relative path, the path is added to the test results folder.
OverrideExisting	Optional. A Boolean value. Indicates whether the captured image should be overwritten if the image file already exists in the test results folder. Possible values: **True** **False** (default)

Return Value: None

Note: The object is captured as it appears in the application when the method is performed. If only part of the object is visible, only the visible part is captured.

Example: Capture an Image of Gmail logo

Browser("Gmail ").Page("Gmail ").Image("Gmail").CaptureBitmap "D:\QTPCompleteRefrence\logo.bmp"

Check Method

Checks whether the actual value of an item matches the expected value.

Syntax: *object*.**Check** (*Verify*)

Argument	Description
object	A test object of type Window.
Verify	Required. A Variant value. The checkpoint object that contains the expected values to be compared and verified during the test run.

Return Value: A Boolean value.

Example: Perform a Checkpoint on a Gmail Sign in Object

```
Browser("Gmail").Page("Gmail").WebButton("Sign in").Check CheckPoint("Sign in")
```

ChildObjects

Returns the collection of child objects contained within the object.

Syntax: *object*.**ChildObjects** ([*Description*])

Argument	Description
object	A test object of type Window.
Description	Optional. An **Object** object.A Properties (collection) object. **Tip:** We can retrieve a Properties collection using the GetTOProperties method or we can build a Properties collection object using the Description object.

Return Value: An object object

NOTE: For Example Please Refer to the Descriptive Programming Chapter.

GetROProperty

Returns the current value of the test object property from the object in the application.

Syntax: ***object***.GetROProperty (***Property***, **[*PropertyData*]**)

Argument	Description
object	A test object of type Window.
Property	Required. A String value. The property to retrieve from the object.

PropertyData	Optional. A Variant value. Not in use.

Return Value: A Variant value

Example: Retrieve the Number of Countries in Google Registration Location Listbox

Location:	India

Msgbox(Browser("Google Accounts").Page("Google Accounts").
WebList("loc").GetROProperty("items count")).

GetTOProperty

Returns the value of the specified property from the test object description i.e from an object present in the object repository.

Syntax: ***object***.GetTOProperty (***Property***)

Argument	Description
Object	A test object of type Window.
Property	Required. A String value. The property whose value is retrieved from the object description.

Return Value: A Variant value

Example: Retrieve Value of the RegExpWndClass Property for a Window

RxpWndClass = Window("Notepad").GetTOProperty("RegExpWndClass")

GetTOProperties

Returns the collection of properties and values used to identify the object.

Syntax: ***object***.GetTOProperties

Argument	Description
Object	A test object of type Window.

Return Value: An Object's properties collection object.

Example: *Retrieve Properties Used to Identify a Window*
set propColection = Window("Notepad").GetTOProperties()

SetTOProperty:

Sets the value of the specified property in the test object description.

Syntax: ***object*.SetTOProperty *Property, Value***

Argument	Description
Object	A test object of type Window.
Property	Required. A String value. The test object property to set.
Value	Required. A Variant value. The value to assign to the listed property.

Return Value: None

Example: Set the Index Property Value for a Window
Window("Notepad").SetTOProperty "Index", 2

Output

Retrieves the current value of an item and stores it in a specified location.

Syntax: ***object*.Output *Verify***

Argument	Description
Object	A test object of type Window.
Verify	Required. A Variant value. The output object that contains the details of the data to output.

Return Value: None
Example: Output Data from Location Field
Msgbox(Browser("Google Accounts").Page("Google Accounts"). WebList("loc").Output CheckPoint("loc").

ToString

Returns a string that represents the current test object.

Syntax: ***object*****.ToString**

Argument	Description
Object	A test object of type Window.

Return Value: A String value. The name of the test object and its generic type, for example, loc list.

Note: The **ToString** method is useful if you want to retrieve the test object name and type from within a function or keyword.

WaitProperty

Waits until the specified object property achieves the specified value or exceeds the specified timeout before continuing to the next step.

Syntax: ***object*****.WaitProperty (*****PropertyName, PropertyValue,*** **[*****TimeOut*****])**

Argument	Description
Object	A test object of type Window.
PropertyName	Required. A String value. The name of the property whose value is checked. The available properties are listed in the Identification Properties page under the Properties section for each test object.
PropertyValue	Required. A Variant value. The value to be achieved before continuing to the next step. You can either use a simple value or you can use a comparison object together with the value to perform more complex comparisons.
TimeOut	Optional. A Long value. The time, in milliseconds, after which QuickTest continues to the next step if the specified value is not achieved. If no value is specified, QuickTest uses the time set in the Object Synchronization Timeout option in the Run tab of the Test Settings dialog box.

Return Value

A Boolean value. Returns TRUE if the property achieves the value, and FALSE if the timeout is reached before the property achieves the value. A FALSE return value does not indicate a failed step.

GetTOProperty Vs GetROProperty

GetTOProperty differs from the **GetROProperty** method. **GetTOProperty** returns the value from the test object's description. **GetROProperty** returns the current property value of the object in the application during the test run. You can use the **GetTOProperty** method to retrieve the values of only those properties that are included in the test object description.

For example WebButton **Google Search** present in the object repository as shown below has only three identification properties type, html tag and name in object repository. By using **GetTOProperty** we can retrieve only these three properties.

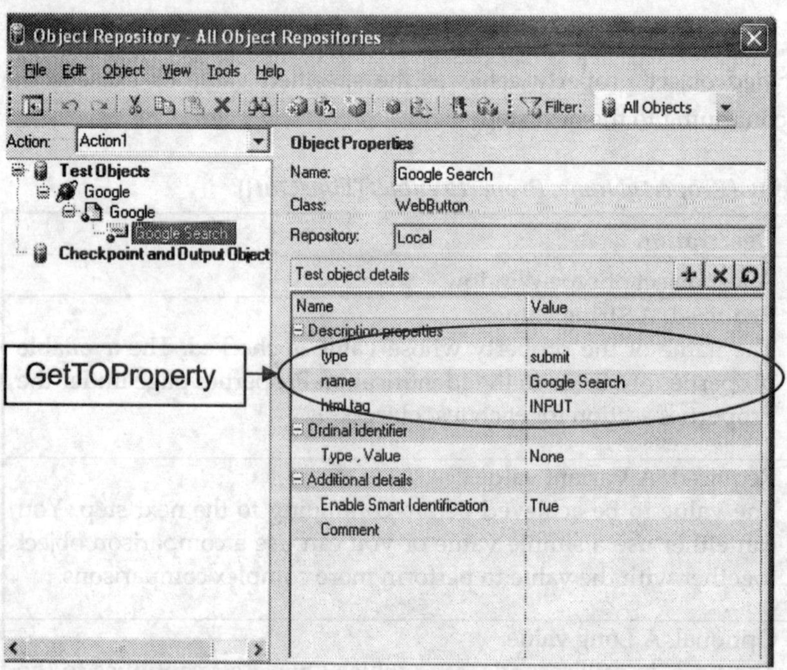

Whereas **GetROProperty** is used to retrieve any of the Identification properties of test object shown by Object spy. In the diagram below we can find many Identification properties for Google Search Object like Class Name, abs_x, abs_y. To retrieve any of those identification properties displayed by Object Spy we will use GetROProperty.

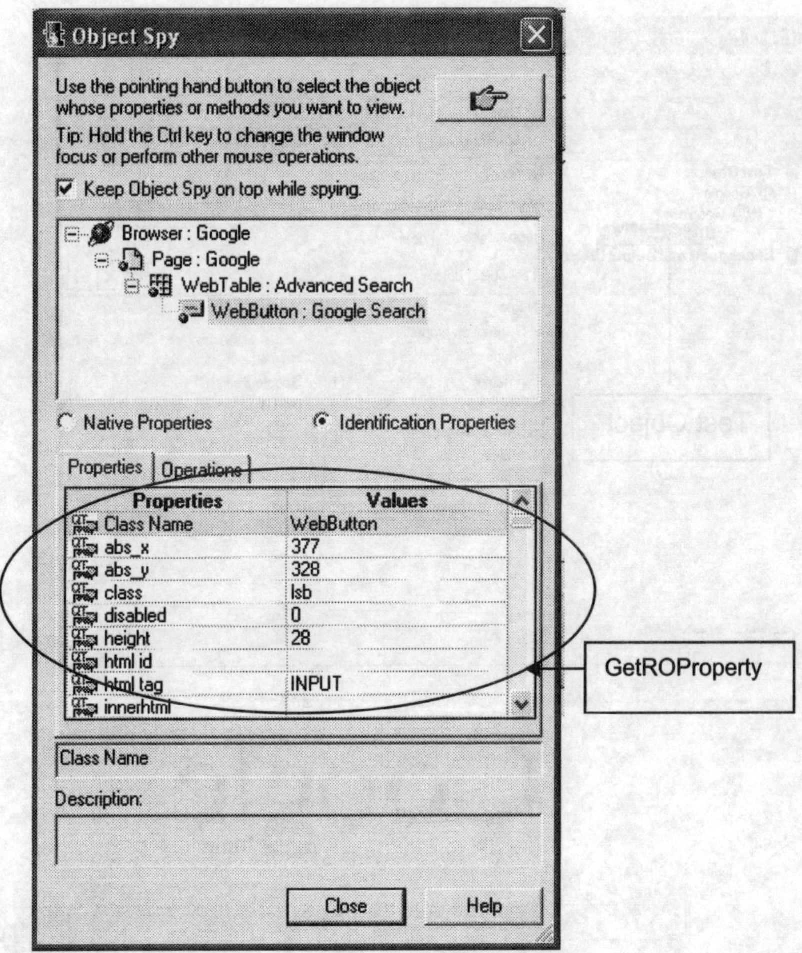

Test object Vs Runtime Object

A *test object* is an object that QuickTest uses to represent an object in your application. In other words this is the object present in the object repository.

A *run-time object* is the actual object in the AUT.

Test object and Run Time Objects are shown below.

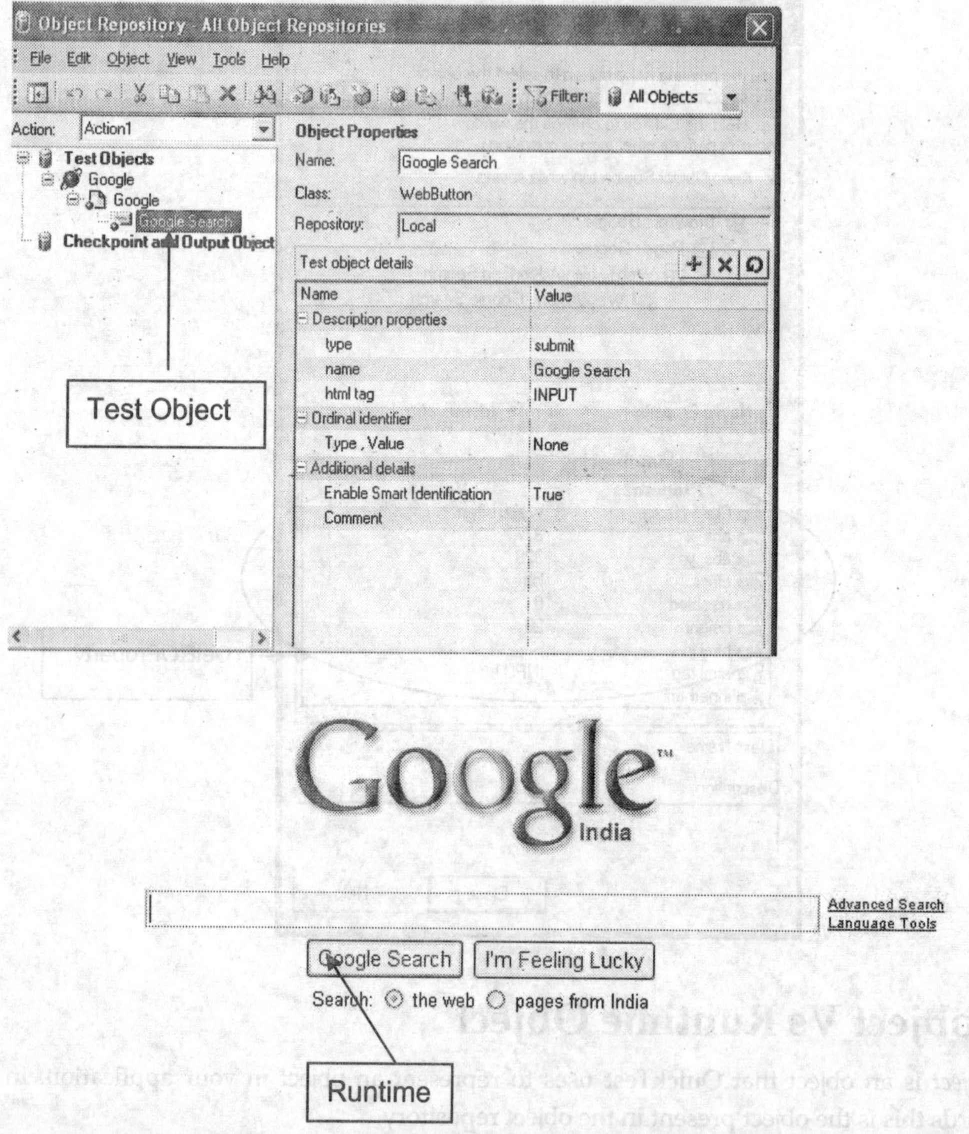

Test objects are the cornerstone of all QTP object operations, but they are sometimes too limited for the task at hand. There are two situations in which we might prefer working with the actual runtime objects of the application, as opposed to the QTP test objects:

There are some objects (especially .Net custom controls), which QTP fails to recognize correctly. For example, some combo-boxes might appear as SwfObjects, or generic ActiveX controls. As QTP fails to recognize the object for what they are (in this example, combo-boxes), the test objects it creates do not have the properties or methods that are required to operate the objects (like "all items" and Select).

Another case is when we are required to perform some non-standard operation with an object. Here it makes no difference if QTP succeeds to correctly recognize the object, as the corresponding test object will only provide us with a standard set of commands and properties. A good example for this case is trying to find the font style of a WebElement. The WebElement test object simply does not carry the information we need, and so we have to resort to unusual measures such as working with the WebElement's runtime object.

Working with Runtime Objects

You can see an object's runtime properties and methods in the native properties tab of the object spy as below:

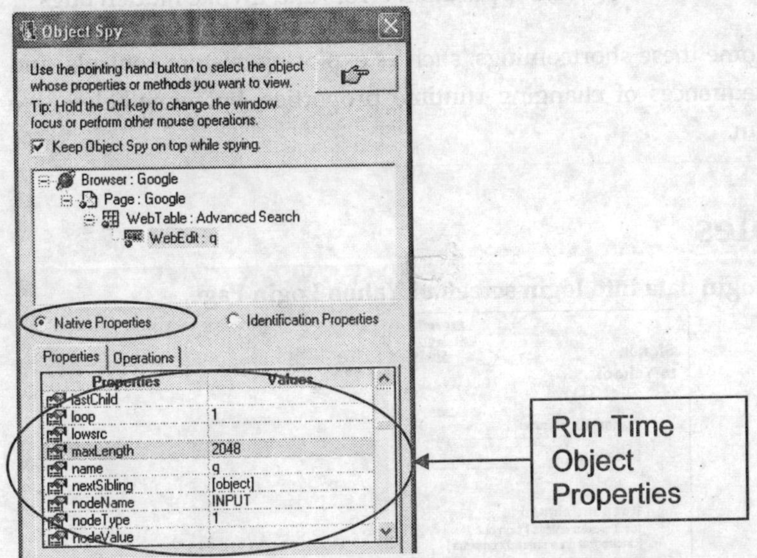

Not all test objects support working with their corresponding runtime objects, but if they do, it can be done via their **.Object** property. This property exposes all the properties and methods of the runtime object "hiding" behind our test object. For example: the maximum characters supported by Google WebEdit box has property maxLength 2048 indicating we can enter maximum of 2048 characters in the edit box. It is important to note that maxLength property is not available in Identification properties of the Test Object.

To read the maxLength of Search Box the VbScript code is as below:

```
set srchRuntimeObj=Browser("Google").Page("Google").WebEdit("q").Object
Msgbox "Length of Google SearchBox "&srchRuntimeObj.maxLength
```

The property Object returns the Runtime object of searchbox into a variable srchRuntimeObj and the property maxLength returns the maximum length of the characters that can be entered in the search box

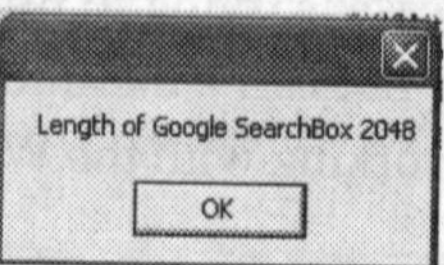

With all their benefits, it is important to remember that working directly with runtime objects can have significant downsides. Unlike the standard and simple test objects, it is unclear how to operate the object, and exactly what properties and methods it has (CurrentStyle.Color is hard to come by). Even when we find the right properties or methods, using them "from behind the scenes" may cause application errors and invoke hidden bugs.

There are ways to overcome these shortcomings, such as exploring custom controls, and carefully mapping the consequences of changing runtime properties, but nonetheless, we must always be aware of them.

Scripting Examples

1: Write a program to enter login data into login screen of Yahoo Login Page.

```
1  Browser("Yahoo").Page("Login").WebEdit("login").Set "testuser"
2  Browser("Yahoo").Page("Login").WebEdit("passwd").SetSecure
   "4723040dbf2e6999bfd2a7d47958c14f493c18dc"
3  Browser("Yahoo").Page("Login").WebButton("Sign In").Click
```

Line 1 : Enter "testuser" in the Login edit box of the Login page of Yahoo. **Set** is the method used to enter text into the edit box.

Line 2 : Enter password using SetSecure in the password edit box of the Login page. **Setsecure** method takes encrypted password hash as an input and decrypts as a normal string and enters into an application. Encrypting password will help in maintaining password confidentiality.

Line 3 : Clicks the "Sign In" button.

NOTE: Use Password Encoder (Start>QTP>Tools>Password Encoder) to get the encrypted string for text for password.

2: Write a program to find the x and y coordinates of a button.

```
1 xcoord=Browser("Yahoo").Page("Login").WebButton("Sign In").GetROProperty("x")
2 ycoord=Browser("Yahoo").Page("Login").WebButton("Sign In").GetROProperty("y")
3 print("xcoord="&xcoord)
4 print("ycoord="&ycoord)
```

Line 1 : Assigns the "x" co-ordinate value of web button "Sign In" to variable "**xcoord**". Method GetROProperty is used to read x coordinate value of the application object.

Line 2 : Assigns the "y" co-ordinate value of web button "Sign In" to variable "**ycoord**". x and y coordinates are measured with respect to Top Left corner of the object.

Line 3&4: Prints "xcoord" and "ycoord".

3: Write a program to Read items in country list box of Yahoo Registration Page.

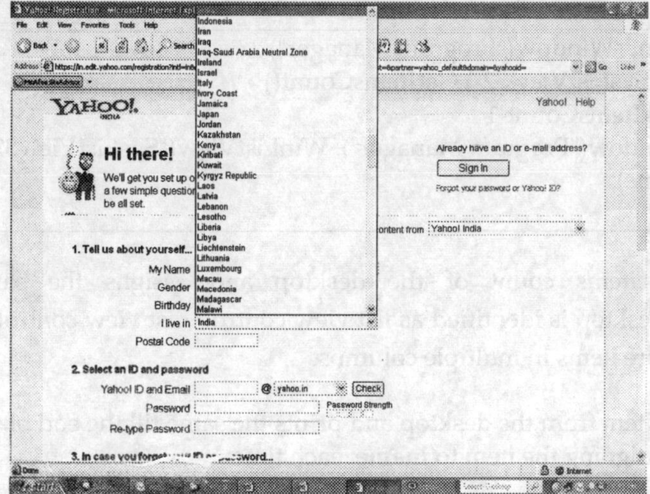

```
1 itemcount=Browser("Yahoo").Page("Registration").WebList("country").GetROProperty("it
  ems count")
2 For i=1 To itemcount
3 itemname=Browser("Yahoo").Page("Registration").WebList("country").GetItem(i)
4 print(itemname)
5 Next
```

Line 1 : Gets the item count from the web list box "country" and assigns that value to variable **itemcount.**

Line 2-5 : **GetItem** function is used to read the value of an item from the list box based on specified index. For loop iterates from the first item to the last item of the 'country' list box items. For every iteration GetIem reads item value from the list box based on the index value specified by 'i' and stores the item value in the variable "itemname". For Example if index is 1, the first country stored in the listbox will be read by GetItem method.

4. Write a program to Read items on a desktop

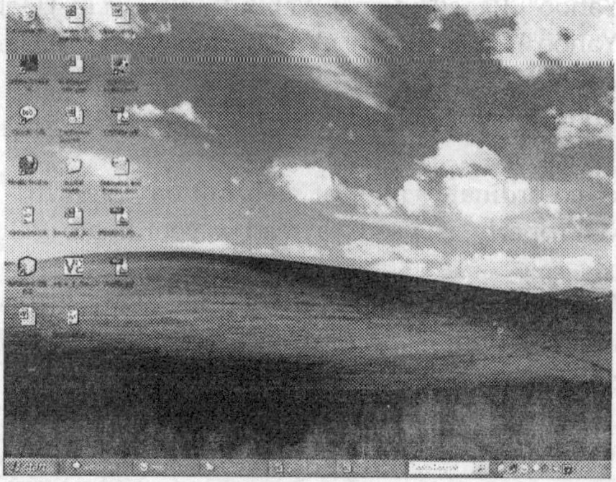

```
1 deskItemsCount=Window("Program Manager").
  WinListView("SysListView32").GetItemsCount()
2 For i=0 To deskItemsCount-1
3     iname=Window("Program Manager"). WinListView("SysListView32").GetItem(i)
4       print(iname)
5 Next
```

Line 1: Gets the items count of the desktop and assigns the same to variable **deskItemsCount**. Desktop is identified as list view control. List view control is like a list box except that it can store items in multiple columns.

Line 2-5 : Gets each item from the desktop and prints the same till the end of the items in Desktop, through assigning the item to **iname** each time.

5. Write a program to Capture Desktop Screen shot

```
Desktop.CaptureBitmap "C:\QTP\printscreen.bmp"
```

Captures the Desktop screen shot and stores it with the name "printscreen.bmp" in the given path. The path given should be a valid path. CaptureBitmap method is used to capture the runtime bitmap of the object and stores the bitmap with extension bmp or png.

6. Write a program to Read tab names from a tabbed window

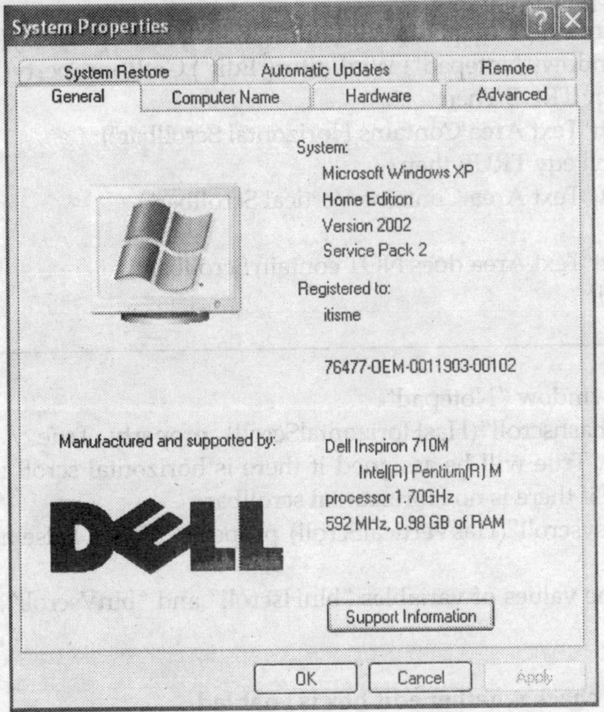


```
1 icount=Dialog("System Properties").WinTab("SysTabControl32").GetItemsCount()
2 For i=0 To icount-1
3 iname=Dialog("System Properties").WinTab("SysTabControl32").GetItem(i)
4 print(iname)
5 Next
```

Line 1: Counts the number of tabs in the "System Properties" Tab window and assigns the same to the variable "icount".

Line 2-5: Getting and printing each tab name from the tab window by iterating through each item of the tab window. Tab Window is a control similar to list box where tab window contains Tabs as items.

7. Write a program to check whether scrollbars exist inside an editor

```
1  Window("Notepad").Activate
2  blnHscroll=Window("Notepad").WinEditor("Edit").GetRoproperty("hashscroll")
3  blnVscroll=Window("Notepad").WinEditor("Edit").GetRoproperty("hasvscroll")
4  If blnHscroll eqv TRUE Then
5              print("Text Area Contains Horizontal Scrollbar")
6  Else if blnVscroll eqv TRUE then
7              print("Text Area Contains Vertical Scrollbar")
8  Else
9              print("Text Area does NOT contain Scrollbar")
10             End if
11 End If
```

Line 1: Activates the window "Notepad".
Line 2: Based on "hashscroll"(HasHorizontalScroll) property True / False assigned to variable "blnHscroll". True will be assigned if there is horizontal scroll in the text area and False will be assigned if there is no Horizoantal scrollbar.
Line 3: Based on "hasvscroll"(HasVerticalScroll) property True / False assigned to variable "blnVscroll".
Line 4-11: Based on the values of variables "blnHscroll" and "blnVscroll", the corresponding Message is displayed.

8. Write a program to check whether edit box is enabled.

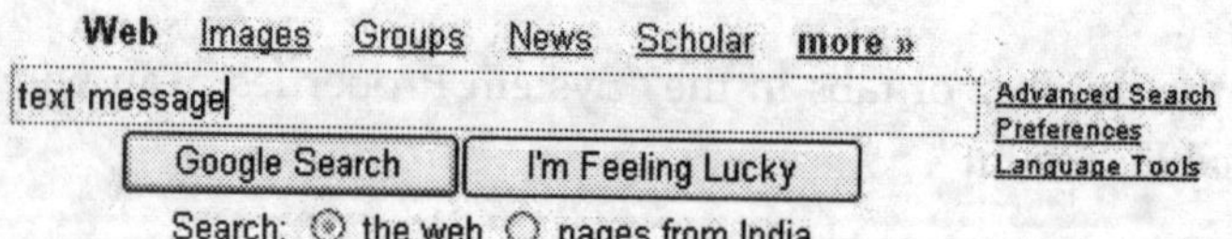

```
1 isDisabled=Browser("Google").Page("Google").WebEdit("search").GetROProperty("disa
  bled")
2 If isDisabled eqv True Then
3     Print ('Edit box is disabled")
4 Else
5     Print ("Edit box is enabled")
6 End If
```

Line 1 : Fetches the value of "disabled" property for the web edit box "search" and places it in variable "isDisabled".

Line 2-6 : Check the value of variable "isDisabled" and prints the appropriate message to the user.

9. Write a program to check whether the image is in the middle of the window.

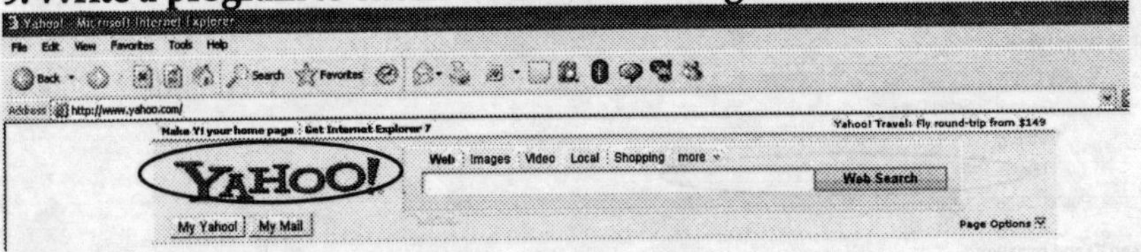


```
1  Dim logo_absx_pos, logo_width,logo_center
2  Dim page_absx_pos, page_width,page_center
3  logo_absx_pos=Browser("Yahoo").Page("Home").Image("Logo_Yahoo").GetROProper
   ty("abs_x")
4  logo_width=Browser("Yahoo").Page("Home").Image("Logo_Yahoo").GetROProperty("
   width")
5  page_absx_pos=Browser("Yahoo").Page("Home").GetROProperty("abs_x")
6  page_width=Browser("Yahoo").Page("Home").GetROProperty("width")
7  logo_center=(logo_absx_pos+logo_width)/2
8  page_center=(page_absx_pos+page_width)/2
9  If logo_center=page_center Then
10     Print ("Logo is at center of the page")
11 Else
12     Print ("Logo is NOT at center of the page")
13 End If
```

Line 1-2: Declaration of variables used throughout the program.

Line 3: Fetching the absolute x position of the image and storing it in the variable "logo_absx_pos".

Line 4: Fetching the width of the image and storing it in the variable "logo_width".

Line 5: Fetching the absolute x position of the page and storing it in the variable "page_absx_pos".

Line 6: Fetching the width of the page and storing it in the variable "page_width".

Line 7: Determining the Horizontal middle point of the image.

Line 8: Determining the Horizontal middle point of the page.
Line 9-11: Comparing the Horizontal middle point of the image and the Horizontal middle point of the page and printing the message accordingly.

10. Check default selection in list box.

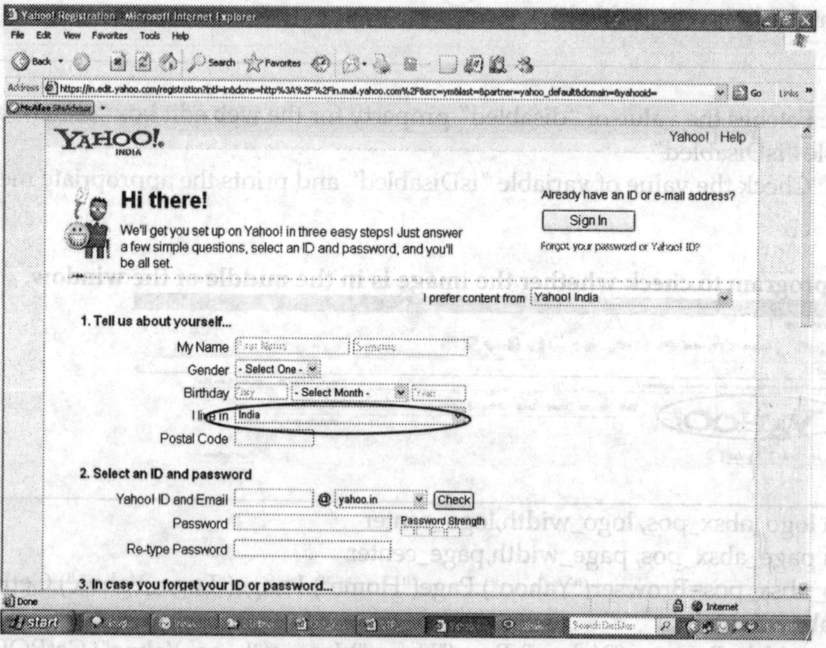


```
1  Dim expDefaultName
2  expDefaultName="India"
3  iselectedindex=Browser("Yahoo").Page("Registration").WebList("country").GetROPro
   perty("selected item Index")
4  itemIndex=CInt(iselectedindex)+1
5  iselectedname=Browser("Yahoo").Page("Registration").WebList("country").GetItem(ite
   mIndex)
6   If iselectedname=expDefaultName Then
7     print("Default Selection in list is correct")
8   Else
9     print("Default Selection in list is wrong")
10  End If
```

Line 1: Declaration of a variable "expDefaultName".
Line 2: Assigning the expected default value to the variable "expDefaultName".
Line 3: Runtime Object property "selected item Index" of web list is assigned to variable "iselectedindex".

Line 4: The value in variable "iselectedindex" is converted into integer and incremented by one and assigned to itemIndex. This is because the selected item index value is counted from 0 as starting and Getitem method used in the next line will count starting index value from 1. For example in Yahoo country list box shown above let us say India is selected. If the **selected item index** returns 99 GetItem requires 100 as input since it counts starting index as 1.
Line 5: Fetches the (itemIndex)th value from the web list and assigns it to the variable "iselectedname".
Line 6-7: Comparison is made between "iselectedname" and "expDefaultname" and accordingly the corresponding message is printed.

11. Find image width and Height

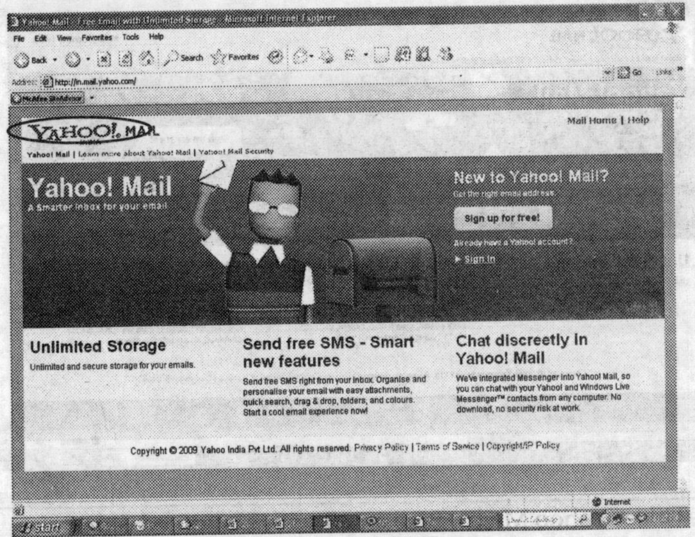


```
1  img_height=Browser("Yahoo").Page("MailHome").Image("Logo_Mail").
   GetROProperty("height")
2  img_width=Browser("Yahoo").Page("MailHome").Image("Logo_Mail").
   GetROProperty("width")
3  print("(Height,Width)"&VbTab&"("&img_height&","&img_width&")")
```

Line 1-2: Get the height and width of the **Mail Logo** image by reading the respective **height** and **width** properties using **GetROProperty** method. GetROProperty is a method used to read the properties of an object.
Line 3 : Print image height and width.

12. Print URL of the page

```
1  urlName=Browser("Yahoo").Page("MailHome").GetROProperty("url")
2  print(urlName)
```

Line 1 : Reads URL name through property url.

Line 2 : Prints the url.

13. Refresh web page

```
1 Browser("Yahoo").Refresh()
```

Line 1 : Refreshes the browser through Refresh method.

14. Verify that page title is displayed correctly

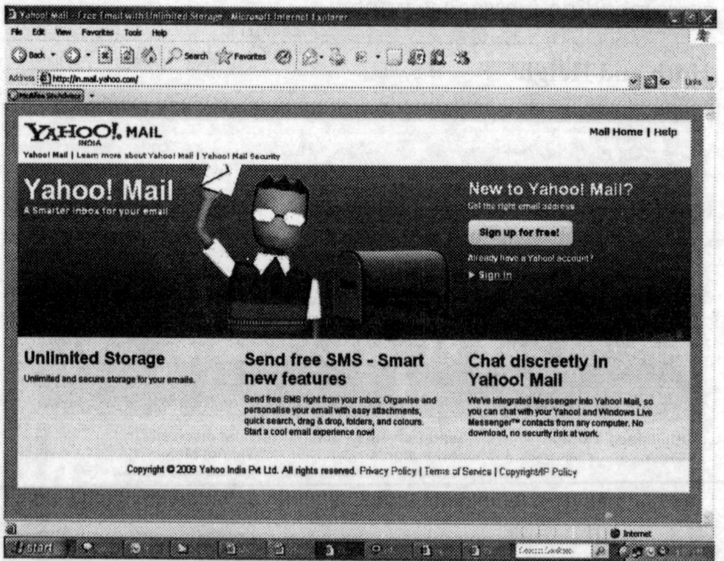


```
1 Dim expPageTitle="Yahoo Mail! – Free email with Unlimited Storage"
2 pageTitle=Browser("Yahoo").Page("MailHome").GetROProperty("title")
3 If pageTitle = expPageTitle Then
4     print("Page Title is Correct")
5 Else
6     print("Page Title is wrong")
7 End If
```

Line 1 : Declaration of variable for expected page title.
Line 2 : Reads title name through property title.
Line 3-7: If pageTitle=expPageTitle, print "Page Title is Correct",else print "Page Title is wrong".

15. Write a program to Invoke the Browser with specified URL.

```
1 SystemUtil.Run "iexplore","www.yahoo.com"
```

Line 1: Invokes the specified application. **SystemUtil.Run** statement runs the specified application from specified location.

16. Write a program to Find whether image contains tool tip.

```
1 logoTooltip=Browser("Yahoo").Page("Home").Image("imgLogo").
    GetRoproperty("alt")
2 If logoTooltip = "" Then
3   print("Tool Tip Not present")
4 Else
5   print("Tool Tip:" &" "&logoTooltip)
6 End If
```

Line 1: Reads tooltip of imglogo through property **alt**. Assign it to a variable.
Line 2-6: If logoTooltip = " " then prints "Tool Tip Not present" else prints Tooltip as the Content of logoTooltip.

17. Write a program to Display the entire data in the web table.

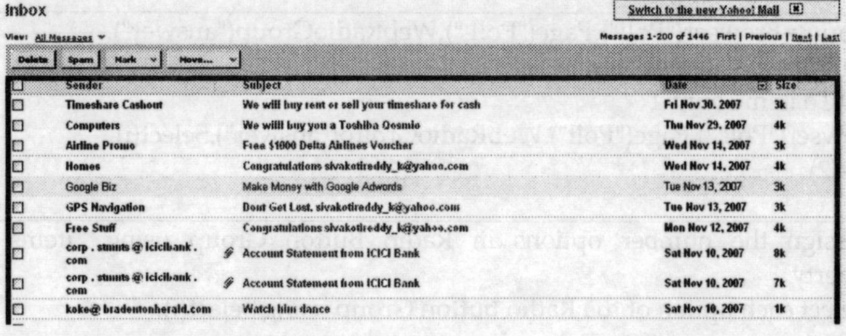


```
1 rowCount=Browser("Yahoo! Mail").Page("Yahoo! Mail Inbox").
  WebTable("Sender").RowCount()
2 For row=1 To rowCount
3    colCount=Browser("Yahoo! Mail").Page("Yahoo! Mail Inbox").
  WebTable("Sender").ColumnCount(row)
4 rowData=""
5     For col=1 To colCount
6  rowData=rowData&vbTab&Browser("Yahoo!Mail").Page("Yahoo! Mail Inbox").
  WebTable("Sender"). GetCellData(row,col)
7     Next
8     print(rowData)
9 Next
```

Line 1: Stores the total number of rows in a given webtable into a variable, which is accessed through the rowcount method.
Line 2-9: Loops through all the rows from the beginning.
Line 3: Stores the number of columns count in a variable.

Line 4: Sets row data to null.
Line 5-7: Sets inner loop which loops through all the columns.
Line 6: Stores a particular cell data into a variable. GetCellData method retrieves the content of the specified cell from the table.
Line 8: Prints row data.

18. Write a program to select items in a Radio Group

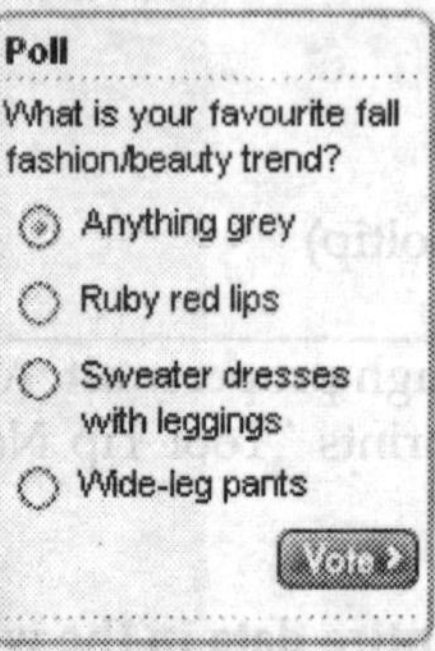


```
1 itemCount=Browser("Poll").Page("Poll ").WebRadioGroup("answer").
  GetROProperty("items count")
2 For i=0 To itemCount-1
3     Browser("Poll ").Page("Poll").WebRadioGroup("answer").Select(i)
4     wait(2)
5 Next
```

Line 1: Assign the number options in Radio Button Group using "items count" of GetROProperty
Line 1-5: Select each option of the Radio button Group using Select(i).

REGULAR EXPRESSIONS

Why Regular Expressions?

A regular expression (regex or regexp for short) is a special text string for describing a search pattern. You can think of regular expressions as wildcard. You are probably familiar with wildcard notations such as *.doc to find all word files in a file manager.

Regular Expression Characters

Regular Expression Character	Definition	Regularized String	Valid Match	Invalid Match
. (Dot)	Matches any Single Character	Amount in .	Amount in $	Amount in Rs

Regular Expressio n Character	Definition	Regularized String	Valid Match	Invalid Match
[xy] (Square braces)	Matches Any Single Character in a List	Order No [567]	Order No 5 Order No 6 Order No 7 (Either 5, 6, or 7)	Order No 10 Order No 2 (Any number other than 5,6,7 is invalid)
[^xy] (Caret with Square braces)	Used for Negation, Matches Any Single Character **NOT** in a List	Order No [^567]	Order No 8 Order No 2 Order No 3 (Any number other than 5,6,7 is valid)	Order No 5 Order No 6 Order No 7 (5,6,7 are invalid)
[x-y] (Hyphen with Square braces)	Matches any Single Character within a **Range**	Order No [4-7]	Order No 4 Order No 5 Order No 6 Order No 7	Any number out of the Range is invalid Order No 2 Order No 3 Order No 8
* (asterix)	Matches the previous character for Zero or more times	abc*	ab abc abccc	The previous character c may occur zero or more times abs
+ (Plus)	Matches the previous character for one or more times	abc+	abc abccc	The previous character c should occur atleast once ab
? (Question mark)	Matches the Previous character for Zero or One time	abc?	ab abc	The previous character may occur either zero or one time. abcc
| (Vertical Line)	Matches One of Several Regular Expressions	(Deposit|W ithdrawal)	Matches one of the string. Deposit or Withdrawal	

Regular Expression Character	Definition	Regularized String	Valid Match	Invalid Match
^ (Caret)	Matches Beginning of a Line	^book	Matches lines Starting with book	
$ (Dollar)	Matches End of a Line	Book$	Matches lines ending with Book	
\w	Matches any Alphanumeric characters & Underscore	EmployeeID \w{6}	Matches 6 occurrences of Alpha Numeric Characters including Underscore. HR_02, RD_05, QA_08	
\W	Matches any character other than Alphanumeric Character & Underscores	Hello\W	Hello@#$%	Hello_siva
\d	Matches digit	EMP\d	EMP1 EMP2 EMP4	EMPX
\D	Matches Non digit	EMP\D	EMPA EMPB	EMP1
\s	Matches space	Jan\s01	Jan 01	Jan01
\S	Matches no space	Jan\S01	Jan01	Jan 01

Grouping Regular Expressions - ()

Multiple Regular Expression Characters can be combined in a Single Expression.

For Example:

Window("text:=.*(Report|Graph)").Close

The above line Closes a Window with Text Report or Graph preceded by any set of alphanumeric characters.

Using the Backslash Character (\ )

The backslash can be used along with a Regular Expression Character to indicate that the next character be treated as a literal character.

For Example:

There is a link with FirstName.LastName to click the script which can be

Browser("Yahoo").Page("Yahoo").Link("text:=.*\..*").Click

Here the backslash is preceded by the .(period) so the .(period) will be considered literal & not a Regular Expression.

Regexp Object

You can use regular expressions in VBScript by creating one or more instances of the RegExp object. This object allows you to find regular expression matches in strings, and replace regex matches in strings with other strings. You can create this object in scripting as shown below:

Regexp Rx= New Regexp

RegExp Object Methods & Properties

Method	Description
Execute	Executes a regular expression search against a specified string.
Replace	Replaces text found in a regular expression search.
Test	Executes a regular expression search against a specified string and returns a **Boolean** value that indicates if a pattern match was found.
Property	**Description**
Global	Sets or returns a **Boolean** value that indicates if a pattern should match all occurrences in an entire search string or just the first one.
IgnoreCase	Sets or returns a **Boolean** value that indicates if a pattern search is case-sensitive or not
Pattern	Sets or returns the regular expression pattern being searched for.

After creating the object, assign the regular expression you want to search for to the **Pattern** property. If you want to use a literal regular expression rather than a user-supplied one, simply put the regular expression in a double-quoted string. By default, the regular expression is case sensitive. Set the **IgnoreCase** property to True to make it case insensitive.

After setting the RegExp object's properties, you can invoke one of the three methods to perform one of three basic tasks.

1) **Test:** The **Test** method takes one parameter as a string to test the regular expression on. **Test** returns True or False, indicating if the regular expression matches (part of) the string. When validating user input, you'll typically want to check if the entire string matches the regular expression. To do so, put a caret at the start of the regex, and a dollar at the end, to anchor the regex at the start and end of the subject string.
   Syntax: myVar= object.Test(string)
   myVar will have value True if match for the pattern is found else it will have value False.
   Example:

```
Option explicit
Dim myRegEx, myVal,str  ' Create variable.
str="HI1 hi2 HI3 hi4"
Set myRegEx = New RegExp  ' Create regular expression.
        myRegEx.Pattern = "hi."      ' Set pattern.
        myRegEx.IgnoreCase = False     ' Set case sensitivity.
        myVal = myRegEx.Test(str)     ' Execute the search test.
If myVal Then
        Print  "Match is found"
Else
        Print  "No match was found."
End If
```

2) **Execute:** The **Execute** method also takes one string parameter. Instead of returning True or False, it returns a **Matches** Collection object. If the regex could not match the subject string at all, **Matches.Count** will be zero. If the **RegExp.Global** property is False (the default), **Matches** Collection will contain only the first match. If **RegExp.Global** is true, **Matches** Collection will contain all matches.
   Syntax: object.Execute(string)
   The execute method returns collection of strings containing every match found in string. If no match is found then execute methods returns empty value.
   Example:

```
Option explicit
Dim regEx, Match, Matches,str,RetStr   ' Create variable.
        str="HI1 hi2 HI3 hi4"
        Set regEx = New RegExp     ' Create a regular expression.
        regEx.Pattern = "hi."        ' Set pattern.
        regEx.IgnoreCase = True         ' Set case insensitivity.
        regEx.Global = True         ' Set global applicability.
        Set Matches = regEx.Execute(str)   ' Execute search.
For Each Match in Matches ' Iterate Matches collection.
        RetStr = RetStr & "Match found at position "
```

```
            RetStr = RetStr & Match.FirstIndex & ". Match Value is '"
            RetStr = RetStr & Match.Value & "'." & vbcrlf
    Next
            print RetStr
```

3) **Replace:** The **Replace** method takes two string parameters. The first parameter is the text string in which the text replacement is to occur, while the second parameter is the replacement text. If the RegExp.Global property is False (the default), **Replace** will return the subject string with the first regex match (if any) substituted with the replacement text. If RegExp.Global is true, **Replace** will return the subject string with all regex matches replaced.

   Syntax: object.Replace(string1,string2)

   The above line will find the string1 in the expression and replace it with string2.

   Example:

```
Option explicit
 Dim regEx, str1,str2 ,newStr              ' Create variables.
       str1 = "Hello, goodmorning."
       str2="Hi"
 Set regEx = New RegExp             ' Create regular expression.
       regEx.Pattern = "Hello"          ' Set pattern.
       regEx.IgnoreCase = True          ' Make case insensitive.
       newStr=regEx.Replace(str1, str2)  ' Make replacement.
       print "String before Replace:"&str1
       print "String after Replace:"&newStr
```

Match Object & Matches Collection

A **Matches** collection contains individual **Match** objects, and can be only created using the **Execute** method of the **RegExp** object. When a regular expression is executed, zero or more **Match** objects can result. Each **Match** object provides access to the string found by the regular expression, the length of the string, and an index to where the match was found.

Match Object Properties

Property	Description
First Index	Returns the position in a search string where a match occurs.
Length	Returns the length of a match found in a search string
Value	Returns the value or text of a match found in a search string.

Using Regular Expressions

Regular Expressions can be used in

1) Expected Result of Check Points (Checkpoint Properties)
2) Physical Description in the Repository (Changing Window Titles)
3) Scripts / Programs

Using Regular Expressions in Checkpoints

During creation of a Standard Checkpoint, the expected value of an object's property can be set as a Regular Expression.

For Example:

A Sales Man in a CRM application does not have permission to enter a value of more than 9999 in the Amount Field. To validate this the Regular Expression in the Text Property of a checkpoint can be

[0-9][0-9][0-9][0-9]

Physical Description in the Repository

Regular Expressions are used in the Physical Description of an object repository to handle objects with varying (dynamic) descriptions.

For Example:

There is a link in a web page with the number of visitors like Visitor 1, Visitor 2, Visitor 3 .... Visitor **n**, for text property in the Physical description (Object Repository) can be Visitor.*

Scripts / Programs

Regular Expressions can also be used in Programming like matching all lines that starts with "QTP".

Scripting Examples

1. Matching an Alphanumeric Test case ID

```
[a-zA-Z0-9]+
```

Description: Matches any alphanumeric string without any spaces.

Matching Text: 10a, ABC, A3fg

Non-Matching Text:

45.3 : This string contains a period(.)

this or that : This string contains spaces

$23 : This string contains a symbol($)

2. Matching an Email Address

```
(\w+)\.(\w+)@(\w+)\.[A-Za-z]{2,4}
```

Description: Matches any email ids in the format firstname.lastname@company.com

(\w+) – matches any Firstname with any Alphanumeric characters & Underscore

\. – treat dot as a literal character. Slash(\) is an escape character which escapes the special meaning of dot(.)

(\w+) – matches any lastname with any Alphanumeric characters & Underscore

@ - email id henceforth should be followed by @

(\w+)- matches any company name with any Alphanumeric characters & Underscore

\. – company name followed by a dot.

[A-Za-z]{2-4} – matches alphabets of both lower case and uppercase. Number of characters can range from two to four.

Matching Text: siva.reddy@iibc.com
Shalini.r@iibc.in

Non-Matching Text: **siva.reddy@iibc.abcde**

The above expression exceeds the range 2-4 hence the expression does not match.

3. Matching 6 Integer PIN code

```
\d{6}
```

Description: Matches 6 numeric digits, such as a 6 digit PIN code.
Matching Text: 560054, 560065
Non-Matching Text:
Abcd : Given string is not a digit
1324 : Number of digits in the given string should be 6
as;lkjdf : Given string is not a digit

4. Matching an HTML Tag

```
<(.*)>.*<\/\1>
```

Description: The above expression Matches HTML Tags.
.* at starting Represents any Tag, and also since it is placed in (), it is the first positional data. 1 represents the end Tag which must be the same as the 1st positional data. For example TABLE tag is stored in the first positional data, 1 indicates that it must also have TABLE.* in between represents any text between two Tags.

Matching Text: <HEAD> Hello World </HEAD>
Non-Matching Text:
<HEAD> Hello World </IMG> : The initial tag is <HEAD> hence the end Tag must also be </HEAD> since the regular expression defines the end tag to be the same as the first positional data.

5. **Matching a Blank Line**

```
^\s*$
```

The above expression matches Blank lines. The symbol ^ indicates from starting and $ indicates till ending. In other words ^ and $ at starting and Ending represents from starting to Ending of the string. \s indicates space i.e blank data which is preceding character to *. Overall above expression represents space from starting to ending of the line i.e the line is Blank.

6. **Matching start of the line**

```
^QTP
```

Description: Matches all lines Starting with QTP. ^ symbol matches strings that are starting with a specified pattern. In the above expression all strings Starting with QTP will be matched.

Matching Text: QTP is primarily used for functional regression test automation.

Non-Matching Text: Quick Test Professional in short is referred to as QTP. The above line does not start with QTP hence this line is not matched.

7. **Matches End of the Line**

```
SUCCESS$
```

Description: Matches all Lines Ending with SUCCESS. The $ symbol matches strings that are ending with a specified pattern. In the above expression all strings ending with SUCCESS will be matched.

Matching Text: DEFINING SUCCESS
Non-Matching Text: WHAT IS SUCCESS IN TODAYS WORLD?
The above line does not end with the string SUCCESS.

8. **Matching Time of Day**

```
([0][0-9])|([1][0-2]) : ([0-5][0-9]) : ([0-5][0-9]) (AM|PM)
```

Time will be in the format 10:25:46 AM where 10 represents Hours, 25 represents Minutes and 46 Represents Secs.

Since Hours are always between 00-12 the regular expression is [0][0-9])|([1][0-2]). It specifies that hours are either 00-09 or 10-12.

Since Minutes and Secs are always between 00-59 the regular expression is [0-5][0-9]).

Always Time Must show either AM or PM. Hence Regular Expression AM|PM represents either AM or PM.

9. Matching a Date in DD-MM-YYYY format

([0][1-9] | [1-2][0-9]) | ([3][0-1]) – ([0][1-9]) | ([1][0-2]) – ([1-9][0-9][0-9][0-9])

Description: Date is in the format DD-MM-YYYY where

DD- is Always between 01-31.

Whenever the first D is 0, the second D can be between 1-9; i.e 01-09; Hence Regular Expression is [0][1-9]

If the first D is 1-2 second D can be between 0-9; i.e 10-29; Hence Regular Expression [1-2][0-9]

If the first D is 3, the second D can be between 0-1; i.e 30-31; Hence Regular Expression [3][0-1]

The above Regular Expression for Day matches any day between 01-31

MM – is Always between 01-12

Whenever the First M is 0, the second M can be between 1-9; i.e 01-09; Representing January To September. Hence Regular Expression will be [0][1-9]

If the first M is 1, the second M can be between 0-2; i.e 10-12; Representing October To December. Hence Regular Expression will be [1-2][0-9]

YYYY – is Between 1000 – 9999 with Regular Expression [1-9][0-9][0-9][0-9]

10. Matching a Floating point number

[-+]?([0-9]*\.[0-9]+)

Description:

In the above regular expression

[-+]? - Indicates either + or – symbol can appear zero or one time.

[0-9]* - Indicates any number between 0-9 can appear zero or more times

\. - Indicates. must be there after the previous number since we are matching a floating point.

[0-9]+ - Indicates that one more number between 0-9 can appear one or more times.

Matching Text:

Floating point numbers will be like 127.234, +127.234, -127.234

Non-Matching Text: 127234

11. Matching Credit Card

([4]{1})([0-9]{12,15})

Description: The above expression validates against a visa card number. Here all visa card numbers should start with a digit 4 and are followed by numbers ranging from 12 to 15 numbers.

Matching Text:

4125632152365, 418563256985214, 4125632569856321

Non-Matching Text:

3125652365214: Here the first digit is not 4 hence the string is not matched.

41256321256: Here the first digit is 4 followed by 10 more numbers whereas the numbers following after 4 should be within the range of 12-15
42563985632156322: The total numbers followed after the first digit 4 is 16 which is out of the given range 12-15.

DESCRIPTIVE PROGRAMMING

When Quick Test learns an object in your application, it adds the appropriate test object to the object repository along with some description on how to recognize that object. QTP cannot take action on an object until it is in the Object Repository. But Descriptive Programming (DP) is used when we want to perform an operation on an object that is not present in the object repository. There are many obvious reasons why an object cannot be in the repository and also why we should use Descriptive programming while working with Automation which we discuss later in this chapter.

How to do Descriptive Programming?

There are two ways for writing code using descriptive programming.

1. Placing the set of properties and values directly in the statement

You can describe an object directly in a statement by specifying **property: =value pairs** describing the object instead of specifying an object's name.

The general syntax is:

TestObject("PropertyName1:=PropertyValue1","...",PropertyNameX:=PropertyValueX")

TestObject - The test object class likes WebButton, Web list, WinEdit, etc...

PropertyName:=PropertyValue. The identification property and its value. Each **property:=value** pair should be separated by commas and quotation marks.

To write a text in Google Search edit box in the home page you can write VbScript statement using logical name of object present in object repository as

Browser("Google").Page("Google").WebEdit("q").Set "QTP Complete Reference"

The same text can be set into the Google Search edit box in the home page using Descriptive Programming as

Browser ("Google").Page ("Google").WebEdit ("type:=text","name:=q", "html tag:=INPUT").Set "QTP Complete Reference"

In the above code we have replaced the logical name of the object by directly entering the property names and values of a search button.

Note that you can enter a variable name as the property value if you want to find an object based on property values you retrieve during a run session. For example:

MyVar="q"

Browser("Google").Page("Google").WebEdit("type:=text","name:="&MyVar,"html tag:=INPUT").Set "QTP Complete Reference"

2. *Using Description object*

You can use the **Description** object to return a **Properties** collection object containing a set of **Property** objects. A **Property** object consists of a property name and value. You can then specify the returned **Properties** collection in place of an object name in a statement.

Using Description object we can set data into the Google Search edit box home page as

```
Set myDesc=Description.Create ()
myDesc("type").value="text"
myDesc("name").value="q"
myDesc("html tag").value="INPUT"
Browser("Google").Page("Google").WebEdit(myDesc).Set "QTP Complete Reference".
```

Hierarchy of specifying test object description

Providing properties and Values directly to QTP script for identifying the object without using object repository is known as **programmatic description.**

When using programmatic descriptions from a specific point within a test object hierarchy, you must continue to use programmatic descriptions from that point onward within the same statement. If you specify a test object by its object repository name after other objects in the hierarchy have been specified using programmatic descriptions, QuickTest cannot identify the object.

For example, you can use the following statement since it uses programmatic descriptions throughout the entire test object hierarchy:

Browser("Title:=Google").Page("Title:=Home").WebEdit("type:=text","name:="&MyVar,"html tag:=INPUT").Set "QTP Complete Reference"

You can also use the statements as below, since it uses programmatic descriptions from a certain point in the description (starting from the Page object description):

Browser("Google").Page("Title:=Home").WebEdit("type:=text","name:="&MyVar,"html tag:=INPUT").Set "QTP Complete Reference"

Browser("Google").Page("Title:=Home").WebEdit(myDesc).Set "QTP Complete Reference"

Observe from the above that both the types of programmatic descriptions (Statement and Description object) are allowed within the same statement.

However, you cannot use the following statement, since it uses programmatic descriptions for Browser and Page objects but then attempts to use an object repository name for the WebEdit test object:

Browser("Title:=Google").Page("Title:=Google").WebEdit("search").Set "QTP Complete Reference"

QuickTest tries to locate the WebEdit object based on its name, but cannot locate it in the repository because the parent objects were specified using programmatic descriptions.

You can use any of the above two methods of descriptive programming. In general if object description is required in 1or 2 statements, placing directly in the statement is good, else using Description object is a best approach.

Identifying Properties and Values to be used in Descriptive Programming

To identify properties to be used to uniquely identify a particular type of object in the application, you can observe the object repository and understand the usual properties being used by QTP. If required you can also use Object Spy to identify additional properties and also the values corresponding to these properties.

The screen below shows how I have picked the properties for search edit box object in Google while doing descriptive programming in the above sections.

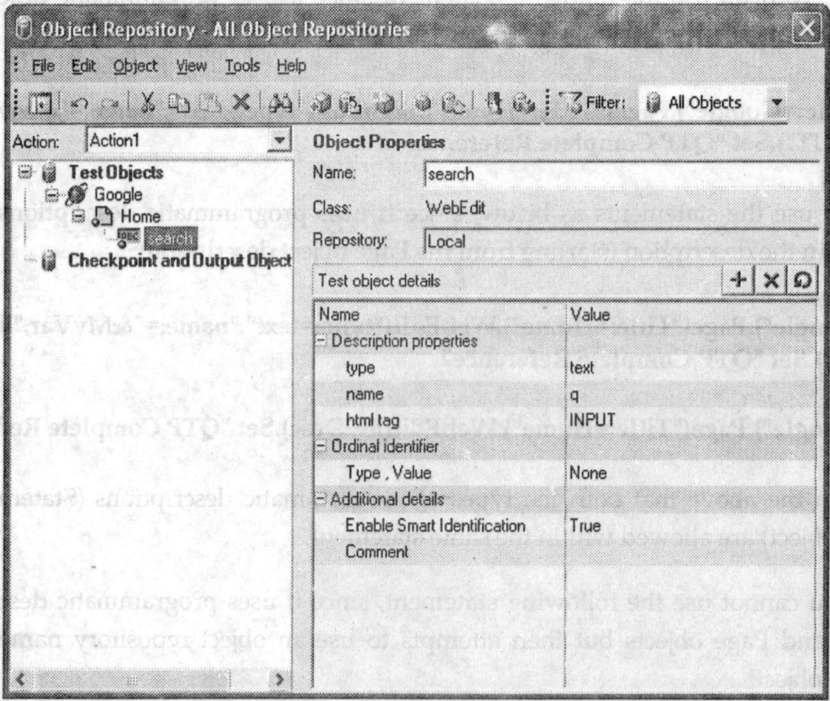

QTP has used three properties - type, name and html tag as shown above to recognize search WebEdit box. I have used the same properties in the above sections to recognize the objects using descriptive programming.

micClass

micClass represents the class type of a test object like Browser, Page, WebList, WebButton. In the below code there are three micClasses named Browser, Page and WebEdit.

```
Browser("Google").Page("Home").WebEdit("search").Set "QTP Complete Reference"
```

In general QTP doesn't use any properties to recognize the browser. So to deal with situations where you need to work with any browser you can use micClass as a dummy property since Descriptive programming expects at least one property. So to refresh the browser using descriptive programming, the code below will NOT work, since there is no logical name or properties to identify the browser.

```
Browser("").Refresh
```

We have to use code as shown below, by giving micClass as dummy property.

```
Browser("micClass:=Browser").Refresh
```

When and Where to use Descriptive programming?

Below are some of the situations where Descriptive Programming can be very useful:

1. Working with Runtime objects created in the application. For example let us say you have a requirement to register 10 users and update personal info of all users by logging into the application with Admin privileges. To update each user personal info we have to click on the link name created in the admin panel with the same name we used during user registration. This username link is called as Runtime Object of the application. We cannot have these user name links in the Object repository because different user names are filled in data table during script execution. So by using descriptive programming we will create these user link objects and work with them as below.

```
Set usrLink=Description.create()
usrLink ("html tag").value="A"
usrLink("text").value=Datatable.GetSheet("User
Info").GetParameter("UserName"). Value
Browser("App").Page("Admin").Link(usrLink).click
```

2. When we want to read child objects of a particular type from webPage or webTable. The code below will read all links from the Google Home Page

```
set linkObjs=Browser("Google").Page("Home").ChildObject("html tag:=A")
```

3. Objects in the application are dynamic in nature. For example, if you have to click on a link as *"Weather Report of Today 1/10/2010"* where the date is changing regularly to today's date we can use Descriptive programming as below.

```
Set weatherLink=Description.create()
weatherLink ("html tag").value="A"
weatherLink ("text").value= "Weather Report of Today "&Date()
Browser("App").Page("Admin").Link(weatherLink).click
```

4. When we are automating applications having localization, instead of creating one object repository for each language we can use descriptive programming and test all the languages of application directly by reading the text of each object from resource bundle files. Resource Bundle is a file where localized strings are stored.
5. Suppose you want to start automation scripting much earlier than the application availability. However this is not very common.
6. When Object repository size is getting huge. For QT. 6.2 and below Mercury recommends that OR size should not be greater than 1.5MB.
7. One place where DP can be of significant importance is when you are creating functions in an external file. You can use these functions in various actions directly, eliminating the need of adding object(s) in object repository for each action [If you are using per action object repository].
8. If more than one object is matching the same properties, QTP will through an error indicating multiple objects are matching the description. Descriptive Programming easily deals with double objects by using the index property. We can add "index:=X" to the description strings (when X is a zero-based counter), and QTP will point to the object #X.
9. When using external functions, you can never count on the relevant object being defined in the calling action's OR may not have the relevant object used by function. And even if the object is defined there, it's logical name might be different, so really, Descriptive Programming remains the only option.
10. Sometime an object will appear under a different parent each time (e.g. – a pop-up which appears under the initiating sub-window). In some applications, the only way to work with such objects is with DP.
11. If we're dealing with an unknown number of checkboxes and need to mark all of them as checked using child objects method and Descriptive Programming, we can loop through all the checkboxes in the screen, and mark all of them easily.

Regular Expressions in Descriptive Programming

QuickTest evaluates all property values in programmatic descriptions as regular expressions. Therefore, if you want to enter a value that contains a special regular expression character (such as *, ?, or +), use the \ (backslash) character to instruct QuickTest to treat the special characters as literal characters. For more information on regular expressions, Refer Chapter on **Regular Expressions.**

Scripting Examples

1. Click Google Search button using properties in the step

Google Search   I'm Feeling Lucky

```
Browser("Google").Page("Google").WebButton("type:=submit","html tag:=INPUT","name:=Google Search").Click
```

In the above line Google Search button was identified using descriptive programming by writing the properties directly into the step. Properties used to recognize the button are type, html tag and name. To identify which properties to be used we can take the help of Object Repository or Object Spy.

Example 2: Click Google Search button using Description object

```
1 Set googleSearchObj=Description.Create()
2 googleSearchObj("type").value="submit"
3 googleSearchObj("html tag").value="INPUT"
4 googleSearchObj("name").value="Google Search"
5 Browser("Google").Page("Google").WebButton(googleSearchObj).Click
```

Line 1: Creates the Properties Collection object (googleSearchObj) using Description Object. PropertiesCollection object is used to store all the properties of an object that should be identified using Descriptive Programming.

Line 2-4: Stores type, html, name property values as submit, INPUT, Google Search respectively in Properties Collection object googleSearchObj.

Line 5: Clicks on the Web Button "Google Search" represented by googleSearchObj.

Example 3: Adding and Removing properties of an Object in Descriptive Programming

```
Set googleSearchObj=Description.Create()

googleSearchObj("type").value="submit"
googleSearchObj("name").value="Google Search"

Set tmpObj=Description.Create()
tmpObj("html tag").value="INPUT"
```

```
8   googleSearchObj.Add tmpObj(0)
9
10  Print("Number of Properties in the Description are: "&googleSearchObj.count)
11  googleSearchObj.Remove "type"
```

Line 1: Create Properties Collection Object, googleSearchObj
Line 3-4: Add 2 properties type, name for properties collection object googleSearchObj. Now googleSearchObj contains 2 properties.
Line 6-8: Add new property html tag to googleSearchObj. Note that properties cannot be added directly to properties collection object. Instead we must create another properties collection object and add this properties collection object to existing properties collection object. In Line 6 we have created a properties collection object tmpObj, in Line 7 we have added a property html tag to tmpObj and in Line 7 properties collection object tmpObj is added to another properties collection object googleSearchObj. Now googleSearchObj contains 3 properties named type,name and html tag.

Line 10: Prints number of properties in googleSearchObj which is 3.
Line 11: Removes Type property from googleSearchObj

Example 4: Display all the links present in Orkut Home Page


```
Set linkDesc=Description.Create()
linkDesc("html tag").value="A"
set orkutLinks=Browser("orkut - login").Page("orkut - login").ChildObjects(linkDesc)
Print("Total Number of Links="& orkutLinks.count)
For i=0 To orkutLinks.count-1
        print(orkutLinks(i).GetROProperty("text"))
Next
```

This program prints all the links present in the Orkut Home Page. Uses ChildObjects method to find all the children of type link.

Line 1: Creates Properties Collection object linkDesc.
Line 2: Sets the html tag property of an object as "A" (Anchor) that represents Link.
Line 3: Use ChildObjects Method on the Page to retrieve all the children of type link since PropertiesCollection Object linkDesc represents link objects as specified in Line 2 . All Links are stored in a collection orkutLinks.
Line 4: Print total number of links in the page.
Line 5-7: Print the name of all links. Each link in the collection is referred with orkutLinks(i) and the text of the link is retrieved with GetROProperty("text").

Example 5: Select all check boxes in Gmail Inbox Page

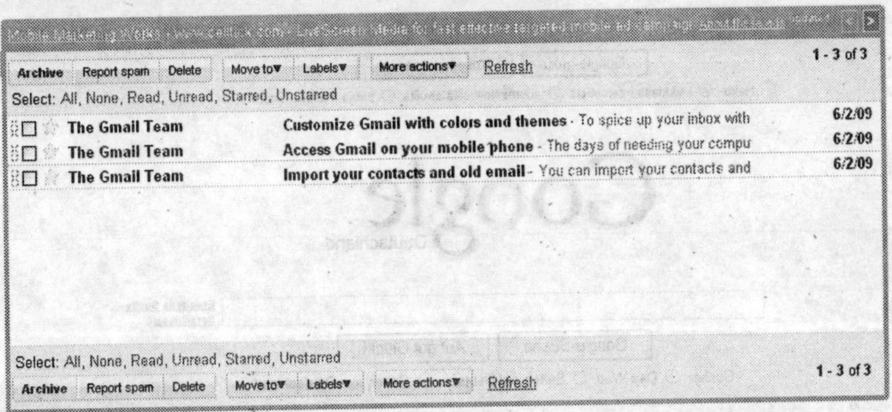


```
1  Set chkboxDesc=Description.Create()
2  chkboxDesc("type").value="checkbox"
3  set chboxCollection=Browser("Gmail").Page("Gmail").Frame("Mails").
   WebTable("Inbox"). ChildObjects(chkboxDesc)
4  For i=0 To chboxCollection.count -1
5          chboxCollection(i).set "ON"
6  Next
```

Line 1-3: Retrieve all the objects of Type checkbox from the webTable Inbox of Google Mailbox into the collection chboxCollection.
Line 4-6: Retrieves from first to Last CheckBox using chboxCollection(i) and selects the checkbox by setting it to ON.

Example 6: Working with multi language of Google Search Button Using Descriptive programming

Google™

Advanced Search
Language Tools

Google Search | I'm Feeling Lucky

Google™ Suomi

Tarkennettu haku
Kielivalinnat

Google-haku | Kokeilen onneani

Haku: kaikkialta internetistä suomenkielisiltä sivuilta sivuja maasta: Suomi

Google™ Deutschland

Erweiterte Suche
Sprachtools

Google-Suche | Auf gut Glück!

Suche: Das Web Seiten auf Deutsch Seiten aus Deutschland

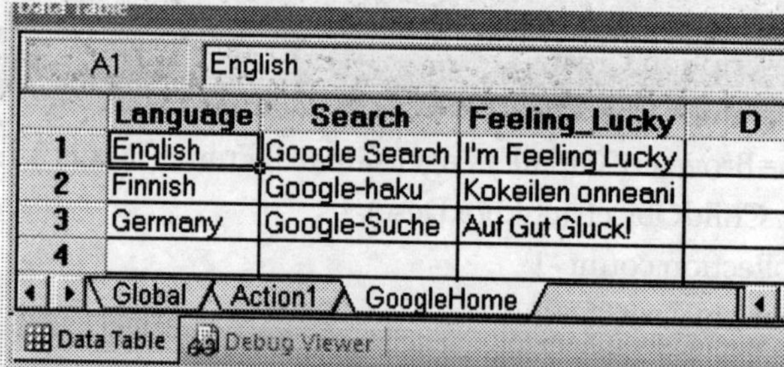

A1 English

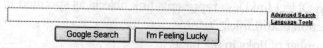

	Language	Search	Feeling_Lucky	D
1	English	Google Search	I'm Feeling Lucky	
2	Finnish	Google-haku	Kokeilen onneani	
3	Germany	Google-Suche	Auf Gut Gluck!	
4				

Global / Action1 / GoogleHome

Data Table | Debug Viewer

```
Datatable.ImportSheet"D:\QTPCompleteReference\Chapter22\GoogleLanguageStr
ings.xls" ,"HomePage","GoogleHome"
appLanguage=Environment("AUTLanguage")
Set btnGoogleSearchDesc=Description.Create()
btnGoogleSearchDesc("type").value="submit"
btnGoogleSearchDesc("html tag:=").value="INPUT"
For i=1 To Datatable.GetSheet("GoogleHome").GetRowCount
If Datatable.GetSheet("GoogleHome").GetParameter("Language").
ValueByRow(i) = appLanguage Then
```

```
8   btnGoogleSearchDesc("name").value=Datatable.GetSheet("GoogleHome").GetParameter("Search").ValueByRow(i)
9               Exit For
10          End If
11  Next
12  Browser("Google").Page("Google").WebButton(btnGoogleSearchDesc).Click
13  Set btnGoogleSearchDesc=Nothing
```

Most of the web applications are localized to make them available for people in their own language. This program demonstrates how to use Descriptive Programming to automate the localized applications by avoiding the unnecessary effort of creating a separate test script for each language. The above Screenshots showthree language versions of Google Home Page; English, Finnish and German respectively. The above program is written to click on Google Search Button irrespective of the localized language of the Google Home Page. The Excel file above shows the language in the first column and the way Google Search button is represented in the corresponding language in the second column.

Line 1: Imports external excel sheet "HomePage" into the DataTable sheet "GoogleHome". This sheet contains representation strings of HomePage objects in various languages.
Line 2: Retrieves the Environment variable that represents the language of the Google Home Page.
Line 3-5: Creates Properties Collection Object btnGoogleSearchDesc and sets two properties type, html tag.
Line 6-11: Go through the entire Excel File and retrieve the text string of the Google Search Object corresponding to the language of the Google Home Page. Line 7 identifies the row corresponding to the Language of the Google Home Page and line 8 retrieves the corresponding text string representation of Google Search object depending on the language of the Google Home Page and assigns as value of the name property. If the Language is Finnish, the text assigned to name property is "Google-haku" and if the language is Germany the text assigned to name property is "Google-Suche". Hence if Google Home Page Langauge is Finnish three properties of Google Search Button are type, html tag and name and their values are respectively submit,INPUT and Google-haku. Similiarly if the Language of Google Home Page is German then three properties of Google Search Button are type, html tag and name and their values are respectively submit, INPUT and Google-Suche.
Line 12: Clicks the Google Search Button based on the language of the Google Home Page.

Example 7: Working With RunTime Objects of Application

Members			
Login	First Name	Last Name	Level
admin	Administrator	Account	Administrator
guest	Guest	Account	Member
kiran	kiran	kumar	Member
sivareddy	SivaKoti	Reddy	Member
Insert			

Data Table

F9

	UserName	FirstName	LastName	Address	E
1	Kiran	Kiran	Kumar	Banglore	
2	SivaReddy	Siva	Reddy	Chennai	
3	Guest	Guest	QTP	Noldea	
4					
5					
6					

This program demonstrates how to use descriptive programming to deal with the RunTime objects created in the Application. RunTime object is the object created in the application while test script is under execution. Let us assume an automation requirement of registering 10 users and Updating their information by clicking on the user name link. 10 users can be registered by having their data in the Excel File. To update these user's information we have to click on the link object of each user and in a general approach these user link objects must be present in the repository. This is fine as long as usernames are known while creating the script. But practically these usernames are part of data file and are filled with new data every time before script execution. Hence we cannot have them in the object repository while creating the script. The best and only solution to deal with this is Descriptive programming. The Above code reads usernames from data table during runtime and creates a user link object and clicks on the user link object.

Line 1-2: Creates Properties Collection object and sets html tag property as "A" representing the object as Link.

Line 3-4: Go through 1st to Last user name in the excel file and reads username then assigns it to the text property. If the username read from the excel file is Kiran the object usrLink represent the link object Kiran.

Line 5-6: Clicks the link represented by object usrLink

Line 7-8: Updates the information of the user represented by usrLink

Example 8: Using Regular Expression in the Descriptive programming

```
Set googleLinkDesc=Description.Create()
googleLinkDesc("html tag").value="A"
googleLinkDesc("text").value=".*Google.*"
googleLinkDesc("text").RegularExpression=True
```

```
5 Set googleLinkCol=Browser("Google").Page("Google").
  ChildObjects(googleLinkDesc)
6 For i=0 To googleLinkCol.count-1
7         print(googleLinkCol(i).GetROProperty("text"))
8 Next
```

This program displays all the links in the Google Home Page which contains Google in their name using Regular Expressions.

Line 1-2: Creates a properties collection object googleLinkDesc that contains html tag property as a representing link.
Line 3: Saves Text property value as a regular expression ".*Google.*". This means all the links that have text Google irrespective of the text before and after them.
Line 4: Sets Regular Expression property to TRUE indicating QTP to recognize property values as regular expression if it encounters any regular expression characters.
Line 5-8: Print all the names matching the property values. In this case all links having Google in their name.

```
Set googleLinkCol=Browser("Google").Page("Google").
ChildObjects(googleLinkDesc)
For i=0 To googleLinkCol.count-1
    print(googleLinkCol(i).GetROProperty("text"))
Next
```

This program displays all the links in the Google Home Page which contains Google in their name using Regular Expressions.

Line 1-2: Creates a properties collection object googleLinkDesc that contains html tag property as a representing link.
Line 3: Saves Text property value as a regular expression ".*Google.*". This means all the links that have text Google irrespective of the text before and after them.
Line 4: Sets Regular Expression property to TRUE indicating QTP to recognize property values as regular expression if it encounters any regular expression characters.
Line 5-8: Print all the names matching the property values, in this case all links having Google in their name.

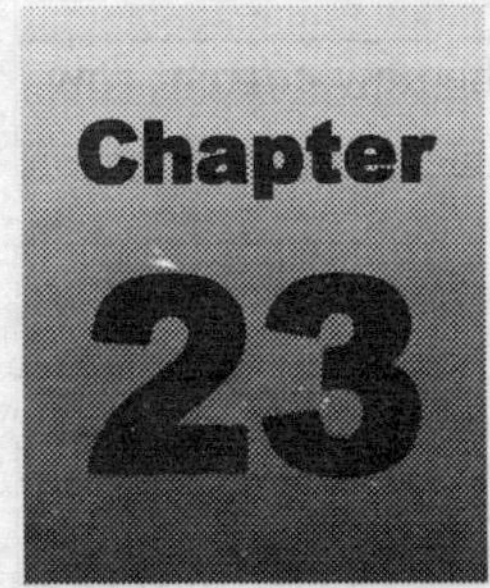

WORKING WITH DATA TABLE

To work with data present in the Data Table QTP supports 3 objects named **Datatable** Object, **DTParameter** object and **DTSheet** Object. These Objects support various methods and properties to interact with data in the data table. With the help of these objects we can add and delete sheets, also add, delete, change data in the cells.

Data table Object

Datatable Object refers to the Entire Run Time Datatable in QTP. Datatable has Sheets in it and you can perform many operations like adding sheet, deleting sheet and exporting sheet on the Datatable object. The tables below will give important methods and properties of a data table.

Method Name	Description
AddSheet	Add new Sheet To Datatable
DeleteSheet	Delete Existing Sheet from Datatable
Export	Export Entire Data Table to an external Excel File
ExportSheet	Export sheet to an external Excel File

GetCurrentRow	Get Current Active Row of Global Sheet. Usually Active Row is identified by Highlighting with black colour
GetRowCount	Get Number of Rows in Global Sheet
GetSheet	Get Any Sheet specified by name or index. Index starts from 1
GetSheetCount	Returns the number of sheets present in the excel file
Import	Imports an external excel file into the Datatable
ImportSheet	Imports a sheet from an external excel file into the Datatable
SetCurrentRow	Set particulr row as active row
SetNextRow	Sets the row after the current (active) row as the new current row in the Global Sheet
SetPrevRow	Sets the row previous to the current (active) row as the new current row in the Global Sheet

Property Name	Description
GlobalSheet	Returns Global Sheet Object
LocalSheet	Returns specified Local Sheet Object
RawValue	Retrieves the *raw value* of the cell. The *raw value* is the actual string written in a cell before the cell has been computed, such as the actual text from a formula.
Value	Retrieves or sets the value of the cell in the specified parameter and the current row of the run-time Data Table.

DTSheet Object

This is a sheet in the Run-Time Data Table. This has the following methods or properties. While reading the description remember that, description always refers to the sheet on which you are using these methods and properties.

Method Name	Description
AddParameter	Adds a Parameter(Column) to the sheet
DeleteParameter	Deletes a Parameter(Column) from the sheet
GetCurrentRow	Returns the current active row of the sheet
GetParameter	Returns the parameter object specified by name or index(1)
GetParameterCount	Returns the number of parameters in the sheet
GetRowCount	Returns the number of rows in the sheet
SetCurrentRow	Makes a particular row as active
SetNextRow	Makes the Next row to current row as active
SetPrevRow	Sets the previous row to current row as active

Property Name	Description
Name	Returns the name of the Sheet

DTParameter Object

This represents a parameter (column) of a sheet in the run-time Data Table. DTParameter object has only properties and there are no methods. Following are the properties associated with the DTParameter object. While reading the description remember that the description always refers to the parameter on which you are using these methods and properties.

Property Name	Description
Name	Returns the name of the Parameter
RawValue	Returns the text string from the active row before executing the formula in the cell.
Value	Returns the value from the current row
ValueByRow	Returns the value from the row specified by index

CSV File

CSV stands for Comma Separated Values, sometimes also called Comma Delimited. A CSV file is a specially formatted plain text file which stores excel file data or basic database-style information in a very simple format, with one record on each line, and each field within that record separated by a comma. It's important that the individual "records" within a CSV file should NOT contain commas, as this may break the simple formatting when using the file in another application.

CSV files are often used as a simple way to transfer a large volume of excel file or database information between programs, without worrying about special file types. For example, transferring a home-made address book from Excel into a database program such as Filemaker Pro could be done by exporting the file as a CSV from Excel, then importing that CSV into Filemaker.

Creating a CSV file from spreadsheet data is very simple and is as follows:

1. Open your spreadsheet document and go to the **File** pull-down menu (or the Windows/Office round button menu in Office 2007), and choose **Save As....**
2. Change the "Save as type" or "Format" field to read: "CSV (Comma delimited)".
3. Enter a name for the document and click **Save**.

4. To check the validity of your CSV file, open the new file from a plain-text reading program such as Notepad or TextEdit. Check to make sure there are no extra commas, other than between fields. Depending on what program you're going to use the CSV file, you may also need to remove any extra quotation marks or other formatting which Excel may have inserted.

Scripting Examples

Example 1: Write a program to Import an excel file to a Data table.

```
Datatable.Import ("D:\QTP\ EmpData.xls")
```

This program imports the excel file EmpData.xls into the Run Time Datatable of QTP from specified location. Import is the method used to import external excel file into QTP. After import, the first sheet of the external excel file will be saved in the Global Sheet and the rest in the Action sheets of a QTP Datatable. Note that the number of sheets imported will be equivalent to numbers of action plus one. i.e if there are 2 actions maximum 3 sheets can be imported from external excel file 3.

Example 2: Write a program to Read data from the first parameter of the Global sheet.

Data Table

C8

	EmpName	EmpPlace	EmpAge	D	E	F	G	H	I	J
1	Emp1	Banglore	28							
2	Emp2	Chennai	30							
3	Emp3	Banglore	24							
4	Emp4	Delhi	29							
5	Emp5	Mumbai	38							
6										
7										

Global / Action1

```
1 set dsGlobal=Datatable.GetSheet("Global")
2 set pmFirst=dsGlobal.GetParameter(1)
3 dsGlobal_RowCount=dsGlobal.GetRowCount()
4 print(pmFirst.Name)
5 For i=1 To dsGlobal_RowCount
6     print(pmFirst.ValueByRow(i))
7 Next
```

Line 1: Stores the Global Sheet object into the variable **dsGlobal**. Getsheet method returns the specified sheet object from the run-time DataTable.
If the return value is an object, Keyword **set** must be used to store the return value.

Line 2: Stores the first parameter object of the Global sheet into the variable **pmFirst.** Getparameter method retrieves the specified parameter from the specified sheet of the run-time Data Table.

Line 3: Stores the number of rows into variable dsGlobal_RowCount variable. Getrowcount method returns the total number of rows in the longest column of the Global sheet.

Line 4: Print the name of the first column. Property **Name** is used to retrieve the name of the parameter

Line 5-7: Loops through all the rows from 1st to last. Each Time reads and prints a value from the cell represented by the First Column and specified Row number. ***Valuebyrow(i)*** retrieves the value of the cell from the row specified by i and the first column.

Example 3: Write a program to Read data from all sheets and all parameters of excel file.

```
1   Datatable.Import("C:\QTP\DataFiles\EmpData.xls")
2   sheetCount=Datatable.GetSheetCount()
3   For sheet=1 To sheetCount
4       set currentSheetObj=Datatable.GetSheet(sheet)
5       paramCount=currentSheetObj.GetParameterCount()
6       rowCount=currentSheetObj.GetRowCount()
7       print(currentSheetObj.Name)
8       For row=1 To rowCount
9           rowData=""
10          For param=1 To paramCount
11              Set currentParamObj=currentSheetObj.GetParameter(param)
12              rowData=rowData&VbTab&currentParamObj.ValueByRow(row)
13          Next
14          print(rowData)
15      Next
16  Next
```

Line 1: Imports the specified excel file into the run time datatable.

Line 2: Returns the count of sheets in the run time datatable to a variable **sheetCount.**

Line 3: Loops through all the sheets.

Line 4: Returns one sheet object every time from the run-time data Table and assigns it to the variable **currentSheetObj.**

Line 5: Stores the total number of parameters(columns) present in the current sheet into a variable **paramCount**. **Getparametercount** method returns the total number of parameters (columns) in the specified sheet of a run-time Data Table.

Line 6: Stores the total number of rows present in the current sheet into a variable **rowCount**. **GetRowCount** method returns the total number of rows in the specified sheet of a run-time Data Table.

Line 7: Prints the current sheet name. Name property returns the name of the sheet.

Line 8: Line 6 and 7 of the program has retrieved the number of column and rows present in a sheet. **For Loop** present in this line loops through the first row to the last row since we need to read the data present in all the rows.
Line 9 : Initialize Row data to NULL.
Line 10-15: Loops through all the columns of the sheet and retrieve the parameter object of each column. **GetParameter** method of Line12 returns Parameter Object and **ValueByRow** method of Line13 retrieves the value present in the cell specified by Column and Row. For Example if row=1 and param=3 then cell represented by the 3rd column of the first row will be returned. In line 12 we are also appending values of all columns corresponding to a specific row and storing the entire row data in a variable **rowData** which is printed in Line15.

Example 4. Write a program to place data in a specific sheet in the excel file.

```
1 Function PlaceData(SheetName,ParamName,RowNumber,DataToAdd)
2     Set paramObj=Datatable.GetSheet(SheetName). GetParameter ( ParamName)
3     paramObj.ValueByRow(RowNumber)=DataToAdd
4 End Function
5 PlaceData "Action1","EmpName",5,"Demo User"
```

Line 1-5 : **PlaceData** is a function to place data in a given row and column of a specified sheet. It takes sheet name, parameter name, row number and data to be added as arguments. Line 2 gets the parameter object and Line 3 assigns the value to the cell represented by the column of **paramObj** and the row of **RowNumber.** From Line3 please observe that **DataToAdd** variable which is at the right side of the expression holds a data to be entered in the cell. ValueByRow returns value from the cell if it is Right Side of the expression as shown in previous program Line 12 and enters value to cell if it is the Left side of the expression as shown above in Line 3.

Line 5 : Calling the function PlaceData where sheetname is Action1;Column Name is EmpName;Row Number is 5 and data to be added is Demo User.

Example 5. Write a program to Read and display the entire data from CSV file
CSV - Comma Separated Values. This kind of file data can be opened with Excel File or text editor. If it opens with text editor each column is separated by comma(,).
NOTE: Use the same program that is used for reading the entire data of an Excel i.e example 3.

COM OBJECTS

What is COM?

The Component Object Model (COM) provides a standard way for applications (.exe files) or libraries (.dll files) to make their functionality available to any COM-compliant application or script. COM makes it possible for nonprogrammers to write scripts for managing Windows operating systems. Objects that make their functionality available through COM are known as COM servers. Applications or scripts that make use of that functionality are referred to as COM clients. COM servers can be implemented in one of two ways:

- **Out-of-process servers**. Out-of-process servers are typically implemented in executable files and run in a different process than the script. For example, when you start a script, an instance of Wscript.exe begins to run. Next, if you instantiate a Microsoft Word object, then you are working with two processes: Wscript.exe and the Winword.exe. Wscript.exe is a process in which the Microsoft Word object runs.
- **In-process servers**. Libraries (.dll files) are known as in-process servers because they run in the same process as the application or script that called them. For example,

when you call the FileSystemObject from within a script, no new process is created. This is because the FileSystemObject (which is found in the Scrrun.dll library) is an in-process server and thus runs in the same process as the script. In-process servers typically run faster than out-of-process servers.

Creating a New Instance of a COM Object

To create a new instance of a COM object, a script can call the WScript CreateObject method and pass it the Programmatic Identifier (ProgID) of the COM object by using the following syntax:

WScript.CreateObject("*ProgID*")

You have to know only how to create a reference to an Automation object. You do not have to worry about how to locate and load the object because the Windows operating system takes care of that for you. For example the following line of code opens Excel Application.

```
Set TestObject = CreateObject("Excel.Application")

Excel.Application is ProgID
```

Server Mode

When an object is created from an executable file, the application is started in a special mode known as Server mode or Embedded mode. This means that although the application is running and fully functional, there is no graphical user interface and nothing is visible on the screen. Server mode allows you to carry out actions without a user seeing graphical user interface of an application. Although server mode is often useful in system administration scripting, sometimes you might want a user interface (for example, if you are displaying data in Internet Explorer). If so, you will need to use the appropriate command for that COM object to make the application appear on screen. For example, the following script creates an instance of Internet Explorer and then uses the Visible command to allow the user to see the application:

```
Set IE = CreateObject("InternetExplorer.Application")

IE.Visible = True
```

Retrieving Existing Instance of a COM Object

If the COM object you want to use is already running, you can use that existing object rather than create a new instance. The WScript **GetObject** method lets you reference and use a previously instantiated object instead of creating a new one as below.

```
Set objIE = Wscript.GetObject("InternetExplorer.Application")
```

Unloading Objects from Memory

In-process servers will automatically unload themselves from memory when the calling script completes. This is because these objects run in the same process as the script; when the script process ends and is thus removed from memory, any in-process servers will also be stopped and removed from memory. For example, the following script creates an instance of the FileSystemObject and then displays a message box. As soon as you dismiss the message box, both the script and the FileSystemObject are removed from memory.

```
Set TestObject = CreateObject("Scripting.FileSystemObject")

Wscript.Echo "Click here to end the script."
```

This is not true, however, for out-of-process servers, Automation objects that run in a different process than the script itself. For example, the following script creates an instance of Microsoft Word and then displays a message box. When you dismiss the message box, the script process is unloaded from memory.

```
Set TestObject = CreateObject("Word.Application")

Wscript.Echo "Click here to end the script."
```

However, the Microsoft Word process (Winword.exe) will continue to run and remain in memory, even though it is not visible on the screen. This is because there is no inherent tie between the script process and the Word process; anything you do to the script process does not affect the Word process and vice versa. You can verify that the process is still running and verify the amount of memory it is still allocated by using Task Manager, as shown below.

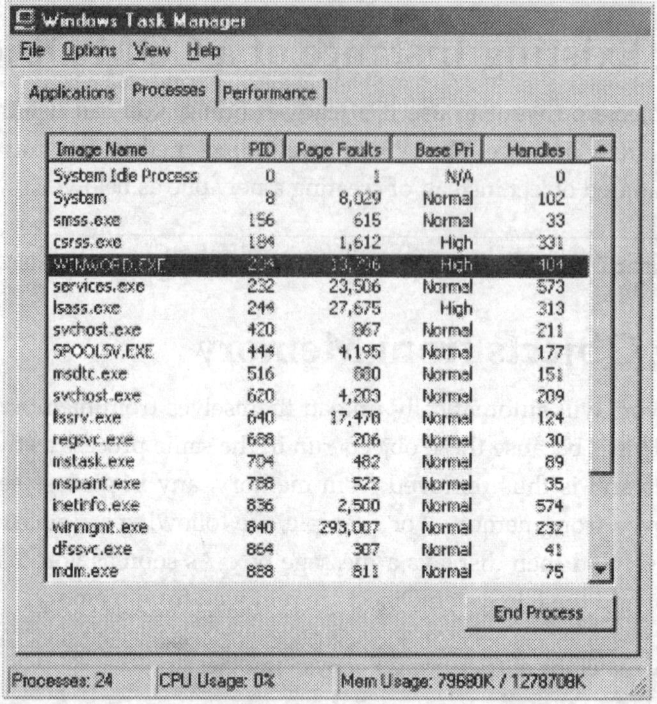

With out-of-process servers, you will typically have to use the method built into the object to explicitly unload it from memory. Microsoft Word, for example, is unloaded from memory by using the Quit method. The following script creates an instance of Microsoft Word and then immediately unloads that instance using the Quit method.

```
Set TestObject = CreateObject("Word.Application")

TestObject.Quit
```

If you run the preceding script and then check the processes running on the computer, you will not see Winword.exe (unless, of course, you had multiple copies of Winword.exe running).

Nothing Keyword

VBscript includes the Nothing keyword, which can be used to disassociate an object reference and an object. After an object variable is set to Nothing, the variable no longer maintains an object reference and thus cannot be used to control the object. For example, the following code creates an instance of Microsoft Word, sets the object variable to TestObject, and then tries to use TestObject to quit Word and unload the object from memory.

```
Set TestObject = CreateObject("Word.Application")

Set TestObject = Nothing

TestObject.Quit
```

When this script runs, the error message shown below appears. The script fails because TestObject no longer represents a valid reference.

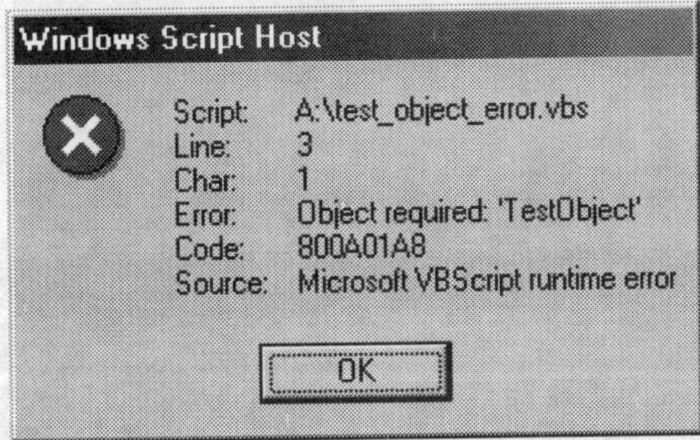

Setting an object variable to Nothing releases a small amount of memory but does not unload the object itself from memory. Because of that, there is generally no reason to set an object variable to Nothing; in effect, object variables (and all other variables, for that matter) are set to Nothing when the script completes. For example, in the following script the last line of code is superfluous: It sets the object variable TestVariable to Nothing, but that would occur anyway as soon as the script ended.

```
Set TestObject = CreateObject("Scripting.FileSystemObject")

Set TestObject = Nothing
```

WORKING WITH FILE SYSTEM

In Automation Scripts it's often important to add, move, change, create, or delete folders (directories) and files in the File System. It may also be necessary to get information about drives attached. Scripting allows you to process drives, folders, and files using the **FileSystemObject** (FSO) object model.

An Object model is a collection of classes or objects which can be controlled or studied by any program. An Object Model gives a facility to control the functionality of an application programmatically.

The FileSystemObject object model allows you to use the familiar *object.method* syntax with a rich set of properties, methods, and events to process folders and files.

The File System Object Model

The **FileSystemObject** (FSO) object model contains the following objects and collections.

Object/Collection	Description
FileSystemObject	Main object. Contains methods and properties that allow you to create, delete, gain information about, and generally manipulate drives, folders, and files.

Drive	Object. Contains methods and properties that allow you to gather information about a drive attached to the system, such as its share name and how much room is available.
Drives	Collection. The **Drives** collection includes all drives available in the system.
File	Object. Contains methods and properties that allow you to create, delete, or move a file. Also allows you to query the system for a file name, path, and various other properties.
Files	Collection. Provides a list of all files contained within a folder.
Folder	Object. Contains methods and properties that allow you to create, delete, or move folders. Also allows you to query the system for folder names, paths, and various other properties.
Folders	Collection. Provides a list of all the folders within a **Folder**.
TextStream	Object. Allows you to read and write text files.

Methods And properties of File System Object.

Method/Property	Description
BuildPath	Builds the specificed folders on to the existing path. **Example:** directory= "c:\test" Set fso = CreateObject("Scripting.FileSystemObject") fso.buildpath(directory)
CopyFile	Copies a file to a new location.
CopyFolder	Copies a folder to a new location
CreateFolder	Creates a new folder in the specified location
CreateTextFile	Creates a textfile in the specified location
DeleteFile	Deletes the specified file
DeleteFolder	Deletes the specified folder
Drives	Returns a collections of drives on which you can use the drives object properties and methods.
DriveExists	Determines whether or not the specified drive exists
FileExists	Determines whether or not the specified file exists
FolderExists	Determines whether or not the specified folder exists
GetAbsolutePathName	Returns a path name that cannot be easily determined from the specified path information. **Example:** subdirectoryname="testagain" directoryname="c:\test\" & subdirectoryname Set fso = CreateObject("Scripting.FileSystemObject") response.write fso.GetAbsolutePathName(directoryname) **Result:**

	c:\test\testagain
GetBaseName	Returns just the name of the object specified. It removes all other information including the extension. **Example:** filename="c:\test\test.html" Set fso = CreateObject("Scripting.FileSystemObject") fso.GetBaseName(filename) **Result:** test
GetDrive	Returns a drive object on which the drive methods and properties can be performed
GetDriveName	Determines the drive letter from the specified path
GetExtensionName	Determines the extension of a file or folder.
GetFile	Returns a file object on which the file methods and properties can be performed.
GetFileName	Returns the name of the specified file.
GetFolder	Returns a file object on which the file methods and properties can be performed.
GetParentFolderName	Determines the parent folder of the specified folder/file
GetSpecialFolder	Determines the input folder type. Windows folder: 0, System Folder: 1, Temporary folder: 2
MoveFile	Moves a file to a new location.
MoveFolder	Moves a folder to a new location.
OpenTextFile	Opens the specified file and returns an object on which the textstream properties and methods can be performed.

Methods And properties of Folder Object

Method/Property	Description
DateCreated	Determines the creation date of the folder.
DateLastAccessed	Determines the date the folder was last accessed by a process
DateLastModified	Determines the date the folder was last modified by a process.
Drive	Returns the drive letter on which the folder is stored.
Files	Returns the files that are stored in the selected folder
IsRootFolder	Determines whether the specified folder is the root folder.
Name	Returns the name of the folder.
ParentFolder	Determines the folder in which the folder resides
Path	Determines the full path of the folder.
Size	Determines the size of the folder in bytes

SubFolders	Returns the subfolders contained in the specified folder.
Type	Returns the folder Type. (Usually Folders are returned as type File)
Copy	Copies the selected folder object to another location.
Delete	Deletes the selected folder.
Move	Moves the selected folder.
CreateTextFile	Creates a text file in a specified folder.

Methods And properties of Files Object

Method/Property	Description
DateCreated	Determines the creation date of the file
DateLastAccessed	Determines the date the file was last accessed by a process
DateLastModified	Determines the date the file was last modified by a process.
Drive	Returns the drive letter on which the file is stored.
Name	Determines the name associated with the file.
ParentFolder	Determines the folder in which the file resides.
Path	Determines the full path of the file
Size	Determines the size of the file in bytes
Type	Returns the file type
Copy	Copies the selected file object to another location.
Delete	Deletes the selected file
Move	Moves the selected file.
OpenAsTextStream	Opens the selected file.

Methods And properties of Drive Object

Method/Property	Description
AvailableSpace	Determines the amount of free space left on the drive in bytes.
DriveLetter	Determines the drive letter associated with the drive.
DriveType	Returns the drive type Unknown: 0, Removable: 1, Fixed Drive: 2, Network: 3, CD-ROM: 4, RAM Disk: 5.
FileSystem	Returns the type of filesystem in which the drive is formatted (FAT16, FAT32, NTFS).
FreeSpace	Returns the amount of free space available on the drive.
IsReady	Determines if the information on the drive can be currently read or written. If the drive contains removeable media, the value becomes true when readable media is placed in the drive.
Path	Returns the Drive Path

	Example: filepath="c:\demo.txt" Set fso = CreateObject("Scripting.FileSystemObject") set maindrive=fso.GetDrive(filepath) response.write maindrive.Path **Result:** C:\
RootFolder	Determines the root folder of the drive.
ShareName	If the drive is shared this returns the share name.
TotalSize	Determines the total amount of bytes on the drive.

Scripting Examples

1)Write a program to read data from a text file.

```
1 Const ForReading = 1
2 Dim fso, ts
3 Set fso = CreateObject("Scripting.FileSystemObject")
4 Set ts = fso.OpenTextFile ("c:\logfile.txt", ForReading)
5 While not ts.AtEndOfStream
6         print(ts.ReadLine())
7 Wend
8 Set fso=nothing
9 Set ts =nothing
```

This program reads line by line from a text file till the end of the file and prints each line to the user.

Line 3: Creates a File System Object which is essential for any operations performed on the file system.

Line 4: Opens Text File in Read Mode and returns Text Stream object which is stored in the variable *ts*.

Line 5: Use **while loop** to Read till the End of Text Stream. ***AtEndoFStream*** property returns **FALSE** if still some data is there to read and returns **TRUE** if text stream is completed and there is no data for further reading. This means we should read if ***AtEndoFStream*** returns ***FALSE*** and stop Reading if it returns **TRUE.** To achieve this we used NOT logical operator.

Line 6: **Readline** method is used to read one line each time from the text stream.

2)Write a program to write data into a text file

```
Const ForWriting = 2
Dim fso, ts
Set fso = CreateObject ("Scripting.FileSystemObject")
Set ts = fso.OpenTextFile ("c:\testfile.txt", ForWriting,true)
For i=1 To 100
        ts.WriteLine("Hello World")
Next
```

```
8  Set fso=nothing
9  Set ts=nothing
```

This program writes string "**Hello World**" 100 times into a text file. Line 4 Opens text file in writing mode and also sets append as true. Line 6 uses **WriteLine** method to write into a text file.

3) Write a program to print all lines that contains a word "Hello"

```
1  Const ForReading = 1
2  Dim fso, ts, strLine
3  Set fso = CreateObject("Scripting.FileSystemObject")
4  Set ts = fso.OpenTextFile ("c:\logfile.txt", ForReading)
5  While not ts.AtEndOfStream
6          strLine=ts.ReadLine()
7          if Instr(1,strLine,"Hello") > 0 then
8                  print(strLine)
9          End if
10 Wend
11 Set fso=nothing
12 Set ts=nothing
```

This program reads all lines from text file and prints only those lines which have "Hello" to the user.

Line 1-4: Open File in Reading Mode.

Line 5-8: Read and Print Lines that have "**Hello**".

Line 7: Use Instr method and search string **Hello** in strLine from the first character. If found return value will be the position of the first character where string is found, else return value is 0.

4)Write a program to print the current folder name

```
1  Dim fso, fdr
2  Set fso = CreateObject("Scripting.FileSystemObject")
3  Set fdr = fso.GetFolder(".")
4  fdrname= fdr.name
5  print(fso.GetAbsolutePathname(fdrname))
6
7  Set fso=nothing
8  Set fdr=nothing
```

This program prints the name of the current folder along with its full path. **GetFolder** method in Line 3 returns Folder object. In Line 4 Name property is used on the Folder object to retrieve it's name. **GetAbsolutePathname** method in Line5 returns the complete path of the folder.

5)Write a program to print files in a given folder.

```
1  Dim fso, fdr, f1, fc
2  Set fso = CreateObject ("Scripting.FileSystemObject")
```

```
3  Set fdr = fso.GetFolder ("c:\testfolder")
4  Set fc = fdr.Files
5  For Each f1 in fc
6          Print(f1.name )
7  Next
```

This method prints all file names present in a given folder.

Line 1-3: Returns Folder object **fdr.**

Line 4: Files property returns all the files present in the folder represented by **fdr** as Files Collection object.

Line 5: Reads each time one file from files collection.

Line 6: Prints file name.

6)Write a program to print subfolders in a given folder

```
1  Set fso = CreateObject("Scripting.FileSystemObject")
2  Set fdr = fso.GetFolder("c:\testfolder")
3  Set fdrc = fdr.SubFolders
4  For Each fd in fdrc
5    Print( fd.name )
6  Next
```

This program prints name of all folders present in a given folder.

Line 1-2: Store Folder object in a variable **fdr.**

Line 3: SubFolders method returns Folder Collection object that stores all the folders present in a folder.

Line 4: Store one folder object in **fd** at a time from folder collection **fdrc.**

Line 5: Name property prints folder name.

7) Write a program to print all drives in the file system

```
1  Dim fso, d, dc
2  Set fso = CreateObject("Scripting.FileSystemObject")
3  Set dc = fso.Drives
4  For Each d in dc
5      print(d.DriveLetter)
6  Next
```

This program prints the name of all drives present in the computer. Line3 uses Drives property to retrieve the collection of all drives present in the computer. Line 4-7 read all drives from drives collection and print the letter used for the drive. **DriveLetter** is a method used to retrieve the letter of the drive like **C, D, E.**

8) Write a program to print current drive name.

```
1  Dim fso, d, s
2  Set fso = CreateObject("Scripting.FileSystemObject")
3  pathName= fso.GetAbsolutePathName(".")
4  drvName=fso.GetDriveName(pathName)
5  Set d = fso.GetDrive(drvName)
6  Msgbox(d.driveletter)
```

This program displays the drive from which the current script is executing.

Line 1-3: Get the absolute path string of the current folder from which the script is executing.
Line 4: Retrieve the name of the Drive from absolute path string.
Line 5: Get the driver object based on Drive Name using **GetDrive** method.
Line 6: Print the Letter of the Drive like **C,D,E** from which the current script is executing.

9)Write a program to print the free space in a given drive

```
1 Dim fso, d, s
2 drvPath="c:\"
3 Set fso = CreateObject("Scripting.FileSystemObject")
4 Set d = fso.GetDrive(fso.GetDriveName(drvPath))
5 s = "Drive " & d. driveletter & vbTab
6 s = s & "Free Space: " & FormatNumber(d.FreeSpace/1024, 0)
7 s = s & " Kbytes"
8 Msgbox(s)
```

Line 2: The Name of the drive for which Free Space Should be printed.
Line 4: Gets Drive Object. GetDriveName gives name of Drive and GetDrive returns Drive object.
Line 6: FreeSpace method prints the number of bytes of Free Space in the Drive. Dividing by1024 prints Space in Kilo Bytes(KB). Format Number formats a given expression as a number. In this line since second parameter is 0 the number of digits after the decimal is zero.

Output:

10) Write a program to display all subfolders in a given folder tree.

```
Function prntfolders(fdrPath)
Dim fso, fd
  Set fso = CreateObject("Scripting.FileSystemObject")
  Set fd=fso.GetFolder(fdrPath)
  Set fc = fd.subfolders
  For each fdr in fc
        print (fdrPath &"\"&fdr.name)
        prntfolders(fdrPath &"\"&fdr.name)
  Next
End Function

prntfolders("D:\QTPCompleteRefrence")
```

This program prints all the folders present in a folder tree of a given folder using recursive programming technique. **Prntfolders** is a function which will print all the folders present in a given folder by calling itself if it finds subfolders.

Line 1-4: Get the Folder Object of a given path.

Line 5: Get Folders Collection object **fc** from **subfolders** method.

Line 6-9: For each sub folder in **fc** prints subfolder name and make a recursive call to same function with sub folder path to verify for any sub folders with in a sub folder. This chain continues until there are no sub folders in the tree.

Output:

```
QuickTest Print Log
File
D:\QTPCompleteRefrence\Chapter18
D:\QTPCompleteRefrence\Chapter20
D:\QTPCompleteRefrence\Chapter24
D:\QTPCompleteRefrence\Chapter30
D:\QTPCompleteRefrence\Chapter30\Exmp4_Create Excel Work book
D:\QTPCompleteRefrence\Chapter30\Exmp4_Create Excel Work book\Action0
D:\QTPCompleteRefrence\Chapter30\Exmp4_Create Excel Work book\Action0\SnapShots
D:\QTPCompleteRefrence\Chapter30\Exmp4_Create Excel Work book\Action1
D:\QTPCompleteRefrence\Chapter30\Exmp4_Create Excel Work book\Action1\SnapShots
D:\QTPCompleteRefrence\Chapter30\Exmpl3_Search_for_a_Value
D:\QTPCompleteRefrence\Chapter30\Exmpl3_Search_for_a_Value\Action0
D:\QTPCompleteRefrence\Chapter30\Exmpl3_Search_for_a_Value\Action0\SnapShots
D:\QTPCompleteRefrence\Chapter30\Exmpl3_Search_for_a_Value\Action1
D:\QTPCompleteRefrence\Chapter30\Exmpl3_Search_for_a_Value\Action1\SnapShots
```

11)Write a program to remove all empty files in the folder.

```
1   Function rmvEmptyFolders(fdrPath)
2   Dim fso
3     Set fso = CreateObject("Scripting.FileSystemObject")
4     Set fd=fso.GetFolder(fdrPath)
5     Set fc = fd.subfolders
6         For each fdr in fc
7             pathName=fdrPath&"\"&fdr.name
8             flc= fdr.files
9                 For each fl in flc
10                    If fl.size = 0 Then
11                        fso.DeleteFile(pathName&"\"&fl.name)
12                    End If
13                Next
14        rmvEmptyFolders(pathName)
15            Next
16    End Function
17  rmvEmptyFolders("D:\QTPCompleteReference")
```

This program deletes all the files of zero size in a given folder tree. This program will go through all the folders in a given folder tree using recursive programming as explained in the previous example. Line8 returns Files Collection object that stores all files present in a folder specified by folder object **fdr**. Line 9-13 goes through each file and deletes the files of size 0. Line10 uses size property to check whether files size is 0 and Line 11 uses DeleteFile method to delete the file.

12) Write a program to display all folders created on a specific date.

```
1  Function findfolders(fdrPath,dateOfCreation)
2    Set fso = CreateObject("Scripting.FileSystemObject")
3    Set fd=fso.GetFolder(fdrPath)
4    Set fc = fd.subfolders
5        For each fdr in fc
6            pathName=fdrPath&"\"&fdr.name
             fdrCreationDate=FormatDateTime(fdr.DateCreated,2)
7              daysDiff=DateDiff("d",dateOfCreation,fdrCreationDate)
8              If daysDiff=0 Then
9                      print(fdr.name & vbTab &fdrCreationDate)
10             End If
11
12           findfolders(pathName,dateOfCreation)
13       Next
14 End Function
15
16 findfolders " D:\QTPCompleteReference","4/23/2006"
17
```

This program prints all the folders created on a specified date in a given folder tree. This program will go through all the folders in a given folder tree using recursive programming as explained in previous examples. Line7 uses **FormatDateTime** method that formats the folder creation date returned by **DateCreated** method of folder object. Line 8 finds the number of days difference between File Creation Date and the Date of creation we are searching for. If the dates are the same then the difference in dates are 0. Line 10 will print those folders created on the date mentioned in the search criteria.

13) Write a program to Copy contents of one folder to other folder

```
FileSystemObject.CopyFolder "c:\folder1\*", "c:\folder2\"
```

Copy Folder Method copies contents of folder1 to folder2.

14) Write a program to check whether a given path represents a file or a folder.

```
On Error Resume Next
Err.Clear
Dim fso, fc,fl
pathName="c:\siva\personal\testfile.txt"
 Set fso = CreateObject("Scripting.FileSystemObject")
Err.clear
Set fc = fso.GetFolder(pathName)
If Err.Number <>0 Then
        Err.clear
```

```
10          Set fl = fso.GetFile(pathName)
11          If Err.Number <>0 Then
12                  Msgbox("Given string does NOT represent a file or a Folder")
13          Else
14                  Msgbox("Given string represents a file")
15          End if
16  Else
17          Msgbox("Given string represents a folder")
18  End If
```

This program checks whether a given path represents a File or Folder.

Line 7: Assume the path is a folder and try to get the Folder object. If it is not a folder then the system throws an error and Err.Number will be set to the number represented by the error.

Line 8: Check the error number. If it is zero go to line 17 and print path as a folder. Otherwise Check whether the path is a file.

Line 10: Assume path as a file and try to get the File object. If it is not a file then the system throws an error and **Err.Number** will be set to the number represented by the error.

Line 11: Check the error number. If it is zero go to line 14 and print path as a file. Otherwise print path is neither a file nor folder.

15) Write a program to rename a folder.

```
1  Dim fso, fdr
2  Set fso = CreateObject("Scripting.FileSystemObject")
3  Set fdr = fso.GetFolder("C:\folderA")
4  fdr.Name="folderB"
```

This program renames **folderA** as **folderB**. Line 3 gets **folderA** object and Line 4 uses Name property to rename it to **folder.**

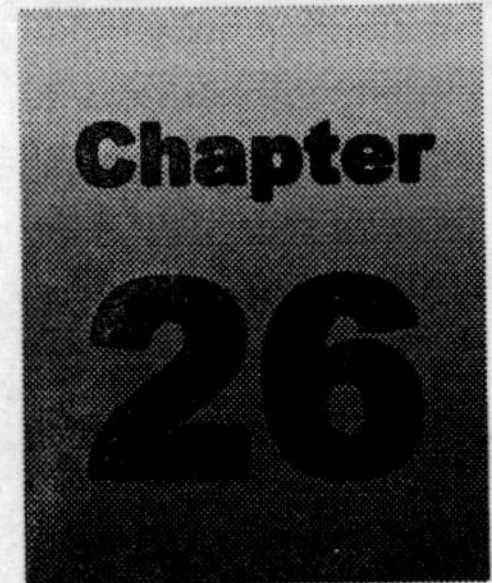

WORKING WITH DATABASE

ADO Object Model

ADO, a data-access technology from Microsoft, offers a less strict data object model than its ancestors, DAO and RDO--which gives the programmer a great deal more flexibility and reduces development time. The Diagram below shows all the objects and collections of ADO object model.

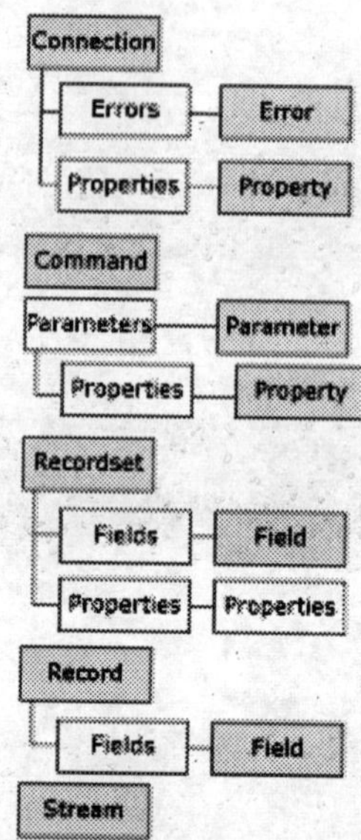

Source: http://msdn.microsoft.com/en-us/library/ ms675944(VS.85).aspx

ADO Objects

Connection	The Connection is actually the hub of ADO, because it provides the methods that allow us to connect to a data store.
Command	The Command object is designed to run SQL statements (assuming the provider supports the Command object), especially those that require parameters. This is an important point, because the use of stored queries and procedures is a great way to improve speed and segment your application.
Recordset	The Recordset object is probably the most frequently used object in ADO; consequently, it has more properties and methods than other objects.
Record	A **Record** object represents one row of data, and has some conceptual similarities with a one-row **Recordset**.
Stream	This represents a stream of binary data or text. In tree-structured hierarchies such as a file system or an e-mail system, a Record may have a default binary stream of bits associated with it that contains the contents of the file or the e-mail. A **Stream** object can be used to manipulate fields or records containing these streams of data.
Field	Each **Field** object corresponds to a column in the Recordset. You use the Value property of **Field** objects to set or return data for the current record.
Error	Any operation involving ADO objects can generate one or more provider errors. As each error occurs, one or more **Error** objects are placed in the **Errors** collection of the **Connection** object. When another ADO operation generates an error, the **Errors** collection is cleared, and the new set of **Error** objects is placed in the **Errors** collection.

ADO Collections

Collection	Description
Errors	Contains all the **Error** objects created in response to a single provider-related failure.
Fields	Contains all the **Field** objects of a **Recordset** object.
Parameters	Contains all the **Parameter** objects of a **Command** object.
Properties	Contains all the **Property** objects for a specific instance of an object.

Recordset Object

The Recordset object is probably the most frequently used object in ADO; consequently, it has more properties and methods than other objects.

Recordset Object Collections, Properties and Methods are

- **Fields Collection:** Contains all the Field objects of a Recordset or Record object. Each **Field** object corresponds to a column in the **Recordset**.
- **RecordCount Property:** Indicates the number of records in a Recordset object. Returns a **Long** value that indicates the number of records in the Recordset.
- **Find Method:** Searches a Recordset for the row that satisfies the specified criteria.
- **Move Method:** Moves the position of the control in a Recordset object.
- **MoveFirst, MoveLast, MoveNext, and MovePrevious Methods:** Moves control to the first, last, next, or previous record in a specified Recordset object and makes that record the current record.

Field Object

Each **Field** object corresponds to a column in the Recordset.. With the collections, methods, and properties of a **Field** object, you can do the following:

- Return the name of a field with the Name property.
- View or change the data in the field with the **Value** property. **Value** is the default property of the **Field** object.
- Return the basic characteristics of a field with the Type, Precision, and NumericScale properties.
- Return the declared size of a field with the DefinedSize property.
- Return the actual size of the data in a given field with the ActualSize property.

Error Object

You can read an **Error** object's properties to obtain specific details about each error, including the following:

- The **Description** property, which contains the text of the error. This is the default property.
- The **Number** property, Indicates the number that uniquely identifies an **Error** object

Example 1: Connecting to the database using DSN

```
1  dim dbConnection
2      on error Resume next
3      ' Opening connection
4      set dbConnection = CreateObject("ADODB.Connection")
5      If Err.Number <> 0 then
6          Msgbox("Error # " & CStr(Err.Number) & " " & Err.Description )
7          Err.clear
8          ExitTest
9  End If
10     dbConnection.Open "DSN=QT_Flight32"
11 If Err.Number <> 0 then
12         Msgbox("Error # " & CStr(Err.Number) & " " & Err.Description )
13         Err.clear
14         ExitTest
15     End If
16 dbConnection.Close
```

This Program Creates Data Base Connection object and Open Connection to Flight Data Base

Line 2: **on error Resume next** ensure that if there is an error in any line program continues to the next line.

Line 4: Create **ADODB.Connection** object.

Line 5 : Check Any Error. If there is an error **Err.Number,** value will be set to a value other than zero.

Line 6: Print Error Number using **Err.Number** and Description of Error using **Err.Description.**

Line 7: Clear Error Number, so that the next Error can be saved.

Line 8: Exit the Test if there is an Error in Creating the Connection object.

Line 10: Use open method of Connection objects and connects to Flight Data Base. DSN is Data Source Name which contains the details like data base driver to be used and name of the Database.

Line 11-15: Check for error in case of opening the connection

Line 16: Close Connection with Data Base.

Example 2: Connecting to SQL Server database from QTP.

```
1  dim dbConnection
2      on error Resume next
3      ' Opening connection
4      set dbConnection = CreateObject("ADODB.Connection")
5        If Err.Number <> 0 then
6          Msgbox("Error # " & CStr(Err.Number) & " " & Err.Description )
7          Err.clear
8          ExitTest
9      End If
10     dbConnection.Open "Driver={SQL Server}; Server=myServerAddress;
   Database=myDataBase; Uid=myUsername; Pwd=myPassword;"
    If Err.Number <> 0 then
11         Msgbox("Error # " & CStr(Err.Number) & " " & Err.Description )
12         Err.clear
13         ExitTest
14     End If
15 dbConnection.Close
16
```

This example works in a similar way to the previous example. The only difference is in Line10 we have used the corresponding driver to connect to SQL Server Data base. In this program **SQL Server** driver is used to connect with SQL Server Data base. Server represent SQL server name and Database represents the name of the database to connect.

Example 3: Connecting to Oracle database from QTP.

```
dim dbConnection
    on error Resume next
    ' Opening connection
    set dbConnection = CreateObject("ADODB.Connection")
    If Err.Number <> 0 then
      Msgbox("Error # " & CStr(Err.Number) & " " & Err.Description)
        Err.clear
        ExitTest
    End If
 dbConnection.Open "provider: MSDAORA.1; Data Source=myORADB;  uid:scott;
pwd:tiger; "
    If Err.Number <> 0 then
      Msgbox("Error # " & CStr(Err.Number) & " " & Err.Description)
        Err.clear
        ExitTest
    End If
dbConnection.Close
Set dbConnection=Nothing
```

This example works in a similar way to the previous example. The only difference is in Line10 we have used MSDAORA is a provider to connect to Oracle Data base.

Note that for connecting to Oracle database you need to have the TNS Setup located in your tnsnames.ora. The file can be found at "<Oracle Client Installation folder> \network\admin". Use the TNSname as the Datasource in your connection string.

A typical tnsnames.ora content will be like

```
myTNSName=
(DESCRIPTION =
  (ADDRESS_LIST =
    (ADDRESS = (PROTOCOL = TCP)(HOST = <YourServerNameOrIP>) (PORT =
<YourPortOrDefault1521>)))
(CONNECT_DATA = (SID = <YourDBSID>) (SERVER = DEDICATED))
)
```

Example 4: Retrieving all the records of a Recordset.

```
dim dbConnection
    on error Resume next
    set dbConnection = CreateObject("ADODB.Connection")
    If Err.Number <> 0 then
        Msgbox("Error # " & CStr(Err.Number) & " " & Err.Description )
        Err.clear
        ExitTest
    End If
    dbConnection.Open("DSN=QT_Flight32")
    If Err.Number <> 0 then
        Msgbox("Error # " & CStr(Err.Number) & " " & Err.Description )
        Err.clear
        ExitTest
    End If
        sqlQuery="SELECT * FROM ORDERS"
        set rs=dbConnection.Execute(sqlQuery)
        If Err.Number <> 0 then
        Msgbox("Error # " & CStr(Err.Number) & " " & Err.Description )
        Err.clear
        ExitTest
    End If
'Column Names
        colCount=rs.Fields.Count
                colHeader=""
                For col=0 To colCount-1
                        colHeader=colHeader&vbtab&rs.Fields(col).Name
```

```
27                  Next
28                  print colHeader
29
30  rs.MoveFirst
31      Do while not rs.EOF
32                  rowData=""
33                  For col=0 To colCount-1
34                    rowData=rowData&vbtab&rs.Fields(col).Value
35                  Next
36
37                print(rowData)
38                rs.MoveNext
39      Loop
40  rs.Close
41  dbConnection.Close
42  Set rs=Nothing
43  Set dbConnection=Nothing
```

Line 1-14: Connect to Flight Database.

Line 15-21: Execute SQL Query SELECT * FROM ORDERS using execute method of the Connection Object. Execute method executes any SQL query given as input parameter. Executed query will return RecordSet as output which is stored in **rs**

Line 23: Find the number of columns using **Fields.Count**

Line 25-27: Retrieve all the column names and assign it to variable **colHeader.**

Line 28: Print all the column names.

Line 30: Place the cursor on the first record.

Line 31: Go from the First Record until the End of Record set.

Line 33-36: Go from First Column To Last Column, Read and Print the Data. **rs.Fields(col)**.Value will give the value of the column in the active row. Loop will go through all the columns and append the values in the cells represented by each column in the current active row.

Line 37-38: Print **RowData** and Move Recordset to the Next Row.

Line 40-43: Close Active Connections.

Example 5: Running Stored procedure from QTP

```
sDatabaseName="dbServer"
sUID="scott"
sPWD="tiger"
nameOfStoredProcedure="SpecialUserInfo"
Set objCommand = CreateObject("ADODB.Command")
objCommand.ActiveConnection = "DRIVER={Microsoft ODBC for Oracle};"
&"SERVER=" & sDatabaseName &";User ID=" & sUID &";Password=" & sPWD &" ;"
objCommand.CommandType = 4
objCommand.CommandText = nameOfStoredProcedure
objCommand.Parameters.Refresh
```

```
10 objCommand.Parameters(0).Value = "paramvalue1"
11 objCommand.Parameters(1).Value = "paramvalue2"
12 objCommand.Execute()
13 Set objCommand = Nothing
```

This program demonstrates how to run stored procedure from QTP.

Line 4: Stores the name of the stored procedure to execute.

Line 5: Creates Command object.

Line 6: Connects to Databases.

Line 7: Command Type 4 means user is going to execute stored procedure. Note: Please Refer Command object explained at the starting of this chapter for more information on command types.

Line 8: Set the name of stored procedure with Command object.

Line 10-11: Parameters to the stored procedure.

Line 12: Executes stored procedure.

Chapter

27

WORKING WITH XML

XML or Extensible Markup Language, is a markup language that you can use to create your own tags. It was created by the World Wide Web Consortium (W3C) to overcome the limitations of HTML, the Hypertext Markup Language that is the basis for all Web pages. XML is not a replacement for HTML and they were designed with different goals. HTML was designed to display data and to focus on how data looks and XML was designed to describe data and to focus on what data is. HTML is about displaying information, XML is about describing information.

A sample XML document

```
<address>
  <name>
    <title>Mrs.</title>
    <first-name>
      Mary
    </first-name>
    <last-name>
      McGoon
    </last-name>
  </name>
  <street>
    1401 Main Street
  </street>
  <city>Any town</city>
  <state>NC</state>
  <postal-code>
    34829
  </postal-code>
</address>
```

Tags, elements and attributes

There are three common terms used to describe parts of an XML document: *tags*, *elements*, and *attributes*.

- A tag is the text between the left angle bracket (<) and the right angle bracket (>). There are starting tags (such as <name>) and ending tags (such as </name>).
- An element is the starting tag, the ending tag, and everything in between. In the sample above, the <name> element contains three child elements: <title>, <first-name>, and <last-name>.
- An attribute is a name-value pair inside the starting tag of an element. In this example, state is an attribute of the <city> element; in earlier examples, <state> was an element.

The root element

An XML document must be contained in a single element. That single element is called the **root element**, which contains all the text and any other elements in the document. In the following example, the XML document is contained in a single element, the <greeting> element. Notice that the document has a comment that's outside the root element; that's perfectly legal.

```
<?xml version="1.0"?>
<!-- A well-formed document -->
<greeting>
 Hello, World!
</greeting>
```

Here's a document that doesn't contain a single root element:

```
<?xml version="1.0"?>
<!-- An invalid document -->
<greeting>
 Hello, World!
</greeting>
<greeting>
 How are you!
</greeting>
```

An XML parser rejects this document, regardless of the information it might contain.

XML elements are case sensitive

In HTML, <h1> and <H1> are the same; in XML, they're not. If you try to end an <h1> element with a </H1> tag, you'll get an error. In the example below, the heading at the top is illegal, while the one at the bottom is fine.

```
<!-- NOT legal XML markup -->
<h1>Elements are
 case sensitive</H1>

<!-- legal XML markup -->
<h1>Elements are
 case sensitive</h1>
```

Attributes must have quoted values

There are two rules for attributes in XML documents:

- Attributes must have values
- Those values must be enclosed within quotation marks

Invalid, valid and well-formed documents

There are three kinds of XML documents:

- **Invalid documents** don't follow the syntax rules defined by the XML specification. If a developer has defined rules for what the document can contain in a DTD or schema, and the document doesn't follow those rules, that document is invalid as well.

- **Valid documents** follow both the XML syntax rules and the rules defined in their DTD or schema.
- **Well-formed documents** follow the XML syntax rules but don't have a DTD or schema.

How XML is used

XML is used in many aspects of web development as follows.

Data Sharing

In the real world, computer systems and databases contain data in incompatible formats. XML data is stored in plain text format. This provides a software- and hardware-independent way of storing data. This makes it much easier to create data that different applications can share.

Data Separation

If you need to display dynamic data in your HTML document, it will take a lot of work to edit the HTML each time the data changes. With XML, data can be stored in separate XML files. This way you can concentrate on using HTML for layout and display, and be sure that changes in the underlying data will not require any changes to the HTML. With a few lines of JavaScript, you can read an external XML file and update the data content of your HTML.

Data Transport

With XML, data can easily be exchanged between incompatible systems. One of the most time-consuming challenges for developers is to exchange data between incompatible systems over the Internet. Exchanging data as XML greatly reduces this complexity, since the data can be read by different incompatible applications.

Enhanced Data Availability

Since XML is independent of hardware, software and application, XML can make your data more available and useful. With XML, your data can be available to all kinds of "reading machines" (Handheld computers, voice machines, news feeds, etc), and make it more available for blind people, or people with other disabilities.

Creating New Internet Languages

A lot of new Internet languages are created with XML.

- XHTML the latest version of HTML
- WSDL for describing available web services
- WAP and WML as markup languages for handheld devices
- RSS languages for news feeds
- RDF and OWL for describing resources and ontology
- SMIL for describing multimedia for the web

Database Development

Databases are a natural use for XML, because XML is all about data. Unlike XML for documentation, XML for databases does not need to be inherently human readable. The data is simply written in such a way to allow machines to read it and make it accessible to a database.

Defining Document Content

To define the elements we are going to use to represent data in XML file, we have two ways.

1. **Document Type Definition** or **DTD:** A DTD defines the elements that can appear in an XML document, the order in which they can appear, how they can be nested inside each other, and other basic details of XML document structure. DTDs are part of the original XML specification and are very similar to SGML DTDs.
2. **XML Schema:** A schema can define all of the document structures that you can put in a DTD and it can also define data types and more complicated rules than a DTD can. The W3C developed the XML Schema specification a couple of years after the original XML spec.

Following is a simple XML document called **"address.xml"**

```
<?xml version="1.0"?>
<address>
  < name>Shiva</name>
  <street>4th Cross, 3rd Main</ street >
  <city>Bangalore</ city >
  < postal-code >560054 </postal-code >
</ address >
```

A DTD File

The following example is a DTD file called "**address.dtd**" that defines the elements of the XML document above ("address.xml"):

```
<!-- address.dtd -->
<!ELEMENT address (name, street, city, postal-code)>
<!ELEMENT name (#PCDATA)>
<!ELEMENT street (#PCDATA)>
<!ELEMENT city (#PCDATA)>
<!ELEMENT postal-code (#PCDATA)>
```

This DTD defines all of the elements used in the sample document. It defines three basic things:

- An <address> element contains a <name>, a <street>, a <city>, and a <postal-code>. All of those elements must appear, and they must appear in that order.
- All elements contain text. (#PCDATA stands for parsed character data; you can't include another element in these elements.)

Although the DTD is pretty simple, it makes it clear what combinations of elements are legal. An address document that has a <postal-code> element before the < city> element isn't legal.

The above XML DTD ("**address.dtd** ") can have a reference in XML document as below.

```
<?xml version="1.0"?>
<!DOCTYPE address SYSTEM
"http:// www.QTPCompleteReference.com/ dtd/ address.dtd">
<address>
 < name>Shiva</name>
 <street>4th Cross, 3rd Main</ street >
 <city>Bangalore</ city >
 < postal-code >560054 </postal-code >
</ address >
```

An XML Schema

The following example is an XML Schema file called "**address.xsd**" that defines the elements of the XML document above ("address.xml"):

```
<?xml version="1.0"?>
<xs:schema xmlns:xs="http://www.w3.org/2001/XMLSchema"
targetNamespace="http://www.QTPCompleteReference.com"
xmlns="http://www.QTPCompleteReference.com""
elementFormDefault="qualified">

<xs:element name="address">
  <xs:complexType>
    <xs:sequence>
      <xs:element name="name" type="xs:string"/>
      <xs:element name="street" type="xs:string"/>
      <xs:element name="city" type="xs:string"/>
      <xs:element name="postal-code" type="xs:string"/>
    </xs:sequence>
  </xs:complexType>
</xs:element>
</xs:schema>
```

The name element is a **complex type** because it contains other elements. The other elements (name, street, city, postal-code) are **simple types** because they do not contain other elements.

This above XML schema ("**address.xsd** ") can have a reference in XML document as below.

```
<?xml version="1.0"?>

<address
xmlns=" http://www.QTPCompleteReference.com"
xmlns:xsi="http://www.w3.org/2001/XMLSchema-instance"
xsi:schemaLocation=" http://www.QTPCompleteReference.com address.xsd">

< name>shiva</name>
  <street>4th Cross, 3rd Main</ street >
  <city>Bangalore</ city >
  < postal-code >560054 </postal-code >
</ address >
```

Important XML Objects in QTP

XMLUtil	This object is used to Load XML File
XMLData	An object representing an XML block
XMLElement	An object representing an XML element
XMLAttribute	An object representing an XML element attribute

Scripting Examples

1) Loading an XML File

```
SetXMLDta=XMLUtil.CreateXMLFromFile("D:\QTP\jdk.xml")
```

Address D:\QTPCompleteRefrence\Chapter25\jdk.xml

```
<?xml version="1.0" encoding="UTF-8" ?>
- <project name="jdk" basedir=".">
  - <target name="-jdk-preinit">
    - <condition property=".exe" value=".exe">
        <os family="windows" />
      </condition>
      <property name=".exe" value="" />
      <property name="nbjdk.javac" value="${nbjdk.home}/bin/javac${.exe}" />
      <property name="nbjdk.java" value="${nbjdk.home}/bin/java${.exe}" />
      <property name="nbjdk.javadoc" value="${nbjdk.home}/bin/javadoc${.exe}" />
      <property name="nbjdk.appletviewer" value="${nbjdk.home}/bin/appletviewer${.exe}" />
      <property name="nbjdk.bootclasspath" value="${nbjdk.home}/jre/lib/rt.jar" />
    </target>
  - <target name="-jdk-presetdef-basic" depends="-jdk-preinit" unless="nbjdk.presetdef.basic.done">
    - <macrodef name="javac-presetdef">
        <attribute name="javacval" />
      - <sequential>
        - <presetdef name="javac">
            <javac fork="yes" executable="@{javacval}" />
          </presetdef>
        </sequential>
      </macrodef>
      <javac-presetdef javacval="${nbjdk.javac}" />
    - <macrodef name="java-presetdef">
        <attribute name="javaval" />
```

CreateXMLFromFile is a method in **XMLUtil** object which takes xml file name as input and returns **XMLData** as the object. **XMLData** represents the entire XML file content which is the basis to work further on elements and attributes of an XML. In the XML file shown above, project is the root element having the attributes **jdk** and **basedir**.

2) Reading name of the root node

```
1 Set XMLDta = XMLUtil.CreateXMLFromFile("D:\QTP\jdk.xml")
2 set XMLRootElmnt=XMLDta.GetRootElement()
3 RootElmntName=XMLRootElmnt.ElementName
4 Msgbox(RootElmntName)
```

This program prints the name of the root element in the XML file. Line 1 Loads XML File and returns XMLData objects which represents the entire data of an XML File.

GetRootElement method in Line 2 returns Root Element object. **ElementName** property of a Root Element returns the name of the Root Element.

3) Enumerate attributes of root node

```
1 Set XMLDta = XMLUtil.CreateXMLFromFile("D:\QTP\jdk.xml")
2 set XMLRootElmnt=XMLDta.GetRootElement
3 set attrCol=XMLRootElmnt.Attributes
4 For i=1 To attrCol.count
5     Set attr=attrCol.Item(i)
6     print(attr.name&"="&attr.value)
7 Next
```

Line 1: Creates XMLData object.
Line 2: Returns the RootElement.
Line 3: Attributes property will return all the attributes of attributes collection object.
Line 4: Loop through first Attribute to Last Attribute.
Line 5: Item method returns the attribute at a specified position from attributes collection.
Line 6: Name property prints attribute name and Value property prints value of the attribute as shown below.

Output:

```
QuickTest Print Log
File
name=jdk
basedir=.
```

4) Enumerate child elements of a root node

```
1 Set XMLDta = XMLUtil.CreateXMLFromFile("D:\QTP\jdk.xml")
2 set XMLRootElmnt=XMLDta.GetRootElement
3 set childCol=XMLRootElmnt.ChildElements()
4 For i=1 To childCol.count
5         Set chldElemnt=childCol.Item(i)
6         print(chldElemnt.ElementName)
7 Next
```

Line 1: Creates XMLData object.
Line 2: Returns RootElement.
Line 3: **ChildElements** method returns all the child elements collection of a Root Element object.
Line 4: Loop through first Element to Last Element of an Elements Collection.
Line 5: **Item** method returns the Element at a specified position from Element collection.
Line 6: Name property prints Element name.

5) **Compare two XML files**

```
1 Set XMLDta1 = XMLUtil.CreateXMLFromFile("D:\QTP\jdk1.xml")
2 Set XMLDta2 = XMLUtil.CreateXMLFromFile("D:\QTP\jdk2.xml")
3
4 res=XMLDta1.Compare(XMLDta2,diffResult)
5 If res  eqv True  Then
6         Msgbox ("TwoXML files are Same")
7 Else
8         Msgbox("Two XML files are different")
9 End If
```

Line 1-2 loads two XML files to be compared.
Line 4: Use Compare method to compare two XML files and returns TRUE if they are same, else FALSE.
Line 5-9: Displays result to the user whether files are same or not.

Compare Method:

Compares the specified XML Data object with the current XMLData object and creates a new XMLData object containing the differences. This method returns a Boolean value indicating whether or not the two files are equal.

Syntax

XMLData.**Compare(***XMLDocument*, *ResultXMLDocument [, Filter]***)**

Argument	Type	Description
XMLDocument	XMLData	The XML document objects that you want to compare to this XMLData object.
ResultXMLDocument	XMLData	An XMLData object containing the differences between the XMLData object and the XML document specified in the XMLDocument argument, according to the specified Filter argument (if any).
Filter	Number or pre-defined constant	**Optional.** The XML DOM node information to be compared: **0** or **micXMLNone**: Compares the elements and document type declaration of the specified XML documents. **1** or **micXMLAttributes:** Compares the attributes of the

		specified XML documents, in addition to their elements and document type declaration. **2** or **micXMLCDataSections**: Compares the CDATA sections of the specified XML documents, in addition to their elements and document type declaration. **4** or **micXMLValues**: Compares the #text nodes of the specified XML documents, in addition to their elements and document type declaration. **Note:** If you do not use this parameter, the Document Type Declaration, Elements, Attributes, #text nodes, and CDATA sections are all compared. You can specify more than one filter, separated by a plus (+) symbol. For example, micXMLValues+micXMLAttributes.

	specified XML documents, in addition to their elements and document type declaration. 2 or micXMLCDataSections: Compares the CDATA sections of the specified XML documents, in addition to their elements and document type declaration. 4 or micXMLValues: Compares the #text nodes of the specified XML documents, in addition to their elements and document type declaration. Note: If you do not use this parameter, the Document Type Declaration, Elements, Attributes, #text nodes, and CDATA sections are all compared. You can specify more than one filter, separated by a plus (+) symbol. For example, micXMLValues+micXMLAttributes.	

UTILITY OBJECTS

Reporter Object

After running the test scripts you have seen many times the output in the test result file. You might have also observed that the result file has a status of steps indicating pass or fail, for example, checkpoint Pass or Fail. This kind of status reporting to results file can also be achieved by using **Reporter Object.** Sending information to test results is a very common requirement since we want to see the status of test execution like pass or fail in the test results file. With the help of Reporter object you can:

- Report the status of step execution like pass, fail, warning to test results file.
- Retrieve the folder path in which the current test's results are stored.
- Retrieve the run status at the current point of the run session.
- Enable or Disable reporting of step(s) in the Test Results.

ReporterEvent

ReporterEvent Method is the only method associated with Reporter Object. This is used most commonly whenever we want to report the results status to the test results file.

Syntax:

Reporter.ReportEvent EventStatus, ReportStepName, Details

Argument	Type	Description
EventStatus	Number or pre-defined constant	Status of the Test Results step: **0** or **micPass:** Causes the status of this step to be passed and sends the specified message to the Test Results window. **1** or **micFail:** Causes the status of this step to be failed and sends the specified message to the Test Results window. When this step runs, the test fails. **2** or **micDone:** Sends a message to the Test Results window without affecting the pass/fail status of the test. **3** or **micWarning:** Sends a warning message to the Test Results window, but does not cause the test to stop running, and does not affect the pass/fail status of the test.
ReportStepName	String	Name of the step displayed in the Test Results window.
Details	String	Description of the Test Results event. The string will be displayed in the step details frame in the Test Results window.
ImageFilePath	String	**Optional**. Path and filename of the image to be displayed in the **Results Details** tab of the Test Results window. Images in the following formats can be displayed: BMP, PNG, JPEG, and GIF.

Example:

Action1

```
1: Reporter.ReportEvent micPass, "Demo Step", "The user-defined step Passed."
2: Reporter.ReportEvent micFail, " Demo Step ", "The user-defined step failed."
3: Reporter.ReportEvent micDone, " Demo Step ", "The user-defined step failed."
4: Reporter.ReportEvent micWarning, " Demo Step ", "The user-defined step has a Warning."
```

In the above example we are printing all the status messages using Report Event method. The results file output is as follows:

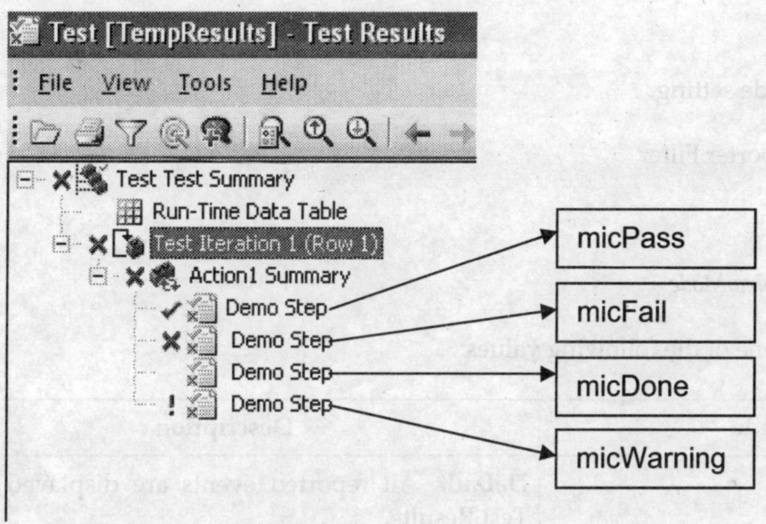

Output put of Line1 with Status **Pass** (micPass) in Test Results file is as follows:

Object	Details	Result	Time
Demo Step	The user-defined step Passed.	Passed	5/22/2010 - 2:39:58

Output put of Line2 with Status **Fail** (micFail) in Test Results file is as follows:

Object	Details	Result	Time
Demo Step	The user-defined step failed.	Failed	5/22/2010 - 2:39:58

Output put of Line3 with Status **Done** (micDone) in Test Results file is as follows:

Object	Details	Result	Time
Demo Step	The user-defined step failed.	Done	5/22/2010 - 2:39:58

Output put of Line4 with Status **Warning** (micWarning) in Test Results file is as follows:

Object	Details	Result	Time
Demo Step	The user-defined step has a Warning.	Warning	5/22/2010 - 2:39:58

Filter property

There can be situations where we don't want the full status to display in the test report. You can use this property to completely disable or enable reporting of steps to be included in the report.

Syntax

To retrieve the mode setting:

CurrentMode = Reporter.Filter

To set the mode:

Reporter.Filter = *NewMode*

The mode can be one of the following values:

Mode	Description
0 or **rfEnableAll**	**Default.** All reported events are displayed in the Test Results.
1 or **rfEnableErrorsAndWarnings**	Only event with a warning or fail status are displayed in the Test Results.
2 or **rfEnableErrorsOnly**	Only events with a fail status are displayed in the Test Results.
3 or **rfDisableAll**	No events are displayed in the Test Results.

Example:

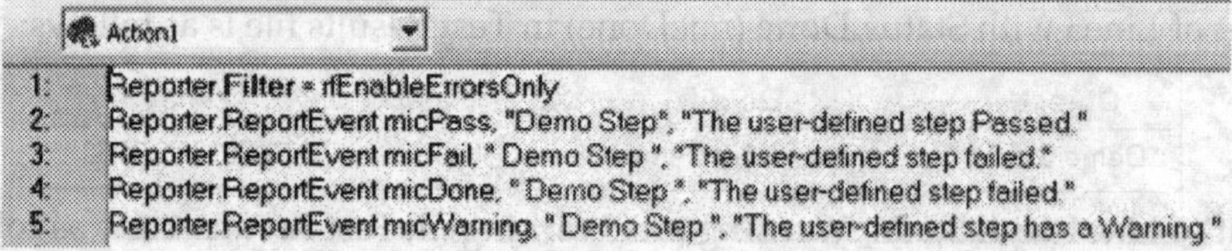

In the above program in line 1 we have set the filter as **rfEnableErrorsOnly.** This means display only errors in the Test Results file. Below is the Test Results file created by running the above program.

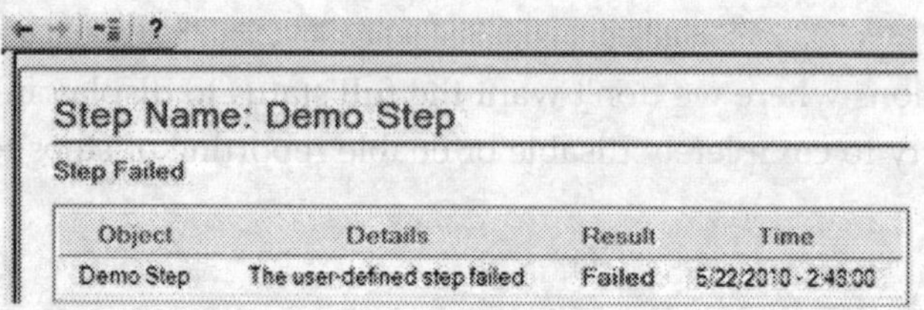

Observe that only Error step is displayed in the results file and other steps like Pass, Warning and Done are filtered.

ReportPath Property

Retrieves the folder path in which the current test's results are stored. Note: Do not use this property to attempt to set the results folder path.

Syntax

*Path = **Reporter.ReportPath***

Argument	Type	Description
Path	String	The folder path in which the current test's results are stored.

Example

The following example uses the ReportPath property to retrieve the folder in which the results are stored and displays the folder in a message box.

```
dim Path
Path = Reporter.ReportPath
MsgBox (Path)
```

RunStatus Property

Retrieves the run status at the current point of the run session.

Syntax

Reporter.RunStatus

For Example below line

If Reporter.RunStatus = micFail Then ExitAction

uses the RunStatus property to retrieve the status of the run session at a specific point and exit the action if the test status is fail.

Crypt Object

This object is used to encrypt strings. It has method Encrypt, which Encrypts a given string.

Example:

```
E_Passwd=Crypt.Encrypt("Passwd")
```

Environment Object

Enables you to work with environment variables. You can set or retrieve the value of environment variables using the Environment object. You can retrieve the value of any environment variable but you can set the value of only user-defined, environment variables.

To set the value of a user-defined, environment variable:

Environment (*VariableName*) = *NewValue*

Or

Environment.Value(*VariableName*) = *NewValue*

Example: Author is the user defined environment variable and we can assign new value for it as shown below.

```
Environment ("Author")="Siva"
        Or
Environment.Value("Author")="Siva"
```

To retrieve the value of a loaded environment variable:

CurrValue = Environment (*VariableName*)

Or

CurrValue =Environment.Value(*VariableName*)

Example: Below code retrieves built-in environment variable OS from the system.

```
OperSys=Environment("OS")
Msgbox(OperSys)
```

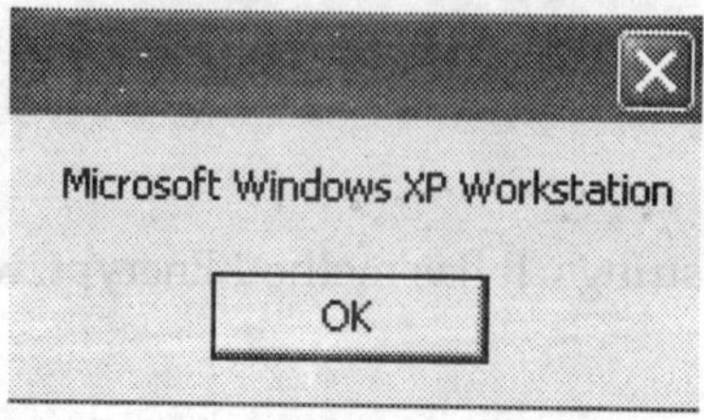

Loading External Environment File

The following example uses the **ExternalFileName** property to check whether an environment variable file is loaded, and if not, loads a specific file and then displays one of the values from the file.

```
1 envFileName = Environment.ExternalFileName
2 If (envFileName = "") Then
3     Environment.LoadFromFile("D:\QTP\Environment.xml")
4 End If
5 msgbox Environment("Author")
```

Line1: **ExternalFileName** property returns File name of the loaded environmental file.
Line 2: Checks whether the environment file loaded if not Loads external environment file using **LoadFromFile** method.

Path Finder

You can use a **PathFinder.Locate** statement in your test to retrieve the full path that QuickTest uses for a specified relative path. The full path is retrieved based on the folders specified in the **Tools>Options>Folders** tab.

QTP AUTOMATION OBJECT MODEL (AOM)

What is Quick Test AOM?

An Object model is a collection of classes or objects which can be controlled or studied by any program. An Object Model gives a facility to control the functionality of an application programmatically.

The Quick Test Automation Object Model is a set of its classes and interfaces, together with their properties, methods and events, and their relationships. All configuration and run functionality provided via the QuickTest interface is in some way represented in its Object Model.

Using Quick Test AOM the functionalities of QTP can be controlled from any other applications/programs by using a scripting or programming language.

When to use Quick Test Automation Programs?

Automation Programs are especially useful for:

Initialization scripts: - These scripts automatically start QuickTest and configure the options and the settings required for testing a specific environment.

Updating values: - This includes updating the tests with the proper add-ins, runs it in update run mode against an updated application, and saves it.

Applying new options to existing tests: - When a test needs to be updated with a new version of QuickTest, and if that newer version offers a new option that needs to be updated in all existing scripts.

Calling QuickTest from other applications: - Sometimes a simple web/windows application may be required to schedule the test runs. This is useful for non technical people.

Some more situations where QuickTest Automation Programs are required:

- To configure multiple tests with same settings
- To configure QTP for different environments/machines
- For passing test parameter values from one test to another
- To define environment variables
- When there are Preconditions to execute before actual test execution
- To configure the test object identification properties

Choosing Language and Development environment

The QuickTest automation scripts can be written in any language and development environment that supports automation. For ex: VBScript, JavaScript, Visual Basic, Visual C++, or Visual Studio .NET

But choosing a development environment that supports referencing a **type library** will provide some more features like Microsoft IntelliSense, automatic statement completion, and status bar help tips while writing script.

A **type library** is a binary file containing the description of the objects, interfaces, and other definitions of an object model. The QuickTest automation object model supplies a type library file named **QTObjectModel.dll**. This file is stored in **<QuickTest installation folder>\bin**.

When developing the automation scripts in such environments, be sure to reference the **QuickTest type library** before writing or running automation script. For example, for Microsoft Visual Basic, select **Project > References** to open the References dialog box for the project. Then select **QuickTest Professional <Version> Object Library** (where **<Version>** is the current installed version of the QuickTest automation type library).

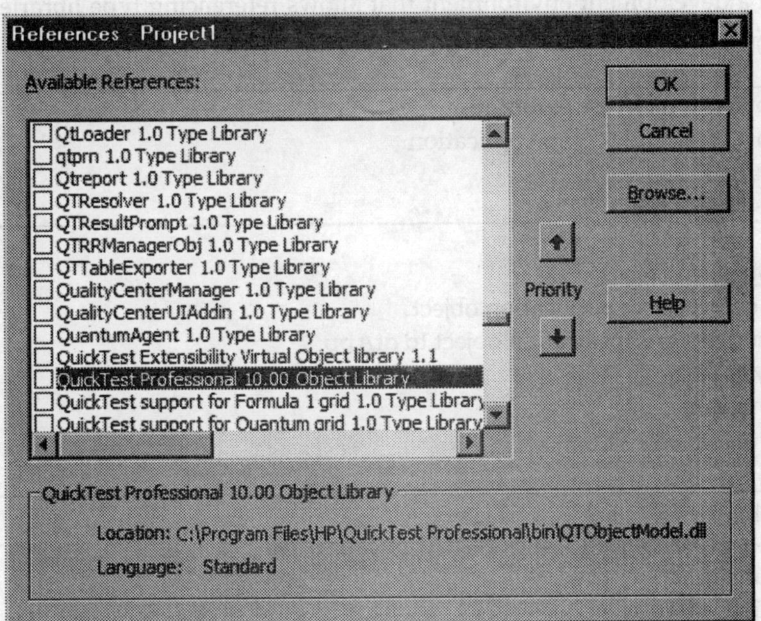

Creating and Launching the Quick Test Application Object

The Application object is a root object which is useful to return other elements of QuickTest such as the **Test** object (which represents a test document), **Options** object (which represents the Options dialog box), or **Addins** collection (which represents a set of add-ins from the Add-in Manager dialog box), and to perform operations like loading add-ins, starting QuickTest, opening and saving tests, and closing QuickTest.

Every automation script begins with the creation of the QuickTest Application object. Creating this object does not start QuickTest. It simply provides an object from which you can access all other objects, methods and properties of the QuickTest automation object model.

Only one instance of the **Application** object can be created. Recreation of QuickTest **Application** object is not required even if QuickTest starts and exits for several times during your script.

Below are some examples for creating the QuickTest **Application** object and starting QuickTest in visible mode, using different programming languages.

Visual Basic

The example below can be used only after setting a reference to the type library. If you are not working in a development environment that allows referencing type libraries, create the Application object as described for VBScript below.

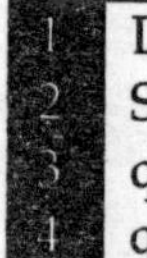

```
1 Dim qtApp As QuickTest.Application
2 Set qtApp = New QuickTest.Application
3 qtApp.Launch
4 qtApp.Visible = True
```

<u>Code Walkthrough</u>

Line 1: Declare qtApp as an application object

Line 2: Create and assign Application object to qtApp

Line 3: Start QuickTest

Line 4: Make it visible

VBScript

```
1 Dim qtApp
2 Set qtApp = CreateObject("QuickTest.Application")
3 qtApp.Launch
4 qtApp.Visible = True
```

<u>Code Walkthrough</u>

Line 1: Declare qtApp

Line 2: Create and assign Application object to qtApp

Line 3: Start QuickTest

Line 4: Make it visible

JavaScript

```
1 var qtApp = new ActiveXObject("QuickTest.Application")
2 qtApp.Launch
3 qtApp.Visible = True
```

<u>Code Walkthrough</u>

Line 1: Declare, Create and assign Application object to qtApp

Line 2: Start QuickTest

Line 3: Make it visible

Visual C++

```
1 #import "QTObjectModel.dll"
2 QuickTest::_ApplicationPtr spApp;
3 spApp.CreateInstance("QuickTest.Application");
4 spApp->Launch();
5 spApp->Visible = VARIANT_TRUE;
```

Code Walkthrough

Line 1: Import the type library

Line 2: Declare the application pointer and assign to spApp

Line 3: Create Application object to spApp

Line 4: Start QuickTest

Line 5: Make it visible

Generating Automation Scripts

The Quick Test Professional provides an easy option to generate automation scripts for few settings.

1. Test Settings dialog box
2. Options dialog box
3. Object Identification dialog box

These dialog boxes contain a **Generate Script** button which generates an automation script file (**.vbs**) by just clicking on it. This file contains the current settings from the corresponding dialog box.

A sample code looks like this

```
Dim App 'As Application
Set App = CreateObject("QuickTest.Application")
App.Launch
App.Visible = True
App.Options.DisableVORecognition = False
App.Options.AutoGenerateWith = False
App.Options.WithGenerationLevel = 2
App.Options.TimeToActivateWinAfterPoint = 500
...
...
App.Options.WindowsApps.NonUniqueListItemRecordMode="ByName"
App.Options.WindowsApps.RecordOwnerDrawnButtonAs="PushButtons"
App.Folders.RemoveAll
```

Scripting Examples

1. Changing the Synchronization Timeout of a Test

```
1 Dim qtApp
2 Set qtApp = CreateObject("QuickTest.Application")
3 qtApp.Launch
4 qtApp.Visible = True
5 qtApp.Open "C:\DemoTest", True
6 qtApp.Test.Settings.Run.ObjectSyncTimeOut = 25000
7 qtApp.Test.Save
8 qtApp.Quit
9 Set qtApp = Nothing
```

This program will open a test and change the synchronization timeout. This is equivalent to changing the synchronization time manually by going to File → Settings →Run → Object Synchronization Timeout.

Code Walkthrough

Line 1 : Declare Variable
Line 2 : Create and assign application object
Line 3 : Start QuickTest
Line 4 : Make it visible
Line 5 : Open an Existing Test
Line 6 : Change the synchronization timeout value
Line 7 : Save the Test
Line 8 : Exit from QTP
Line 9 : Release Application Object

2. Enumerating the Libraries used by the script

```
Dim qtApp
 Set qtApp = CreateObject("QuickTest.Application")
qtApp.Launch
qtApp.Visible = True
qtApp.Open "C:\DemoTest", True
Set qtLibraries = qtApp.Test.Settings.Resources.Libraries
For qtLibraryIndex=1 to qtLibraries.Count
      print qtLibraries.Item(qtLibraryIndex)
Next
qtApp.Quit
Set qtApp = Nothing
```

Code Walkthrough

Line 1 : Declare Variable
Line 2 : Create and assign application object
Line 3 : Start QuickTest
Line 4 : Make it visible
Line 5 : Open an Existing Test
Line 6 : Get the Libraries Collection
Line 7-9 : Get the Associated Library files for a test
Line 10 : Exit from QTP
Line 11 : Release Application Object

3. Execute a Test with a specified Result Folder

```
1  Dim qtApp
2  Set qtApp = CreateObject("QuickTest.Application")
3  qtApp.Launch
4  qtApp.Visible = True
5  qtApp.Open "C:\Tests\Test1", True
6  Set qtResultsOpt = CreateObject("QuickTest.RunResultsOptions")
7  qtResultsOpt.ResultsLocation = "C:\Tests\Test1\Res1"
8   qtTest.Run qtResultsOpt
9  MsgBox qtTest.LastRunResults.Status
10. qtApp.Quit
11 Set qtResultsOpt = Nothing
12 Set qtApp = Nothing
```

Code Walkthrough

Line 1 : Declare Variable
Line 2 : Create and assign application object
Line 3 : Start QuickTest
Line 4 : Make it visible
Line 5 : Open an Existing Test
Line 6 : Get the Result Options Object
Line 7 : Specify test results location
Line 8 : Run the test with the specified result location
Line 9 : Check the results of the test run
Line 10 : Exit from QTP
Line 11 : Release result options Object
Line 12 : Release Application Object

Chapter 30

HTML DOM

What is DOM?

The Document Object Model (DOM) is an Application Programming Interface (API) developed by the World Wide Web Consortium (W3C) to create and modify HTML pages and XML documents. It defines the logical structure of documents in the way a document is accessed and manipulated.

With the Document Object Model, programmers can create and build documents, navigate their structure, and add, modify, or delete elements and content. Anything found in an HTML or XML document can be accessed, changed, deleted, or added using the Document Object Model. The Document Object Model can be used with any programming or scripting languages.

HTML DOM: - A Standard object model for HTML documents.
XML DOM: - A Standard object model for XML documents.

When can we use DOM?

An object in a HTML document will have lot of properties and supported methods. But QTP captures only limited properties that are useful to find the object. All native methods and properties of an html object cannot be captured or performed directly by QTP.

DOM is especially useful for identifying:
1. Event handlers
2. Parent Nodes
3. Previous and Next Elements
4. Ready State
5. Source Index

These properties will not be captured by QTP and so DOM is the only alternative.

In html, web tables are the complex objects which will have more internal objects and configurations. The table captions, background images, background colors, column names, rows and tags may not be captured some times by using QTP. In this situation the DOM is useful to work with every object in web table with a specific hierarchy.

When we cannot use DOM?

Not for Browser Compatibility Testing

In QTP, DOM methods and properties can work only for Internet Explorer. So if the application needs to be tested in different browsers then the DOM should not be used in the scripts because it may affect the result.

Not for FireEvents

QTP performs DOM operations on application in offline mode i.e. when performing DOM operations QTP will not activate the browser. In this case fire events will not work properly.

Not for Edit box, Combo box Validations

The edit and combo boxes accept any value which is coming from DOM methods, even if the objects are disabled or restricted to use specific characters.

HTML DOM Objects

A HTML document is made up of Frames, Tables, Links, Buttons, and Input Data Fields…etc. But when it comes to DOM, every object is a node in a HTML document. The relations between the nodes are Parent, Children, Previous sibling and next sibling. The table below describes the structure of a node tree:

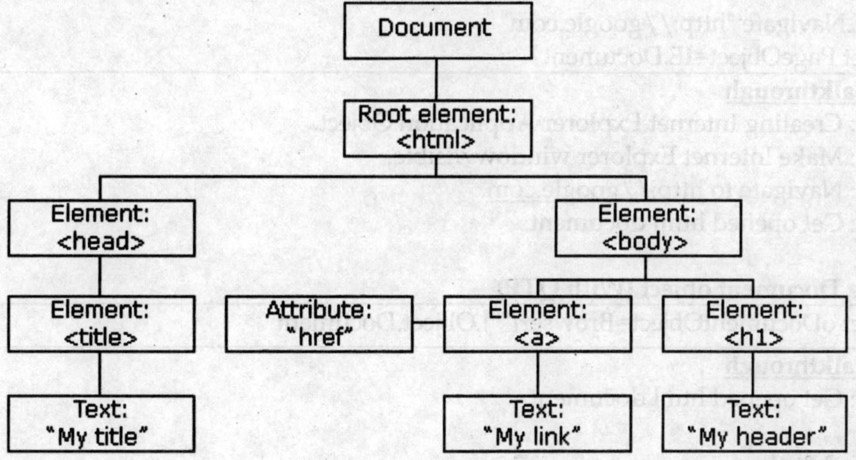

Source: w3schools

- A node tree has one root node.
- A node can have only one parent node except root node.
- A node can have any number of child nodes.
- A node which does not have any children is called as Leaf.
- Nodes which have the same parent are called as siblings.

Accessing DOM Methods and Properties

In QTP for every web object there is a property called "**object**". Using this property the internal methods and properties can be accessed for any web object.

Syntax:
WebObjectClass("").Object

Parameters
WebObjectClass: - Any test object class related to web
Object: - A property to access internal methods and properties of a web object

The Document Object

The document object refers to the HTML Document. This will provide an access to all objects inside the document.

Creating Document object for IE (Without QTP)

```
1 Set IE=CreateObject("internetexplorer.application")
2 IE.Visible=True
3 IE.Navigate "http://google.com"
4 Set PageObject=IE.Document
```

Code Walkthrough

Line 1 : Creating Internet Explorer Application Object.
Line 2 : Make Internet Explorer window visible.
Line 3 : Navigate to http://google.com.
Line 4 : Get opened html document.

Creating Document object (With QTP)

```
1 Set oDocumentObject=Browser("").Object.Document
```

Code Walkthrough

Line 1 : Get opened html document.

HTML Node

Every object is a node in a HTML document. The entire document is a document node. A node can be an element or text or attribute in the element. Elements are element nodes, text and attributes for the elements are text nodes and attribute nodes.

HTML Element0

An element is a node in html document which has a *start tag (open tag)* and *end tag (closed tag)*. Everything in between the start and end tags are called as element content. An element with no content can be closed in the start tag. Elements can have attributes to provide additional information for the element.

A Sample HTML Document Code

```
<HTML>
  <title>Sample Document</title>
  <BODY>
    <h1> A Sample HTML </h1>
      <a href="www.hp.com" >HP</a>
  </BODY>
</HTML>
```

In the above HTML document:

- "HTML"," title", "BODY", "h1" and "a" are the element nodes.
- "Sample Document","A Sample HTML" and "HP" are the text nodes.
- href="www.hp.com" is an attribute for the element "a".

Accessing HTML element using DOM

```
1 Dim oDocument
2 Dim oLnkObjectList
3 Dim oObjectIndex
4 Set oDocument=Browser("Sample Document").Object.Document
5 Set oLnkObjectList=oDocument.getElementsByTagName("a")
6 For oObjectIndex=0 to oLnkObjectList.length-1
7     msgbox oLnkObjectList.item(oObjectIndex).outerText
8 Next
```

The above code displays all the available elements with the tag "a".

Code Walkthrough

Line 1-3: Declare Variables.

Line 4 : Get document object using ".object" property.

Line 5 : Get "a" tag elements from the document.

Line 6 : Start for loop from index 0 to length of the elements.

Line 7 : Display the outer text of the element.

Line 8 : Iterate the for loop till end of elements length.

Reading HTML Element attributes

```
Dim oDocument
Dim oLnkObjectList
Dim oObjectIndex
Dim oElementObject
Dim oAttributeLength
Dim oAttributeIndex
Dim oAttributeName
Dim oAttributeValue
Set oDocument=Browser("Sample Document").Object.Document
Set oLnkObjectList=oDocument.getElementsByTagName("a")
For oObjectIndex=0 to oLnkObjectList.length-1
  Set oElementObject=oLnkObjectList.item(oObjectIndex)
  print "Element Name :- " & oElementObject.outerText
  oAttributeLength=oElementObject.attributes.length
  For oAttributeIndex=0 to oAttributeLength-1
    Set oAttribute=oElementObject.attributes.item(oAttributeIndex)
    print "Attribute Name:-" & oAttribute.name
    print "Attribute Value:-" & oAttribute.value
  Next
Next
```

The above code displays all the available elements with the tag "a" and prints all available attribute names and values.

Code Walkthrough

Line 1-8 : Declare Variables.
Line 9 : Get document object using ".object" property.
Line 10 : Get "a" tag elements from the document.
Line 11 : Start for loop from index 0 to length of the elements.
Line 12 : Get the element object.
Line 13 : Print the outer text of the element.
Line 14 : Get the attribute length for the element.
Line 15 : Start for loop from index 0 to length of the attributes.
Line 16 : Get the attribute object.
Line 17 : Print name of the attribute.
Line 18 : Print value of the attribute.
Line 19 : Iterate the for loop till end of attributes length.
Line 20 : Iterate the for loop till end of elements length.

Scripting Examples for DOM

The picture below is a sample registration form which has object types of Edit, Link, Checkbox, Listbox, Button and Radio buttons.

Registration Form Sample

First Name
Middle Name
Last Name
Gender ○ Male ○ Female
Country Select One
Interests Movies ☐ Games ☐
☐ Accept Terms and Conditions
Submit

Form details:

The title of the form is **"Sample Document"**.
Almost every object in the document has attributes type, Id and Name
Type: - Type of the object
Id: - Unique Id for the object
Name: - Name of the Object

All the objects in the document are placed in a table. The table can be identified using the attribute Id. Below is the HTML Code for the above document.

```
<HTML>
<title>Sample Document</title>
<BODY>
<h2 align="center">Registration Form Sample</h2>
  table align="center" cellpadding="2" cellspacing=10 id="UserDetails" >
  <tr> <td><label>First Name</label></td>
    <td><input name="FirstName" type="text" id="FirstName" size="15"></td> </tr>
  <tr><td><label>Middle Name</label></td>
    <td><input name="MiddleName" type="text" id="MiddleName" size="15"></td> </tr>
  <tr> <td><label>Last Name</label></td>
        <td><input name="LastName" type="text" id="LastName" size="15"></td> </tr>
  <tr> <td><label>Gender</label></td>
    <td><input type="radio" name="Gender" id="Male" value="Male">Male</button> <input
name="Gender" type="radio" id="Female" value="Female">Female</button></td> </tr>
  <tr> <td><label>Country</label></td>
  <td ><select id="Country" name="Country">
  <option value="Select One" >Select One</option>
  <option value="India">India</option>
  <option value="United States">United States</option>
  <option value="Others">Others</option> </td> </tr>
  <tr > <td ><label>Interests</label></td>
  <td> Movies<input name="Movies" type="checkbox" id="Movies" value="1">
  Games<input name="Games" type="checkbox" id="Games" value="1"> </td>
  </tr>
 <tr>  <td  colspan="2" align="center">
    <input type="checkbox" name="t&c" id="t&c" >
    <a href="www.hp.com"> Accept Terms and Conditions</a>
    </input>
    </td> </tr>
  <tr><td colspan="2" align="center"><button type="button" name="btn1" >Submit</button></td>
</tr>  </table>
</BODY> </HTML>
```

HTML Code for the Document

Ex1: Print Specific type of object names from the Registration Form.

```
Function GetObjectsByType(oTagName)
  Dim oDocObj
  Dim oTagObjectsList
  Dim oTagObject
 Set oDocObj=Browser("SampleDocument").Object.Document
 Set oTagObjectsList= oDocObj.getElementsByTagName(oTagName)
 For each oTagObject in oTagObjectsList
```

```
8        print oTagObject.Name
9      Next
10     Set oDocObj =Nothing
11     Set oTagObjectsList =Nothing
12    Set oTagObject = Nothing
13   End Function
14
15   GetObjectsByType("input")
```

Description: The above code prints the names of the objects with tag "input".

Parameters:

oTagName: A HTML Tag name. Every element in the html document will have a tag name. Ex: <Input> tag is for Edit, radio, button and checkboxes.

Code Walkthrough

Line 1 : A Function **GetObjectsByType** which prints names of the objects of a specific type.
Line 2,3,4 : Declare Variables.
Line 5 : Get document object.
Line 6 : Get elements based on the provided Tag value.
Line 7 : Initiate a for loop to get objects from the Tag objects list.
Line 8 : Print name of the object.
Line 9 : Iterate the for loop.
Line 10,11,12 : Release the variables.
Line 13 : Function End.
Line 14,15 : Calling Function.

Ex 2: Get all elements from the Registration Form

```
Function GetAllObjects()
   Dim oDocObj
   Dim oAllObjects
   Set oDocObj =  Browser("SampleDocument").Object.Document
   Set oAllObjects= oDocObj.all
   For each oObject in oAllObjects
      print oObject.tagName
   Next
  Set oDocObj =Nothing
  Set oAllObjects=Nothing
End Function

GetAllObjects()
```

Description:

The above code prints the tag names of the all elements available in the document.

Code Walkthrough

Line 1	: Started a Function GetAllObjects.
Line 2,3	: Declare Variables.
Line 4	: Get document object.
Line 5	: Get all elements from the document.
Line 6	: Initiate a for loop to get objects from the all objects list.
Line 7	: Print the tag name of the object.
Line 8	: Iterate the for loop.
Line 9,10	: Release the variables.
Line 11	: Function End.
Line 12,13	: Calling Function.

Ex 3: Get Specific object from Registration Form using the Attribute Id

```
1  Function GetObjectById(oObjectId)
2  Dim oDocObj
3  Dim oObject
4  Set oDocObj = Browser("Sample Document").Object.Document
5  Set oObject= oDocObj.getElementById(oObjectId)
6  print oObject.Name
7  Set GetObjectById=oObject
8  Set oDocObj =Nothing
9  End Function
10
11 Set oFirstName=GetObjectById("FirstName")
12 oFirstName.value="hi"
```

Description:

The above code returns the object from HTML document based on HTML id of the object.

Parameters:

oObjectId : HTML Id attribute of an object.

> *Note:*
> There is no rule that every element should have an id. But an object which has a unique id can be easily handled by a script or CSS style sheets.

Code Walkthrough

Line 1	: Started a Function GetObjectById.
Line 2,3	: Declare Variables.
Line 4	: Get document object.
Line 5	: Get elements based on the provided Tag value.
Line 6	: Print name of the object.
Line 7	: Store the object in function.
Line 8	: Release the variables.
Line 9	: Function End.

Line 10,11 : Calling Function and store object in variable.
Line 12 : Enter text in to the object.

Ex 4: Select All Checkboxes in a Document

```
1  Function SelectCheckBox(oCheckBoxName)
2    Dim oDocObj
3    Dim oInputTagObjectsList
4    Dim oInputTagObject
5    Set oDocObj= Browser("Sample Document").Object.Document
6    Set oInputTagObjectsList= oDocObj.getElementsByTagName("input")
7    For each oInputTagObject in oInputTagObjectsList
8      If oInputTagObject.type="checkbox" and oInputTagObject.name= oCheckBoxName then
9        oInputTagObject.checked=true
10       Exit for
11     End If
12 Next
13 Set oDocObj =Nothing
14 Set oInputTagObjectsList=Nothing
15 Set oInputTagObject = Nothing
16 End Function
17
18 SelectCheckBox("movies")
```

Description:

The above code switches on the checkbox.

Parameters:

oCheckBoxName: Name attribute of a checkbox.

Code Walkthrough

Line 1 : Start a Function SelectCheckBox.
Line 2,3,4 : Declare Variables.
Line 5 : Get document object.
Line 6 : Get input tag elements.
Line 7 : Initiate a for loop to get object by object from the objects list.
Line 8 : Verify type and name of the object.
Line 9 : select the checkbox if the type and name matched.
Line 10,11 : Exit for, End If.
Line 12 : Iterate the for loop.
Line 13,14,15 : Release the variables.
Line 16 : Function End.
Line 17,18 : Calling Function.

Ex 5: Enter Text in the Edit box

```
1  Function SetTextInEditBox(oEditBoxName,oValueToSet)
2  Dim oDocObj
3  Dim oInputTagObjectsList
4  Dim oInputTagObject
5  Set oDocObj = Browser("Sample Document").Object.Document
6  Set oInputTagObjectsList= oDocObj.getElementsByTagName("input")
7  For each oInputTagObject in oInputTagObjectsList
8    If oInputTagObject.type="text" and oInputTagObject.name= oEditBoxName then
9        oInputTagObject.Value= oValueToSet
10       Exit for
11   End If
12 Next
13 Set oDocObj =Nothing
14 Set oInputTagObjectsList=Nothing
15 Set oInputTagObject = Nothing
16 End Function
17
18 SetTextInEditBox "FirstName","QTP"
```

Description:

The above code enters the text in the Edit box.

Parameters:

oEditBoxName	:	Name attribute of an Edit box.
oValueToSet	:	Value to be entered in Edit box.

<u>Code Walkthrough</u>

Line 1	: Start a Function SetTextInEditBox.
Line 2,3,4	: Declare Variables.
Line 5	: Get document object.
Line 6	: Get input tag elements.
Line 7	: Initiate a for loop to get object by object from the objects list.
Line 8	: Verify type and name of the object.
Line 9	: Set the value of edit if the type and name matches.
Line 10,11	: Exit for, End If.
Line 12	: Iterate the for loop.
Line 13,14,15	: Release the variables.
Line 16	: Function End.
Line 17,18	: Calling Function.

Ex 6: Select Radio Button

```
1  Function SelectRadioButton(oRadioButtonValue)
2  Dim oDocObj
3  Dim oInputTagObjectsList
4  Dim oInputTagObject
5  Set oDocObj = Browser("Sample Document").Object.Document
6  Set oInputTagObjectsList= oDocObj.getElementsByTagName("input")
7  For each oInputTagObject in oInputTagObjectsList
8    If oInputTagObject.type="radio" and oInputTagObject.Value= oRadioButtonValue then
9       oInputTagObject.checked=true
10      Exit for
11   End If
12 Next
13 Set oDocObj =Nothing
14 Set oInputTagObjectsList=Nothing
15 Set oInputTagObject = Nothing
16 End Function
17
18 SelectRadioButton ("Female")
```

Description:

The above code selects the radio button.

Parameters:

oRadioButtonValue: Value attribute of a Radio Button.

Code Walkthrough

Line 1 : Starta Function SelectRadioButton.
Line 2,3,4 : Declare Variables.
Line 5 : Get document object.
Line 6 : Get input tag elements.
Line 7 : Initiate a for loop to get object by object from the objects list.
Line 8 : Verify type and name of the object.
Line 9 : select the Radio button if the type and name matches.
Line 10,11 : Exit for, End If.
Line 12 : Iterate the for loop.
Line 13,14,15: Release the variables.
Line 16 : Function End.
Line 17,18 : Calling Function.

Ex 7: Select List Value

```
1  Function SelectListValue(oListName,oValueToSelect)
2  Dim oDocObj
3  Dim oSelectTagObjectsList
4  Dim oSelectTagObject
5  Set oDocObj = Browser("Sample Document").Object.Document
6  Set oSelectTagObjectsList= oDocObj.getElementsByTagName("select")
7  For each oSelectTagObject in oSelectTagObjectsList
8   If oSelectTagObject.Name= oListName then
9     oSelectTagObject.Value=oValueToSelect
10    Exit for
11  End If
12 Next
13 Set oDocObj =Nothing
14 Set oSelectTagObjectsList=Nothing
15 Set oSelectTagObject = Nothing
16 End Function
17
18 SelectListValue "Country","Others"
```

Description:

The above code selects the list box item based on its value.

Parameters:

oListName : Name attribute of a List box.

oValueToSelect : Value attribute of an item to be selected in List box.

<u>Code Walkthrough</u>

Line 1 : Starta Function SelectListValue.

Line 2,3,4 : Declare Variables.

Line 5 : Get document object.

Line 6 : Get the select tag elements.

Line 7 : Initiate a for loop to get object by object from the objects list.

Line 8 : Verify name of the object.

Line 9 : Select the value of list if the type and name matches.

Line 10,11 : Exit for, End If.

Line 12 : Iterate the for loop.

Line 13,14,15 : Release the variables.

Line 16 : Function End.

Line 17,18 : Calling Function.

Ex 8: Click Link

```
Function ClickLink(oLinkOuterText)
Dim oDocObj
Dim oATagObjectsList
Dim oATagObject
```

```
5  Set oDocObj = Browser("Sample Document").Object.Document
6  Set oATagObjectsList= oDocObj.getElementsByTagName("A")
7  For each oATagObject in oATagObjectsList
8    If oATagObject.outerText= oLinkOuterText then
9      oATagObject.Click
10     Exit for
11   End If
12 Next
13 Set oDocObj =Nothing
14 Set oATagObjectsList=Nothing
15 Set oATagObject = Nothing
16 End Function
17
18 ClickLink "Accept Terms and Conditions"
```

Description:

The above code clicks a link in the HTML document.

Parameters:

oLinkOuterText : Outertext attribute of a link.

Code Walkthrough

Line 1	: Start a Function oLinkOuterText.
Line 2,3,4	: Declare Variables.
Line 5	: Get document object.
Line 6	: Get the tag elements with tag name "A".
Line 7	: Initiate a for loop to get object by object from the objects list.
Line 8	: Verify outer text of the link.
Line 9	: Click on the link if the name is matched.
Line 10,11	: Exit for, End If.
Line 12	: Iterate the for loop.
Line 13,14,15	: Release the variables.
Line 16	: Function End.
Line 17,18	: Calling Function

Ex 9: Click Button

```
Function ClickButton(oButtonValue)
Dim oDocObj
Dim oButtonTagObjectsList
Dim oButtonTagObject
Set oDocObj = Browser("Sample Document").Object.Document
Set oButtonTagObjectsList= oDocObj.getElementsByTagName("Button")
For each oButtonTagObject in oButtonTagObjectsList
 If oButtonTagObject.Value= oButtonValue then
   oButtonTagObject.Click
```

```
9       Exit for
10    End If
11  Next
12  Set oDocObj =Nothing
13  Set oButtonTagObjectsList=Nothing
14  Set oButtonTagObject = Nothing
15  End Function
16
17  ClickButton "Submit"
18
```

Description:

The above code clicks on a button in the HTML document.

Parameters:

oButtonValue : Value attribute of a button.

<u>Code Walkthrough</u>

Line 1 : Starta Function oLinkOuterText.
Line 2,3,4 : Declare Variables.
Line 5 : Get document object.
Line 6 : Get the tag elements with tag name “button”.
Line 7 : Initiate a for loop to get object by object from the objects list.
Line 8 : Verify value of the button.
Line 9 : Click on the button if the value is matched.
Line 10,11 : Exit for, End If.
Line 12 : Iterate the for loop.
Line 13,14,15 : Release the variables.
Line 16 : Function End.
Line 17,18 : Calling Function.

Note:

In HTML, Buttons can be created with <Input> and <button> tags. The above script will work for the buttons which are created using <button> tag.

WORKING WITH EXTERNAL DLLs AND WINDOWS API

Fundamentals of DLL

Dynamic-Link Library (DLL), is Microsoft's implementation of the shared library concept in the Microsoft Windows operating systems. These libraries usually have the file extension DLL and OCX. For instance, Windows has many DLL files built-in which other programs can access and utilise. A common example of this is spool32.dll, which is used for printing control within Windows 95/98/XP/Vista, by other applications.

The use of DLLs helps promote modularization of code, code reuse, efficient memory usage, and reduced disk space. Therefore, the operating system and the programs load faster, run faster, and take less disk space on the computer.

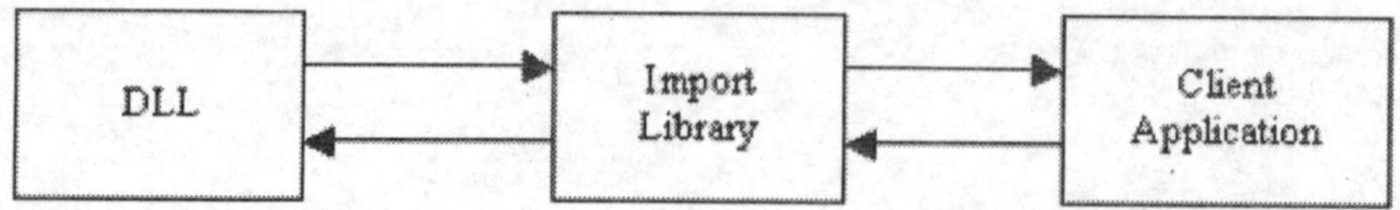

Along with dll, the import library is created, which contains information about each available function included in the DLL. When an application needs to use a function contained in the DLL, it presents its request to the import library. The import library checks the DLL for that function. If the function exists, the client program can use it. If it doesn't, the library communicates this to the application and the application presents an error.

Windows API

The **Windows API**, informally **WinAPI**, is Microsoft's core set of application programming interfaces (APIs) available in the Microsoft Windows operating systems. It was formerly called the **Win32 API**; however, the name Windows API more accurately reflects its roots in 16-bit Windows and its support on 64-bit Windows. Almost all Windows programs interact with the Windows API. The Microsoft Windows SDK (Software Development Kit) is available for Windows, which provides documentation and tools to enable developers to create software using the Windows API and associated Windows technologies.

The functionality provided by the Windows API can be grouped into eight categories.

Base Services

Provide access to the fundamental resources available to a Windows system, which include things like file systems, devices, processes and threads, and error handling. These functions reside in kernel.exe, krnl286.exe or krnl386.exe files on 16-bit Windows, and kernel32.dll on 32-bit Windows.

Advanced Services

Provide access to functionality that is an addition on the kernel. Included are things like the Windows registry, shutdown/restart the system (or abort), start/stop/create a Windows service, manage user accounts. These functions reside in advapi32.dll on 32-bit Windows.

Graphics Device Interface

Provides functionality for outputting graphical content to monitors, printers and other output devices. It resides in gdi.exe on 16-bit Windows, and gdi32.dll on 32-bit Windows in user-mode. Kernel-mode GDI support is provided by win32k.sys which communicates directly with the graphics driver.

User Interface

Provides the functionality to create and manage screen windows and most basic controls, such as buttons and scrollbars, receive mouse and keyboard input, and other functionality associated with the GUI part of Windows. This functional unit resides in user.exe on 16-bit Windows, and user32.dll on 32-bit Windows. Since Windows XP versions, the basic controls reside in comctl32.dll, together with the common controls (Common Control Library).

Common Dialog Box Library

Provides applications the standard dialog boxes for opening and saving files, choosing color and font, etc. The library resides in a file called commdlg.dll on 16-bit Windows, and comdlg32.dll on 32-bit Windows. It is grouped under the User Interface category of the API.

Common Control Library

Gives applications access to some advanced controls provided by the operating system. These include things like status bars, progress bars, toolbars and tabs. The library resides in a DLL file called commctrl.dll on 16-bit Windows, and comctl32.dll on 32-bit Windows. It is grouped under the *User Interface* category of the API.

Windows Shell

Component of the Windows API allows applications to access the functionality provided by the operating system shell, as well as change and enhance it. The component resides in shell.dll on 16-bit Windows, and shell32.dll on 32-bit Windows. The Shell Lightweight Utility Functions are in shlwapi.dll. It is grouped under the User Interface category of the API.

Network Services

Give access to the various networking capabilities of the operating system. Its sub-components include NetBIOS, Winsock, NetDDE, RPC and many others.

Web API

The Internet Explorer web browser also exposes many APIs that are often used by applications, and as such could be considered a part of the Windows API. Internet Explorer has been included with the operating system since Windows 98 Second Edition, and has provided web related services to applications since Windows 98. Specifically, it is used to provide:

- An embeddable web browser control, contained in shdocvw.dll and mshtml.dll.

- The URL monitor service, held in urlmon.dll, which provides COM objects to applications for resolving URLs. Applications can also provide their own URL handlers for others to use.
- A library for assisting with multi-language and international text support (mlang.dll).
- DirectX Transforms, a set of image filter components.
- XML support (the MSXML components, held in msxml*.dll).
- Access to the Windows Address Book.

Multimedia API

Microsoft has provided the DirectX set of APIs as part of every Windows installation since Windows 95 OSR2. DirectX provides a loosely related set of multimedia and gaming services, including:

- **Direct3D** for access to 3D hardware accelerated graphics.
- **DirectDraw** for hardware accelerated access to the 2D frame buffer. As of DirectX 9, this component has been deprecated in favor of Direct3D, which provides more general high-performance graphics functionality (as 2D rendering is a subset of 3D rendering).
- **DirectSound** for low level hardware accelerated sound card access.
- **DirectInput** for communication with input devices such as joysticks and gamepads.
- **DirectPlay** as a multiplayer gaming infrastructure. This component has been deprecated as of **DirectX 9** and Microsoft no longer recommends its use for game development.
- **DirectShow** which builds and runs generic multimedia pipelines.
- **DirectMusic** - allows playing of MIDI files, deprecated.

Windows Handle

A window handle (usually shortened to hWnd) is a unique identifier that Windows assigns to each window created. By window in this case we are referring to everything from command buttons and textboxes, to dialog boxes and full windows.

The window handle is used in APIs as the sole method of identifying a window. It is a Long (4 byte) value.

Extern Object

QTP's **Extern** object enables you to declare calls to external procedures from an external Dynamic-Link Library (DLL). Extern object is extremely useful for extending the power of QTP by exposing all of the Win32 API.

Declare method

Declares references to external procedures in a Dynamic-Link Library (DLL). After you use the **Declare** method for a function in the DLL, you can use the Extern object to call the function present in the DLL.

Syntax

Extern.Declare(RetType, MethodName, LibName, Alias [, ArgType(s)]**).**

Argument	Type	Description
RetType	String	Data type of the value returned by the method. For available data types, see Data Types from below table
MethodName	String	Any valid procedure name to be used to reference function in the DLL.
LibName	String	Name of the DLL or code resource that contains the declared procedure.
Alias	String	Name of the procedure in the DLL or code resource. **Note:** DLL entry points are case sensitive. **Note:** If ***Alias*** is an empty string, ***MethodName*** is used as the Alias.
ArgType(s)	String	A list of data types representing the data types of the arguments that are passed to the procedure when it is called. **Note:** For out arguments, use the **micByRef** flag.

Following are the Data Types used by Declare method with appropriate conversions.

Declare Constant	Value	Win API Data Type
micVoid	0	Void
micInteger	2	int
micLong	3	long
micFloat	4	float
micDouble	5	double
micString	8	CHAR*
micDispatch	9	IDispatch*
micWideString	18	WChar*
micChar	19	char
micUnknown	20	IUnknown
micHwnd	21	HWND
micVPtr	22	void*
micShort	23	short

micWord	24	WORD
micDWord	25	DWORD
micByte	26	BYTE
micWParam	27	WPARAM
micLParam	28	LPARAM
micLResult	29	LRESULT
micByRef	0X4000	out
micUnsigned	0X8000	unsigned
micUChar	micChar+micUnsigned	unsigned char
micULong	micLong+micUnsigned	unsigned long
micUShort	micShort+micUnsigned	unsigned short
micUInteger	micInteger+micUnsigned	unsigned int

Calling DLL Functions

To call a function present in the DLL first we must understand the declaration of the function within the DLL. Then we must declare the function in DLL with Extern object using declare method present in the extern object as follows.

For Instance *FindWindowA* is the function present in the *user32.dll* which is used to find the existence of the window with specified Class type and Title. It has the following declaration:

HWND FindWindowA(CHAR, CHAR*")*

Return value ***HWND*** is Handle To Window.
First Argument CHAR* is Class of the window to be identified.
Second Argument CHAR* is the Title of the window to be identified.

To call the above DLL function from QTP you have to use declare function as below

Extern.Declare micHwnd,"MYFindWindow","user32.dll","FindWindowA", micString, micString

Argument	Type	Description
MicHwnd	HWND	Data type of the return value of the *FindWindowA* function.
MYFindWindow	String	Any valid procedure name used in the QTP script

user32.dll	String	Name of the DLL
FindWindowA	String	Name of the procedure in the DLL
micString	String	Class of the Window to be Identified
micString	String	Title of the Window to be Identified

The above line declares ***FindWindowA*** function in the DLL with Extern object as ***MYFindWindow***. Here after you can call FindWindowA function in the DLL with Extern object as below.
hwnd=Extern.MYFindWindow("Notepad","Untitled – Notepad")

Passing Arguments to DLL functions

A value can be passed to a DLL function from QTP in two ways i.e **ByVal** and **ByRef.** When a value is passed ByVal, the actual value is passed directly to the procedure, and when passed **ByRef**, the address (pointer) of the value is passed. Always pass out **String** as **micByRef** since API extracts the address of the first character while reading the string. **ByRef** in declare method is represented as **micByRef.**

CallBack Functions

A callback function is a routine in your program that Windows calls. More generally, a callback is a means of sending a function as a parameter into another function.

We can determine whether an API function requires a callback function by looking at its parameters. Parameter that takes a pointer to a callback function is a long pointer, usually prefaced with the prefix "lp". Also, the name of the parameter usually ends in "Func", indicating that it takes a pointer to a function.

For example, take a look at the declaration for the EnumWindows function. The **lpEnumFunc** parameter indicates that the function requires a callback function.

```
BOOL EnumWindows(
  WNDENUMPROC lpEnumFunc,
  LPARAM lParam
);
```

Limitations of Extern Object

The QuickTest Extern object does not support API functions with CallBack mechanism, and also does not support any function with a structure parameter, and a pointer to function parameter.

For Example Extern Object cannot be used on the following two procedures:
BOOL EnumWindows(WNDENUMPROC lpEnumFunc,LPARAM lParam);
*BOOL GetCursorInfo(**PCURSORINFO** pci);*
Because *EnumWindows* argument ***lpEnumFunc*** is a function pointer and *GetCursorInfo* argument ***PCURSORINFO*** is a structure.

QuickTest Extern object has one drawback that can make development a little tricky: because Extern is a reserved object in QTP, it is instantiated once when QTP starts and persists through all your test runs. When you're doing your development, you might need to play with the DLL call signature you pass into Extern. When you make your changes and run the code again, you will notice that Extern does not always pick up the new signature and you often have to restart QTP. This can become a real time sink.

You can work around this problem by creating your own instance of the Extern object. Because this instance only exists while the test is running, you can change your extern declarations and simply re-run the script to see your changes. The Extern object is contained in the Mercury.ExternObj control. Here's some example code to illustrate:

Dealing with Extern object Instantiation issues

```
Option Explicit

Const FILENAME = "C:\Program Files\HP\QuickTest Professional\bin\wrls_ins.ini"
Const SECTION  = "ProductInformation"
Const KEYNAME  = "SerialNumber"

Dim myExtern
Dim serialNum
Dim numOfBytes

Set myExtern = CreateObject("Mercury.ExternObj") 'Create the extern instance
myExtern.Declare micInteger,"GetPrivateProfileStringA",
"kernel32.dll","GetPrivateProfileStringA", micString, micString, micString,
micString+micByRef, micInteger, micString
serialNum = String(255, " ")
numOfBytes = myExtern.GetPrivateProfileStringA(SECTION, KEYNAME, "", serialNum,
```

```
255, FILENAME)
msgbox numOfBytes
serialNum = Left(serialNum, numOfBytes)
 print "QTP Serial Number: "& serialNum
Set myExtern = Nothing
```

In the above code we are creating our own instance of the Extern object using the statement ***CreateObject("Mercury.ExternObj")*** and storing the extern object in a variable ***myExtern*** which will be used further to refer to the functions present in the DLL.

Scripting Examples

1. Write a program to find whether the window with specified title exists.

```
Extern.Declare micHwnd, "FindWindow", "user32.dll", "FindWindowA", micString, micString

hwnd = Extern.FindWindow("Notepad", “Hello – Notepad”)

If hwnd = 0 then
    MsgBox "Window with Title Hello - Notepad is  Not found"
Else
    Msgbox "Window with Title Hello - Notepad is found"
end if
```

<u>Description:</u>

This program checks whether a window with specified class and title exists and returns handle to the window if the window exists. If the window exists the handle will be a nonzero value.

The **FindWindow** function retrieves a handle to the top-level window whose class name and window name match the specified strings. This function does not perform a case-sensitive search. This function is available in user32.dll. If the function succeeds, the return value is a handle to the window that has the specified class name and window name. If the function fails, the return value is NULL.

Syntax

HWND FindWindow(LPCTSTR *lpClassName*,LPCTSTR *lpWindowName*);

Parameters

lpClassName

[in] Pointer to a null-terminated string that specifies the class name.

If *lpClassName* is NULL, it finds any window whose title matches the *lpWindowName* parameter.

lpWindowName

[in] Pointer to a null-terminated string that specifies the window name (the window's title). If this parameter is NULL, all window names match.

Code Walkthrough:

Line 1: Declares external method *FindWindowA* as *FindWindow* with Extern Object
where **'micHwnd'** is the return type,
'FindWindow' is the procedure name used in the script,
'user32.dll' is the Name of the DLL
'FindWindowA' is the Name of the function in the DLL
micString, micString are arguments ; class name and title of window.

Line 3: Check whether Window Exists on the desktop and assigns return value (Window handle) to the variable *hwnd.*

Line 5-9: Prints a message whether window exists or not based on the value of the ***hwnd***. If it is a nonzero value then window exists else window doesn't exist.

2. Write a program to change the title of the Window.

```
Extern.Declare micLong, "SetWindowText", "user32.dll", "SetWindowTextA",
micHwnd, micString
Extern.Declare micHwnd, "FindWindow", "user32.dll", "FindWindowA", micString,
micString

hwnd = Extern.FindWindow("Notepad", "Hello – Notepad")

If hwnd = 0 then
    MsgBox "Window with Title Hello - Notepad is  Not found"
Else
    Msgbox "Window with Title Hello - Notepad is found"
    ExitTest
end if
Extern.SetWindowText(hwnd, "HelloWorld - Notepad")
```

This program finds the window with specified title and changes the name of the window to a new name.

The **SetWindowTextA** function changes the text of the specified window's title bar. If the specified window is a control, the text of the control is changed. However, **SetWindowTextA** cannot change the text of a control in another application. This function is available in user32.dll. If the function succeeds, the return value is nonzero. If the function fails, the return value is zero.

Syntax

```
BOOL SetWindowText(HWND hWnd, LPCTSTR lpString);
```

Parameters

hWnd

[in] Handle to the window or control whose text is to be changed.

lpString

[in] Pointer to a null-terminated string to be used as the new title or control text.

Code Walkthrough

Line 1 : Declares external method *SetWindowTextA* as *SetWindowText* where **'micLong'** is the return type, **'SetWindowText'** is the procedure name used in the script, **'user32.dll'** is the Name of the DLL ***'SetWindowTextA'*** is the Name of the function in the DLL Argument **MicHWnd** refers to handle of the window whose name is to be changed and Argument **micString** refers to new Title of the window.

Line 2-11: Returns the handle of the window whose name is to be changed.

Line 12: Change the name of the window to new name **"HelloWorld - Notepad".**

3. Write a program to find the Last opened or Active window name

```
Extern. Declare
micLong,"GetForegroundWindow","user32.dll","GetForegroundWindow"
Extern. Declare micInteger,"GetWindowText", "user32.dll", "GetWindowTextA",
micLong, micString+micByRef, micInteger
wait(2)
hwnd=Extern.GetForegroundWindow()
tln=Extern.GetWindowText(hWnd,winname,100)

print("Foreground Window Name is:  " &winname)
```

This program displays the name of the window or application which was last accessed or which is currently active.

The **GetForegroundWindow** function returns a handle to the foreground window (the window with which the user is currently working). This function is available in user32.dll.

The return value is a handle to the foreground window. The foreground window can be NULL in certain circumstances, such as when a window is losing activation.

Syntax

```
HWND GetForegroundWindow(VOID);
```

The **GetWindowTextA** function copies the text of the specified window's title bar. If the function succeeds, the return value is the length, in characters, of the copied string, not including the terminating NULL character. If the window has no title bar or text, if the title bar is empty, or if the window or control handle is invalid, the return value is zero.

Syntax

```
int GetWindowText(HWND hWnd, LPTSTR lpString, int nMaxCount);
```

Parameters

hWnd

[in] Handle to the window or control containing the text.

lpString

[out] Pointer to the buffer that will receive the text. If the string is as long or longer than the buffer, the string is truncated and terminated with a NULL character.

nMaxCount

[in] Specifies the maximum number of characters to copy to the buffer, including the NULL character. If the text exceeds this limit, it is truncated.

Code Walkthrough

Line 1: Declares **'GetForegroundWindow'** that returns the Handle of the window which is on the foreground of the desktop with Extern Object.

Line 2: Declares **'GetWindowTextA'** that returns the Title of the window with Extern Object. The second argument is the title of the window which is an out parameter which is filled by the function GetWindowTextA. The argument Type **micString+micByRef** indicate that you are passing the address of the string buffer to GetWindowTextA to fill the name of the foreground window.

Line 4: Returns the foreground window handle to hwnd.

Line 5: Copies foreground window name to variable *'winname'* and the length of the window title to variable *'tln'*.

Line 7: Prints the Name of the Foreground Window.

4. Write a program to Get the color of a pixel

```
Dim hDC, hWnd
Dim X,Y,pixVal
Extern.Declare micLong,"GetForegroundWindow","user32.dll",
"GetForegroundWindow"
Extern.Declare micInteger,"GetWindowText","user32.dll", "GetWindowTextA",
micLong, micString+micByRef, micInteger
Extern.Declare MicLong, "GetPixel", "gdi32.dll", " GetPixel",MicLong, MicLong,
MicLong
Extern.Declare MicLong, "GetDC", "user32.dll"," GetDC", MicLong
Extern.Declare micLong,"ReleaseDC","user32.dll"," ReleaseDC",micLong,micLong

hwnd=Extern.GetForegroundWindow()
hDC = Extern.GetDC(hWnd)

 X = 5
 Y = 5
pixVal=Extern.GetPixel (hDC, X,Y)

Extern.ReleaseDC hWnd, hDC
```

It's the simple things which often seem impossible. A good example would be checking the color of a certain element in our application. This program will present a more delicate mechanism than a bitmap check - getting the color of a given pixel in the screen with the help of WinAPI functions **GetPixel, GetDC** and **ReleaseDC**.

The **GetPixel** function retrieves the Red, Green, Blue (RGB) color value of the pixel at the specified coordinates. The return value is the RGB value of the pixel. If the pixel is outside of the current clipping region, the return value is CLR_INVALID. The pixel must be within the boundaries of the current clipping region. Not all devices support **GetPixel**. An application should call **GetDeviceCaps** to determine whether a specified device supports this function. A bitmap must be selected within the device context, otherwise, CLR_INVALID is returned on all pixels.

Syntax

```
COLORREF GetPixel(
                              __in HDC hdc,
                              __in int nXPos,
                              __in int nYPos
              );
```

Parameters

hdc [in]

A handle to the device context.

nXPos [in]

The x-coordinate, in logical units, of the pixel to be examined.

nYPos [in]

The y-coordinate, in logical units, of the pixel to be examined.

The **GetDC** function retrieves a handle to a device context (HDC) for the client area of a specified window or for the entire screen. If the function succeeds, the return value is a handle to the DC for the specified window's client area. If the function fails, the return value is NULL.

An HDC is basically a handle to something you can draw on; it can represent the entire screen, an entire window, the client area of a window, a bitmap stored in memory, or a printer.

Syntax

```
HDC GetDC(__in HWND hWnd );
```

Parameters

hWnd [in]

A handle to the window whose DC is to be retrieved. If this value is NULL, **GetDC** retrieves the DC for the entire screen.

The **ReleaseDC** function releases a device context (DC), freeing it for use by other applications. The return value indicates whether the DC was released. If the DC was released, the return value is 1. If the DC was not released, the return value is zero.

Syntax

```
int ReleaseDC(__in HWND hWnd,__in HDC hDC);
```

Parameters

hWnd [in]

A handle to the window whose DC is to be released.

hDC [in]

A handle to the DC to be released.

Code Walkthrough

Line 1-7: Declares various WinAPI functions with Extern Object and also declares some of the variables.

Line 9: Get Handle to Foreground Window

Line 10: Get the device context with the help of GetDC function. This is very essential to work on the Graphics of windows.
Line 12-13: X,Y coordinate of a pixel whose color you want to know.
Line 14: Returns the RGB value of the Pixel.
Line 15: Release device context so that another application can use the same.

5. Read a Specific Key from ini file.

```
1 C Const FILENAME = "C:\Program Files\HP\QuickTest
  Professional\bin\wrls_ins.ini"
2 Const SECTION = "ProductInformation"
3 Const KEYNAME  = "SerialNumber"
4
5 Extern.Declare micInteger,"GetPrivateProfileString",
  "kernel32.dll","GetPrivateProfileStringA", micString, micString, micString,
  micString+micByRef, micInteger, micString
6
7 numOfBytes = Extern.GetPrivateProfileString(SECTION, KEYNAME, "", serialNum,
  255, FILENAME)

8 print "QTP Serial Number: "& serialNum
```

ini files, also called as Initialization files. are used to store initialization information of an application. Data is stored in the form of sections and key value pairs for easy maintenance and retrieval. Please refer to the ini file mentioned in line 1 of this program. This program reads value of a key **SerialNumber** present in the **ProductInformation** section of the **wrls_ins.ini** file.

GetPrivateProfileString Function retrieves a string from the specified section in an initialization file. The return value is the number of characters copied to the buffer, not including the terminating null character.

Syntax

```
DWORD WINAPI GetPrivateProfileString(
  __in  LPCTSTR lpAppName,
  __in  LPCTSTR lpKeyName,
  __in  LPCTSTR lpDefault,
  __out LPTSTR lpReturnedString,
  __in  DWORD nSize,
  __in  LPCTSTR lpFileName
);
```

Parameters

lpAppName [in]

The name of the section containing the key name.

lpKeyName [in]

The name of the key whose associated string is to be retrieved.

lpDefault [in]

A default string. If the *lpKeyName* key cannot be found in the initialization file, **GetPrivateProfileString** copies the default string to the *lpReturnedString* buffer. If this parameter is NULL, the default is an empty string, "".

lpReturnedString [out]

A pointer to the buffer that receives the retrieved string.

nSize [in]

The size of the buffer pointed to by the *lpReturnedString* parameter, in characters.

lpFileName [in]

The name of the initialization file. If this parameter does not contain a full path to the file, the system searches for the file in the Windows directory.

Code Walkthrough

Line 1-3: Name of the ini file, section and key name to retrieve.
Line 5: Declare GetPrivateProfileString function with Extern Object. 4th parameter is the out parameter that contains the value of the key. Since out parameter is a string data type it is mentioned as **micString+micByRef**.
Line 7: Calls *GetPrivateProfileStringA* function from kernel32.dll and reads the *SerialNumber* key from section *ProductInformation* of *wrls_ins.ini* file to a string buffer ***serialNum***. ***numOfBytes*** variable contains the actual number of characters read i.e size of the keyname. If this is greater than 0 function is successful and the key name is read.
Line 8: Print the value of the key serial number.

6. **Write Key and Value to particular section of an ini file.**

```
Const FILENAME = "C:\Program Files\HP\QuickTest Professional\bin\wrls_ins.ini"
Const SECTION  = "ProductInformation"
Const KEYNAME  = "Vendor"

Extern.Declare micInteger,"WritePrivateProfileStringA",
"kernel32.dll","WritePrivateProfileStringA", micString, micString, micString,micString
RetVal = Extern.WritePrivateProfileStringA(SECTION, KEYNAME, "HP", FILENAME)

If CInt(RetVal) > 0 Then
```

```
9           print ("Key has written Successfully")
10      Else
11          print("Key Writing Failed")
12      End If
```

This program updates the value of a key if the key exists else creates new key and value in the ini file under the section specified.

WritePrivateProfileString function copies a string into the specified section of an initialization file. If the function successfully copies the string to the initialization file, the return value is nonzero.

Syntax

```
BOOL WINAPI WritePrivateProfileString(
  __in  LPCTSTR lpAppName,
  __in  LPCTSTR lpKeyName,
  __in  LPCTSTR lpString,
  __in  LPCTSTR lpFileName
);
```

Parameters

lpAppName [in]

The name of the section to which the string will be copied. If the section does not exist, it is created. The name of the section is case-independent; the string can be any combination of uppercase and lowercase letters.

lpKeyName [in]

The name of the key to be associated with a string. If the key does not exist in the specified section, it is created. If this parameter is NULL, the entire section, including all entries within the section, is deleted.

lpString [in]

A null-terminated string to be written to the file. If this parameter is NULL, the key pointed to by the *lpKeyName* parameter is deleted.

lpFileName [in]

The name of the initialization file.

Code Walkthrough

Line 1-3: Name of the ini file, section and key name.

Line 5: Declares ***WritePrivateProfileString*** function which takes 4 arguments. Section Name, Key Name, Key Value and Filename of an Initialization file. Adds a new key ***Vendor*** and a value ***HP*** under section ***ProductInformation*** of ***wrls_ins.ini*** file.

Line 6: Return status of key updation will be stored to a variable ***RetVal.***

Line 8-12: Checks and Prints whether Key Writing is successful or not. If ***RetVal*** is nonzero then key writing is successful.

7. Minimize a given Window.

```
1  Extern.Declare micInteger,"CloseWindow","user32.dll" ,"CloseWindow",micHwnd
2  Extern.Declare micHwnd, "FindWindow", "user32.dll", "FindWindowA", micString,
   micString
3
4  hwnd = Extern.FindWindow("Notepad", VbNullString)
5  RetVal=Extern.CloseWindow(hwnd)
6
7  If CInt(RetVal) > 0 Then
8      print ("Notepad Window is minimized successfully")
9  Else
10     print("Failed to minimize Notepad Window")
11 End If
```

Minimize the window whose handle is specified by a variable hwnd. **CloseWindow is the Win API function which is part of user32.dll and is used to minimize the window.**

The **CloseWindow** function minimizes (but does not destroy) the specified window. If the function succeeds, the return value is nonzero. If the function fails, the return value is zero.

Syntax

```
BOOL CloseWindow(
  HWND hWnd
);
```

Parameters

hWnd

[in] Handle to the window to be minimized.

Code Walkthrough

Line 1: Declare ***CloseWindow*** function which takes handle of the window to be minimized as argument and returns Boolean value as output. Returns true if the window is minimized, else false. Since BOOL doesn't have any direct mapping in declaration types we are using micInteger as a return type. A value nonzero indicates True and 0 indicates false.

Line 2: Declares ***FindWindow*** Method

Line 4: Stores the handle of the window to be closed in a variable *hwnd.*

Line 5: Calls ***CloseWindow*** function on a window whose handle is represented by *hwnd.* If the window exists and window is minimized return value *RetVal* is set to 1 else it is set to 0

Line 7-11: Prints the status whether window is minimized or not.

8. Determine whether a given window is Minimized.

```
1  Extern.Declare micInteger,"IsIconic","user32.dll","IsIconic",micHwnd
2  Extern.Declare micHwnd, "FindWindow", "user32.dll", "FindWindowA", micString,
   micString
3
4  hwnd = Extern.FindWindow("Notepad", VbNullString)
5  RetVal=Extern. IsIconic (hwnd)
6
7  If CInt(RetVal) > 0 Then
8       print ("Window is Minimised")
9  Else
10      print("Window is NOT Minimised")
11 End If
```

This program checks whether a window represented by its handle *hwnd* is minimized or not. The Program uses **IsIconic** Win API function to determine whether the window is minimized.

The **IsIconic** function determines whether the specified window is minimized (iconic). If the window is iconic, the return value is nonzero. If the window is not iconic, the return value is zero.

Syntax

```
BOOL IsIconic(
  HWND hWnd
);
```

Parameters

hWnd

[in] Handle to the window to test.

Code Walkthrough

Line 1: Declares *IsIconic* function which takes handle of the window to be verified for minimize status as argument and returns Boolean value as output. Returns true if the window is minimized, else false. A value nonzero indicates True and 0 indicates false.

Line 2-4: Stores the handle of the window to be verified for minimize status in a variable *hwnd.*

Line 5: Calls *IsIconic* function on a window whose handle is represented by *hwnd.* If the window exists and the window is minimized, return value *RetVal* is set to 1 else it is set to 0.

Line 7-11: Prints the status whether window is minimized or not.

9. Determine whether window is Maximized.

```
1  Extern.Declare micInteger,"IsZoomed","user32.dll","IsZoomed",micHwnd
2  Extern.Declare micHwnd, "FindWindow", "user32.dll", "FindWindowA", micString,
   micString
3
4  hwnd = Extern.FindWindow("Notepad", VbNullString)
5  RetVal=Extern.IsZoomed(hwnd)
6
7  If CInt(RetVal) > 0 Then
8      print ("Window is Maximised")
9  Else
10     print("Window is NOT Maximised")
11 End If
```

This program checks whether a window represented by its handle *hwnd* is maximized or not. The program uses **IsZoomed** Win API function to determine whether the window is maximized.

The **IsZoomed** function determines whether a window is maximized. If the window is zoomed, the return value is nonzero. If the window is not zoomed, the return value is zero.

Syntax

```
BOOL IsZoomed(
  HWND hWnd
);
```

Parameters

hWnd

[in] Handle to the window to test.

Code Walkthrough

Line 1: Declares ***IsZoomed*** function which takes handle of the window to be verified for maximized status as argument and returns Boolean value as output. Returns true if the window is maximized, else false. A value nonzero indicates True and 0 indicates false.

Line 2-4: Stores the handle of the window to be verified for maximized in a variable *hwnd*.

Line 5: Calls ***IsZoomed*** function on a window whose handle is represented by *hwnd*. If the window exists and window is maximized return value *RetVal* is set 1 else it is set to 0

Line 7-11: Prints the status whether window is maximized or not.

10. Forcibly Close a window

```
1  Extern.Declare micInteger, "EndTask", "user32.dll", "EndTask", micHWnd,
   micInteger, micInteger
2
3  Browser("estore").Close
4
5  Wait 5
6
7  If Browser("estore").Exist( 0 ) Then
8    hwnd = Browser("estore").GetROProperty( "hwnd" )
9    Retval = Extern.EndTask( hWnd, False, True )
10 End If
```

This program forcibly closes the application or window specified by its handle. This is equivalent to closing of the program from the TaskManager in windows operating system. The program uses Win API function **EndTask** to close the application window.

The **EndTask** function is called to forcibly close a specified window. If the function succeeds, the return value is nonzero. If the function fails, the return value is FALSE.

Syntax

```
BOOL EndTask(
  HWND hWnd,
  BOOL fShutDown,
  BOOL fForce
);
```

Parameters

hWnd

[in] Handle to the window to be closed.

fShutDown

[in] Ignored. Must be FALSE.

fForce

[in] A TRUE for this parameter will force the destruction of the window if an initial attempt fails to gently close the window using WM_CLOSE. With a FALSE for this parameter, only the close with WM_CLOSE is attempted.

Code Walkthrough

Line 1: Declare *EndTask* function which takes arguments like Handle to the window to be terminated.

Line 2: Try to close browser window normally.

Line 7: Check browser window still exists.

Line 8: If exists get the handle to the browser window.

Line 9: Close the browser window forcibly using *EndTask* function.

11. Bring Application Window to Top.

```
Extern.Declare micInteger,"BringWindowToTop","user32.dll",
"BringWindowToTop",micHwnd
Extern.Declare micHwnd, "FindWindow", "user32.dll", "FindWindowA", micString,
micString

If Browser("Yahoo").Exist Then
  hwnd = Browser("Yahoo").GetROProperty( "hwnd" )
  RetVal=Extern.BringWindowToTop(hwnd)

      If CInt(RetVal) > 0 Then
          wait(10)
          print ("Application  has come to Top")
      Else
          print("Application  has NOT come to Top")
      End If
Else
    print("Application Doesn't Exist")
End If
```

This program checks whether the window specified exists and if it exists brings it to the top of all the windows on the screen. Then program uses **BringWindowToTop** Win API function to bring the window with specified handle to the top of the screen.

The **BringWindowToTop** function brings the specified window to the top of the screen. If the function succeeds, the return value is nonzero. If the function fails, the return value is zero.

Syntax

```
BOOL BringWindowToTop(
  HWND hWnd
);
```

Parameters

hWnd

[in] Handle to the window to bring to the top of the Z order.

Code Walkthrough

Line 1-2: Declares *BringWindowToTop, FindWindowA* functions with extern object.

Line 4 : Check whether Browser window "Yahoo" exists.

Line 5 : If Exists; Get Handle to the Window.

Line 6: Bring the window with specified handle to the top of the screen. *RetVal* is nonzero if function is successful else 0

Line 7-13: Print the status **message** to printlog

Line 14-16: Prints that "Application Doesn't Exist" if browser window "Yahoo" doesn't exist.

Chapter 32

WORKING WITH EXCEL OBJECT MODEL

To develop solutions that use Microsoft Office Excel, you can interact with the COM objects provided by Microsoft Office Excel object model. The following are the objects related to Microsoft Office Excel object model:

- Excel.Application
- Excel.Workbook
- Excel.Worksheet
- Excel.Range

For the most part, the object model directly emulates the user interface. For example, the **Application** object represents the entire excel application, and each **Workbook** object contains a collection of **Worksheet** objects. **Range** object allows you to work with individual cell or group of cells.

For complete information about the Excel 2003 object model, see the VBA documentation that is installed with Excel or see "Welcome to the Microsoft Office Excel 2003 VBA Language Reference": **http://go.microsoft.com/fwlink/?linkid=27951**

For complete information about the Excel 2007 object model, see the VBA documentation that is installed with Excel or see the 2007 Microsoft Office system developer content on the MSDN Web site.

http://go.microsoft.com/fwlink/?LinkId=72870

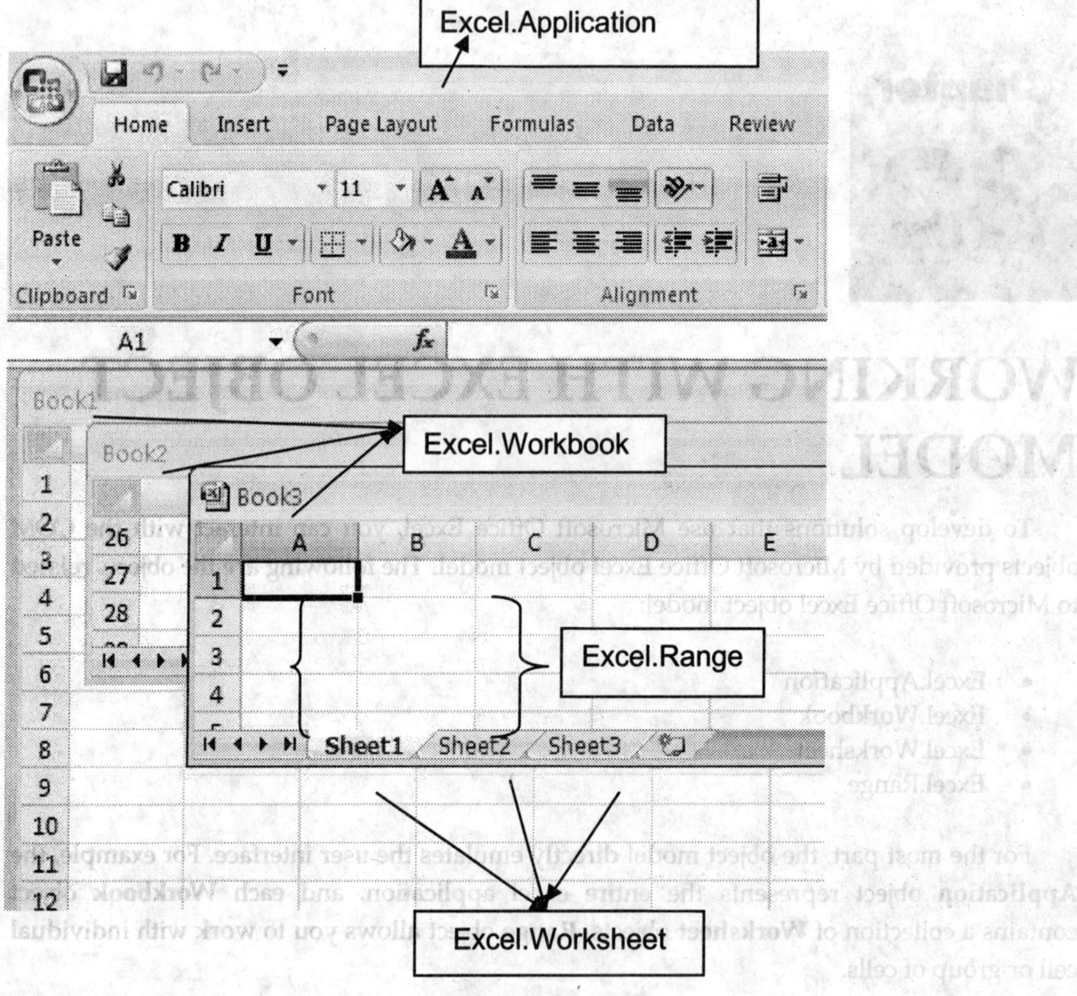

Scripting Examples

Example 1: Open Excel Application.

```
1 Set ExcelApp = CreateObject("Excel.Application")
2 ExcelApp.Visible = True
3 Wait(5)
```

This program creates a COM object called Excel using CreateObject method and makes it visible to the end user. Line1 creates a COM object Excel and Line 2 makes it visible to the end user by setting visible property to True. Line 3 shows excel application to the user for 5secs.

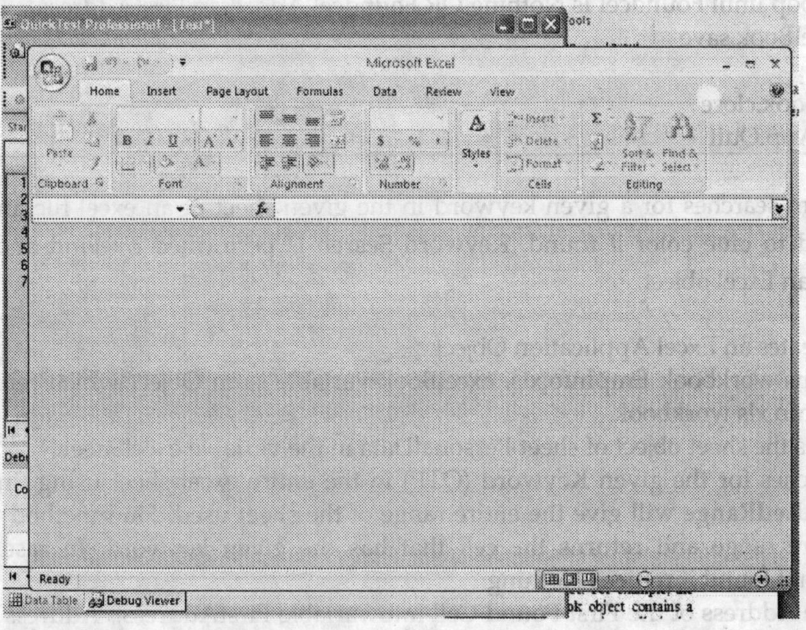

Example 2: Close Microsoft Excel Document.

```
1 Set ExcelApp = CreateObject("Excel.Application")
2 ExcelApp.Workbooks.Add
3 ExcelApp.Visible = True
4 wait(5)
5 ExcelApp.Quit
```

Line 1 creates an Excel COM object and Line 2 Adds workbook to Excel Application. Line 3 and 4 make the Excel visible to the end user for 5 secs. Line 5 removes the Excel object from memory using Quit Method.

Example 3: Search for a particular value in Excel file.

```
1  Set ExcelApp = CreateObject("Excel.Application")
2  ExcelApp.visible=true
3   Set excelBook  = ExcelApp.Workbooks.Open ("D:\QTP\ EmpInfo.xls")
4   Set excelSheet  = ExcelApp.Sheets("PersonalData")
5
6  Set Foundcel =excelSheet.UsedRange.Find ("QTP")
7  FirstAddress=Foundcel.Address
8  If Not Foundcel Is Nothing Then
9       Do
10      Foundcel.Font.Color=VBBlue
11      Set Foundcel=excelSheet.UsedRange.FindNext(Foundcel)
12      Loop until Foundcel Is Nothing OR Foundcel.Address= FirstAddress
13    excelBook.save
14 End If
15 excelBook.close
16 ExcelApp.Quit
```

This program searches for a given keyword in the given sheet of an excel file and converts the keyword to blue color if found. Keyword Search is performed by Find and FindNext Methods of an Excel object.

Line 1-2: Creates an Excel Application Object.
Line 3: Opens workbook EmpInfo.xls. excelBook variable is an Object which represents the entire EmpInfo.xls workbook.
Line 4: Stores the sheet object of sheet PersonalData in the variable excelSheet.
Line 6: Searches for the given Keyword (QTP) in the entire excel sheet using find method. **excelSheet.UsedRange** will give the entire range of the sheet used. Find method will search for the entire range and returns the cell that has the given keyword. In case the given keyword is not found it returns Nothing.
Line 7: Store Address of the First Found Cell into variable FirstAddress. Address of the Cell is returned by Address property of a Cell Object in the form of string as $Column$Row
Line 8: Check whether search keyword is found by Find method while comparing with **Nothing.**
Line 9-12: Loop entire sheet and set the font color of the Keyword to Blue. Line 10 sets the font color to Blue. Line 11 Find the next cell with given Keyword. Line 12 check whether any next cell is available with given keyword by comparing Foundcel with Nothing and also checks if found, next cell address is same as first cell address which is stored in line number 7. This is because FindNext method will search from the starting of the sheet if it reaches the end of the sheet. Hence we will come out of the loop if search starts again from the starting of the sheet.
Line 13: Save the changes made in the Sheet.
Line 15&16: Close the work book and Exit Excel Application.

Example 4: Create a New WorkBook in Excel File.

```
1 Set ExcelApp = CreateObject("Excel.Application")
2 ExcelApp.Visible = True
3 set excelWorkbook=ExcelApp.Workbooks.Add()
4 excelWorkbook.SaveAs "D:\QTP\EmpInfo.xls"
5 excelWorkbook.close
6 ExcelApp.Quit
```

Line 1-3: Open Excel File and Adds Default Workbook.
Line 4: Save the name of the workbook as "EmpInfo.xls" in the specified folder.
Line 5: Close Excel Work Book.
Line 6: Quit Excel Application.

Example 5: Copy an Excel Sheet of one Excel File to another Excel File.

```
1 Set ExcelApp = CreateObject("Excel.Application")
2 ExcelApp.Visible = True
3 Set excelWorkbook1= ExcelApp.Workbooks. Open("D:\QTP\EmpInfo.xls")
4 Set excelWorkbook2= ExcelApp.Workbooks. Open("D:\QTP\EmpInfoBAK.xls")
5 excelWorkbook1.Worksheets("PersonalData").UsedRange.Copy
6 excelWorkbook2.Worksheets("Sheet1").Range("A1"). PasteSpecial Paste =xlValues
7 excelWorkbook1.save
8 excelWorkbook2.save
9 excelWorkbook1.close
10 excelWorkbook2.close
11 ExcelApp.Quit
```

This Program copies the entire data from a sheet of an excel file to another sheet of an excel file. This copy is performed by using Copy and PasteSpecial method of an Excel Object.

Line 1-4: Opens two Excel Workbooks EmpInfo.xls and EmpInfoBAK.xls and stores the work book objects in excelWorkbook1 and excelWorkbook2 respectively.
Line 5: Copy the entire data from PersonalData sheet of excelWorkbook1 using Copy method.
Line 6: Paste the entire copied data into Sheet1 of excelWorkbook2 using Paste Special method. Paste Special pastes the contents of the Clipboard onto the sheet, using a specified format. Use this method to paste data from other applications or to paste data in a specific format. Pasting starts from Column A and Row 1 as Specified in Range.
Line 7-11: Save and Close WorkBooks. Also Quit Excel Application.

Example 6: Compare Two Excel Sheets Cell by Cell.

```
Set ExcelApp = CreateObject("Excel.Application")
ExcelApp.Visible = True
Set excelWorkbook1= ExcelApp.Workbooks.Open("D:\QTP\EmpInfo.xls")
set sheet1=ExcelApp.Worksheets.Item("PersonalData")
set sheet2=ExcelApp.Worksheets.Item("EmploymentData")
If sheet1 Is Nothing Or sheet2 Is Nothing Then
```

```
7            ExitTest
8      End If
9      startRow=1
10     numberofRows=7
11     startColumn=1
12     numberOfColumns=2
13     For r = startRow to (startRow + (numberOfRows - 1))
14          For c = startColumn to (startColumn + (numberOfColumns - 1))
15               Value1 = sheet1.Cells(r, c)
16               Value2 = sheet2.Cells(r, c)
17                Value1 = Trim(Value1)
18                 Value2 = Trim(Value2)
19              If Value1 <> Value2 Then
20                     sheet2.Cells(r, c).Font.Color = vbRed
21               End If
22          Next
23       Next
24     excelWorkbook1.save
25     excelWorkbook1.close
26     ExcelApp.Quit
```

This Program Compares two sheets of an excel file cell by cell and marks the conflicted cell with Red Color. We can also specify range of the cells to be compared by using variables defined between Line9 to Line 12.

Line 1-5: Opens two sheets PersonalData and EmploymentData from excel workbook EmpInfo.xls

Line 6-8: Checks whether Sheets are available. Else Exits the Test.

Line 9-12: Define the Range(Rows, Columns) to be compared in both excel sheets.

Line 13-14: Loop Through all the rows and Columns of the sheet using two For Loops.

Line 15-18: Read the values of a given cell from both the sheets and trim the values for unnecessary spaces.

Line 19-21: Compare the values in both the sheets if not the same change cell values in Sheet2 to Red Color.

Line 24-26: Save and Close Excel Work Book and Excel Application.

Example 7: Delete rows from Excel Sheet.

```
Set ExcelApp= CreateObject("Excel.Application")
ExcelApp.DisplayAlerts = False
Set excelWorkBook = ExcelApp.Workbooks.Open("D:\QTP\EmpInfo.xls")
ExcelApp.Rows("3:6").Delete
excelWorkBook.SaveAs ("D:\QTP\EmpInfoRowsModified.xls")
ExcelApp.Workbooks.Close()
ExcelApp.Quit
```

This program deletes a specified number of Rows from the first sheet of an excel file and saves the modified sheet as a new excel work book. Line 2 sets Display Alerts Property as False; this suppresses any dialogs displayed by Excel like Save. Line 4 Deletes the Rows 3-6 from the First Sheet. If you want to delete from any other sheet you can activate that sheet by using Activate method on the Sheet Object.

Example 8: Add and Delete an Excel Sheet.

```
1  Set ExcelApp = CreateObject("Excel.Application")
2  ExcelApp.Visible = True
3  ExcelApp.DisplayAlerts=False
4  Set excelWorkbook= ExcelApp.Workbooks.Open("D:\QTP\EmpInfo.xls")
5  set newSheet=excelWorkbook.Sheets.Add
6
7  newSheet.Name="TestSheet"
8  wait(10)
9  Set delSheet=excelWorkbook.Sheets("TestSheet")
10 delSheet.delete
11 wait(5)
12 ExcelApp.Quit
```

This Program demonstrates how to add a new sheet to an existing sheet of a work book and also to delete a sheet. Line 5 will add a new sheet using Add method of a sheet object. Line 7 sets the name of the sheet to TestSheet. Line 9 retrieves the Sheet object of the TestSheet and line 10 deletes the sheet using delete method of the sheet object.

Example 9:Sort Excel Sheet By Column

```
1  Const dataAscending = 1
2  Set ExcelApp = CreateObject("Excel.Application")
3  ExcelApp.Visible = True
4  Set excelWorkBook = ExcelApp.Workbooks.Open("D:\QTP\EmpInfo.xls")
5  Set excelSheet = excelWorkBook.Worksheets("PersonalData")
6  Set dataRange =excelSheet.UsedRange
7  Set colRange = ExcelApp.Range("B1")
8  dataRange.Sort colRange,dataAscending
9  wait(20)
10 ExcelApp.Quit
```

This program sorts the data of an excel sheet based on a specified column in Ascending Order. Line6 gets the entire range of the excel sheet that has data. Line 7 gets the range of the column from B1 on which sorting has to happen. Line 8 uses Sort method of the Range object and sorts all the columns based on column B1 specified in Line7. Line 9 helps you to view the sorted data for 20Secs. In any case to save permanently you can use save method of the workbook.

Example 10: Reading Data from Password Protected Excel File

```
1  Set ExcelApp = CreateObject("Excel.Application")
2  ExcelApp.Visible = True
3  ExcelApp.DisplayAlerts=False
4  filePasswd="confidential123"
5  Set excelWorkBook = ExcelApp.Workbooks.
   Open("D:\QTP\EmpInfo.xls",0,False,5,filePasswd)
6  Set excelWorkSheet=ExcelApp.Worksheets.Item("PersonalData")
7  usedColumnsCount = excelWorkSheet.UsedRange.Columns.Count
8  usedRowsCount = excelWorkSheet.UsedRange.Rows.Count
9  top = excelWorkSheet.UsedRange.Row
10 lft = excelWorkSheet.UsedRange.Column
11 Set Cells = excelWorkSheet.Cells
12 For row = 0 to (usedRowsCount-1)
13         rdata=""
14         For col = 0 to usedColumnsCount-1
15                 curRow = row+top
16                 curCol = col+lft
17                 word = Cells(curRow,curCol).Value
18                 rdata=rdata&vbtab&word
19     Next
20                 print(rdata)
21 Next
22 ExcelApp.Quit
```

This program demonstrates how to open and read data from a password protected Excel Work Book. Line 5 opens Password protected work book with appropriate parameters to Open Method of a work book. Below are the five parameters used for Open method respectively.

Filename - The file name of the workbook to be opened.
UpdateLinks – Optional. Specifies the way links in the file are updated. If the argument is 0, no charts are created.
ReadOnly - Optional .Use Boolean value True to open the workbook in read-only mode.
Format - Optional. If Microsoft Excel is opening a text file, this argument specifies the delimiter character, as shown in the following table. If this argument is omitted, the current delimiter is used.
Password - Optional. A string that contains the password required to open a protected workbook. If this argument is omitted and the workbook requires a password, the user is prompted for the password.
Line 6-21: Reads all the data from an Excel Sheet and Display to the user.

WORKING WITH WORD OBJECT MODEL

To develop solutions that use Microsoft Office Word, you can interact with the objects provided by the Word object model. Word objects are arranged in a hierarchical order, and the two main classes at the top of the hierarchy are the Application and Document classes. These two classes are important because most of the time you either work with the Word application itself, or manipulate Word documents in some way.

The Word object model closely follows the user interface. The **Application** object represents the entire application, each **Document** object represents a single Word document, the **Paragraph** object corresponds to a single paragraph, and so on. Each of these objects has many methods and properties that allow you to manipulate and interact with it.

For complete information about the Word 2003 object model, see the Visual Basic for Applications (VBA) documentation that is installed with Word or see "Welcome to the Microsoft Office Word 2003 VBA Language Reference" (http://go.microsoft.com/fwlink/?linkid=27950). For complete information about the Word

2007 object model, see the VBA documentation that is installed with Word or see the 2007 Microsoft Office system developer content on the MSDN Web site

(http://go.microsoft.com/fwlink/?LinkId=72870)

Word provides hundreds of objects with which you can interact. The following sections briefly describe the top-level objects and how they interact with each other. These include:

- Application object
- Document object
- Selection object
- Range object
- Bookmark object

Application Object

The **Application** object represents the Word application, and is the parent of all of the other objects. Its members usually apply to Word as a whole. You can use its properties and methods to control the Word environment.

Document Object

The **Microsoft.Office.Interop.Word.Document** object is central to programming Word. When you open a document or create a new document, you create a new **Microsoft.Office.Interop.Word.Document** object, which is added to the Documents collection in Word. The document that has the focus is called the active document and is represented by the ActiveDocument property of the **Application** object.

Selection Object

The **Selection** object represents the area that is currently selected. The **Selection** object is always present in a document. If nothing is selected, then it represents the insertion point. In addition, it can also be multiple blocks of text that are not contiguous.

Range Object

The **Range** object represents a contiguous area in a document, and is defined by a starting character position and an ending character position. You are not limited to a single **Range** object. You can define multiple **Range** objects in the same document

Bookmark Object

The **Microsoft.Office.Interop.Word.Bookmark** is used to mark a location in a document, or as a container for text in a document.

Scripting Examples

Example1: Creating a Microsoft Word Document

```
1 Dim objMsWord
2 Set objMsWord = CreateObject("Word.Application")
3 objMsWord.Visible=True
4 wait(20)
5 objMsWord.Quit
```

Line 1-2: Create a COM Object of MSWord
Line 3: Displays Word Application since the Visible Property is True.
Line 4-5: Displays MSWord for 20 Secs and Quits the Word Application

Example 2: Writing simple text to windows word

```
1 Dim objMsWord
2 Set objMsWord = CreateObject("Word.Application")
3 objMsWord.Visible=True
4 objMsWord.Documents.Add
5 objMsWord.Selection.TypeText "QTP for Professionals is the Best Book to learn QTP"
  objMsWord.ActiveDocument.SaveAs "D:\QTP \QTPWord.doc"
6 wait(20)
7 objMsWord.Quit
8
```

This program creates Word Document and Add simple Text to it using the method TypeText.
Line 1-3: Create and Display MS Word Application
Line 4: Add New Document to MS Word
Line 5: Enter a simple Text into Word Document using **TypeText** method. Selection object represents area selected in the document; if nothing is selected it represents the cursor position.
Line 6: Saves the word Document as **QTPWord.doc** in a specified Folder
Line 7-8: Displays MSWord for 20 Secs and Quits the Word Application

Example 3: Setting the Font Color and Font Type to a String

```
1 Dim objMsWord
2 Set objMsWord = CreateObject("Word.Application")
3 objMsWord.Visible=True
4 set objWordDoc=objMsWord.Documents.Add()
5 Set objSelection = objMsWord.Selection
6
7 objSelection.TypeParagraph()
8 objSelection.Font.Name = "Arial"
9 objSelection.Font.Size = "8"
10 objSelection.Font.color=Vbred
```

```
11 objMsWord.Selection.TypeText "QTP for Professionals is the Best Book to learn QTP"
   objSelection.TypeParagraph()
12
13 objSelection.Font.Size = "14"
14 objSelection.Font.color=VbBlue
15 objSelection.TypeText "" & Date()
16 objSelection.TypeParagraph()
17
18 objMsWord.ActiveDocument.SaveAs
19 "D:\QTPCompleteReference\Chapter33\QTPLearningFont.doc"
   objWordDoc.close
20 objMsWord.Quit
21
```

This Program Creates a new Word Document and Type a Text and Date of the system .Then change the font Name, Color and Size. Finally saves into a file named QTPLearningFont.doc. The output will be as below.

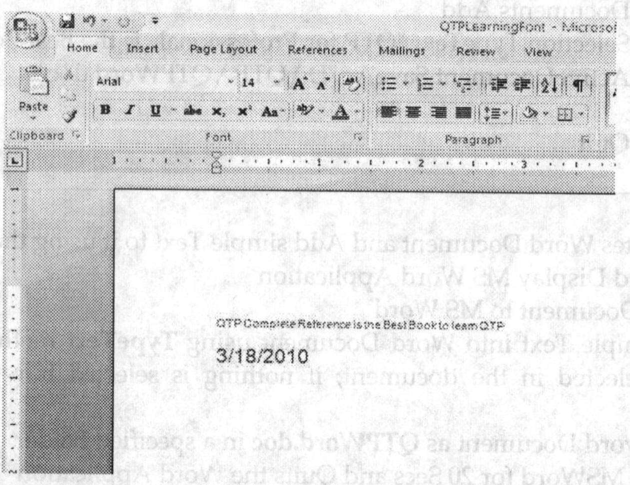

Line 1-5: Creates a Word Application and a new Document
Line 7: TypeParagraph() will type the paragraph separator i.e. New Line
Line 8: sets Font Name as Arial using Font.Name property
Line 9-10: sets Font Size and Color as 8 and Vbred using Font.Size and Font.Color properties respectively. VbRed is VbScript constant for the Red color
Line 11: Types the text into the Document. Since you have already defined the Font properties typed text will be of Arial, red Color with Size 8.
Line 12: Again types a new line
Line 14-15: Change Font Size and Color to 14 and Blue.
Line 16: Print the Date in the Document. Date will be printed from the current cursor position with new Font Size and Color.

Line 19: Saves the Word Document as QTPLearningFont.doc
Line 20: Close Word Document using Close Method
Line 21: Exits Word Application.

Example 4: Writing a table to windows word

```
Dim objMsWord
Set objMsWord = CreateObject("Word.Application")
objMsWord.Visible=True
set objWordDoc=objMsWord.Documents.Add()
Set objDocSelection = objMsWord.selection

objDocSelection.TypeParagraph()
objDocSelection.TypeParagraph()

objDocSelection.TypeText "EmpInfo"
objDocSelection.TypeParagraph()

Set objRange = objDocSelection.Range
objWordDoc.Tables.Add objRange,6,4
Set objDocTable = objWordDoc.Tables(1)
  For i=1 To 6
          For j=1 To 4
                    objDocTable.Cell(i, j).Range.Text="cell"&i&j
          Next
  Next
          objDocTable.borders(1).LineStyle=8 'Top
          objDocTable.borders(2).LineStyle=5  'Left
          objDocTable.borders(3).LineStyle=8 'Bottom
          objDocTable.borders(4).LineStyle=5 'Right
          objDocTable.borders(5).LineStyle=1  'Center Horizontal
          objDocTable.borders(6).LineStyle=1  'Center Vertical

objMsWord.ActiveDocument.SaveAs "D:\QTP \QTPTable.doc"
objWordDoc.close
objMsWord.Quit
```

This program prints a table in the word document and sets the borders with appropriate border styles. Table is the Object that represents the Table in the word document, borders object represent the border of the Table and LineStyle property represents the border style. The output will be as follows.

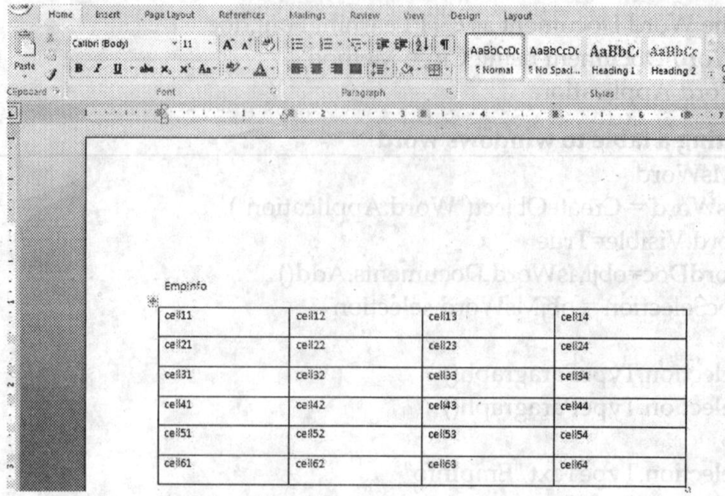

EmpInfo

cell11	cell12	cell13	cell14
cell21	cell22	cell23	cell24
cell31	cell32	cell33	cell34
cell41	cell42	cell43	cell44
cell51	cell52	cell53	cell54
cell61	cell62	cell63	cell64

Line 1-11: Create a word document and Type the text “EmpInfo”
Line 13: Create A range object for defining the area to create the Table.
Line 14: Add a Table with 6 Rows and 4 Columns using Table.Add method.
Line 15: Store the Table Object Created into a Variable objDocTable
Line 16-20: Add Value to each cell of the Table
Line 21-26: Set the Style of the table border using LineStyle Property
Line 28: Saves word Document as QTPTable.doc
Line 29-30: Close the word document and Exit Word Application

Example 5: Search a Specific String in the Microsoft word Document

```
Dim objMsWord
Set objMsWord = CreateObject("Word.Application")
objMsWord.Visible=False
objMsWord.DisplayAlerts=False
set objWordDoc=objMsWord.Documents.
Open("D:\QTP\DemoData.doc")
strToSearch = "QTP"
flagFound=False

For i = 1 To objWordDoc.Paragraphs.Count
    paragraphStart=objWordDoc.Paragraphs(i).Range.Start
    paragraphEnd=objWordDoc.Paragraphs(i).Range.End
     Set searchRange = objWordDoc.Range(paragraphStart,paragraphEnd)

   searchRange.Find.Text = strToSearch
   searchRange.Find.Execute
```

```
16      If searchRange.Find.Found Then
17              flagFound=True
18              Exit For
19      End If
20  Next
21  If flagFound Then
22              Msgbox("Search String "&strToSearch&"  is Found")
23  Else
24              Msgbox("Search String "&strToSearch&"  is NOTFound")
25  End If
26  objWordDoc.Close
27  objMsWord.Quit
```

This program searches for QTP string in the entire document and prints whether the String is available or not. This program uses Count method of Paragraphs object and iterates through all paragraphs of the word document.

Line 1-3: Creates Word Application and sets visible property to False. So the user cannot see this Word Application.
Line 4: Sets Display Alerts Property to False so that no dialogs will be displayed by word.
Line 5: Opens Excel Word Document named DemoData.doc
Line 6: Sets the String to Search in the Document as QTP
Line 7: Sets the flag flagFound as False with the Assumption that QTP keyword is not found in the document. If QTP keyword is found later we will set the flagFound to true.
Line 9: Iterates from First Paragraph to Last Paragraph of the document using Paragraphs.Count property.
Line 10-12: Sets the Search Range of a Keyword as One Paragraph.
Line 14: Sets the String to Search to Find Method.
Line 15: Executes the Find Operation on the Paragraph.
Line 16-19: If Search Keyword is Found set flagFound as True and Exit For Loop. Else Search for the Next Paragraph.
Line 21-25: Displays whether Search Keyword is Found or Not.
Line 26-27: Close Word Document and Quit Word Application.

WORKING WITH OUTLOOK OBJECT MODEL

To perform any operation on Microsoft Office Outlook, you can interact with the objects that are provided by the Outlook object model. The Outlook object model provides classes that represent items in the user interface. For example, the **Application** class represents the entire application, the **MAPIFolder** class represents a folder that contains e-mail messages or other items, and the **MailItem** class represents an e-mail message.

Outlook provides many classes with which you can interact. To use the object model effectively, you should be familiar with the following top-level classes:

- Application
- Explorer
- Inspector
- MAPIFolder
- MailItem™

- AppointmentItem
- TaskItem
- ContactItem

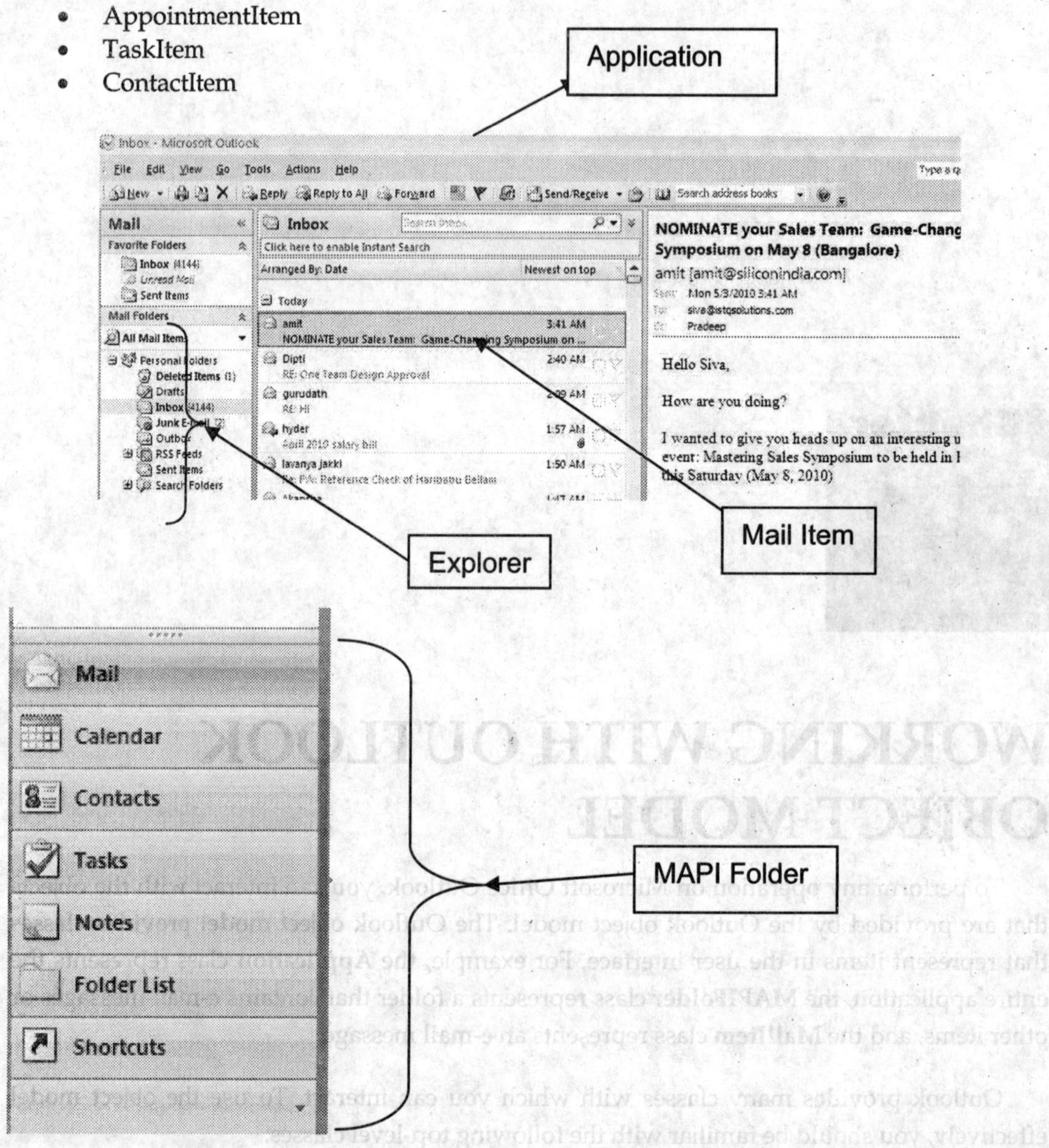

Application Class

The **Application** class represents the Outlook application, and it is the highest-level class in the Outlook object model. Some of the most important members of this class include:

- The **CreateItem** method which you can use to create a new item such as an e-mail message, task, or appointment.

- The **Explorers** property, which you can use to access the windows that display the contents of a folder in the Outlook user interface (UI).
- The **Inspectors** property, which you can use to access the windows that display the contents of a single item, such as an e-mail message or meeting request.

MAPIFolder Class

The **MAPIFolder** class represents a folder that contains e-mail messages, contacts, tasks, and other items. Outlook provides 16 default **MAPIFolder** objects.

The following Table Specifies the folder type for the current Outlook profile.

Name	Value	Description
olFolderCalendar	9	The Calendar folder.
olFolderConflicts	19	The Conflicts folder (subfolder of Sync Issues folder). Only available for an Exchange account.
olFolderContacts	10	The Contacts folder.
olFolderDeletedItems	3	The Deleted Items folder.
olFolderDrafts	16	The Drafts folder.
olFolderInbox	6	The Inbox folder.
olFolderJournal	11	The Journal folder.
olFolderJunk	23	The Junk E-Mail folder.
olFolderLocalFailures	21	The Local Failures folder (subfolder of Sync Issues folder). Only available for an Exchange account.
olFolderManagedEmail	29	The top-level folder in the Managed Folders group. For more information on Managed Folders, see Help in Microsoft Outlook. Only available for an Exchange account.
olFolderNotes	12	The Notes folder.
olFolderOutbox	4	The Outbox folder.
olFolderSentMail	5	The Sent Mail folder.

olFolderServerFailures	22	The Server Failures folder (subfolder of Sync Issues folder). Only available for an Exchange account.
olFolderSyncIssues	20	The Sync Issues folder. Only available for an Exchange account.
olFolderTasks	13	The Tasks folder.
olFolderToDo	28	The To Do folder.
olPublicFoldersAllPublicFolders	18	The **All Public Folders** folder in the Exchange Public Folders store. Only available for an Exchange account.
olFolderRssFeeds	25	The RSS Feeds folder.

MailItem Class

The **MailItem** class represents an e-mail message. **MailItem** objects are usually in folders, such as Inbox, Sent Items, and Outbox. **MailItem** exposes properties and methods that can be used to create and send e-mail messages.

AppointmentItem Class

The **AppointmentItem** class represents a meeting, a one-time appointment, or a recurring appointment or meeting in the Calendar folder. The **AppointmentItem** class includes methods that perform actions such as responding to or forwarding meeting requests, and properties that specify meeting details such as the location and time.

TaskItem Class

The **TaskItem** class represents a task to be performed within a specified time frame. **TaskItem** objects are located in the Tasks folder.

ContactItem Class

The **ContactItemclass** represents a contact in the Contacts folder. **ContactItem** objects contain a variety of contact information for the people they represent, such as street addresses, e-mail addresses, and phone numbers.

Scripting Examples

Example 1: Launching the Outlook Application.

```
Set outlookApp=CreateObject("Outlook.Application")
Set outlookNamespace=outlookApp.GetNamespace("MAPI")
outlookNamespace.Logon
set fdrInbox=outlookNamespace.GetDefaultFolder(6)
fdrInbox.Display
wait(60)
outlookApp.Quit
```

This Program Creates the Outlook COM object and attaches to the MAPI Name Space which contains e-mail messages, contacts, tasks, and other items represented by Outlook Application. Logs in to Outlook and Displays Inbox folder to the user as shown below.

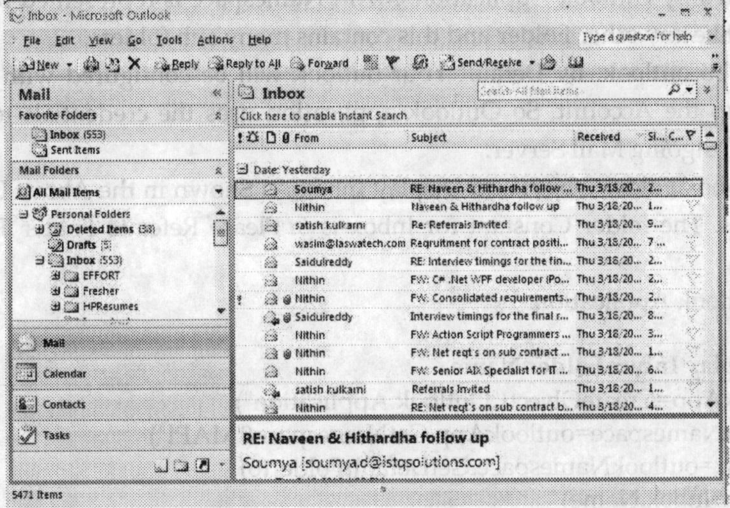

Logon Method

Logs the user on to MAPI and obtains a MAPI session.

NameSpace.**Logon(Profile, Password, ShowDialog, NewSession)**

NameSpace **MAPI NameSpace** object.

Profile Optional **Variant**. The MAPI profile name is a **String** to be used for the session.

Password Optional **Variant**. The password (if any) is a **String** associated with the profile. This parameter exists only for backward compatibility and for security reasons, it is not recommended for use. Microsoft Oultook will prompt the user to specify a password in most system configurations. This is your logon password and should not be confused with PST passwords.

ShowDialog Optional **Variant. True** to display the MAPI logon dialog box to allow the user to select a MAPI profile.

NewSession Optional **Variant. True** to create a new Outlook session. Since multiple sessions cannot be created in Outlook, this parameter should be specified as True only if a session does not already exist.

Line 1: Creates Outlook Application object. This COM object represents the entire Outlook Application.
Line 2: Get MAPI Name Space which contains e-mail messages, contacts, tasks, and other items represented by Outlook Application. MAPI Namespace is represented by MAPIFolder Class which is like any other Folder and this contains many sub folders.
Line 3: Logon To outlook. By Default Your outlook will be configured with Logon details while setting up the Account. So Outlook application uses the credentials to logon to the Incoming and Outgoing Mail Server.
Line 4-6: Get Inbox Folder Object and Display Inbox As Shown in the Above Diagram to the user for 60 Secs. The folder Constant for Inbox is 6. Please Refer to Folder Types table for other folders.
Line 7: Exit Outlook Application.

Example2: Display Inbox Folder Name.

```
1 Set outlookApp=CreateObject("Outlook.Application")
2 Set outlookNamespace=outlookApp.GetNamespace("MAPI")
3 set fdrInbox=outlookNamespace.GetDefaultFolder(6)
4 Msgbox (fdrInbox.Name)
5 outlookApp.Quit
```

Line 1-4 will be used to initialize outlook Application and to retrieve the Inbox Folder Object. Line 4 uses Name Property of the Folder and Displays the folder name. Line 5 Exits the Outlook Application.

Example 3: Enumerating all Folders in a Mailbox.

```
1  Set outlookApp=CreateObject("Outlook.Application")
2  Set outlookNamespace=outlookApp.GetNamespace("MAPI")
3  For each fldr in outlookNamespace.Folders
4          print(fldr.name)
5          GetFoldrsTree(fldr)
6  Next
7  outlookApp.Quit
8
9  Function GetFoldrsTree(fdr)
10   For each foldr in fdr.folders
11           print(foldr.name)
12           GetFoldrsTree(foldr)
13   Next
14 End Function
```

This program displays all Folders present in the Outlook by going through every sub folder in the MAPI Folder Tree. This program uses Recursive Programming Technique to display the entire Folder Tree.

Line 1-2: Initialize Outlook Application and Get MAPI Namespace which contains all Sub Folders.

Line 3-6: Go through each folder in MAPI Name Space and print the Sub Folders under each Folder by using **GetFoldrsTree** recursive function. Recursive function is the function which calls itself. This is very essential while reading tree like data which is represented by Menus, XML Files and Folders.

Example 4: Count number of emails in any folder.

```
1  Set outlookApp=CreateObject("Outlook.Application")
2  Set outlookNamespace=outlookApp.GetNamespace("MAPI")
3  set fdrInbox=outlookNamespace.GetDefaultFolder(6)
4  Msgbox ("Number of Emails in Inbox:"&fdrInbox.Items.Count)
5  outlookApp.Quit
```

This program Displays the number of emails present in the Inbox. Line 1-3 Initializes Outlook and gets Inbox Folder Object. Line 4 Displays the number of emails in the Inbox by using **fdrInbox.Items.Count**. Items Represent the collection of each email and count gives the number of emails in the collection.

Example 5: Read subject of All Emails from outlook

```
1 Set outlookApp=CreateObject("Outlook.Application")
2 Set outlookNamespace=outlookApp.GetNamespace("MAPI")
3 set fdrInbox=outlookNamespace.GetDefaultFolder(6)
4 For each mailItem in fdrInbox.Items
5         print(mailItem.subject)
6 Next
7 outlookApp.Quit
```

This Program prints the Subject of All Emails in the Inbox. Line 1-3 Initializes Outlook and gets the Inbox Folder Object. Line 4-6 goes through each email and prints the subject of his email. **MailItem** variable in Line 4 represents one mail at a time from mails collection represented by fdrInbox.Items. Line 5 uses subject property and print the subject of the email

Example 6: Read content of first unread Email from Inbox.

```
1  Set outlookApp=CreateObject("Outlook.Application")
2  Set outlookNamespace=outlookApp.GetNamespace("MAPI")
3  set fdrInbox=outlookNamespace.GetDefaultFolder(6)
4  For each mailItem in fdrInbox.Items
5      If mailItem.unread Then
6              print(mailItem.body)
7              Exit For
8      End If
9  Next
10 outlookApp.Quit
```

This program prints the content of a first unread email it encountered in the Inbox. Line 1-3 Initializes Outlook and gets the Inbox Folder Object. Line 4-9 goes through each email and checks for the first unread email and prints its content. **mailItem** variable in Line 4 represents one mail at a time from mails collection represented by *fdrInbox.Items*. Line 5 uses unread property and checks whether the mail is read or unread. If Unread, Line 6 prints the content of the email using body property. Line7 Exits the For Loop since we encountered first unread mail and there is no need to loop through further mails.

Example 7: Download an email attachment from a Mail with specific subject

```
1  Set outlookApp=CreateObject("Outlook.Application")
2  Set outlookNamespace=outlookApp.GetNamespace("MAPI")
3  set fdrInbox=outlookNamespace.GetDefaultFolder(6)
4  For each mailItem in fdrInbox.Items
5          If mailItem.subject="Best Way To Learn QTP" Then
6                  For each attachmnt in mailItem.attachments
7                      attachmnt.saveasfile "D:\QTP\attachmnt.FileName
8                  Next
9                  Exit For
10         End If
11 Next
12 outlookApp.Quit
```

This Program saves the attachments from a mail with specified subject in the specified folder. Line 1-3 Initializes Outlook and gets the Inbox Folder Object. Lines 4-11 goes through each email and checks for the email with specified subject and saves all its attachments in a specified folder. Line 5 uses subject property and checks for the email with specified subject. If found, Line 6 uses attachments property to represent all the attachments collection and loops through one attachment at a time. Line 7 Saves the Attachment in the specified folder. Name of the attachment will be retrieved by using FileName property of the attachment. Line9 Exits the For Loop since we encountered email with specified subject and there is no need to loop through further mails.

Example 8: Send an Email from outlook.

```
Set outlookApp=CreateObject("Outlook.Application")
Set outlookNamespace=outlookApp.GetNamespace("MAPI")
outlookNamespace.Logon
set fdrInbox=outlookNamespace.GetDefaultFolder(6)
fdrInbox.Display
set mailMsg=outlookApp.CreateItem(olMailItem)
mailMsg.Recipients.Add("QTPCompleteReference@yahoo.com")
mailMsg.subject="Feed Back"
mailMsg.body="This book is very useful for my QTP learning"
mailMsg.send
outlookApp.Quit
```

This program sends an email from outlook with specified Subject, body to specified Recipient.

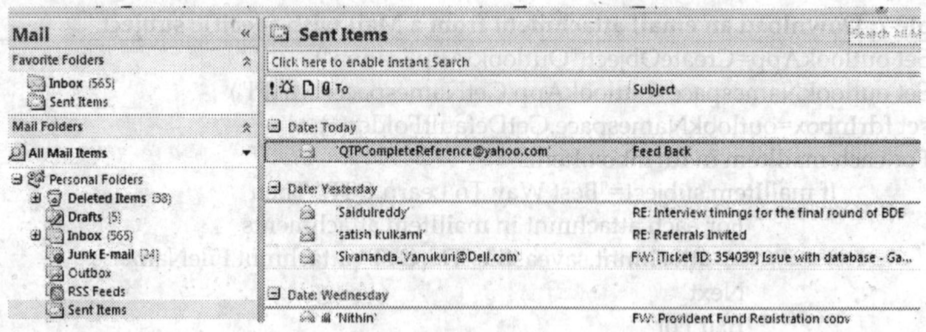

Line 1-5: Initialize outlook and display Inbox.
Line 6: Creates a New Mail Message using CreateItem Method.
Line 7: Add Recipient's Email Address.
Line 8: Add Mail subject.
Line 9: Add Mail body.
Line 10: Send Email using send property.

Example 9: Send an Email from outlook with Attachment.

```
1  Set outlookApp=CreateObject("Outlook.Application")
2  Set outlookNamespace=outlookApp.GetNamespace("MAPI")
3  outlookNamespace.Logon
4  set fdrInbox=outlookNamespace.GetDefaultFolder(6)
5  fdrInbox.Display
6  set mailMsg=outlookApp.CreateItem(olMailItem)
7  mailMsg.Recipients.Add("QTPCompleteReference@yahoo.com")
8  mailMsg.subject="Feed Back"
9  mailMsg.body="This book is very useful for my QTP learning"
10 mailMsg.Attachments.add "D:\QTP\qtpmanual.doc"
11 mailMsg.send
12 outlookApp.Quit
```

This program sends an email from outlook with specified Subject, body to specified Recipient along with Attachment.

Line 1-5: Initialize outlook and display Inbox.
Line 6: Create a New Mail Message using CreateItem Method.
Line 7-9: Add Recipient's Email Address, Mail subject, Mail body.
Line 10: Add the Attachment.
Line 11: Sends Email using send property.

Chapter 35

USER DEFINED METHODS

Function Definition Generator

QuickTest provides a Function Definition Generator, which enables you to generate definitions for new user-defined functions. You can then register these functions to a test object, if needed. After you register a function to a test object, it is displayed in the Keyword View, as well as in IntelliSense and in the Step Generator.

Finally, you can document your user-defined function by defining the tooltip that displays when the cursor is positioned over the operation in the Step Generator, in the Keyword View, and when using IntelliSense. You can also add a sentence that describes the purpose of the function. This sentence is then displayed in the Keyword View in the Documentation column.

Using the Function Definition Generator

1. To open the Function Definition Generator Select **Insert > Function Definition Generator** or click the **Function Definition Generator** icon. The Function Definition Generator opens as below

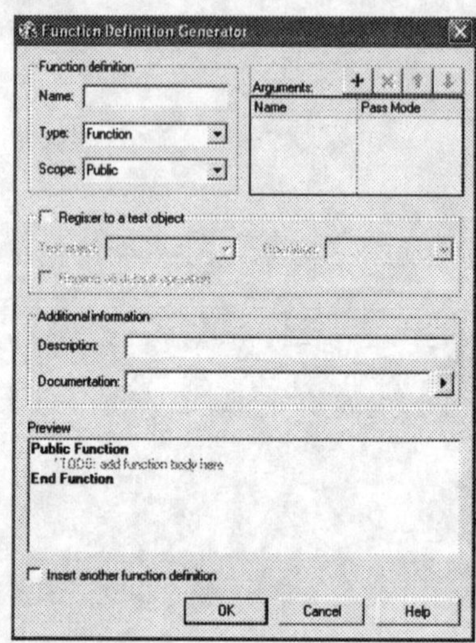

2. Enter Name of the function in Name field like **GetCountOfItems**, select Type as Function or Sub and scope as public

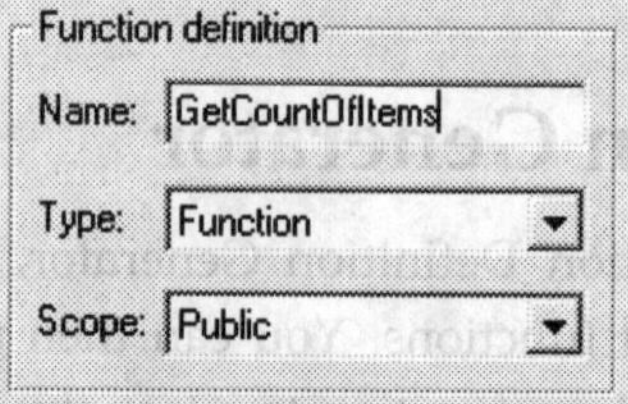

3. Select TestObject from the list of available objects and write method name to be displayed in the list of object methods in the operation list box. For Ex: **MyGetItemsCount**. Most of the times we give method name the same as the function name. If you want the function to be displayed as the default operation, select the check box **Register as default operation.**

4. Specify the function's arguments under the Arguments section

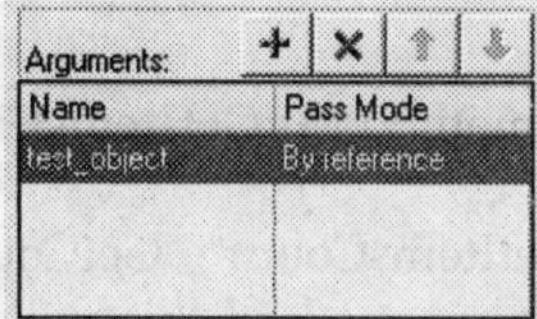

5. Specify the text that you want to display in the **Documentation** column in the section below. Therefore, the sentence must be clear and understandable.

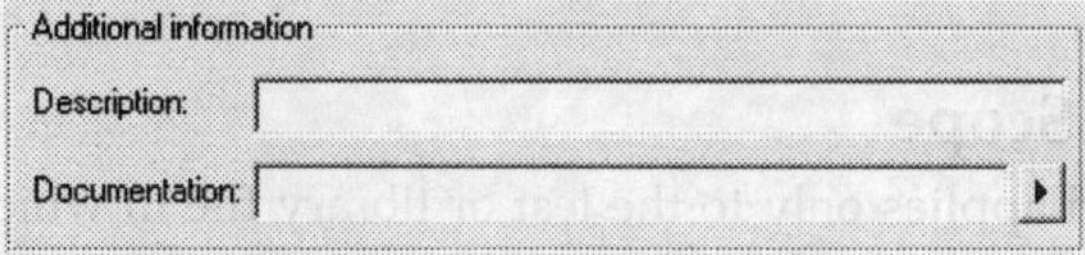

6. Click OK. Code something like below will be displayed in the Expertview Editor

```
Public Function GetCountOfItems(ByRef test_object)
    ' TODO: add function body here
End Function
RegisterUserFunc "WebList", "MyGetItemsCount", "GetCountOfItems"
```

RegisterUserFunc

RegisterUserFunc allows you to add a new method or overwrite the existing method of a test object. Syntax is:

RegisterUserFunc TOClass, MethodName, FunctionName, SetAsDefault

Item	Description
TOClass	Any test object class.
MethodName	The name of the method you want to register (and display in QuickTest, for example, in the Keyword View and IntelliSense). If you enter the name of a method already associated with the specified test object class, your user-defined function overrides the existing method. If you enter a new name, it is added to the list of methods that the object supports.
FunctionName	The name of the user-defined function that you want to call from your component. The function can be located in any function library associated with your component's application area.
SetAsDefault	**Optional.** Indicates whether the registered function is used as the default

	operation for the test object. **Default = False**

The following Code registers a new method **MyGetItemsCount** to WebList object.

RegisterUserFunc "WebList", "MyGetItemsCount", "GetCountOfItems"
When the user calls **MyGetItemsCount** method this will indirectly call **GetCountOfItems** function which actually returns the number of items in a list box. Also note that the method you registered is applicable to all the objects of type WebList, not specific to a particular list object of the application.

RegisterUserFunc Scope

A registered method applies only to the test or library file in which you register it or to any tests calling an action containing a **RegisterUserFunc** statement. For tests, if you register a function within a reusable action, it is recommended that you unregister the method at the end of the action. QuickTest clears all function registrations at the beginning of each run session.

UnregisterUserFunc Statement

This is used to unregister the method which you already registered to Test Object. The Syntax is:

UnRegisterUserFunc *TOClass, MethodName*

Argument	Type	Description
TOClass	String	The test object class for which you want to unregister the method.
MethodName	String	The method you want to unregister.

The following Code Unregisters **MyGetItemsCount method** from **the WebList** Test Object.

UnRegisterUserFunc "WebList", "MyGetItemsCount".

Scripting Examples

Example1: Add MyGetItemsCount method to WebList

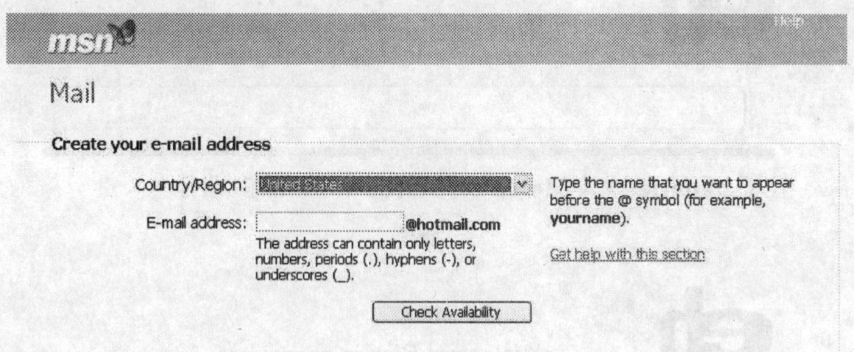


```
1 Public Function GetCountOfItems(ByRef test_object)
2         GetCountOfItems=test_object.GetROProperty("items count")
3 End Function
4
5 RegisterUserFunc "WebList", "MyGetItemsCount", "GetCountOfItems"
6 countryCount=Browser("MSN").Page("SignUp").WebList("pff00000000010004").MyGetIt
  emsCount()
7 Msgbox("Number of Countries in Country List Box Are: "&countryCount)
```

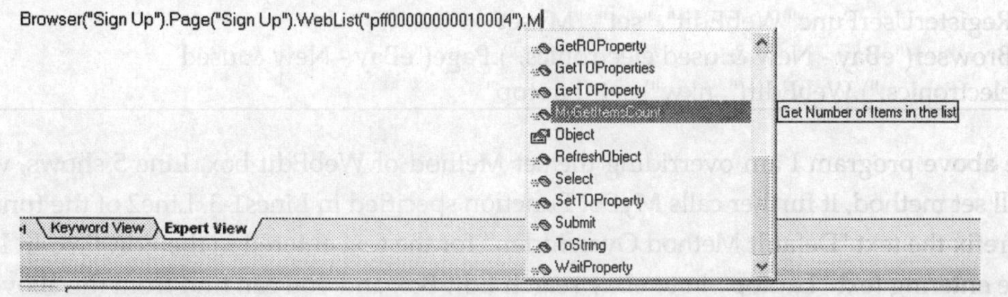

This program demonstrates how to add user defined method **MyGetItemsCount** to WebList TestObject. After adding this method to WebList you can find this method from WebList methods in QTP Script Editor as shown in the above Fig. **MyGetItemsCount** method will return the number of items present in the WebList Box on which it is called. Line6 shows usage of **MyGetItemsCount** method with Country/Region WebList box present in MSN Sign Page Shown in the above Fig. **RegisterUserFunc** statement specified in Line5 register user defined method **MyGetItemsCount** with Function **GetCountOfItems.** When the user calls **MyGetItemsCount** method this indirectly calls function **GetCountOfItems** which in turn returns the number of items present in the list box.

Example 2: Overriding default set method of a WebEdit object

Welcome! Sign in or register.

Categories ▾ | Motors | Stores | Daily Deal

Welcome! Sign in or register.

Default Method Overridden Laptop

Categories ▾ | Motors | Stores | Daily Deal

```
1 Public Function Myset(ByRef test_object, ByRef textToSet)
2         test_object.set "Default Method Overridden "&textToSet
3 End Function
4 
5 RegisterUserFunc "WebEdit", "set", "Myset"
6 Browser("eBay - New & used electronics,").Page("eBay - New & used electronics,").WebEdit("_nkw").set "Laptop"
```

In the above program I am overriding the set Method of WebEdit box. Line 5 shows, when we call set method, it further calls **MySet** Function specified in Lines1-3. Line2 of the function will prefix the text "Default Method Overridden" for the text entered in the Edit Box. In Line6 we are entering text "Laptop" in to eBay search Edit Box and you can find from the above Fig that the overridden WebEdit box set method enters "Default Method Overridden Laptop".

WORKING WITH WINDOWS SCRIPT HOST (WSH)

Windows Script Host (WSH) is a Windows administration tool. WSH creates an environment for hosting scripts. That is, when a script arrives at your computer, WSH plays the part of the host — it makes objects and services available for the script and provides a set of guidelines within which the script is executed. Among other things, Windows Script Host manages security and invokes the appropriate script engine.

WSH is language-independent for WSH-compliant scripting engines. It brings simple, powerful, and flexible scripting to the Windows platform, allowing you to run scripts from both the Windows desktop and the command prompt. We can program in QTP using Windows Script Host objects.

WSH Object Model

Windows Script Host provides several objects for direct manipulation of script execution, as well as helper functions for other actions. Using these objects and services, you can accomplish tasks such as the following:

- Print messages to the screen
- Run basic functions such as CreateObject and GetObject
- Map network drives
- Connect to printers
- Retrieve and modify environment variables
- Modify registry keys

The illustration that follows represents the Windows Script Host Object Model hierarchy:

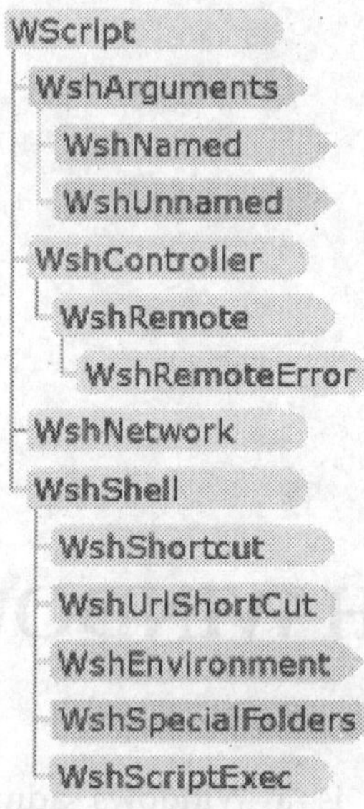

Source: http://msdn.microsoft.com/en-us/library/a74hyyw0(VS.85).aspx

WSH provides the following nice runtime objects to allow your VBScript code to interact with the environment:

- **WScript** - The root object in the WSH runtime hierarchy to hold other WSH objects. WScript also contains some important properties to access script execution level information, like standard input and output, connection to external COM objects, etc.
- **WScript.Shell** - Creates a new WshShell object to run commands and manage registry keys on the local machine.
- **WScript.Network** - Creates a new WshNetwork object to access resources on the network, including the local machine.
- **WScript.Arguments** - A WshArguments object representing command line arguments as a collection.

WSH Objects Services

Using these objects and services, you can accomplish tasks such as the following:

- Print messages to the screen
- Run basic functions such as CreateObject and GetObject
- Map network drives
- Connect to printers
- Retrieve and modify environment variables
- Modify registry keys

Send Keys Method

Use the **SendKeys** method of **WshShell** object to send keystrokes to applications that have no automation interface. Below is the table for Key and its representation in SendKeys method.

Key	Argument
BACKSPACE	{BACKSPACE}, {BS}, or {BKSP}
BREAK	{BREAK}
CAPS LOCK	{CAPSLOCK}
DEL or DELETE	{DELETE} or {DEL}
DOWN ARROW	{DOWN}
END	{END}
ENTER	{ENTER} or ~
ESC	{ESC}
HELP	{HELP}
HOME	{HOME}
INS or INSERT	{INSERT} or {INS}
LEFT ARROW	{LEFT}
NUM LOCK	{NUMLOCK}
PAGE DOWN	{PGDN}
PAGE UP	{PGUP}
PRINT SCREEN	{PRTSC}
RIGHT ARROW	{RIGHT}
SCROLL LOCK	{SCROLLLOCK}
TAB	{TAB}

UP ARROW	{UP}
F1	{F1}
F2	{F2}
F3	{F3}
F4	{F4}
F5	{F5}
F6	{F6}
F7	{F7}
F8	{F8}
F9	{F9}
F10	{F10}
F11	{F11}
F12	{F12}
F13	{F13}
F14	{F14}
F15	{F15}
F16	{F16}

To send keyboard characters that of a regular keystroke in combination with a SHIFT, CTRL, or ALT, create a compound string argument that represents the keystroke combination. You do this by preceding the regular keystroke with one or more of the following special characters:

Key	**Special Character**
SHIFT	+
CTRL	^
ALT	%

To send the keystroke combination Q,T and P with SHIFT key is held down send the string argument "+(QTP)". To send a space, send the string " ".Also note you cannot send the PRINT SCREEN key {PRTSC} to an application.

The **SendKeys** method uses some characters as modifiers of characters. This set of special characters consists of parentheses, brackets, braces, and the:

- plus sign "+",
- caret "^",
- percent sign "%",
- and tilde "~"

Send these characters by enclosing them within braces "{}". For example, to send the plus sign, send the string argument "{+}". Brackets "[ ]" have no special meaning when used with **SendKeys**, but you must enclose them within braces to accommodate applications that do give them a special meaning (for dynamic data exchange (DDE) for example).

- To send bracket characters, send the string argument "{[}" for the left bracket and "{]}" for the right one.
- To send brace characters, send the string argument "{{}" for the left brace and "{}}" for the right one.

Read more about **sendkeys** method at below link
http://msdn.microsoft.com/en-us/library/ 8c6yea83%28VS.85%29.aspx

Comparing VBScript CreateObject and GetObject Functions with WSH

Both VBScript language and WSH provides CreateObject and GetObject functions. The VBScript CreateObject function and the WScript CreateObject method both instantiate COM objects when they are called with a single parameter, the ProgID of the COM object to instantiate. For example, from below two lines of code the first uses the VBScript version of CreateObject and the second uses the WSH version; both are functionally identical and instantiate an instance of the FileSystemObject:

```
Set objFSO = CreateObject("Scripting.FileSystemObject")
Set objFSO = Wscript.CreateObject("Scripting.FileSystemObject")
```

Both versions of CreateObject can also accept a second parameter; however, each interprets this second parameter in a completely different way. Consider these two lines of code. The first line uses VBScript, and the second uses WSH:

```
Set objExcel = CreateObject("Excel.Application", "Parameter2")
Set objExcel = Wscript.CreateObject("Excel.Application", "Parameter2")
```

The VBScript CreateObject function interprets the second parameter as a remote computer name and tries to create the COM object on that remote computer; in this example, it tries to instantiate an instance of Microsoft Excel on a remote computer named Parameter2. The WScript CreateObject method interprets a second parameter as a subroutine prefix to be used in handling events from the object. The two GetObject functions are similarly related.

To simply create a COM object, you can either use the VBScript function or the WScript CreateObject method. After the object has been created, there are no differences in capabilities; all the methods and properties available for the object created using Wscript CreateObject are also available using VBScript CreateObject. Furthermore, these properties and methods are all called in identical fashion.

Scripting Examples

Example 1: Send Keys Method to open the Date and Time Dialog

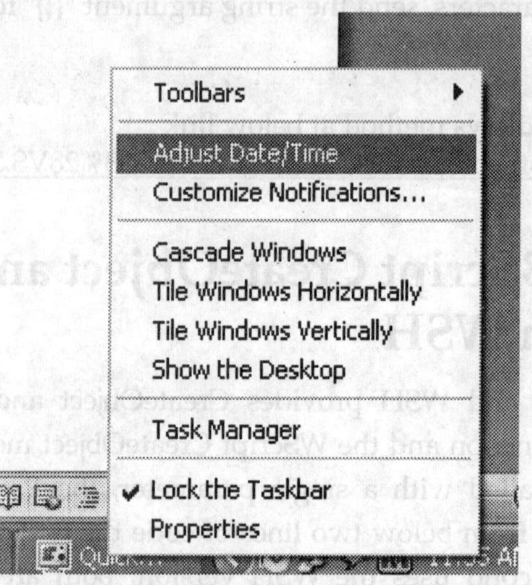

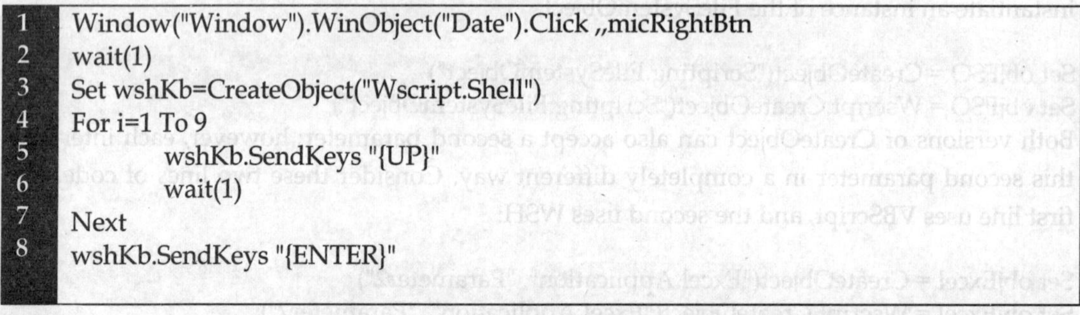

```
1 Window("Window").WinObject("Date").Click ,,micRightBtn
2 wait(1)
3 Set wshKb=CreateObject("Wscript.Shell")
4 For i=1 To 9
5         wshKb.SendKeys "{UP}"
6         wait(1)
7 Next
8 wshKb.SendKeys "{ENTER}"
```

This program demonstrates how to use keyboard keys on the application. In Line1 we are clicking the Date object which is present at the bottom right of your windows using Right Mouse Button. Line 3 Creates a Shell object which is part of windows script host. Lines 4-9 send UP key from key board for 9 times with a delay of 1 sec for each key press event. Line 8 presses **Enter** key in the keyboard and this displays Date and Time Properties Dialog.

Using SendKeys method is one of the most powerful techniques that help solving many automation problems. If your application supports Key Strokes then you can automate that application using SendKeys method as shown above. Note, you cannot send the PRINT SCREEN key {PRTSC} to an application using SendKeys method.

Example 2: Pressing Right Mouse Key

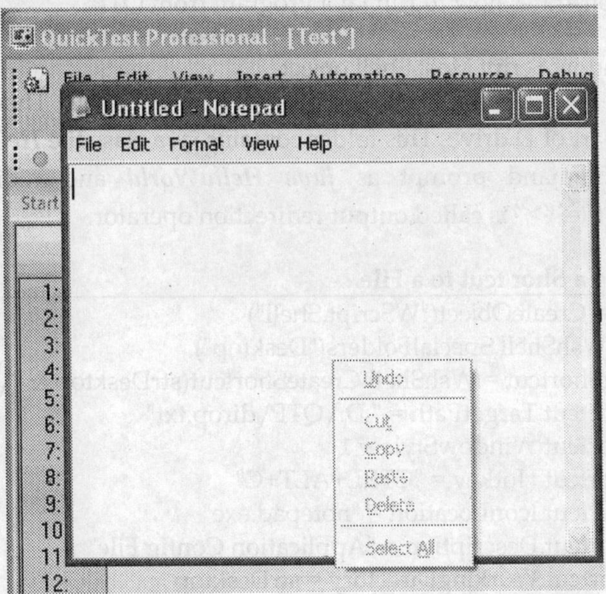


```
1 Window("Notepad").WinEditor("Edit").SetCaretPos 0,0
2 Set wshShell=CreateObject("Wscript.Shell")
3 wait(2)
4 wshShell.SendKeys "+{F10}"
5 wait(10)
```

In the above program presses Right Mouse button. Right Mouse button is referred to with SHIFT+F10 from the key board. Since the Cursor is placed in the Notepad, the above screenshot shows the Menu appeared in the Notepad when the Right Mouse button is pressed. Line4 sends RightMouse Button press event to application.

Example 3: Running Java program from QTP.

HelloWorld - Notepad

File Edit Format View Help

```
public class HelloWorld{
        public static void main(String args[]){
        System.out.println("QTP Complete Reference");
        }
}
```

```
1 Set wshCmd=CreateObject("Wscript.Shell")
2 wshCmd.Run "cmd /K d: &cd D:\ &java HelloWorld > D:\QTP \javapgmop.txt"
3 wait(2)
4 Set wshCmd=Nothing
```

This program demonstrates how to run Java Program from QTP.

Line 1: Creates Window Script Host Shell object.
Line 2: Use Run method to run a command prompt from the shell. Then we change to folder **D:\QTP** which is part of D drive. This folder contains java class file ***HelloWorld***. We run this class file from command prompt as ***java HelloWorld*** and redirect the output to ***javapgmop.txt*** text file. ">" is called output redirection operator.

Example 4: Creating a Shor tcut to a File.

```
1  set WshShell = CreateObject("WScript.Shell")
2  strDesktop = WshShell.SpecialFolders("Desktop")
3  set appConfigShortcut = WshShell.CreateShortcut(strDesktop & "\AppConfig.lnk")
4  appConfigShortcut.TargetPath = " D:\QTP\dirop.txt"
5  appConfigShortcut.WindowStyle = 1
6  appConfigShortcut.Hotkey = "CTRL+ALT+C"
7  appConfigShortcut.IconLocation = "notepad.exe"
8  appConfigShortcut.Description = "Application Config File"
9  appConfigShortcut.WorkingDirectory = strDesktop
10 appConfigShortcut.Save
```

This program demonstrates how to create Shortcut to a specific file on the Desktop using CreateShortcut method. Simply calling the **CreateShortcut** method does not result in the creation of a shortcut.To create a shortcut, you must:

1. Create an instance of a **WshShortcut** object.
2. Initialize its properties.
3. Save it to disk with the Save method.

Line 1: Create windows script Host object
Line 2: Get the path of the Special Folder Desktop, using SpecialFolders method.
Line 3: Create Shortcut ***AppConfig.lnk*** on the desktop using CreateShortcut method of the shell Object. This method return appConfigShortcut which is of the type **WshShortcut.**
Line 4-10: Set various properties of the shortcut object.

TargetPath - The path to the shortcut's executable.

WindowStyle - Sets the window style for the program being run. 1-Activates and displays a window. 3- Displays as a maximized window. 7- Minimizes the window.

Hotkey - A string representing the key-combination to assign to the shortcut.

IconLocation - Assigns an icon to a shortcut.

Description - Returns a shortcut's description.

WorkingDirectory - Directory in which the shortcut starts.

Line 10: Saves the Shortcut properties.

Example 5: Print logged in username, domain name and computer name

```
1 Set WshNetwork = CreateObject("WScript.Network")
2 print "Domain = " & WshNetwork.UserDomain
3 print "Computer Name = " & WshNetwork.ComputerName
4 print "User Name = " & WshNetwork.UserName
```

This program uses Network object of Windows Script Host and Prints three properties of the computer in the network namely Domain, Computer Name and User Name. Line1 Returns WshNetwork Object. Line2 displays Domain Name, Line3 Computer Name and Line4 returns Logged in UserName. The Output is as shown below:

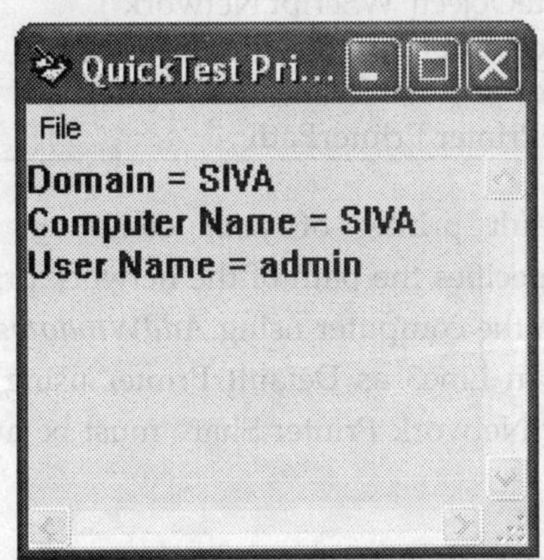

Example 6: Print Mapped Network Drives.

```
1 Set WshNetwork = CreateObject("WScript.Network")
2 Set oDrives = WshNetwork.EnumNetworkDrives
3 print "Network drive mappings:"
4 For i = 0 to oDrives.Count - 1 Step 2
5     print "Drive " & oDrives.Item(i) & " = " & oDrives.Item(i+1)
6 Next
```

This Program Prints all the mapped Network drives in the computer. Line 2 uses EnumNetworkDrives method of WshNetwork Object and stores the list of Network Drives in oDrives. Line 4-6 prints all the drive names and their network share path. Please observe that in Line4 Loop is incremented by 2. The first increment is for Drive Name like Z and the second increment is for network share path like \\server\public.

Example 7: Map a network Drive to a local computer

```
1 Dim WshNetwork
2 Set WshNetwork = CreateObject("WScript.Network")
3 WshNetwork.MapNetworkDrive "Z:", \\Server\Public
4 Wait(20)
5 WshNetwork.RemoveNetworkDrive "Z:"
```

This program demonstrates how to Add or Remove Network drives in the computer using the methods of WshNetwork object. Line 3 Maps **\\server\public** share to Z drive using MapNetworkDrive method and Line 6 Removes Z drive mapping using RemoveNetworkDrive method. Note that **\\server\public** Network Share must be available for this program to execute successfully.

Example 8: Set Default Printer

```
1 Set WshNetwork = CreateObject("WScript.Network")
2 PrinterPath = "\\myoffice\public"
3 WshNetwork.AddWindowsPrinterConnection PrinterPath
4 WshNetwork.SetDefaultPrinter PrinterPath
```

This program sets the default printer of your computer using printer methods of ***WshNetwork*** Object. Line 2 specifies the path of the network printer. Line 3 adds printer to the list of printers available in the computer using ***AddWindowsPrinterConnection*** method. Line4 sets the Printer added in Line3 as Default Printer using ***SetDefaultPrinter*** method. Note that **\\myoffice\public** Network Printer Share must be available for this program to execute successfully.

Example 9: Add, Read and Delete Registry Keys.

```
Dim WshReg
Set WshReg = CreateObject("WScript.Shell")
WshReg.RegWrite "HKCU\MyRegKey\", 1, "REG_BINARY"
WshReg.RegWrite "HKCU\MyRegKey\QTPCompleteReference\Author", "Siva", "REG_SZ"
Msgbox WshReg.RegRead("HKCU\MyRegKey\QTPCompleteReference\Author")
Wait(50)
WshReg.RegDelete "HKCU\MyRegKey\QTPCompleteReference\Author"
WshReg.RegDelete "HKCU\MyRegKey\QTPCompleteReference\"
WshReg.RegDelete "HKCU\MyRegKey\"
```

This Program Adds and assigns a value to the Registry Key. It Displays the Value of the Registry Key by reading from registry and Delete the Registry Key from Registry. This program uses RegWrite, RegRead and RegDelete Methods of Windows Script Host Shell object.

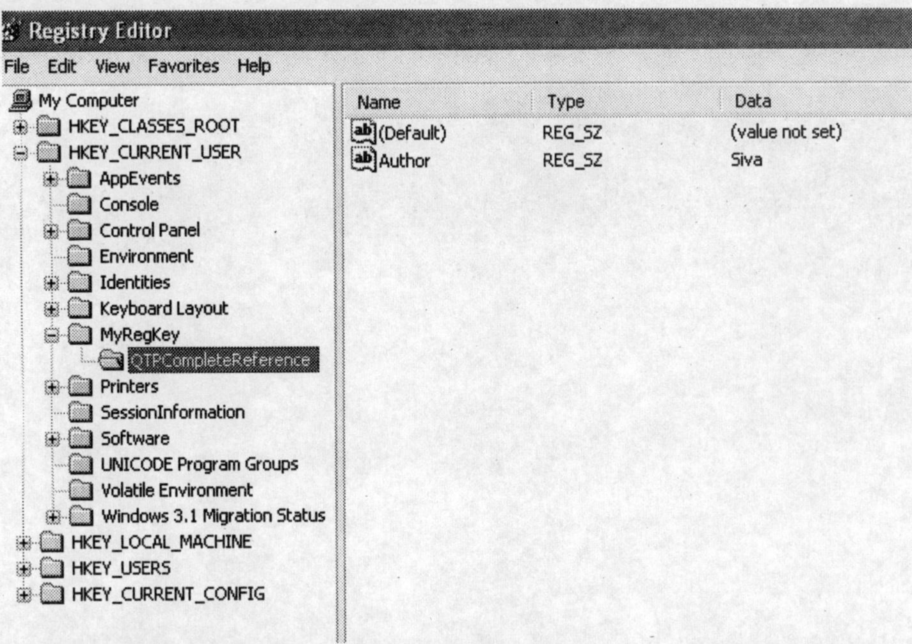

Line 3: Creates a Registry Entry MyRegKey under HKCU.
Line 4: Adds a RegistryKey Author under **HKCU\ MyRegKey\ QTPCompleteReference** and Assigns the Value as Siva. You can view these entries by opening windows registry with regedit command.
Line 5: Read and Display value of Registrykey Author.
Line 7-9: Deletes Registry Key Values.

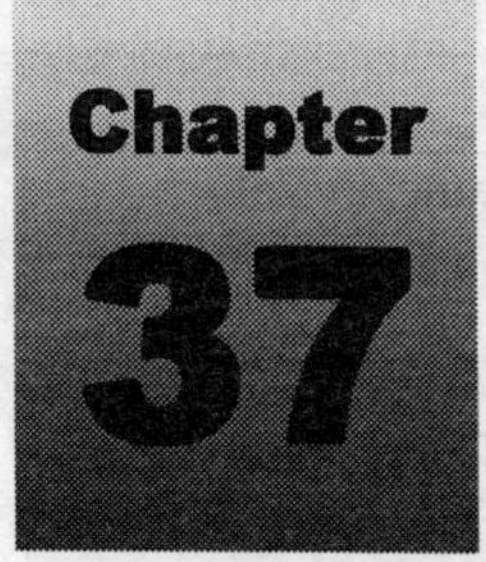

CUSTOM CHECK POINTS AND SYNCHRONISATION

We have already learnt how to use inbuilt features of QTP like checkpoints and synchronization. This chapter explains to the reader how to implement their own check points called custom checkpoints. Custom Checkpoints offer an easier and highly flexible way of constructing your object verifications, which is a core concept of test automation. This chapter also unveils the code behind QTP implementation of check points and synchronization.

Where do you need custom check points?

You may use custom check points in various instances as below:

- To compare two or more objects with respect to their properties. For example, you may want to check whether groups of edit boxes and list boxes in the page are left aligned.
- To write your own algorithm to compare bitmaps with some tolerance like RGB color and % of pixels deviation.

- To compare a bitmap with one or more bitmaps of the same page or a different page.
- To make some custom checks like NULL validation on the database content.
- To custom compare XML files content like some tolerance in the attributes value or number of children.

Understanding Code behind Standard Checkpoint

We have seen in the Checkpoints chapter how to use a standard checkpoint which is used to check the property values of an object. Below is the code snippet to create your own standard check point named **MyPropertyCheck** for Webbutton object which checks the property value of a given object.

```
1  Public Function MyPropertyCheck(ByRef TestObject, ByVal PropName, ByVal
   ExpValue)
2      ActValue=TestObject.GetROProperty(PropName)
3  If ExpValue=ActValue Then
4      Reporter.ReportEvent micPass,PropName&" Check","Property Check Passed"
5  Else
6      Reporter.ReportEvent micFail,PropName&" Check","Property Check Failed"
7  End If
8  End Function
9  RegisterUserFunc"WebButton","MyPropertyCheck","MyPropertyCheck"
10
11 Browser("Google").Page("Google").WebButton("Google Search").MyPropertyCheck
   "Disabled",False
12
13 Browser("Google").Page("Google").WebButton("Google Search"). MyPropertyCheck
   "Height",25
```

In the above program from Line1-8 we have created a user defined method **MyPropertyCheck** which checks whether the specified Property has specified expected value and reports PASS/FAIL to the results file. This function takes 3 arguments:

TestObject - Name of the object for which the property has to be verified

PropName - Name of the property to be verified
ExpValue - Expected value of the property

In Line 2 GetROProperty returns the property value of the object in the application corresponding to the property name specified. This return value is called actual value since we have read it from the application object.

Line 3-7 compares the Expected Value with Actual Value and reports PASS/FAIL to the results fail.

Line 11 checks **Disabled** property of Google Search button. Expected value of Disabled property is False. Check point used in this line will pass since it's expected value is same as the Actual Value. Output in Test Results file is as below.

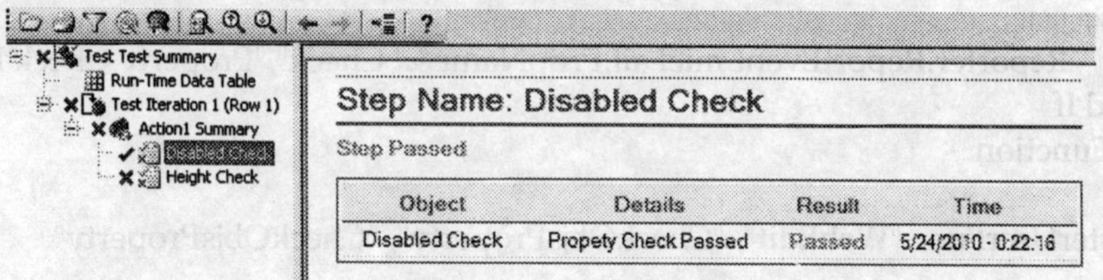

Line 13 checks **Height** property of Google Search button. Expected value of property Height is 30 and check point will Fail since Actual Value of GoogleSearch button is not 30. Output in Test Results file is as below.

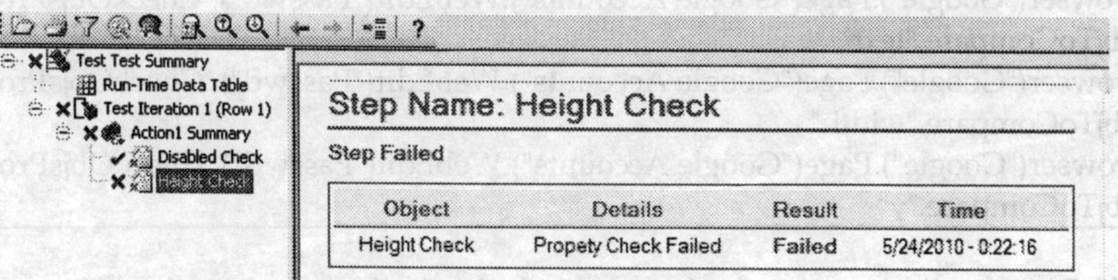

Please note that in the above checkpoint we did not use time out value which you usually find while applying standard check point. This can also be achieved by passing an additional parameter timeout. How to manage the timeout value can be learnt later in this chapter while learning synchronization point.

Creating Custom Check Point

Now Let us create a Custom Check Point which compares the Specified property for Two objects and reports PASS to results file if property value is same or else reports FAIL to results file. Code for this custom check point is as below...

```
1  Public Function CheckObjsProperty(ByRef TestObject1, ByRef TestObject2,ByVal
   PropName)
2          ActValue1=TestObject1.GetROProperty(PropName)
3          ActValue2=TestObject2.GetROProperty(PropName)
4    If ActValue1=ActValue2 Then
5        Reporter.ReportEvent micPass,PropName&" Check","Property Check Passed"
6    Else
7        Reporter.ReportEvent micFail,PropName&" Check","Property Check Failed"
8    End If
9  End Function
10
11 RegisterUserFunc "WebEdit", "CheckObjsProperty", "CheckObjsProperty"

12 set ObjToCompare=Browser("Google").Page("Google Accounts").
   WebEdit("PasswdAgain")
13
14
15 Browser("Google").Page("Google Accounts").WebEdit("Passwd"). CheckObjsProperty
   ObjToCompare,"text"
16 Browser("Google").Page("Google Accounts").WebEdit("Passwd"). CheckObjsProperty
   ObjToCompare,"width"
17 Browser("Google").Page("Google Accounts").WebEdit("Passwd"). CheckObjsProperty
   ObjToCompare,"y"
```

CheckObjsProperty is custom check point which checks whether the property value represented by PropName for both the application objects TestObject1, TestObject2 is same or not. Line2,3 retrieves property values for both TestObject1 and TestObject2 and stores in variables ActValue1, ActValue2 respectively. Line 4-8 compares the property value of both objects and reports result of checkpoint as PASS/FAIL to results file.

Below is the password section of Google registration screen with two WebEdit boxes Password and PasswordAgain.

Choose a password: •••••••• Password strength:

Minimum of 8 characters in length.

Re-enter password: ••••••••

Line 15, 16 and 17 checks text, width and y property values for both objects Password and PasswordAgain. Below is the TestResults screen.

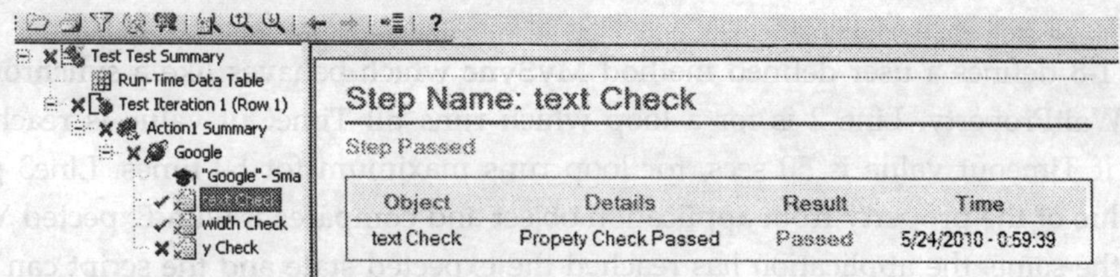

It is clear from the test results file that check point is pass for two properties **text and width** and failed for **y**.

Understanding Code behind Synchronization Point

We have learnt about synchronization in the previous chapters as it is a mechanism to control the speed of the script execution so that it matches with the application speed. We have also learnt that when a synchronization point is created the code will look as below:

Browser("Yahoo").Page("Home").WebButton("SignIn").WaitProperty"Disabled",False,50000

In the above statement;

- Waitproperty is the method which represents the synchronization point.
- Property name: Disabled
- Expected value: False
- Timeout: 50000 milli seconds

Now let us create a synchronization method MySync for WebButton. Code for the same will look as below:

```
Public Function MySync(ByRef TestObject, ByVal PropName, ByVal ExpValue, ByVal TimeOut)
    For i=1 To TimeOut
        If  TestObject.GetROProperty("PropName") = ExpValue Then
                Exit For
            Else
                wait(1)
            End If
        Next
End Function
RegisterUserFunc "WebButton", "MySync", "MySync"

Browser("Yahoo").Page("Home").WebButton("SignIn").MySync "Disabled",False,50
.........
.........
```

Line 1-8 defines a user defined method **MySync** which behaves like a synchronization method WaitProperty. Line 2 is for a loop which runs till TimeOut value is reached. For example if Timeout value is 50 secs, for loop runs maximum for 50 times. Line3 gets the actual value of the property from application object and compares it with Expected Value. If they are the same, the application has reached the expected state and the script can execute the next statement without further delay i.e script moves from line12 to line 13 in the above example. If they are not the same, application has not reached to the expected state and the script must wait for further time. Hence code goes to else condition specified in Line 5 and sleeps for 1 sec at Line 6 using wait statement before the next iteration of for loop executes. For example if maximum time out is 50 secs, the property is disabled and the expected value is False; the script gets disabled property value for every 1 sec and compares this value to expected state False. If the comparison turns a success then for loop and function exits, so script goes to the next line i.e 13. If the property value never matches the expected value even after number of iterations equal to time out, the for loop and function exits. So the script goes to the next line i.e 13 in the above example because of timeout.

We can create our own synchronization point known as custom synchronization point like the above in case the given synchronization doesn't serve our synchronization requirements. But in most of the cases synchronization provided by QTP must be more than sufficient.

PROGRAMMING WITH REPOSITORIES COLLECTION AND RECOVERY OBJECTS

Repositories Collection Object

QTP has provided RepositoriesCollection Object to program with Object Repository. This object is used to associate or disassociate shared object repositories with an action during a run session. This helps for more efficient automation. For example, suppose you want to test a Web application that supports twenty different languages. Instead of creating twenty different tests (one for each supported language), you can create one test and run multiple iterations of that test—one for each language version of your application. If you create one or more shared object repository files for each version, you can use the RepositoriesCollection object to load the required shared object repository files for each iteration. Then, when each iteration finishes, you can use the RepositoriesCollection object to remove these object repository files prior to loading the object repository files required for the next iteration.

The Program below demonstrates how to work with RepositoriesCollection object:

```
1  Rep1Path = "\\QTP\Google\Google1.tsr"
2  Rep2Path = "\\QTP\Google\Google2.tsr"
3  Rep3Path = "\\QTP\Google\Google3.tsr"
4
5  RepositoriesCollection.RemoveAll()
6
7  RepositoriesCollection.Add(Rep1Path)
8  RepositoriesCollection.Add(Rep2Path)
9  RepositoriesCollection.Add(Rep3Path)
10
11 Pos = RepositoriesCollection.Find(Rep1Path)
12 RepositoriesCollection.MoveToPos Pos,3
13
14 RepositoriesCollection.Remove(1)
```

Line 1-3 represents 3 Shared Repositories Google1.tsr, Google2.tsr and Google3.tsr stored in a network share \\QTP\Google

Line 5: RemoveAll method removes all repositories which are already associated with current action

Line 7-9: Add methods adds 3 shared repositories to current action.

Line 11: Find method returns the position of the specified repository in the list of available repositories list of the action. First repository position starts with 1.

Line 12: MoveToPos Moves repository at position 1 to position 3

Line 14: Removes or De-associates Repository present at position 1

Recovery Object

This enables you to control the recovery scenario mechanism programmatically during the run session. The following example demonstrates how to use the recovery object:

```
RecCount=Recovery.Count
Msgbox ("Number of Recoveries="&RecCount)

isRecEnabled = Recovery.Enabled
Msgbox ("IsRecoveryEnabled="&isRecEnabled)
If isRecEnabled Eqv False Then
        Recovery.Activate
End If
ScenariosStatus=""
for Iter = 1 to Recovery.Count
    Recovery.GetScenarioName Iter, ScenarioFile, ScenarioName
    Position = Recovery.GetScenarioPosition( ScenarioFile, ScenarioName )
```

```
13      isSenEnabled=Recovery.GetScenarioStatus( Position )
14      ScenariosStatus=ScenariosStatus&ScenarioName&"=" &isSenEnabled&"; "
15      ScenarioFile = Empty
16      ScenarioName = Empty
17  Next
18  Msgbox( ScenariosStatus)
19  Recovery.SetScenarioStatus 2, False
20  Recovery = False
```

This program checks whether Recovery Scenario is enabled for the test. If not enabled, enables the Recovery Scenario. It goes through each recovery and returns its name and position. It also disable recovery at position 2, during run time. The following shows the recovery scenarios configured for one Test.

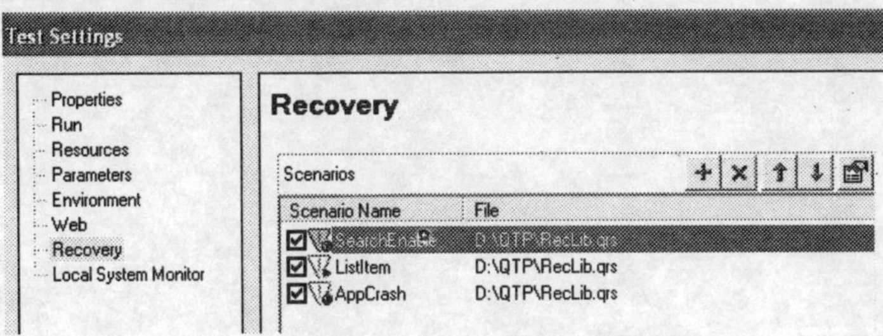

Line 1-2: Count property in Line 1returns how many recovery scenarios are present in the test and Line 2 prints the same. Output of Line 2 is as below:

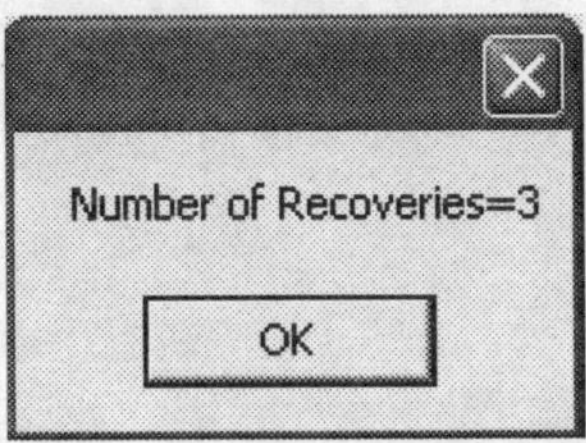

Line 4: Line4 returns whether Recovery Scenario is Enabled for test.

Line 5: Prints whether Recovery Scenario is Enabled or Not. Output of Line 5 is as below

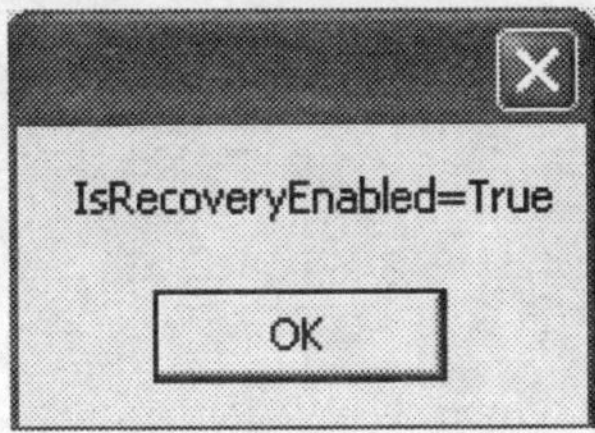

Line 6-8: Enables Recovery Scenario for test if it is not enabled already.

Line 10-17: Loop iterates from First Recovery Scenario to Last Recovery Scenario. Line 11 returns one Recovery Scenario Name and the File Name in which it was stored. Line 12 returns the position of the Recovery Scenario in the list of Recovery scenarios. Line 13 prints whether the Recovery Scenario is enabled or not. Line 14 saves the status of all recoveries in to one string which is printed in Line18. Output of Line18 is as below.

SearchEnable=True; ListItem=True; AppCrash=True;

OK

Line 19: Sets the status of Recovery Scenario at position 2 as False.

Line 20: Disables the entire Recovery Scenario of the test.

WORKING WITH HP QUALITY CENTER

HP Quality Center, the Web-based test management tool, simplifies and organizes test management by giving you systematic control over the testing process.

Quality Center helps you to maintain a project requirements, manual and automation tests, test results, application defects and various reports & graphs.

Quality Center offers integration with HP testing tools (WinRunner, QuickTest Professional, LoadRunner, and Visual API-XP) as well as third party and custom testing tools and requirement and configuration management tools.

Quality Center guides you through the releases specification, requirements specification, test planning, test execution, and defect tracking phases of the testing process.

Connecting QTP with QC

Prerequisites to connect QC & QTP

1. Select the checkbox **Allow other Mercury products to run tests and components** present under **Tools > Options > Run** in QTP.

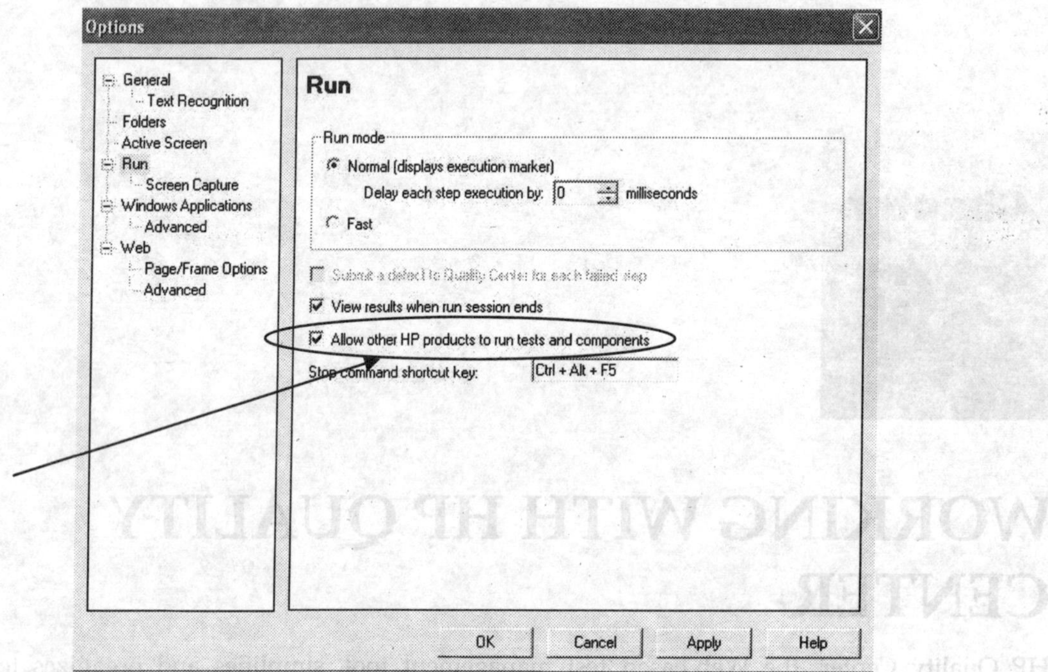

2. QTP Connectivity Add-In and QTP Add-ins are installed

QC and QTP can be connected in 4 ways:

1. From QC test plan
2. From QC test lab
3. From QTP File menu option
4. From QTP script

1. Connecting QTP from QC Test Plan

1 In the test plan tree, choose the manual test that you want to automate.

2 Click the Design Steps tab and click the Generate Script button.

3 Choose an automated test type QUICKTEST_TEST to convert to QTP automation test.

4 Click the Test Script tab to view the test script.

5 Click the launch button to edit the test script in QTP tool.

2. Connecting from QC Test Lab

1 You can run tests automatically on your machine or on a remote machine.

2 You can select the tests you want to run from the Execution Grid.

3 You can include both automated and manual tests.

4 When you run an automated test, Quality Center opens the selected testing tool automatically, runs the test on your local machine or on a remote machine and exports the results to Quality Center.

3. From QTP File menu option

1 Go to File -> Quality Center Connection.

2 Enter QC URL and click Connect.

3 Log in with valid user credentials.

4 Select the Domain and Project.

To connect to the QC project automatically select the check box **Reconnect to server on start-up.**

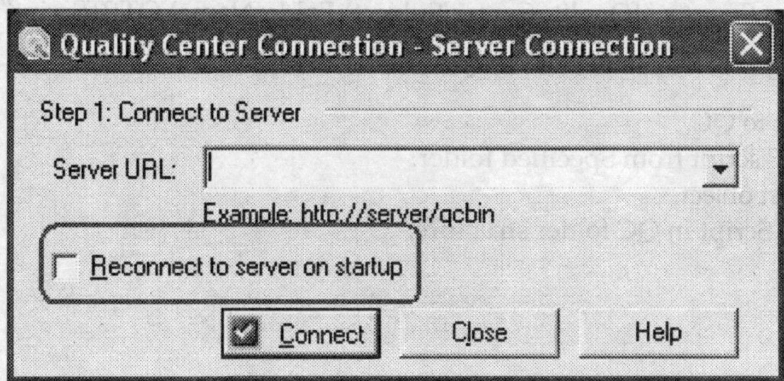

4. From QTP script

The following Code lines will explain how to connect to QC from QTP through scripting.

```
1 Set qtqcApp = CreateObject("QuickTest.Application")
2 qtqcApp.Launch
3 qtqcApp.Visible = True
4 qtqcApp.TDConnection.Connect "http://QualityCenterServer/tdbin", "FR",
  "Flights", "learnqtp", "welcome", False
```

Line 1: Create the QuickTest Professional application object.
Line 2: Launch QTP.
Line 3: Make it visible.
Line 4: Connect to Quality Center. Syntax is as below:
qtqcApp.TDConnection.Connect <QC Server path>, <Domain name that contains QC project>,<Project Name in QC you want to connect to>, <UserName>, <Password>, <Whether password is entered in encrypted or normal. Value is true for encrypted and FALSE for normal>

Uploading QTP Scripts to QC

The code below will demonstrate how to upload QTP script to QC:

```
1 Set qtqcApp = CreateObject("QuickTest.Application")
2 qtqcApp.Launch
3 qtqcApp.Visible = True
4 qtqcApp.TDConnection.Connect "http://QualityCenterServer/tdbin", "FR", "Flights",
  "learnqtp", "welcome", False
5 qtqcApp.Open "C:\Temp\Project\QTPTestScript1, True
6 Set qtqcTest = qtqcApp.Test
7 qtqcApp.Test.SaveAs "[QualityCenter]Subject\FolderName\QTPTScript"
```

Line 1-4: Connect to QC.
Line 5: Open QTP script from Specified folder.
Line 6: Create Test object.
Line 7: Save QTP Script in QC folder structure.

Running scripts from QC

Automation and manual tests can be executed in the QC Test Lab module.

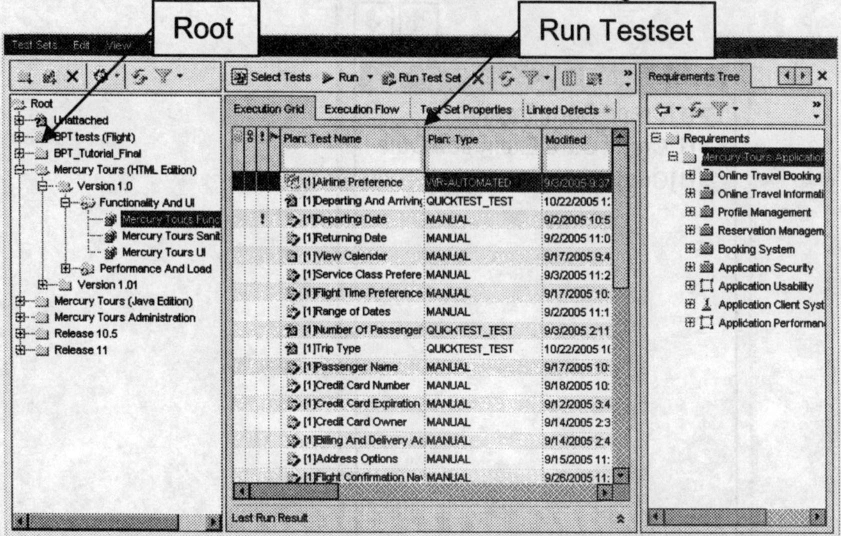

Test execution process

1. CREATE TEST SET
2. SCHEDULE TESTS
3. RUN TESTS
4. ANALYSE RESULTS

Test set is a set of tests in the QC project. Test set can be defined based on the types of testing that will be performed in the project, for example smoke test, regression test… or modules in the project. Assign test set folders to cycles in the release module.

The uppermost level in a test sets tree is the Root folder. You cannot delete the Root folder or add test sets directly to it. Under the Root folder, the *unattached* folder contains all test sets no longer associated with a folder. You cannot add a test set to the *unattached* folder.

You can set the sequence in which to execute the tests in Execution Flow tab.

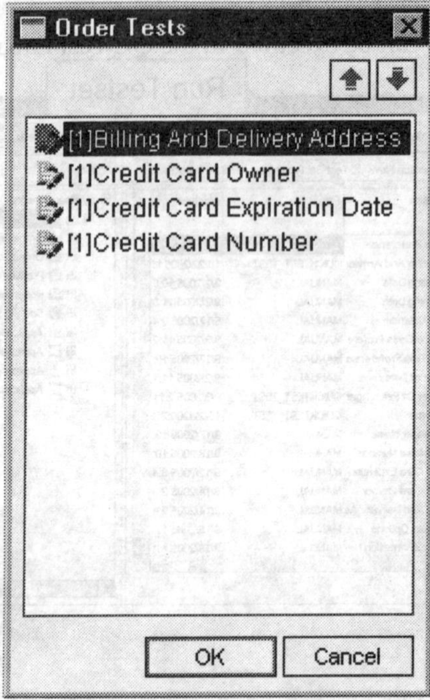

You can set conditions, and schedule the date and time for executing the tests in Execution Flow tab.

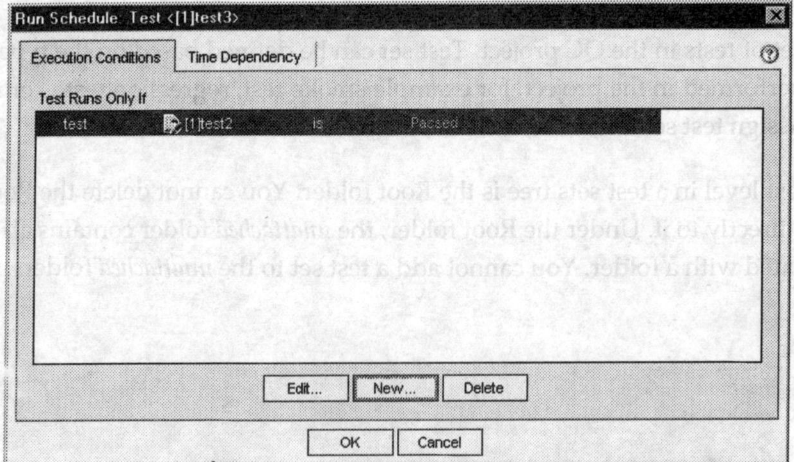

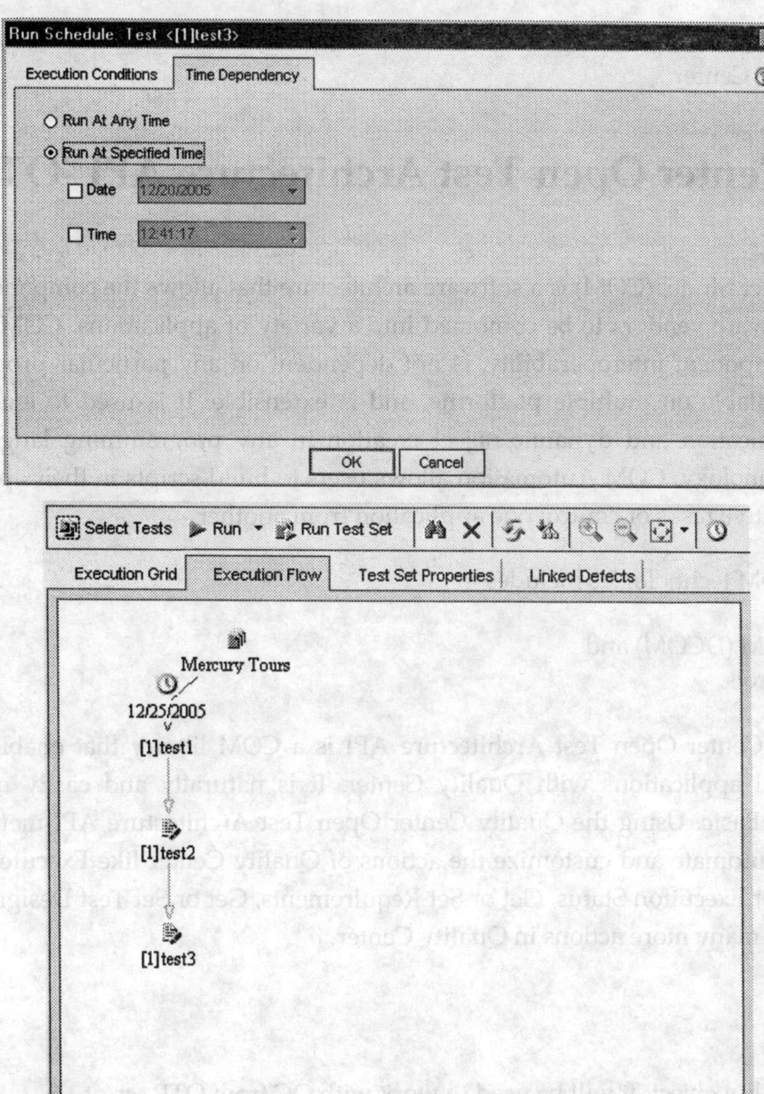

A dashed line arrow indicates that the test is to be executed after the previous test, with no conditions. A solid line arrow indicates a condition and can be blue or green. If the solid line is blue, it indicates that the test is to be executed only if the previous test has status Finished. If the solid line is green, it indicates that the test is to be executed only if the previous test has status Passed.

Once you have defined test sets, you can begin executing the tests by clicking **RunTestSet**. You can configure the host to run the test by providing host details in the Dialog opened after clicking RunTestSet button. After the test run is complete, you can view a summary of test results in Quality Center.

Quality Center Open Test Architecture API -OTA COM 9.0

Component Object Model (COM) is a software architecture that allows the components made by different software vendors to be combined into a variety of applications. COM defines a standard for component interoperability, is not dependent on any particular programming language, is available on multiple platforms, and is extensible. It is used to enable inter-process communication and dynamic object creation in any programming language that supports the technology. COM Automation allows users to build scripts in their applications to perform repetitive tasks or control one application from another.

The family of COM technologies includes
- COM+
- Distributed COM (DCOM) and
- ActiveX® Controls.

The Quality Center Open Test Architecture API is a COM library that enables you to integrate external applications with Quality Center. It is naturally and easily used with Microsoft Visual Basic. Using the Quality Center Open Test Architecture API methods and classes one can automate and customize the actions of Quality Center like Execute TestSets, Execute Tests, Get Execution Status, Get or Set Requirements, Get or Set Test Design Steps or Attachments and many more actions in Quality Center.

QCUtil

QCUtil is QTP utility object. It will be used to work with QC from QTP script.

Script to list the test cases and number of runs in the test set folder

```
Set oTdc = QCUtil.TDConnection
Set oTestSetTreeMgr = oTdc.TestSetTreeManager
Set oTestSetFolder = oTestSetTreeMgr.nodebypath(sTestSetPath)
Set oTestList = oTestSetFolder.FindTestInstances("")
For each oTest in oTestList
     Set oRunFact = oTest.RunFactory
    Set oRuns = oRunFact.NewList("")
    print oTest.Name & " - " & oRuns.count
Next
```

```
10 Set oTest = nothing
11 Set oTestSet = nothing
12 Set oTestList = nothing
13 Set oTestSetFolder = nothing
14 Set oTestSetTreeMgr = nothing
15 Set oTdc = nothing
```

This Program Returns all the tests present in a TestSet and the number of times they have been executed.

Line 1: Create TDConnection object.

Line 2: Get The Testset Tree Manager Object.

Line 3: Get the TestSetFolder object that represents the TestSet Folder.

Line 4: Get the collection of all test objects present under Testset Folder.

Line 5-9: Run through each test in the test. Line 6 and 7 gets the Run object. Line 8: Prints the Test Name and Number of Runs.

Line 10-15: Release the objects from memory.

Function to get the attachment in QC.

```
Public Function GetAttachment(sAttPath,sFileName)
  Dim oTreeManager, oSysTreeNode, oAttachmentFactory, oAttachmentFilter, oAttachmentList, oAttachment
  Dim iNdId, ErrMsg
  Dim  sAttachment
Err.clear
Print "Get Tree Node"
Set oTreeManager = QCUtil.TDConnection.TreeManager
Set oSysTreeNode = oTreeManager.NodeByPath(sAttPath)
Set oAttachmentFactory = oSysTreeNode.Attachments
Set oAttachmentFilter = oAttachmentFactory.Filter
 iNdId = oSysTreeNode.NodeID
oAttachmentFilter.Filter("CR_REFERENCE") = "'ALL_LISTS_" & iNdId & "_" & sFileName & "'"
 Set oAttachmentList = oAttachmentFilter.NewList
 If oAttachmentList.Count > 0 Then
          Print "XML attachment is found in HPQC"
          Set oAttachment = oAttachmentList.Item(1)
          oAttachment.Load True, " "
          sAttachment = oAttachment.FileName
          'Print "XML attachment: " & sAttachment
 Else
         Reporter.ReportEvent 1,"Failed to find the attachment '" & sFileName & "' in folder '" & sAttPath ,"Failed to find the attachment '" & sFileName & "' in folder '" & sAttPath
         ErrMsg = "Failed to find the attachment '" & sFileName & "' in folder '" & sAttPath
```

```
23 End if
24 Set oAttachment = nothing
25 Set oAttachmentList = nothing
26 Set oAttachmentFilter = nothing
27 Set oAttachmentFactory = nothing
28 Set oSysTreeNode = nothing
29 Set oTreeManager = nothing
30 GetAttachment = sAttachment
31 End Function
```

This function takes attachment path and attachment filename and check the attachment availability in QC Test Script. If available return the attachment.

Line 1-4: Variable Declaration.
Line 5: Free up Error object.
Line 7: Get Test Tree.
Line 8: Get the Test node referenced by specified Path.
Line 9,10: Get all attachments stored under TestNode.
Line 11: Get the ID of the Node.
Line 12: Set the filter to filter attachment with specified name.
Line 13: Get the list of all attachments.
Line 14-23: Check the number of attachments matched with given FileName. If the number of attachment matched are not zero then print attachment found else attachment not found.
Line 24-30: Free up memory resources.

QTP Script to upload the file in the current run attachment

```
1  Public Function UploadFile(FilePath)
2  On Error Resume Next
3  Dim obj_Afact
4  Dim obj_Att
5  Err.clear
6  Set obj_Afact = QCUtil.Currentrun.Attachments
7  If IsObject(obj_Afact) Then
8          Set obj_Att = obj_Afact.AddItem(Null)
9          obj_Att.FileName = FilePath
10         obj_Att.Type = 1
11         obj_Att.Post
12         Set obj_Afact = nothing
13         Set obj_Att = nothing
14 End If
15 End Function
```

This script takes path for attaching the file and attaches the file from the current test run in the specified path. Line 6 gives attachments from current run. Line 8-10 adds attachment to QC.

Script to add defect in QC

```
1 Dim TDConnection
2 Set TDConnection = CreateObject("TDApiOle.TDConnection")
3 TDConnection.InitConnection "http://yovav/tdbin" ' URL for the DB
4 TDConnection.ConnectProject "TD76","bella","pino"
5 Set BugFactory = TDConnection.BugFactory
6 Set Bug = BugFactory.AddItem (Nothing)
7 Bug.Status = "New"
8 Bug.Summary = "Connecting to TD"
9 Bug.Priority = "4-Very High" ' depends on the DB
10 Bug.AssignedTo = "admin" ' user that must exist in the DB's users list
11 Bug.DetectedBy = "admin" ' user that must exist in the DB's users list
12 Bug.Post
13 Set Bug = Nothing
14 Set BugFactory = Nothing
15 Set TDConnection = Nothing
```

This program connects to QC and report the defect information automatically.

Line 1-4: Connect to Quality Center Line 5 Gets Bug Factory object which is used to manage Bugs.
Line 6: Add new Bug.
Line 7-1: Sets bug attributes.
Line 12: Add the bug to QC.
Line13-15: Free up objects from memory.

Script to add defect in QC

```
Dim TDConnection
Set TDConnection = CreateObject("TDApiOle.TDConnection")
TDConnection.InitConnection "http://yovav/tdbin" ' URL for the DB
TDConnection.ConnectProject "TD76", "bella", "pino"
Set BugFactory = TDConnection.BugFactory
Set Bug = BugFactory.AddItem (Nothing)
Bug.Status = "New"
Bug.Summary = "Connecting to TD"
Bug.Priority = "4-Very High" ' depends on the DB
Bug.AssignedTo = "admin" ' user that must exist in the DB's users list
Bug.DetectedBy = "admin" ' user that must exist in the DB's users list
Bug.Post
Set Bug = Nothing
Set BugFactory = Nothing
Set TDConnection = Nothing
```

This program connects to QC and report the defect information automatically.

Line 1-4: Set object of Quality Center creates its BugFactory object which is used to manage Bug.
Line 5: Add new bug.
Line 6-11: Set bug setting.
Line 12: Add the bug to QC.
Line 13-15: free up objects from memory.

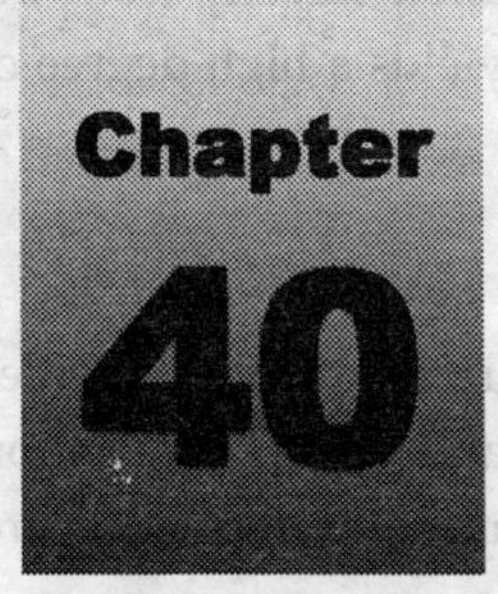

AUTOMATION FRAMEWORK

Automation Framework is nothing but the approach to automate an application in a systematic way with proper planning like Initial Setup, Tool configuration, Test Data files, library files, Script generation, Synchronization, Exception handling, Batch test, Reporting, Maintaining the scripts....all whichever related to our application automation.

There are so many classifications on the type of frame work; some of them are:

1. Test Script Modularity driven.
2. Library Architecture
3. Data driven.
4. Keyword driven.
5. Hybrid driven.(Data driven + Keyword driven)

1. Test Script Modularity

The test script modularity framework is the most basic of the frameworks. When working with test scripts (in any language or proprietary environment) this can be achieved by creating small, independent scripts that represent modules, sections, and functions of the application-under-test. Then these small scripts are taken and combined in a hierarchical fashion to construct larger tests. The use of this framework will yield a higher degree of modularization and add to the overall maintainability of the test scripts.

2. Library Architecture

The test library architecture framework is very similar to the test script modularity framework and offers the same advantages, but it divides the application-under-test into procedures and functions instead of scripts.

This framework requires the creation of library files that represent modules, sections, and functions of the application-under-test. These library files are then called directly from the test case script. Much like script modularization this framework also yields a high degree of modularization and adds to the overall maintainability of the tests.

3. Data Driven

A data-driven framework is where test input and output values are read from data files (ODBC sources, CVS files, Excel files, DAO objects, ADO objects, and such). Navigation through the program, reading of the data files, and logging of test status and information are all coded in the test script.

Advantages:

- Scripts may be developed while application development is still in progress.
- Utilizing a modular design, and using files or records to both input and verify data, reduces redundancy and duplication of effort in creating automated test scripts.
- If functionality changes, only the specific "Business Function" script needs to be updated.
- Data input/output and expected results are stored as easily maintainable text records.

Disadvantages:

The demerits of the Data-Driven test automation framework are as follows:

- Requires proficiency in the Scripting language used by the tool (technical personnel).
- Multiple data-files are required for each Test Case. There may be any number of data-inputs and verifications required, depending on how many different screens are accessed. This usually requires data-files to be kept in separate directories by Test Case.

- The Tester must not only maintain the Detail Test Plan with specific data, but must also re-enter this data in the various required data-files.

4. Keyword Driven

This requires the development of data tables and keywords, independent of the data and the application under test. Keyword-driven tests look very similar to manual test cases. In a keyword-driven test the entire process is data-driven, including functionality. The diagram below shows architecture of a keyword driven frame work.

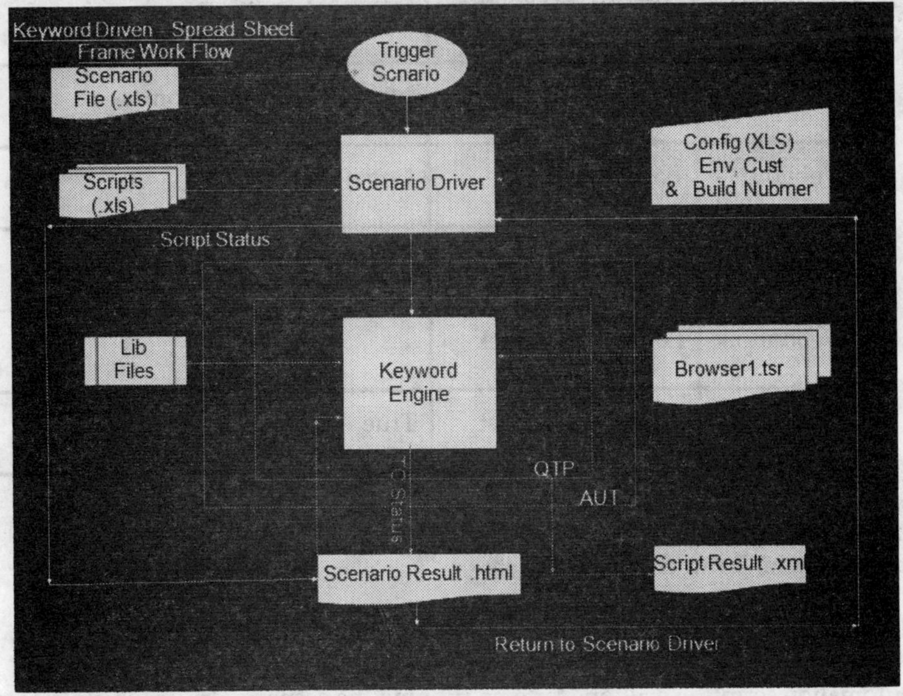

ScenarioFile.xls contains the steps for the scenario to be executed like

1. Open Application
2. Register User
3. Login User

Scripts.xls contains the actions to be performed for each step in the scenario. These actions are like Keywords.

For example the Login User step mentioned above contains actions like

1. Enter Login Name
2. Enter Password

3. Click Login button
4. Check Inbox page displayed.

The keyword table for the above test requirement will be as follows:

Test Table for Yahoo Login

Object	Control	Action	Arguments
Browser		Invoke	IE
Page		Open	http://mail.yahoo.com
WebEdit	Login	Set	DemoUser
WebEdit	Password	Set	Demo123
WebButton	Login	Click	
Page	Inbox	Exist	True

Config.xls indicates the configuration information like path of the application, Build Number, Operating System, Browser to be used, etc.

LibFiles represents the library files that contain reusable function libraries.

Automation scripts execution starts by running the scenario driver which triggers one by one all scenarios in the scenarios.xls file. Each scenario file contains a path to the scripts file. Driver loads the script file based on this path and reads each keyword present in the Script file. Keyword Engine uses these Keywords and also uses any other library files required and converts these keywords into VBscript code (For other tools, a different language is used depending on the support of the tool). This code will be further executed by Keyword Driven Engine and performs operations accordingly on the application under test. It is important to note that we have not written the test script with program language like VBScript. We have just mentioned the actions to be performed on the application like Keywords in the excel file and the rest is taken care by Keyword Engine developed.

At the end of execution, results of execution are outputted to XML file by each script and it will be further converted into HTML or any other format like CSV using Results API.

Advantages:

- The Detail Test Plan can be written in Spreadsheet format containing all input and verification data.
- If "utility" scripts can be created by someone proficient in the automated tool's Scripting language prior to the Detail Test Plan being written, then the tester can use the Automated Test Tool immediately via the "spreadsheet-input" method, without needing to learn the Scripting language.
- The tester need only learn the "Key Words" required, and the specific format to use within the Test Plan. This allows the tester to be productive with the test tool very quickly, and allows more extensive training in the test tool to be scheduled at a more convenient time.

Disadvantages:

- Development of "customized" (Application-Specific) Functions and Utilities requires proficiency in the tool's Scripting language.
- If the application requires more than a few "customized" Utilities, this will require the tester to learn a number of "Key Words" and special formats. This can be time-consuming, and may have an initial impact on Test Plan Development. Once the testers get used to this, however, the time required to produce a test case is greatly improved.

5. Hybrid (Data & Keyword) driven

The most commonly implemented framework is a combination of all of the above techniques, pulling from their strengths and trying to mitigate their weaknesses. This hybrid test automation framework is what most frameworks evolve into over time and multiple projects. The most successful automation frameworks generally accommodate both Keyword-Driven testing as well as Data-Driven scripts.

This allows data driven scripts to take advantage of the powerful libraries and utilities that usually accompany a keyword driven architecture. The framework utilities can make the data driven scripts more compact and less prone to failure than they otherwise would have been.

The utilities can also facilitate the gradual and manageable conversion of existing scripts to keyword driven equivalents when and where that appears desirable. On the other hand, the framework can use scripts to perform some tasks that might be too difficult to re-implement in a pure keyword driven approach, or where the keyword driven capabilities are not yet in place.

Critical Steps in Test Automation Framework

- **Clear vision of what needs to be achieved out of this automation:** It should address core questions like testing model, types of testing, which areas need to be automated, etc.
- **Tool identification and Recommendation:** This means considering critical factors like creating a standard tool evaluation checklist, types of testing, and acquiring multiple tools and adds/ ins to perform different types of testing.
- **Good Framework design:** This involves identifying requirements from multiple areas like identification of necessary utility/ components, types of input data store to be communicated, communication between the systems and third party interfaces/ utility/component development, etc.

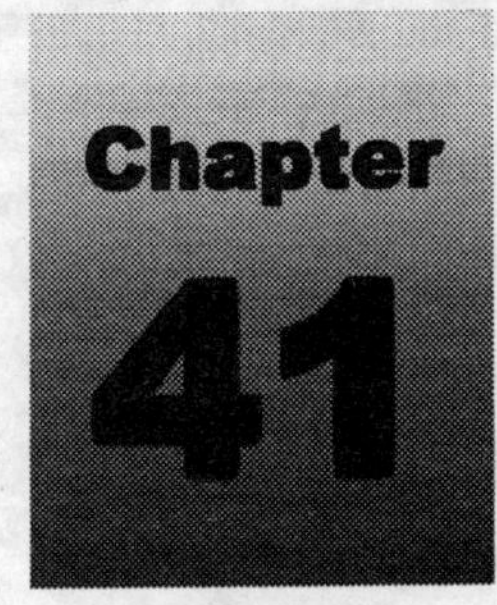

NEW IN QTP 9.5 AND QTP 10.0

What is New in QTP 9.5

1. Test Flow Pane

The Test Flow pane is comprised of a hierarchy of actions and action calls in the current test, and shows the order in which they are run. Each action is displayed as a node in a tree, and includes calls to all of a test's actions. The steps of the action that you double-click in the Test Flow pane are displayed in the Keyword View and Expert View. To view the Test Flow pane select **View > TestFlow**.

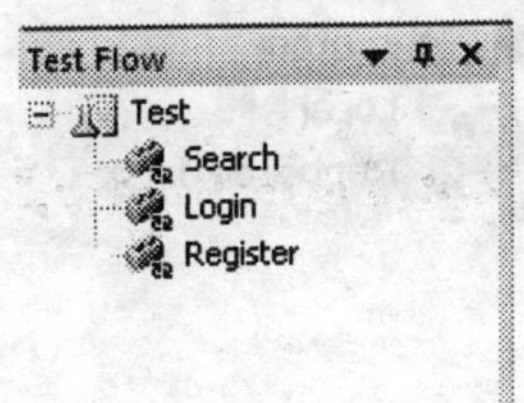

2. Available Keywords Pane

The Available Keywords pane enables you to drag and drop objects or calls to functions into your test. When you drag and drop an object into your test, QuickTest inserts a step with the default operation for that object. When you drag and drop a function into your test, QuickTest inserts a call to that function. To view the Available Keywords pane select **View > Available Keywords**.

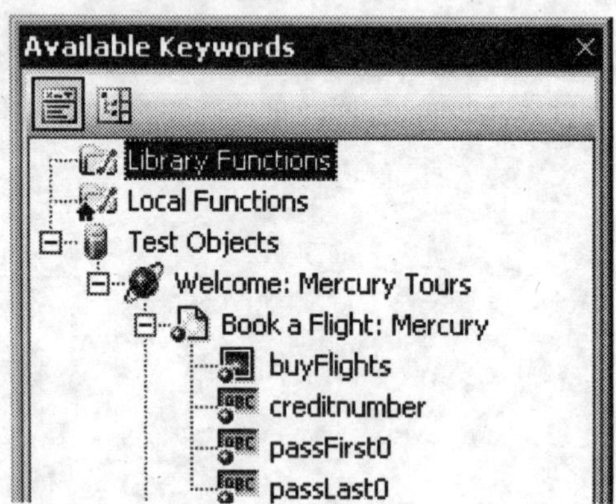

3. Resources Pane

Tests and actions are associated with resources such as function libraries, recovery scenarios, and object repositories. QuickTest displays all the resources associated with a test in the Resources pane. The Resources pane enables you to add, remove, and manage all of the resources in your test. To view the Resources pane select **View > Resources**.

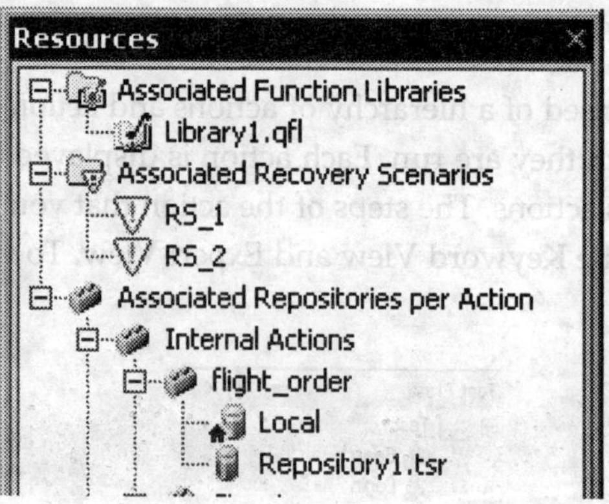

4. The Object Repository - Checkpoint and Output Objects

Using object Repository now we can see all checkpoints and output values in the script. You can even update checkpoints and output values from the object repository.

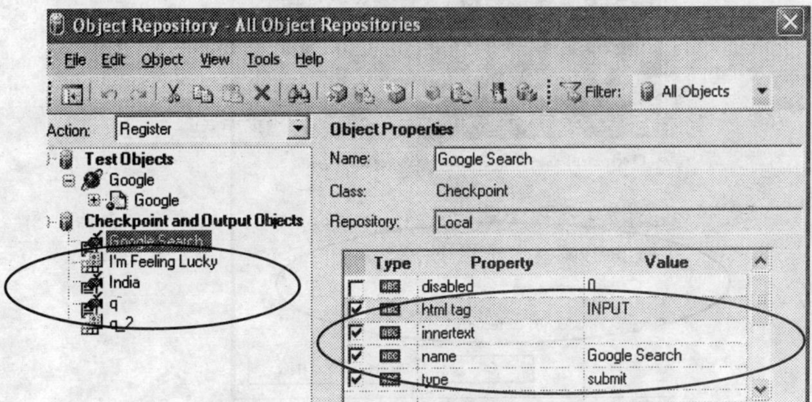

5. Add Existing Checkpoint

Now we can reuse an existing checkpoint in QTP from Resources>Add Existing Checkpoints. When you select Add Existing Checkpoints, the following dialog will open. On the left side, select test object and on the right, select check point from the dropdown list.

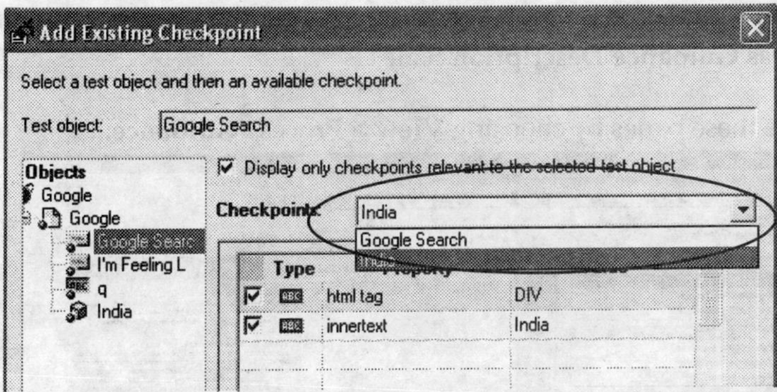

6. Bit Map Checkpoint

A bitmap checkpoint compares the actual and expected bitmaps pixel by pixel and fails if there are any differences. QuickTest 9.5 has new bitmap enhancements that enable its users to define tolerance levels for bitmap checkpoints to refine the bitmap comparison and make it more flexible.

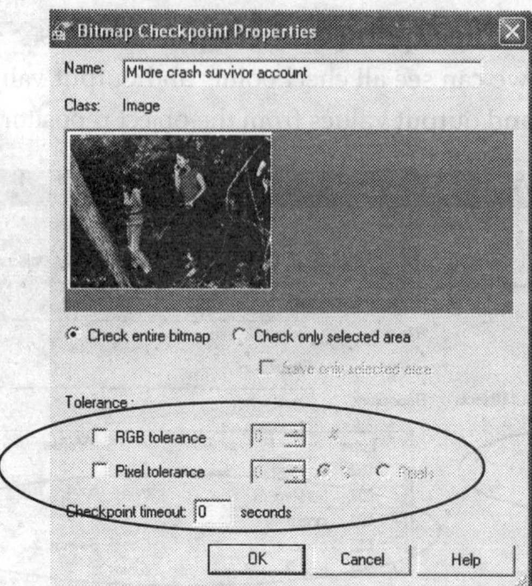

7. Process Guidance Panes

Process guidance is a tool that provides procedures and descriptions on how to best perform specific processes. You use process guidance to learn about new processes and to learn the preferred methodology for performing processes with which you are already familiar.

In QuickTest, process guidance is displayed in two panes: the **Process Guidance Activities** pane and the **Process Guidance Description** pane.

You display or hide these panes by choosing **View > Process Guidance.**

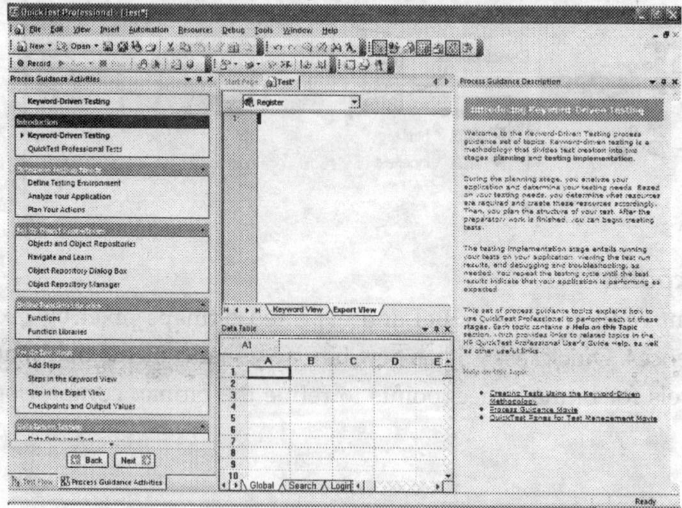

8. Maintenance run mode - Maintenance Run Wizard

The Maintenance Run Wizard helps you to maintain your test when it encounters the following problems and provides the following solutions:

Problem	Solution
The step failed because the object in your test cannot be identified in the application.	The Maintenance Run Wizard helps you identify the object in the application that you want your test to use.
The step failed because the object in your test is missing from your associated object repositories.	The Maintenance Run Wizard helps you add the missing object to the repository. You can also choose to add a comment to your test before the failed step.
The object in your step exists in the application, but can be identified only through Smart Identification.	Identifying objects using Smart Identification may cause tests to run slower. The Maintenance Run Wizard helps you modify the description of the object, so that Smart Identification is not needed.

9. Support for tabbed browsing

10. **QTP 9.5 supports MS Vista 64 bit edition also, in comparison to QTP 9.2's support for 32 bit edition only.**
11. **QTP 9.5 offers all add-ins integrated with the core installation package. Though you still need to buy add-ins separately to get them activated.**
12. **For installing QTP 9.5 you have to do a clean uninstall (as mentioned in the HP KB) of previous versions.**
13. **Web Add-in Extensibility: Using this feature you can configure and extend the supports to those 3rd party custom web controls (and new technologies like AJAX) which were not supported with the earlier versions. You need to possess a fair amount of JavaScript knowledge to handle this.**
14. **Support for Automating Eclipse based application.**

What's New in QTP10?

1. Local System Monitoring While Running Your Tests

The new local system monitoring feature (File > Settings > Local System Monitor) enables you to monitor the local (client-side) computer resources used by the application instance you are testing during a run session.

You can monitor a number of different system counters to view the effects your application has on the system. You can also define upper limits for the counters. If any of the specified counters exceed these limits, the test run will fail.

Monitors will appear in the Test Results file as below:

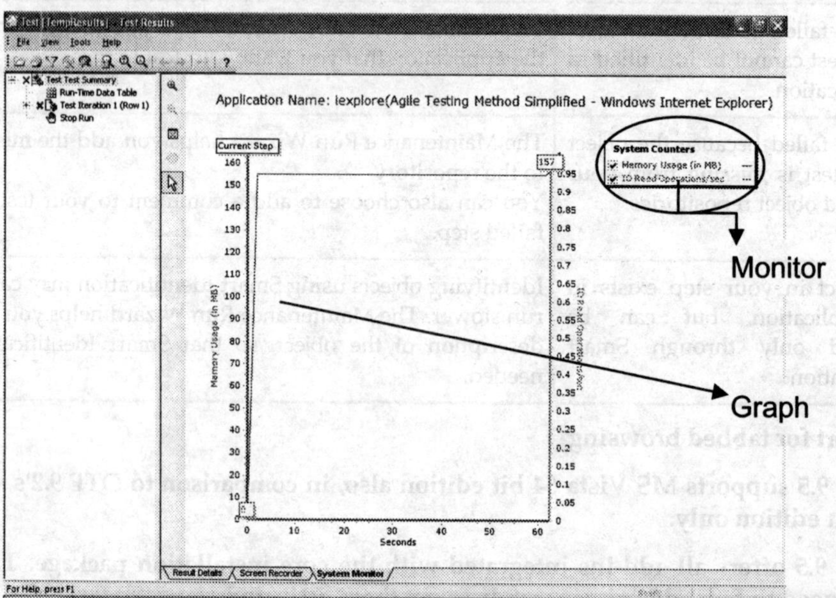

2. Custom Toolbars

In QTP 10 the user has the provision to customize the toolbars and button layouts. Any menu command can be planted in any of the toolbars. The process basically requires you to locate the relevant command and drag it to the toolbar you want it in. Customize dialog can be opened through Tools>Customize.

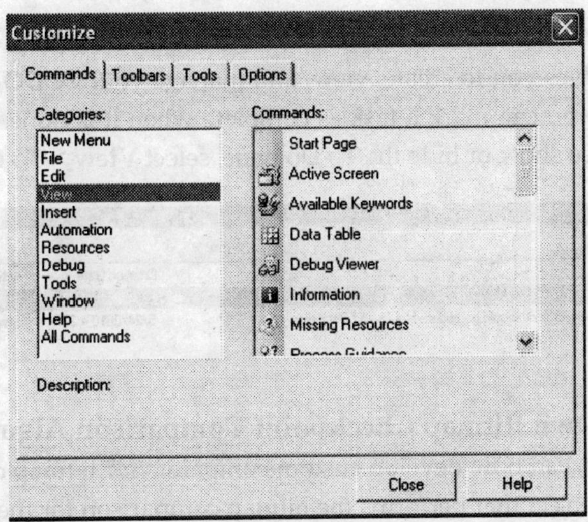

3. Managing Versions of Assets in Quality Center

When QuickTest is connected to a Quality Center project with version control support, you can update and revise your QuickTest assets while maintaining earlier versions of each asset. This helps you keep track of the changes made to each asset and see what was modified from one version to another. Assets can include tests, function libraries, shared object repositories, recovery scenarios, and external Data Tables. Version control can be accessed through **File>Quality Center Version Control.**

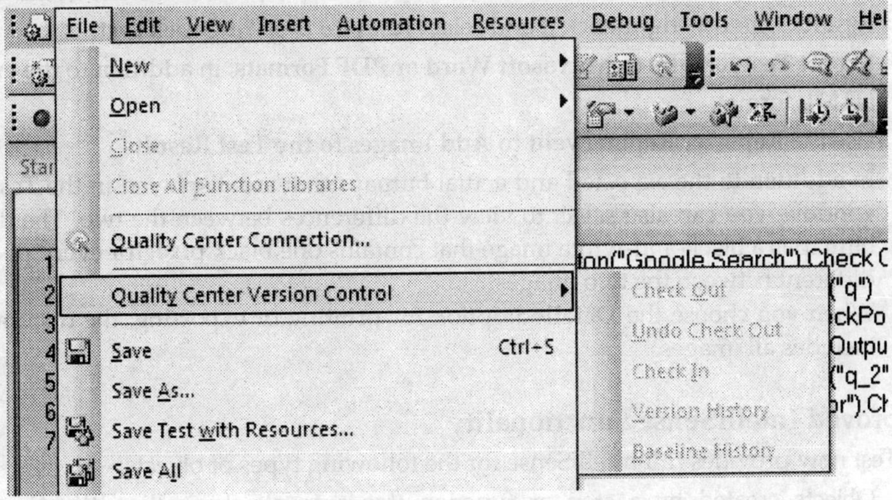

4. To Do Pane

The To Do pane enables you to create, view, and manage your TODO tasks.. You can assign tasks to others, and you can mark a task as complete when it is done. Your TODO tasks are saved with the test. To show or hide the To Do pane, select **View > To Do.**

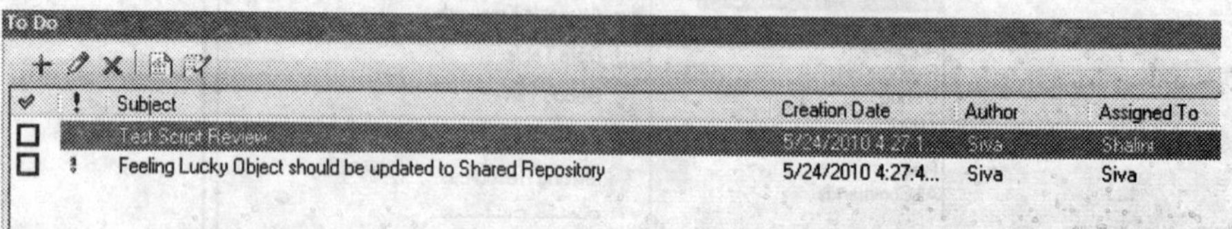

5. Develop Your Own Bitmap Checkpoint Comparison Algorithm

You (or a third party) can now develop custom comparers for bitmap checkpoints. A custom comparer is a COM object that performs the bitmap comparison for the checkpoint according to your testing requirements. For example, you could define a custom comparer that allows a bitmap checkpoint to pass even if the image in the application shifts by an amount specified when the checkpoint is defined.

4. ImproveTest Results Analysis with New Reporting Functionality

QuickTest 10.00 includes a powerful set of new reporting options that help you analyze and manage your run results more thoroughly and efficiently. These include:

- **Jump to step**. When you want to know more about a particular node in the Test Results window, right-click it and select **Jump to Step in QuickTest**.
- **Export Test Results to Microsoft Word or PDF Formats**, in addition to the existing HTML format.
- Use the **Reporter.ReportEvent to Add Images to the Test Results.**
- In addition to the expected and actual bitmaps that are displayed in the Test Results window, you can also select to view the differences between the two. The difference bitmap is a black-and-white image that contains one black pixel for every pixel that is different between the two images.
- When you choose the **Detailed** option for printing or exporting, the document now includes all images.

5. Improved IntelliSense Functionality

QuickTest now provides full IntelliSense for the following types of objects:

- Objects created by a step or function (for example, by calling the CreateObject method)
- Variables to which an object is assigned
- Reserved objects

- COM objects
- Properties that return objects

1. The Debug Viewer pane has a new look, including icons to help you identify the type of information displayed.
2. You can now set all text recognition configuration settings from the QuickTest Options Dialog Box (**Tools > Options > General > Text Recognition**), including new options for selecting the text block mode and specifying the languages to be used with the OCR mechanism. This makes it easier to make any necessary adjustments and to optimize the way that QuickTest identifies text in your application.
3. New Look for Options, Settings, and File Dialog Boxes

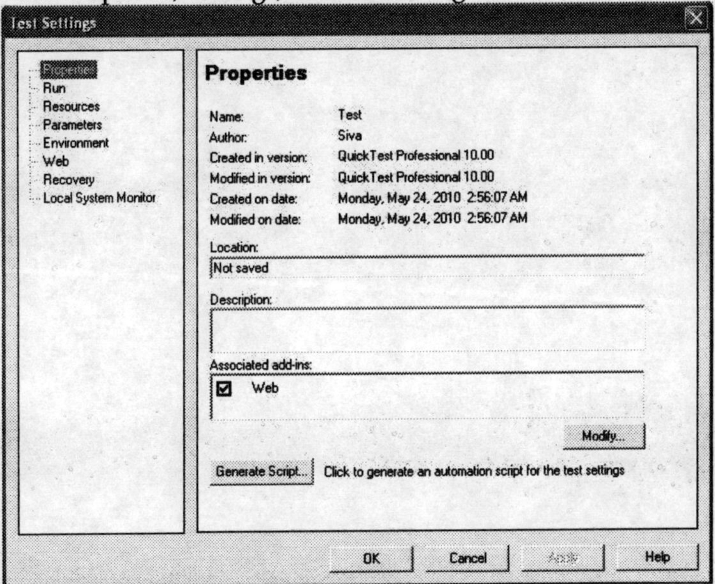

4. **LoadAndRunAction** statement to load an action only when the step runs, and then run that action.

6. New Supported Operating Systems and Environments

QuickTest Professional 10.00 now offers support for the operating systems, browsers, and development environments listed below.

- Microsoft Windows 2008 Server 32-bit Edition
- Microsoft Windows 2008 Server 64-bit Edition
- Microsoft Windows Vista, Service Pack 1, 32-bit Edition
- Microsoft Windows Vista, Service Pack 1, 64-bit Edition
- Microsoft Windows XP Professional 32-bit Edition—Service Pack 3
- Citrix Presentation Server 4.5

- Microsoft Internet Explorer 8, Beta 2
- Mozilla Firefox 3.0.x
- **Delphi**: IDE, versions 6, 7, and 2007 (for controls based on the Win32 VCL library)
- **SAP**: CRM 2007 (For controls that support test mode enhancements. Requires SAP notes: 1147166, 1066565, and 1002944. Later SAP notes related to test mode enhancements are not supported.)
- **Java**: IBM 32-bit JDK 1.5.x, SWT toolkit version 3.4
- **Java Extensibility:** Eclipse IDE 3.4
- **.NET**: .NET Framework 3.5—Service Pack 1

Shroff Reprints & Original Titles

The X Team Series
(An Imprint of Shroff Publishers)

Computers

ISBN	Title	Author	Year	Price
9788184041569	Ajax for Beginners **(B/CD)**, 452 Pages	Bayross	2006	375.00
9788184041972	Application Development with Oracle & PHP on Linux for Beginners, 2/ed **(B/CD)**, 940 Pages	Bayross	2007	650.00
9789350233733	**Blogging for Beginners, 268 Pages**	**Harwani**	**2011**	**350.00**
9788184046397	C for Beginners, 532 Pages	Mothe	2009	350.00
9788184046564	C++ for Beginners, 403 Pages	Harwani	2009	375.00
9789350231012	Core Java for Beginners, **(B/CD)**, 892 Pages	Shah	2010	450.00
9788184046694	Database Concepts and Systems for Students, 3/ed, 428 Pgs	Bayross	2009	300.00
9788184048780	HTML for Beginners, 2/Ed, 416 Pages	Aibara	2010	350.00
9788184047059	Hibernate 3 for Beginners - Covers Java Persistence API **(B/CD)**, 680 Pages	Shah	2009	500.00
9788184045697	Java EE 5 for Beginners, Revised & Enlarged 2/ed **(B/CD)**, 1,192 Pages	Bayross	2008	575.00
9788184049398	Java EE 6 for Beginners, **(B/CD)**, 1092 Pages	Shah	2009	625.00
9788184049411	Java EE 6 Server Programming for Professionals (B/CD), 1,328 Pages	Shah	2010	750.00
9788184048063	Java EE Project using EJB 3, JPA and Struts 2 for Beginners, **(B/CD)**, 1,258 Pages	Shah	2009	750.00
9788184043174	Java for Beginners **(B/CD)**, Covers Java SE 6 JDK, 600 Pages	Chavan	2007	450.00
9788184045932	Java for Professionals: A Practical Approach to Java Programming (Covers Java SE 6), 790 Pages	Harwani	2008	525.00
9789350233719	**Java for Students, 2/ed, 850 Pages**	**Pherwani**	**2011**	**600.00**
9788184047097	Java Persistence API in EJB 3 for Professionals, **(B/CD)** 756 Pgs	Shah	2009	550.00
9788184045925	JavaServer Pages Project for Beginners, **(B/CD)**, 746 Pages	Shah	2008	550.00
9788184045598	Java Server Programming for Professionals, Revised & Enlarged 2/ed (Covers Java EE 5) **(B/CD)**, 1,612 Pages	Bayross	2008	700.00
9788184043594	Java Server Pages for Beginners **(B/CD)**, 872 Pages	Bayross	2007	500.00
9788184048438	Lamp Programming for Professionals, **(B/CD)**, 1,284	Shah	2009	800.00
9788184040142	MySQL 5 for Professionals **(B/CD)**, 770 Pages	Bayross	2005	550.00
9788184045260	Oracle for Professionals (Covers Oracle 9i, 10g & 11g) **(B/CD)**, 1,420 Pages	Shah	2008	750.00
9788184043228	PC Hardware for Beginners, 308 Pages	Sangia	2007	225.00
9788184040753	PHP 5.1 for Beginners **(B/CD)**, 1,284 Pages	Bayross	2006	650.00

ISBN	Title	Author	Year	Price
9788184048445	PHP Project for Professionals, (B/CD), 1,200 Pages	Shah	2010	750.00
9788184047073	Practical ASP.NET 3.5 Projects for Beginners, **(B/CD)**, 550 Pgs	Harwani	2009	425.00
9788184048070	Practical EJB Project for Beginners, 312 Pages	Harwani	2009	325.00
9788184043426	Practical Java Project for Beginners **(B/CD)**, 164 Pages	Harwani	2007	150.00
9788184043419	Practical Web Services for Beginners, 168 Pages	Harwani	2007	150.00
9788184049725	QuickTest Professional (QTP) Version 10, 116 Pages	Mallepally	2010	125.00
9789350231241	QTP for Professionals, 480 Pages	Reddy	2010	450.00
9788184048100	SAP SD for Beginners, 324 Pages	Samad	2009	350.00
9788184047448	Struts 2 for Beginners, 2/ed, **(B/CD)**, 566 Pages	Shah	2009	450.00
9788184046960	Struts 2 with Hibernate 3 Project for Beginners, **(B/CD)**, 1,042 Pgs	Shah	2009	675.00
9788184041071	Visual Basic 2005 for Beginners **(B/CD)**, 1,172 Pages	Bayross	2006	150.00

Other Computer Titles

ISBN	Title	Author	Year	Price
9789350230237	A Primer on Software Quality Models & Project Management, 640 Pages	Mehta	2010	600.00
9788184044270	Advancements in Information Technology and Information Security, 400 Pages	Gopal	2008	750.00
9788184048827	Art of Creative Destruction: Illustarted Software Testing, Test Automation & Agile Testing, 2/ed, 348 Pages	Puranik	2010	400.00
9788173660030	AS/400 Architecture & Applications, 332 Pages	Lawrence	1993	250.00
9788173660047	AS/400: A Practical Guide to Programming & Operations, 284 Pgs	Zeilenga	1993	225.00
9789350232859	**Beginning Web Development for Smartphones Developing Web Applications with PHP, MySQL and jQTouch, 252 Pages**	**Harwani**	**2011**	**300.00**
9789350231029	**C# 4.0 Programming Made Easy, 624 Pages**	**Kadam**	**2011**	**350.00**
9789350230244	Computer Architecture and Maintenance, 320 Pages	Kadam	2010	200.00
9788173660016	CICS: A How-To for Cobol Programmers, 428 Pages	Kirk	1993	300.00
9788184048957	FAQ's in MFC and MFC Solutions, Vol I (B/CD) 510 Pages	P. G. Naik	2010	350.00
9788173666810	First Encounter with Java Including BlueJ, 386 Pages	Bhutta	2006	225.00
9789350230275	Instant Oracle, 100 Pages	Shah	2010	50.00
9788173664632	Introducing MySQL, 96 Pages	Oak	2005	50.00
9789350230251	Management Information Systems (MIS)	Kadam	2010	150.00
9789350231258	**Maximum Oracle with Oracle Best Practices, 772 Pages**	**Puranik**	**2011**	**500.00**
9788173660023	MVS / VSAM for the Application Programmer, 504 Pages	Brown	1993	325.00
9788184047899	Operating Systems, 2/ed, 408 Pages	Sumitradevi	2009	300.00
9789350234242	**Oracle Financials 11i A Practical Guide for the Beginners, 428 Pgs**	**Srikanth Peri**	**2011**	**650.00**
9788173668012	Software Defect Prevention Concepts and Implementation, 180 Pages **(H/B)**	Kane & Bajaj	2003	300.00
9789350230237	Software Quality Models & Project Management in a Nutshell, 640 Pages	Mehta	2010	600.00
9788173668814	Strategic Bidding: A Successful Approach, 192 Pgs	Garg	2004	250.00
9788173660078	TCP/IP Companion: A Guide For The Common User, 284 Pages	Arick	1993	225.00
9789350231005	Testing in 30+ Open Source Tools, (B/CD), 1080 Pages	Shende	2010	675.00
9788173660429	Vijay Mukhi's ERP Odyssey: Implementing. PeopleSoft Financials 7.0/7.5, 528 Pages	Mukhi	1999	350.00

ISBN	Title	Author	Year	Price

Business, Management & Finance

ISBN	Title	Author	Year	Price
9788184046977	An Introduction to Foreign Exchange & Financial Risk Management, **(B/CD)**, 348 Pages	Lakshman	2009	400.00
9789350230268	Bootstrapping A Software Company, 348 Pages	Yadav	2010	425.00
9788184044287	Breaking the Black Box, (B/CD), 276 Pages	Pring	2008	500.00
9789350230220	Complete Guide to Technical Analysis: An Indian Perspective, 612 Pages	Pring	2010	500.00
9788184040425	Developing Analytical Skills: Case Studies in Management, 636 Pages	Dr. Natarajan	2008	500.00
9788173660993	Doing Business with the French, 150 Pages	Jhangiani	1999	150.00
9788184044744	Ethics, Indian Ethos and Management, 252 Pages	Balachandran	2008	175.00
9789350231227	Financial Decision Modeling Operations Research & Business Statistics, 696 Pages	Sridhar	2010	350.00
9788184048094	Financial Management: Problems & Solutions, 3/ed, 1,108 Pgs	Sridhar	2009	550.00
9789350230794	Financial Management: Problems & Solutions, 4/ed, 1,228 Pgs	Sridhar	2010	600.00
9788184045611	Futures & Options: Equities & Commodities, 3/ed, 410 Pages	Sridhar	2008	450.00
9789350232965	**Futures & Options, 4th Edition, Pages 392**	**Sridhar**	**2011**	**450.00**
9789350233917	**Globally Distributed Work: Concepts, Strategies & Models, 276 Pages**	**Jain**	**2011**	**425.00**
9788184040432	How to Eat The Elephant? The CEO's Guide To An Enterprise Sys Implementation, 104 Pages	Tulsyan	2007	325.00
9789350230459	How to Learn Management from your wife, 96 Pages	Rangnekar	2010	125.00
9789350233108	How to Learn Management from your wife (HB), 96 Pages	Rangnekar	2010	275.00
9788184044447	How to Select Stocks Using Technical Analysis, **(B/CD)**, 338 Pages	Pring	2008	500.00
9788184044164	Logistics in International Business, 2/ed, 428 Pages	Aserkar	2007	450.00
9788184047547	Magic and Logic of Elliott Waves, The, 204 Pages	Kale	2009	500.00
9788184048568	Management Accounting & Financial Analysis for C.A.Final (June 2009), 9/ed, 540 Pages	Sridhar	2009	400.00
9788184044454	Momentum Explained, Volume I **(B/CD)**, 366 Pages	Pring	2008	600.00
9788184044461	Momentum Explained, Volume II **(B/CD)**, 338 Pages	Pring	2008	550.00
9788184047066	Purchasing and Inventory Management, 338 Pages	Menon	2009	375.00
9788173666797	Rules of Origin in International Trade, 238 Pages	Dr. Sathpathy	2005	300.00
9789350233580	**Services Marketing, 448 Pages**	**Balachandran**	**2011**	**425.00**
9789350233115	**Soft Skills In Management, 148 Pages**	**Rangnekar**	**2011**	**125.00**
9789350230213	Strategic Financial Management for C.A. Final, 4/ed 1244 Pgs	Sridhar	2010	575.00
9789350231036	**Strategic Financial Management for C.A. Final, 5/ed 1288 Pgs**	**Sridhar**	**2011**	**600.00**
9788173668814	Strategic Bidding: A Successful Approach, 192 Pages	Garg	2004	250.00
9788184043211	Time Your Trades With Technical Analysis **(B/CD)**, 348 Pages	Pradhan	2007	600.00

Catering & Hotel Management

ISBN	Title	Author	Year	Price
9788173668739	Careers in Hospitality - Hotel Management Entrance Exam Guide, 332 Pages	Rego	2004	200.00
9789350230817	**Marvels of Indian Snacks, 264 Pages**	**Shankaran**	**2011**	**350.00**
9788184044751	Marvels of South Indian Cuisine, 220 Pages	Shankaran	2008	250.00
9788184046687	Marvels of North Indian Cuisine, 196 Pages	Shankaran	2009	250.00

ISBN	Title	Author	Year	Price

Civil Engineering

9789350233252	**Concrete for High Performance Sustainable Infrastructure, 312 Pages**	**Newlands**	**2011**	**750.00**
9789350233245	**New Developments in Concrete Construction, 296 Pages**	**Dhir**	**2011**	**750.00**
9788184048056	Raina's Concrete Bridge Practice: Construction, Maintenance & Rehabiliation 2/ed, 452 Pgs (H/B) [14 Color]	Dr. Raina	2010	600.00
9788184048049	Raina's Concrete Bridge: Inspection, Repair, Strengthening, Testing, Load Capacity Evaluation 2/ed, 800 Pages (H/B) [32 Full Color Inserts]	Dr. Raina	2010	1,200.00
9788184047530	Raina's Concrete for Construction: Facts and Practice, 400 Pages **(H/B)**	Dr. Raina	2009	650.00
9788184047875	Raina's Construction & Contract Management, 2/ed Inside Story, 585 Pages **(H/B)**	Dr. Raina	2009	750.00
9788184043785	Raina's Concrete Bridge Practice, 3/ed : Analysis, Design & Economics, 856 Pages **(H/B)**	Dr. Raina	2007	1,000.00
9788184046618	Raina's Field Manual for Highway and Bridge Engineers, 3/ed,1,404 Pages **(H/B)**	Dr. Raina	2009	1,800.00
9788184040135	The World of Bridges, 300 Pages **(H/B)** [4 color]	Dr. Raina	2006	500.00
9789350231180	Using Primavera 6: Planning, Executing, Monitoring and Controlling Projects, 228 Pages	Al-Saridi	2010	275.00
9788184043167	Using Primavera Project Planner Version 3.1 Courseware, 256 Pages	Hamad	2010	300.00
9788184047042	Using STAAD Pro 2007: Courseware with American Design Codes, 356 Pages	Hamad	2009	375.00

Communication

9789350231265	**Knowing Your Word's Worth: A Practical Guide to Communicating Effectively in English, 180 Pages**	**Shirodkar**	**2011**	**175.00**

Dental / Health / Medical

9788173669798	The Balancing Act "A Win Over Obesity", 296 Pages	Dr. Gadkari	2005	225.00
9788184049480	The Balancing Act "Know Your Heart", 368 Pages	Dr. Gadkari	2010	250.00
9788173668975	Splinting Management of MOBILE & Migrating Teeth, 104 Pgs	Dr. Kakar	2004	150.00

Economics

9788184043266	Analysing Macroeconomics: A Toolkit for Managers, Executives & Students **(H/B)**, 156 Pages	Rakesh Singh	2007	500.00
9788184044171	Analysing Macroeconomics: A Toolkit for Managers, Executives & Students **(P/B)**, 156 Pages	Rakesh Singh	2007	250.00

Electrical Engineering

9788184043235	Basic Electrical Circuits, 2/ed, 368 Pages	Dr. Salam	2007	250.00

ISBN	Title	Author	Year	Price

Electronics & Communication

ISBN	Title	Author	Year	Price
9788173669002	Electronic Components and Materials, 3/ed, 404 Pages	Joshi	2004	175.00

Environmental Engineering

ISBN	Title	Author	Year	Price
9788173663772	Principles of Environmental Science Engineering and Maintenance, 288 Pgs	Dr. Thirumurthy	2004	175.00

Event Management

ISBN	Title	Author	Year	Price
9788184044959	Enabling Event-ful Experiences, 250 Pages	Balachandran	2008	250.00

General Titles

ISBN	Title	Author	Year	Price
9788184045642	Hello Police Station (Marathi), 118 Pages	Shinde	2008	100.00
9789350231760	Mom Don't Spoil Me, 140 Pages	Dr. Mishra	2010	150.00

HRD

ISBN	Title	Author	Year	Price
9788184047080	Departmental Enquiries: Concept, Procedure & Practice, 534 Pages	Goel	2009	475.00
9788184046229	How To Improve Trainer Effectiveness, 170 Pages	Balachandran	2008	200.00

Law

ISBN	Title	Author	Year	Price
9789350230800	A Handbook on the Maintenance & Welfare of Parents and Senior Citizens Act, 2007.	Gracias	2010	150.00
9788173664151	Customs Valuation in India 3/ed, 262 Pages	Satapathy	2002	375.00
9788184042481	Laws Of Carriage Of Goods By Sea & Multimodal Transport In India, 92 Pages	Hariharan	2007	60.00
9788173661426	Law of Sale of Goods & Partnership, 228 Pages	Chandiramani	2000	150.00
9789350231289	**Social Security, Insurance & The Law, 460 Pgs**	**Gopalakrishna**	**2011**	**600.00**

Marine

ISBN	Title	Author	Year	Price
9788184043242	Containerisation, Multimodal Transport and Infrastructure Development in India, 5/ed, 852 Pages	Hariharan	2007	650.00
9788173660375	M.S. (STCW) Rules, 1998 incl. Training & Assessment Programme - 1,216 Pages	DG Shipping	1998	225.00
9788173661419	Maritime Education, Training & Assessment Manual (TAP) - Vol II, 474 Pages	DG Shipping	1999	400.00
9788184043136	Marine Control Technology, 336 Pages	Majumder	2007	400.00
9788173669279	Marine Diesel Engines, 428 Pages	Aranha	2004	250.00
9788184048544	Marine Electrical Technology, 5/ed, 1,250 Pages	Fernandes	2010	750.00
9788173660801	Marine Internal Combustion Engines, 272 Pages	Kane	2003	150.00
9788173660146	Safety Management Systems - An Underconstruction Activity, 98 Pages	Capt. Singhal	1998	95.00
9788173665516	A Textbook on Container & Multimodal Transport Management, 522 Pgs	Dr. Hariharan	2002	500.00

ISBN	Title	Author	Year	Price

Motivation

ISBN	Title	Author	Year	Price
9788184044249	Break Your Negative Attitude, 114 Pages	Dr. Mishra	2007	125.00
9788184044768	Hard-Knocks Communication: Thirty Six Timeless Rules for Success **(H/B)**, 222 Pages	Subramanian	2008	250.00
9788173665271	Heads You Win, Tails You Win, 2/ed, 200 Pages	Dr.Mishra	2005	200.00
9789350230206	Nothing Is Absolute, 274 Pages	Balachandran	2010	300.00

Parenting

ISBN	Title	Author	Year	Price
9789350231760	Mom Don't Spoil Me, 140 Pages	Dr. Mishra	2010	150.00

Patent

ISBN	Title	Author	Year	Price
9788184047882	Breeding Innovation and Intellectual Capital, 2/ed 196 Pgs	Dr.Batra	2009	600.00

Physics

ISBN	Title	Author	Year	Price
9788184043259	Gravitation Demythicised: An Introduction to Einstein's General Relativity and Cosmology for Common Man, 258 Pages	Shenoy	2007	250.00
9788184047929	Study Aid Theoretical Physics - Volume I: Relativistic Theory and Electrodynamics, 418 Pgs	Prof Fai	2010	300.00
9788184047912	Theoretical Physics - Volume I: Relativistic Theory and Electrodynamics, 490 Pages	Prof Fai	2010	400.00

Project Management

ISBN	Title	Author	Year	Price
9789350230237	A Primer on Software Quality Models & Project Management, 640 Pages	Mehta	2010	600.00
9788184048568	Management Accounting & Financial Analysis for C.A.Final 9/ed, 540 Pages	Sridhar	2009	400.00

Self-Help

ISBN	Title	Author	Year	Price
9788184047905	Enhancing Soft Skills, 346 Pages	Biswas	2009	375.00

- **All Prices are in Indian Rupees**
- **Titles Released after January 2011 are marked in Bold.**